IN THE SPIRIT OF GODSHILL
The Journal of Christopher Pan Charman

In the Spirit of Godshill
The Journal of Christopher Pan Charman

A New Forest Life

MILLERSFORD PRESS

In the Spirit of Godshill. The Journal of Christopher Pan Charman.
A New Forest Life.
© Christopher Charman, 2019

Typeset, edited and designed
by Sonia Aarons-Green

Images are from the Charman Family Archive unless stated otherwise.

ISBN 978-0-9572736-3-4
A CIP record of this book is available from the British Library.

First published in the United Kingdom in 2019 by
Millersford Press, Woodgreen Road, Godshill, Fordingbridge,
Hampshire, SP6 2LP.

Printed by Biddles Books Ltd., Norfolk.

Cover photograph: Looking towards The Ridge, Godshill, from Godshill
Inclosure and Millersford Bottom in the New Forest. © Sonia Aarons-Green

Inset: Christopher Charman at the potters wheel. © Salisbury Journal

To all those kind people within my family and friends,
especially Danae and Sonia, who gave so much help in
getting this epistle on the road.

CONTENTS

FOREWORD

Christopher Charman, the Master Potter, was the first person I interviewed for a feature in the *New Forest Magazine* when I came to live in Godshill twenty years ago. His sense of place, of self, and love of what he did was immediately evident. So I was already intrigued by the story of the Godshill Pottery.

Chris's sister, Danae, was aware he had written a journal when he was confined to a chair for six months after a cycling accident, and had asked to read it. It was not until 2018, when he asked her to 'sort out his office', that the ideal opportunity arose to recover what turned out to be a disordered pile of closely-typed paper, USBs and ancient disks, some of which she eventually managed to transcribe. The 'jumble' was brought to me by Danae in July 2018. It looked daunting, but irresistible. It was indeed a challenge for Danae, her partner Peter and I to restore it to an orderly book but when we presented Chris and Kate with a spiral-bound proof on his 86th birthday at the beginning of 2019 it was completely worthwhile. He said he had no idea he'd written so much.

Chris has written a frank and sometimes difficult account of his colourful life and that of his parents, growing up in remarkable surroundings, educated at a Quaker school, falling in love, working on the land with the Commoners of the New Forest, and finding out how to be an individual. It is also a record of an extraordinary union of families, the Westlakes and the Charmans, and of a world we appear to be in danger of losing and even worse forgetting.

So many people, residents and visitors alike, have called in at Godshill Pottery over the years, purchasing a pot or a mug, a plate or a dish. For me, and perhaps others too, there is a little bit of the spirit of Godshill which comes with it. It has been an unforgettable experience and an honour to work on this book and help conserve a little piece of the history of Godshill and the New Forest.

Sonia Aarons-Green
Godshill, New Forest, July 2019

Chapter 1
My Father, 1863 onwards

Dear family and friends,

I find as I grow older, in common with many people, that the past comes ever more sharply into focus. That is not to say that I do not look forward to the future, but as the years left to one become fewer, memories and associations with one's parents and grandparents become more important because so much of one's own identity is bound up with them. This last summer of 1998, my first year as a pensioner, was spent on a sofa with a broken leg, so I thought it as good a time as any to try and write down memories of my childhood and family history, before an active life again intervenes.

My father, Tom Charman, the youngest of a family of six, was a Sussex man born in Horsham in 1863. His father owned a small grocer's shop and was a strict Methodist, ruling the family with joyless Protestant zeal. Great-grandfather Charman was a yeoman farmer who, I am told, used to plough in top hat, smock frock and gaiters, which must have been quite a sight. I am the proud inheritor of one of his smocks made out of tough, now yellowing, raw linen, smocked in Sussex pattern and fastened at the neck with hand-made, pearl shell buttons. Although I can squeeze into it, it's a bit tight across the shoulders, which makes me conclude that men in the 1820s must have been a lot smaller in stature and muscle than now, probably owing to poor nutrition in childhood. Such an outfit must have quickly become muddy and greasy from farming activities.

As well as the smock, I have great-grandfather's 'turnip watch', a simple, heavy, solid, silver-cased fob watch, wound and set with a tiny key. The face is hand-painted in black enamel on a white background with a separate second dial. Its weight in your pocket is such that you certainly know that you have a watch on your person! I also have a small primitive dark oak desk with a sloping top that was passed on to my Dad from his grandfather's timber-framed farm house, deep in the Sussex countryside.

My father, in spite of being brought up in the fear of the Lord, and who, in practice, was his own martinet of a father, grew up to be something of a rebel within the confines of the strict Methodist doctrines of the time. He had a vivid imagination and was of a romantic inclination, forming at a very early age a love of the stage and the popular music hall entertainment flocked to by the working classes of the period. As a teenager, he would save up his pennies and escape the stultifying religious atmosphere of home to pay clandestine visits to 'the halls', to see such artists as Dan Leno, Marie Lloyd and George Robey. His arrival back home from these innocent evenings of fun more often than not ended in a beating from his humourless father, and dire warnings as to what would happen to his soul if he continued to sell himself to the devil by consorting with the acting profession.

The only good memory my Dad had of his own father was of a race to which he challenged all his sons. The young men, cocky in their youthful strength, underestimated the old man's sprinting prowess and lost the race, having to admit a grudging admiration. My father's formal education was basic and minimal, and he left at the age of twelve eager for whatever life had to offer. His kindly old school teacher, on Father's last day at school, set him a simple arithmetical problem: "If a pound of butter cost ninepence, how much would a quarter cost?" Father racked his brains and fortunately came up with the right answer: "Tuppence-farthing, sir," at which the teacher beamed, patted him on the head and said: "You will find your way through life, my boy, goodbye and good luck."

Infant nutrition in Victorian times was very inadequate, either through poverty or ignorance, and children who survived the infant killer maladies of the time, such as diphtheria, whooping cough, pneumonia and TB, often grew up with some disability or predisposition to bronchial problems. My Dad survived all these childhood dangers, growing to a healthy manhood, his only problem being a rather dodgy digestion which he said he owed to being weaned on salt pork, a grocer's basic stand-by. He was small by today's standards, 5ft 6ins, of wiry build, fair-haired with a handsome well-boned face; quite a dandy in his bowler hat, high wing collar and cane walking stick.

By the time he left home, his religious father had managed to turn Tom into a free-wheeling atheist, a young man with no profession, a passion for vaudeville and a lot of natural charm. Such a casual attitude to life meant that young Tom was often skint and at times desperate for any sort of work. At one point, he became a door-to-door sewing machine salesman, managing to sell one machine in the course of a week to a poor family to whom he gave overnight credit. When he went to claim his money, the family had decamped their squat and he had to pay for the machine out of his own pocket.

On more than one occasion Dad spent a night in a Salvation Army refuge with the local 'down and outs', not having the money to pay for proper lodgings. As part of the deal for staying the night and a bit of bread and soup, you had to attend a religious service the following morning. Part of the service was devoted to the saving of souls, their numbers rather thin on the ground of late. The Chief Army Officer was a bit irritated with his Lord that the message of salvation had not made any converts that week, and was heard to declaim irritably: "Lord save souls, LORD, SAVE SOULS and don't keep us messing about like you did last week and the week before that!" At which such outburst of human frailty you can guess my father was greatly amused.

My grandmother Charman, by all accounts, was one of those gentle, pragmatic women who loved her children dearly, and obediently put up with the excesses of her autocratic religious husband, as so many did in those days. She was loved in return by her children, whereas her husband was universally feared or, at most, grudgingly respected. Whereas she was a sensitive, educated person, her husband, hiding behind his religious morality, was crude and unimaginative in his relationship with her.

My father nursed his mother, by then a widow, through her last illness, and was finally able to make a real relationship with her. Through those last months together she imparted her love of literature to him. He used to read for long hours to her, and mother and youngest child were at last able to express their love and companionship without fear of autocratic censure. Grandmother bequeathed my father her wedding ring, which he gave to my mother on their union, and now my Kate has it, so celebrating at least 170 years continuity of marriage, symbolised in a tiny thin band of gold, unusually decorated in strange hieroglyphics.

In the free bohemian society of the 1880s, there were inevitably those who were of a 'gay' disposition, albeit covertly because of the harsh laws appertaining to homosexuality and mainstream society prejudice. My father, because of his youthful good looks, suffered some much resented advances from homosexuals, and suddenly realised how much of his puritanical upbringing had rooted itself in his being. In contrast to this puritanical sense of morality and values, my father was, paradoxically, quite able to accept the erotic drawings of Aubrey Beardsley, the tuberculosis-riddled young artist whose work was just beginning to be published and put on display. My father was fired by them to try some drawing for himself, and he found that he had a natural aptitude, particularly for cartoon work, rather in the style of Thomas Rowlandson. He started to earn a few pounds here and there doing the odd cartoons or illustration for newspapers. Always on the bread line, but with no dependants, he scraped by. He liked to dress as well as his meagre resources would allow. If his collar wore out and he couldn't afford another, he cut one out of cartridge paper and folded it origami-style to attach it with a stud to his shirt. When his mother died she left him a small legacy, part of which Dad spent on a passage to America, where he was advised his cartoons would sell like 'hot cakes'.

He found lodgings in Atlantic City, New Jersey, and, on the strength of a portfolio of his drawings, a newspaper took him on, giving him free rein to produce a weekly strip cartoon. It was a heaven-sent opportunity to invent his own character and story line. However, upon finding himself with a deadline and routine, he found his talent and facility for drawing seemed frighteningly to dry up. Such work as he took along to the editor was rejected with the self-evident remark: "You can do better than this."

My father said a type of artistic paralysis set in, and it began to effect him physiologically; his skin turned yellow like parchment. About the same time he began to have bad dreams, not only about deadlines. A voice would say to him: "This man is poisoning you." It went on for a month, and he became increasingly lethargic and ill, as though he was, indeed, being poisoned. The voices of warning continued. One morning, looking out of his bedroom window into the courtyard of his digs, he spied, with paranoid horror, his landlord purposefully sharpening an axe. A voice in his ear said: "Get out of here, or you are a dead man!" In his very weakened state, my father struggled out of bed, threw on his clothes, gathered together his money and what few possessions he had, and dashed out of the building. "Not going?" said the landlord, seeing him disappear through the door into the crowded street. "Gone!" yelled back my terrified father.

Paranoia? Maybe, but from that day on my father's health gradually improved, and he remained convinced his landlord had been slowly poisoning him with arsenic. The intention, he believed, was to reach the point where he could be easily murdered in order to steal the remainder of his legacy, which he always kept on his person. If it was arsenic poisoning, that may well have been part of the reason for his artistic paralysis. As this biography is based on anecdotal evidence we will never get to the real facts of the matter, but it remains a good story.

Dad had dozens of American comics full of classic characters like Popeye, Little Abner, Little Annie Rooney and others; I remember rolls of them on top of the large book case in our living room. Lots of the cartoons featured aircraft from the First World War in dog fights, the Hun in the person of von Richthofen, the 'Red Baron', going down a 'flamer' to the guns of a plucky Yank or British airman. The graphics were superb, particularly with the War Series of stories. My father must have thought a lot of those comics to keep them in such pristine condition for nearly forty years. They went the way of all paper periodicals when we children got our hands on them during the Second World War. They would be worth a packet now on the bygones market if they were still around - imagine, original American comics from 1914, a mouth-watering chance for a collector! We can only imagine, unfortunately.

The voices in my father's dreams convinced him that he was being looked after by some spiritual force outside the normal, and consequent with the fashion for spiritualism at the time, he decided to investigate. He went to a seance and received the usual messages providing 'irrefutable proof' of life after death, and that, moreover, he was a psychic himself. This revelation changed his life, gave him back a faith, and made him a life long proselytiser for spiritualist precepts.

Dad's love of the theatre remained unabated. He met and teamed up with a Mr Pain. As Morecambe and Wise, so Charman and Pain, the two men were perfect foils for each other, my father taking the lead part, and Pain the feed. They billed themselves as *Charman and Pain's Refined Dramatic Company*, performing at many venues around the home counties. After the highly successful partnership ended, Pain emigrated to America where he married and lived out the rest of his life. It was he who sent the comics to my father. His widow, many years later, mailed me some memorabilia including a poster advertising an evening's entertainment given by the two men at the Royal Military Academy theatre in Brighton just before the turn of the century. Front seats were reserved for officers and their friends only and were 4d; the rest of the corps, wives and their families and other services in uniform had the second best seats at 2d and 3d, and civilians had what remained, at a penny extra for each seat. The type of entertainment offered took the form of a series of character sketches, examples of titles running thus: *Never happy unless he's miserable*, Messrs. Charman and Pain; also, *The Quack Doctor*, Mr Tom Charman; another, *The vicar and the curate*. These sketches were interspersed with ventriloquial acts and my father doing lightning sketches on a blackboard. DOORS OPEN AT 6.30pm - COMMENCE AT 7pm…CARRIAGES AT 9PM, it says at the foot of the poster. No late nights for the army it would seem!

At one point in his early manhood, Dad became fitness conscious and joined a club. I have a photo of him with a group of other enthusiasts, flexing their biceps in a rather self-conscious manner. According to my mother, from whom I received all the anecdotal information that enables me to write this sketchy history of my father's life, the fitness classes seem to have included frequent visits to certain pubs, where large quantities of beer were consumed. The period of the 'keep fit' classes was the only time, my mother said, that my Dad admitted to getting fat, and he put it down to the nutritional 'beer'!

Of course, in Victorian times there were no dentists, only itinerant 'tooth pullers', who operated their trade with no anaesthetics. My father had reasonable teeth, but his life style and poor nutritional intake, coupled with lack of care, led to their premature decay, and one agonising day the 'tooth puller' was called in. While an assistant sat on Dad's legs, the 'tooth puller' sat on his chest and pulled all his remaining teeth in one unforgettable, bloody session, without any anaesthetic to dull the pain. Victorian times were hard. The cost of a pair of dentures crippled my father financially for many months, and he, on more than one occasion, had to pawn them and ask his latest host to redeem them in order to eat the supper to which he had been invited!

Dad moved within a large and varied milieu of people and one of his friends was a mystic priest called Macbeth Bain, or Brother James, who wrote the *Brother James Air*, the alternative, haunting setting of the 23rd Psalm from Crimond. Brother James was a strange eccentric and his unorthodox behaviour could be quite embarrassing at times for his friends. My Dad recalled a walk with him through one of the many parks in London. On passing by some municipal flower beds, Brother James helped himself to a big bunch. When Dad mildly expostulated, James replied: "But flowers belong to everyone, Brother", and so saying gave them, with a beatific smile, to a surprised, but delighted old lady passing by in the street.

So the years passed and all my father's brothers and sisters married and had children while he fought shy of the commitment, remaining 'foot loose and fancy free'. He was, by all accounts, a popular uncle, often called in to mind his numerous nephews and nieces with whom he was able to share his vivid imagination and sense of fun. He was

Tom Charman's first sighting of Ernest Westlake as he collected water from the spring at Godshill.
Below: An early promotional poster for the dramatic duo of Charman and Pain.

Above and below: Charman and Pain appeared on stage in numerous theatrical sketches.

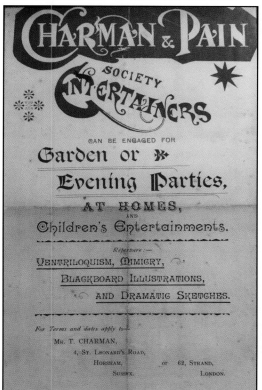

Marmaduke, Tom Charman's 'hideous' ventriloquist's puppet has survived.

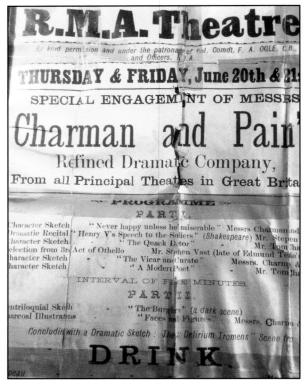

An early poster for the Charman and Pain duo at the Royal Military Academy Theatre. Tom continued performing well into the 1900s.

Cedric Rose (left) and Tom. Chris didn't know Cedric was his out of wedlock half-brother. 'We were all good friends.'

Some of Tom's extraordinary Forest carvings now preserved at the New Forest Heritage Centre in Lyndhurst.

an excellent ventriloquist and brought to life a fascinating, if hideous, doll, known as Marmaduke and still very much with us, whose toothy lantern jaw and eyeballs could be activated and rolled by the pulling of hidden strings. It sported horrible, moth-eaten, carroty-red hair and a forelock that stood on end, also at the pull of a string. Marmaduke's bony face is made up in the classic music hall 'artiste' style, the prominent cheek bones and beaky nose a bucolic shade of red. I was born too late to see and hear Dad and Marmaduke in their double act, but I discovered him much later in the back of a cupboard during my childhood. My sister and I used him to scare the daylights out of a particularly obnoxious youngster living with us during the war. By then, Marmaduke was even more moth-eaten and mangy-looking; he had several teeth missing and in the gloom, with his eyes rolled up into his head in a ghastly leer, he must have been quite frightening to a small child.

Kate and I gave the old fellow a refurbishment a few years ago, and discovered his legs and arms were stuffed with 1880 documents listing share prices relating to a box and bottle factory belonging to Dan Rylands Ltd., Bolton. So Marmaduke is a centenarian and quite a valuable musical hall 'artiste'!

My father hired himself out as an entertainer at children's parties, and besides Marmaduke he used to do his 'Bee in bottle' routine, catching an imaginary 'Bee' in a jam jar, from which it escaped. Realistic sound effects followed to make everyone think it was a genuine bee. Another party act was to get members of his audience to draw a squiggle on a blackboard, which he would proceed, as quick as a flash, to turn into one of his cartoons, to gasps of admiration at his speed and skill. He was a natural showman and story-teller with an empathy for children. The late Jean Westlake, my cousin, was old enough to have enjoyed, and remembered with pleasure, the visits of 'Uncle Tom', his stories and entertainment.

The Victorian era ended with the death of the Queen at the turn of the century, while the bohemian element in society continued to flourish in Edwardian England. In 1903, my father was forty and still footloose and single. Because of his friendly charm and innate decency, coupled with his gift for entertaining, he seems to have been a man well liked by whomever he came in contact.

The Edwardian era spawned a great number of alternative 'movements' in art, literature and education, as well as being the period when the quasi-scientific theories of Spiritualism were at their fashionable peak. My father swallowed all the elements of Spiritualism and its showmanship, which supposed to offer scientific proof of life after death, from levitation, materialisation, automatic writing, spiritual healing, and mediumship in all its aspects. He also held a belief in the existence of fairies, which he claimed to be able to see clairvoyantly and used to draw. 'Elementals' he used to call them, or 'Nature spirits'. According to him, they existed on a different plane of vibration from us human beings, so only those endowed with psychic powers who could tune into those vibrations were able to see them.

Some time during the first decade of the new century, my father joined a group of actors and society eccentrics, looking for an Arcadian life-style holiday; they camped in waggons and caravans in the New Forest. Our family have faded sepia photos from that summer, showing tableaux of actors, the ladies in corseted, long dresses round a camp fire in the beech woods, like the witches in Macbeth. Other tableaux show the men dressed as Red Indians having a fierce altercation, judging by the raised knives, tomahawks and pugilistic expressions! I would love to know more about this period of my Dad's life and who the various characters were that he was having such a good time with.

It would be interesting to know how they sustained their life style. Some of the ladies are extremely beautiful with their long fair hair, and my father, leaning against a large beech tree in a white cheese-cloth suit, looks happy and handsome.

I had often wondered how my Dad managed to remain unentangled with the ladies, and suspected he must have had some romantic entanglements along the way before he met my mother, but it wasn't until a year or two ago that Trudy, Mother's old Swiss friend, told me that I had a step-brother. It appears that my father succumbed to the attractions of a well-to-do, independent-minded lady in Brighton called Ruby Rose, a flamboyant, lively young woman with a sense of humour that matched my Dad's to a tee. She was also a convinced Spiritualist and medium for good measure. They had an 'affair' from which a child resulted, named Cedric. My father never married Ruby, who not only brought up her son on her own but remained on the best of terms with her erstwhile lover, and my mother. She simply became Mrs Rose instead of Miss, and appears to have had no problems. My father said he never got married as a young man as most of the women he met wanted too expensive a life style for him to be able to sustain economically. I can only guess that Ruby had enough private means to rear Cedric on her own and was a feisty enough lady not to worry too much about the prevailing social stigma of bearing an illegitimate child.

I do remember my mother showing me enthusiastic child-like letters to 'Darling Uncle Tom' from Cedric. I wonder if Cedric's mother ever confessed to her son that the Uncle he so passionately wrote to was, in actual fact, his father. I am sad that my mother never revealed that I had a half-brother in Cedric. Maybe the social mores of the thirties precluded her from being open with me, or maybe she mistakenly didn't want to destroy my idealistic concept of my father. At this stage in my life, I bless the fact that my Dad fell in love and had a child out of wedlock, as it somehow makes him that much more accessible as a human being. Cedric paid a visit once with his wife and two teenage children. I was in my early twenties and he must have been in his forties. I would have given anything to have known he was my half-brother, but it's too late now, alas.

At the beginning of the 1914-1918 Great War, my father was fifty-one. One of his sisters was married to a native of Nomansland in the New Forest. Her husband was the village baker, but he suffered from increasing bouts of epilepsy. Dad went to live with them and took over the baking of the bread for the village when his brother-in-law was incapacitated, helping his sister with whatever nursing was needed. In exchange, he earned his keep and had plenty of time to wander about the Forest and enjoy its beauty and solitude. He was on friendly terms with the keepers and forestry workers and, on one occasion, met up with the legendary Brusher Mills, the bearded, alcoholic, snake catcher of the Forest, who lived in a 'Clotten' house made of withy wands, clad with turf. Gypsies roamed the Forest fairly freely in the early years of the century, living in their 'benders', tarpaulin-clad, hazel-hooped tents. Dad enjoyed their company too, on his lone wanderings, and they accepted him to the extent of being approached by some of the younger men to write love letters for them to their girl friends, which he did, to their somewhat embarrassed, hesitant dictation. Most of the letters opened with the inevitable hackneyed opening gambit thus: "Dear Rosy, I loves yer as the flowers in May", after which, the muse tended to dry up, and Dad had to make a few discreet suggestions, which were usually received with relieved enthusiasm.

On one occasion, Dad was asked to be Godfather to a small Gypsy babe, an honour indeed, and went along to the christening. When it came to the ceremony, the vicar asked what the infant was to be called. "Moreover," came the reply. "Moreover?" queried the vicar. "That's a strange name." "You know, yer Reverend", said the father, "like from the

Good Book: 'Moreover the lion licked his sores'!" My mother, who related this story to me, never told me whether the christening went ahead. I do know that Gypsies often choose some strange names. I remember one lad was christened Oxo!

Besides his general handyman-cum-baker role, Dad was responsible for procuring firewood for the winter months. You could buy a whole oak tree from a stand that was being cut down, for 2/6d, twelve and a half pence by today's reckoning. Dad would buy one from the local Forester and, with just an axe and wheelbarrow, gradually chop it up each day and push a load back to the village, a quarter of a mile away.

One of the Nomansland characters was an old Forester called Giddings, a horse knacker by trade. To feed his pigs, he would boil up the carcasses of the horses in a large cauldron over a wood fire in his back yard. My Dad never forgot his first introduction to Giddings. On a gloomy winter's evening, coming into the yard, he was confronted with this vast cauldron, the flames licking round it, bubbling like a witches' brew, and a horse's head, its teeth bared, jutting out of the top in macabre grimace! Giddings raised a few dozen cockerels each year for Christmas, and a week before the festivities, he would be found in one of the out-houses in a sea of feathers, killing and plucking the unfortunate birds, wringing their necks with as little thought as he would have given to the snapping of an old bean stick for kindling. If he was talking to you at the time, his conversation hardly checked as he grabbed another bird and deftly dispatched it. For all his grim, but necessary trade, Giddings was a great one for personal cleanliness, and indeed declared a virtue of it. It was almost obsessive, but he negated this virtue by hardly, if ever, changing his vile, sweaty and greasy, blood-stained clothes, so Dad found him an almost impossible companion downwind!

So here we are, with the First World War over and Dad into his early fifties, living with his sister and brother-in-law in Nomansland on the north-west border of the New Forest. One spring day in 1919, or thereabouts, Tom Charman set off to walk the eight miles to Fordingbridge. Just before coming off The Ridge into Godshill, he espied a recently erected bungalow and large Gypsy caravan amongst the gorse. What really caught his attention, was the sight of a bearded, middle-aged, balding gentleman walking along to the house, carrying a couple of pails of water suspended from a yoke. He was wearing nothing but a loin cloth. "That looks like an interesting eccentric," thought my father, and he stepped aside from the dirt road, hailed my grandfather, Ernest Westlake, and asked him the way to Fordingbridge, which he knew perfectly well already. So we reach the point at which my Mother and Father were converging, as inevitably as day follows night.

Chapter 2
Margaret Agnes Westlake, My Mother, 1896 Onwards

I now come to my mother, Margaret Westlake. She was born in October 1896 in Hampstead, London, the second child of Lucy and Ernest Westlake. Aubrey, her brother, had been born three years before. Ernest Westlake (1855-1922), was the son of a Quaker worthy, Thomas Westlake (1826-1892), who owned East Mills on the Avon River at Fordingbridge, where they manufactured sail cloth and mattress ticking from locally grown flax.

Thomas owned a large property, Oaklands House, on the edge of town and employed (at minimal wages consistent with the day) a large labour force of 200 hands. As a young man it was hoped that Ernest would take over the family business but, as he showed no aptitude, his indulgent father, in true Victorian style, provided him with a very adequate private income enabling him to follow whatever interest he chose. Ernest had received a classical education at University College, London, and sustained a life-long interest in anthropology, palaeontology, geology and the natural sciences. He became a 'gentleman' scientist and an expert amateur field collector.

At the age of thirty-seven he courted, and finally won, the affections of one Lucy Rutter, who came from a Quaker family of solicitors in Mere, Dorset. Lucy had fallen in love with a chemist earlier in her life, but the family quickly steered her away from this attachment as the young man in question was 'in Trade'. Lucy did not take to Ernest at first, and Ernest's love and persistence had to sustain an enforced separation while Lucy went on an eventful cruise of the Antipodes. Ernest, an almost pathologically shy young man, must have been at his most despairing of ever winning his lovely lady when he stole into the grounds of her home one night, in the late autumn of the year of her absence, and planted a bed of daffodils outside her bedroom window as a gesture of his love. Whether or not Lucy ever knew of, or witnessed the result of her lover's romantic gesture, I don't know, but it has always struck me as a lovely action on his part. Ernest persisted with his attentions in his shy way and Lucy who by all accounts was a social 'live wire', finally succumbed to the young man's advances. Lucy's parents gave their consent and blessing to the union and she and Ernest were married in Mere, Wiltshire, in 1891.

Ernest and Lucy rented a large house in the vale of wealthy Hampstead, complete with visitor's book, for Lucy was an extremely lively lady (the complete antithesis of a Quaker), who loved to entertain in style. Ernest and Lucy, with their two children, Aubrey and Margaret, seemed to have everything going for them.

Ernest, financially secure, foolishly thought to increase his family fortunes by borrowing, at two per cent from the bank, the equivalent of his entire capital assets, investing it in supposedly 'rock solid' shares. The market crashed, the bank foreclosed, and Ernest lost all his money. Lucy's money from her marriage settlement, invested in the Wilton carpet factory, also evaporated when the factory went bankrupt. Her brother-in-law and owner of the factory, Pardoe Yates, had been paying out dividends from capital for years, it was discovered at his death. So the family were reduced from a generous life style to having to subsist on £40 a year. Disaster! Lucy hated to leave the comfort of their grand Hampstead home, Vale Lodge, and tried taking in paying guests to make ends meet. Finally, they had to leave London and rent a small house in Salisbury. The stress told on Lucy, who was never very robust, and when Margaret was only five years of age her mother contracted pneumonia which quickly turned to pleurisy. Within 24 hours she tragically died. She was only thirty-six years old.

A distraught Ernest was left with two young children to bring up. The rest of the family thought Ernest an incompetent husband and father and tried to gain custody of his two children, which he resisted with a fierce determination. He loved his children dearly but he was not a practical man, nor was he naturally child-orientated, being a shy, reclusive academic. Realising he needed help, he advertised for a governess to look after five-year-old Margaret and eight-year-old Aubrey. The lady who answered the advert was a middle-aged Russian who was known as Fraulein Sass, or to my mother, just Fraulein. She was a severe, but competent, woman who introduced my mother to a new and hard regime of upbringing, which included a cold sponge-down each morning. This habit my mother kept up for most of her life, though at the time she said it was a shock as she had been brought up rather softly until then. In the fashion of the day, she sported hair down to her waist; it was so long at one stage, she could sit on it. This, of course, had to be brushed thoroughly each day, which was quite an ordeal. Fraulein was fluent in German and taught Mother the language, pulling her hair and making her cry if she declined her verbs inaccurately. Ironically, the text book she used, she told me, was called *German without tears*. Fraulein was rather a hard woman, whose behaviour my mother was, in later years, to characteristically excuse with: "She meant well", but if the truth be known, my mother must have found Fraulein a severe and frightening substitute for her own dear, warm and loving late mother.

I don't know how Aubrey fared under Fraulein. He was a sensitive young boy and no doubt losing his mother was as great a trauma as it was for his sister. Ernest moved yet again, this time back to the family home, Oaklands, now in the possession of cousin Sidney Rake from whom he rented a part of the large house. Aubrey and Margaret were very close in the early years and participated in quite extraordinary projects together on occasions, in spite of Fraulein. Ernest could be a very liberal father, and he let the two children make their own fireworks, giant roman candles in old treacle tins, encouraging them in the science of pyrotechnics. It's hard to imagine, in the nanny climate of today, any parent instructing children of primary school age in the handling of saltpetre, but it was an unforgettable, wonder-filled lesson that stayed with my mother for life. She retained a love of candles and fireworks into her late eighties.

In the grand family home of Oaklands, Mother had a very lonely childhood, the trauma of her mother's early death leaving a scar that marked her for life. Like many lonely children, she invented an inner world to which she could escape, in which her mother featured as an ever-present guardian angel who ameliorated all the miseries of Fraulein's strict treatment, and the pain of maternal loss. Her father lived so much in his head he was probably absent-minded enough to be unaware of some of the harsher aspects of Fraulein Sass's regime with his children. Or maybe he was only too thankful to have a practical woman round the house and was diplomatic enough not to interfere, providing the regime seemed, in adult terms, tolerable.

Ernest had a bicycle and used to carry my mother on the crossbar, riding all round the locality, particularly visiting gravel pits, which he would scour for hours in the search for flint implements and fossils, or other evidence of past life or civilisation. My mother used to tell me of the cold and boredom of those endless hours spent in gravel pits, and how she longed to do something more interesting. On one of their excursions she caught her foot in the spokes of the bicycle wheel, damaging her foot and ankle quite badly. Although she went to the doctor, it was never to set properly and gave her a certain amount of trouble throughout her life, particularly in her last years. Mother's flat feet were something of an oddity anyway, so much so that her father took her to Harley Street where she was placed on a table and her feet looked at by a group of consultants, who prodded them and nodded sagely to each other, discussing the cause of their flatness. It was an ordeal that caused her much embarrassment, and no remedial treatment was ever offered.

The Westlake family plus Fraulein were intrepid, if unorthodox, travellers on the Continent. Ernest was frugal in his life style, and often the cost of living abroad was cheaper than at home. However, if he conceived a project that needed certain equipment, he always bought the best for the job. Their trips on the Continent were on state-of-the-art bicycles with three-speed gears, with racks and wicker baskets front and rear to carry tents and all camping equipment. Aluminium canteens were just coming on the market; expensive, but so much lighter than anything else. The actual holiday expenses being very modest, his priorities seem to have been infinitely sensible and justified.

Round about 1905, when Mother was nine years old, Ernest, thinking it would be a good educational experience for his daughter, organised a cycling expedition to go across France and into Spain. Older brother Aubrey was, by this time, at a Quaker co-educational boarding school, Sidcot in Somerset. Ernest, my mother and Fraulein set off on their bicycles, camping and staying in bug-infested boarding houses. When they were two-thirds of the way across the centre of France they were held up, through lack of money, in the town of Aurillac in the Cantal region. Whilst waiting for fresh funds to come through from England, Ernest discovered a rich seam of prehistoric flint implements embedded in strata dating from the Eocene period (56 to 35.4 million years ago). He was so fired that he immediately hired lodgings in the village and put my mother into the local girls' grammar school, digging happily for the next two years. He discovered a rich seam of prehistoric evidence for man's existence in the vicinity, seeming to predate existing evidence by two million years.

Sometime during the two years, Mother and Fraulein moved to fresh lodgings and a school just outside Paris. Ernest seems to have been rather a detached sort of father during this period of his fruitful fieldwork. My mother and Fraulein, in the meantime thrown together more than ever, thankfully began to grow closer. Life in rural France was very much at subsistence level and consequently rather drab and colourless. I think that drabness got to my mother, as years later when Kate and I went cycle camping in France, she couldn't understand why we were so enthusiastic about its colourful countryside. The France of the first decade of the century was forever fixed in her mind's eye, when people were so poor they had no time for cultivating flowers, and all towns and villages had cobbled streets - impossible to cycle on!

Aubrey spent his holidays from Sidcot with his large clan of Rutter cousins in Wincanton, with whom he got on extremely well, which was fortunate, seeing how preoccupied his father was. Ernest accumulated a mass of material over the two years, carrying away 'half the soil of France' for collation in specimens. In 1907, Mother and Fraulein were back in England. Margaret was fluent in French to the point where she could speak and write it better than her native tongue. In 1908, at the age of twelve, she too went off to Sidcot.

No sooner had he returned from France, and with his two children settled at boarding school, Ernest, seeing the similarities between the flint implements from the Eocene layers in Aurillac and those of Tasmania, determined to visit the island; he sailed there in 1908, staying until 1910. The Tasmanian aborigines had been subject to a policy of genocide and Ernest discovered it was too late to see any implements in use. However, he was able to do some anthropological research and amass a large collection of flint implements which he brought back with him. A slow boat home enabled him to write up his conclusion on his field work in France earning him, on his return, a fellowship to the Royal Anthropological Institute. During their father's absence, Aubrey and Margaret continued to holiday with their much-loved cousins in Wincanton - Lesley, Dorothy, Rachael, John and Cuthbert - where they had a very happy time.

Boarding school was, for my mother, like heaven. For the first time in her life she had friends and companions, apart from Fraulein and her brother. With both children at boarding school, Fraulein's period of useful service was more or less at an end, and she went back to France to look after a French family. Although Mother enjoyed the companionship found at Sidcot, she soon came to rebel at what she saw as the social strictures imposed by the new headmaster, Bevan Lean. She quickly became too self-confident and outspoken for her own survival within the climate of social mores prevailing at the school. "I was considered too argumentative," she wrote later. "I thought them too fussy about particular children behaviour and that there should be more freedom." She found plenty of things to rail against - not being able to sew during Nature Society meetings, for example - and was so at odds with Bevan Lean that at one point he sent her to the sanatorium because he considered her morally infectious.

Mother and a friend set up a society called 'The Famous Fooling Society', whose aim was to perform pranks without being found out. They concocted a programme which they were going to use to disrupt a certain Miss Leadbetter's upper third class. Unfortunately Bevan Lean got hold of it, and without realising its humorous nature, he read it out in front of the whole school, which caused much open amusement. My mother remembers: "He considered it a very serious matter and two of my friends were expelled for half a term. For some reason I got off with a severe reprimand." Although Mother wasn't expelled, about a year later Bevan Lean very politely suggested to Ernest that he thought she would get on better at another school, and he reluctantly agreed.

So in 1912, after four years at Sidcot, my mother transferred at the late age of sixteen, to the new and innovative co-educational school of Bedales near Petersfield, whose recently appointed liberal headmaster, Badderley, didn't believe in exams. Bedales was certainly a different kettle of fish from Sidcot, and she soon learnt to appreciate the manners of the boys at her former school, after putting up with the loutish behaviour of the Bedales lads. Part of the problem of entering a new school at sixth form level, as opposed to working one's way up through the various forms, meant that one made no long-standing friendships, and was a bit of a fish out of water. Mother was such a one, and endured one year at Bedales without getting much academic work under her belt. However, she did gain a smattering of Greek and started to learn the violin.

Aubrey had by this time passed through Sidcot with honours, having been head prefect and the apple of Bevan Lean's eye. In 1913 he gained entrance to Cambridge University to take a BA degree, with a view of going on to study medicine. Under the influence of her father, Mother decided to try for a place at Oxford University, some of whose colleges had started to take women students. Women at that period, although taking a degree course, only qualified for a lower status diploma, a last ditch sexist attempt to deny women their full intellectual equality with men.

As it was questionable whether my mother would pass the entrance exam for Oxford, owing to her sketchy last year at Bedales, and with Greek required to a certain standard, she spent her 18th year on a series of cramming courses. She divided her time between taking lessons in Latin and Greek, and peddling into Downton each week for a violin lesson. She kept a diary of the period which describes making her way to Downton when the river overflowed its banks along the Avon Valley and the road was flooded. She sadly dropped her violin lessons when she entered Oxford, always saying she wasn't musical enough to get anywhere with the instrument. Who knows?

Finally, in June 1914 Mother took her entrance exam for Oxford and passed in the five required subjects, Maths, General Science, French, Latin and Greek. She was a borderline pass in the written Greek paper so fortunately qualified for a second bite at the cherry with an oral exam which, to her relief, she passed with flying colours. Not due to start at University until 1916, she had time on her hands. Her father suggested that a profitable way to fill in the time would be to visit Germany and imbibe some of its culture, a strange proposition, as I am sure Ernest would have been aware of the perilous political state in Europe. To this end Fraulein was contacted in France with a view to asking her to accompany my mother on a trip to that country. This idea had to be abandoned of course, as on 3 August 1914 the First World War began.

Meanwhile, Ernest bought 42 acres of scrub, gorse and heather land, known as Brune's Purlieu, adjoining the New Forest. It was just outside Godshill village, and alongside what is now the busy B3078 road, in those days a quiet gravel track winding its way across the ridges of the Forest to Southampton. The parcel of land cost him £800 and was divided off from the Forest by an open ditch. It belonged to an ancient estate owned by the family of a Colonel Prideaux-Brune since the 12th century - a gift from Henry III.

Having a piece of land of their own, the Westlake family moved to The Ridge above Godshill. Clearing a level space of gorse near their boundary ditch to avoid building very large foundations as the ground fell away steeply, a second-hand, simple, single-roomed bungalow was erected. While the building was in progress, the family lived in a large Gypsy caravan that had been built many decades earlier as a present for a young Gypsy couple on their wedding. Tragically, the young lady concerned died before the marriage could take place, so the van never got on the road. It led a chequered, uncared-for life until one day in 1891, Ernest, seeing it mouldering, rescued it and had it renovated. Mother remembered waking up to find her sheets had frozen to the uninsulated walls of the van in the icy condensation which formed on winter mornings. From a well-to-do, middle-class, childhood in London to a spartan Gypsy caravan, was all part of the rich pageant which formed the circumstances of the Westlake family's life.

At least now they had the prospect of a settled home. When the hut was botched together, Ernest had a large open fireplace built on the south-facing wall, with a massive, foot square, oak beam supporting the draughty inglenook. He had a heavy, hand-forged pair of 'fire dogs' made by the local blacksmith to support the long logs he aimed to burn on the open fire. We still have a long, twisted-wire, toasting fork from those times. "The longest you have in the shop please, as I don't want to burn myself while making toast!" Ernest is reputed to have said to Mr Alexander, the ironmonger in Fordingbridge.

A crazy, impractical, installation of Ernest's was a back boiler that held four gallons of water that you filled with buckets and which, when it did get hot, could be run off into a narrow concrete bath let into the floor of the lean-to wood shed. To get at the bath, you raised a hatch on leather hinges in the floor. The problem was, scientist although he thought himself to be, my grandfather had never thought about the amount of heat that a large concrete bath would absorb in moments, to leave one with a tepid puddle in which to do one's ablutions. The plumbing, amazingly, was of hardened glass which, of course, froze and split on the first winter's nights as the bungalow had no insulation. The concept of an open fire is always romantic in theory, but, in practice, it is notorious for sulkily smoking if the wind is in the wrong quarter, or it's a still night of heavy drizzle, or again, if the chimney is too small in diameter, which in this case it was. Mother told me that the only way they could get the fire to draw on occasions, was by the self-defeating expedient

Oaklands, where Margaret had a lonely childhood. The house was owned first by Thomas Westlake, and then by cousin Sidney Rake. After Lucy's death in 1901, Sidney rented part of it to Ernest and his two children.

Members of the Rake family at a birthday celebration at Oaklands.

Margaret is pictured left, seated second row, next to her brother Aubrey. Centre are Rachel and Clarence Rutter. Standing second left are Lesley and Dorothy Rutter. Seated cross legged are their sons Cuthbert (left) and John (Joseph). Seated far right is Rachael and Rachael's Chinese boyfriend in front of Nancy (Agnes Rutter), standing.

Fraulein Sass.

The young Margaret Westlake.

of putting on their overcoats and having the door open to create more draught!

Water supplies came from strategically-placed water butts, positioned under the gutters round the house, eventually replaced by a large, open, rain water reservoir of two foot deep and with a 200-gallon capacity by the side of the house. Drinking water had to be carried up from a well on the hillside, a few hundred yards below the house. Ernest's skill as a geologist, and interest in water divining (the latter useless without the former), came to the fore. He forecast accurately that a spring would be found within a horseshoe cut made at a certain point in the hill. A circular hole was dug, about three foot deep in the cut, and lined with dry red bricks, and sure enough a small sharp jet of water spurted into the cavity. It was soon filled with lovely clear water. With a wooden lid to cover it and keep out the leaves, for the next decade this was the source of good drinking water carried up each day in two buckets on a yoke.

Just after the bungalow was finished, an old housekeeper, who had been in service with Ernest and Lucy and had taught Lucy as a girl, asked if he would re-employ her as she was in straitened circumstances. So old 'Tattsie', as she was affectionately called, joined the household, her keep and a bit of pocket money provided in lieu of wages.

The first winter began to show up the cowboy standard of building that had (or had not!) gone into the bungalow. One stormy night, the roof threatened to lift off and blow away and was found not to have been bolted down. Margaret, Aubrey, and a student friend who happened to be on vacation from Cambridge, took it in turns to sit on the roof until they could lash it down with ropes. An exhausting, cold and frightening experience.

Life was a bit too communal for Grandfather to be able to study and he resolved to get a room of his own, particularly in order to get away from Tattsie's eternal, bossy, scolding chat that drove him to despair. To further this project, he bought another second-hand wooden building and had it erected on some strong diagonally-braced oak scaffolding, the upright piles being dug into the gravel subsoil. The room was reached from the outside by a stout oak stairway, built deliberately too steep for old Tattsie to negotiate.

Grandfather had a conventional open-grated fireplace built at one end, the construction of which he monitored with irritating insistence, nearly driving the poor builder spare. He, poor man, used to creep into the house early in the morning to try and get a few courses of bricks laid before being interfered with yet again. Grandfather, whose hearing was good, used to dash up the stairs at the first slight noise, so the poor brickie never stood much of a chance to work unobserved. As he was being paid a predetermined price for the job, the poor man resented being overseen by a complete amateur who insisted on offering him advice. I can only say that between the pair of them they made an excellent fireplace that draws like a dream. How the base of the hearth is insulated from the wooden floor on which the fireplace rests remains a mystery, but whatever it is, it works!

From its inception the 'upstairs room' became Grandfather's den and bolt hole from Tattsie, where he could write and formulate his educational ideas that culminated in the foundation of a movement which, in a modest way, was to make him a name to remember. A derivative of Ernest Thompson's American Woodcraft movement, Grandfather recreated his English version calling it 'The Order Of Woodcraft Chivalry'. This organisation, unlike the scouts, embraced whole families, boys and girls, men and women, as equals. It introduced them to the natural world with simple, social pioneering activities like camping, cooking on an open fire and building shelters from natural materials. It was not held together, as the scouts, by jingoist patriotism and allegiance to a national flag and colonial values, but by a democratic, almost pantheistic idealism, centred around the tribal ritual of a yearly gathering, or folk moot camp. Within its circle, a fire lit from an ember from last year always burned for the duration of the gathering, to symbolise continuity. A keeper of the fire was appointed each year whose job it was to organise fuel and helpers to make sure the fire was kept alive while festivities lasted, rather like the Olympic flame. At the head of the gathering, a democratically-elected chieftain would preside and coordinate the running of the camp. Under him were all the appointed officers in charge of different aspects of administration.

Adult members of the order were given names, rather in the North American Indian tradition, consistent with their character and disposition. Uncle Aubrey, chieftain at one stage, was known as Golden Eagle and his wife, my Aunt Marjorie, was called Apple Blossom; another flamboyant character, who paraded in a skin leotard, was known as Leaping Leopard. All infants were referred to as elves and woodlings; new babes-in-arms were offered up each year to be blessed and accepted into the movement with the Order's cry of approbation *"BLUE SKY!"*

The concepts of the Order look rather innocent and naïve in the climate of cynicism that exists today, but for many years the movement fulfilled a great need. Uncle Aubrey was closely connected with his father in the formation of the movement and they discussed for hours the practical and philosophical issues involved in its realisation. He was to recruit many families from the slums of Bermondsey, the area of his first practice as a qualified doctor, and they were to form their own Lodge as part of the initial intake into the Order in the post-Great War years, many of them tasting their first experience of the natural world. Sidcot, the Quaker school, was to form its own Lodge too, and contribute to the interesting social experiment.

As my mother matured, so she was able to relate to her father more readily, and they formed a strong intellectual rapport, based inevitably on Greco-Christian concepts. Besides flint implements and the Greek classics, Ernest Westlake had a scientific interest in Spiritualism, drawn to it, maybe, by his wife's early death. He became a founder member of the Society for Psychical Research, and spent many nights in reputedly haunted houses, or where poltergeist activity was supposed to occur. Sadly, nothing ever occurred when he was around. A convinced spiritualist would have said that Ernest's sceptical vibrations produced the wrong atmosphere for phenomena to manifest themselves!

Part of Ernest needed to believe in an after-life, if only to relieve his personal sense of loss. Many quasi-scientific experiments were carried out with complete, if naïve integrity by the Society for Psychical Research. Sir Oliver Lodge, the eminent scientist and philosopher of his day, and inventor of the spark plug, was among them. Some Psychics were 'exposed' as frauds, but many survived the badly constructed experiments, to be held forth as genuine, truly gifted, mediums, demonstrating the paranormal as evidence of life after death; after all, seeing is believing!

One must remember that the fashion of Spiritualism as a belief received a huge boost in its ranks as a result of the 1914-1918 Great War, when thousands of mothers' sons were being slaughtered on the battlefields of France, and parents were desperate for some proof of their loved one's survival.

Sir Oliver Lodge's son Raymond, was one of those killed, which prompted him to carry out his own research. Ernest, in spite of drawing a blank with his own investigation, still retained a chink of fascination with the subject. My mother's need for belief in an after-life was as strong as her father's, and the subject was obviously a meeting point for endless discussion between them. Whereas my grandfather's approach to Spiritualism was

any admission or physical expression of love out of her 'dear one', i.e. Mallik. Reading between the lines, I have a feeling he was one of that rare breed, a natural celibate. Trying to read his obscure, philosophical books he comes across, to me, as being emotionally impoverished, a man who could only really relate at an academic level.

In the summer of 1919, Mother took her final exam and gained her diploma in anthropology. In 1919 too, 94 acres of mixed woodland on the edge of Godshill, called Sandy Balls and belonging to the Hulse Estate, came up for sale. My grandfather saw the area of woodland, overlooking and dropping down to the Avon valley with the river as its south west boundary, not only as the perfect venue for establishing a centre for the OWC, but also the perfect environment for an educational experiment, which was to become Forest School. Ernest went along to the auction but was forced to pull out of the bidding at a certain stage owing to lack of funds. Mother told me the story of how, when her father found out that the main bidder against him was a timber merchant intent on making a financial killing by clear-felling the entire wood, Grandfather was so angered by this he approached the timber merchant afterwards and offered him a tempting price over and above what he had just paid. The timber merchant accepted the offer and signed over the wood, only to regret his hasty decision and plead with Grandfather the next day to let him have it back, to no avail. Grandfather had his dream location and he wasn't going to let it go in a hurry. However, he crippled himself financially to do it, leaving an outstanding mortgage with no money left to pay the interest, a nightmare of financial juggling for Clarence Rutter, his brother-in-law and monetary adviser.

So we reach the year 1919. The great and bloody European war of attrition had finally ended with an armistice signed in November of the previous year. Shattered young men were desperately trying to come to terms with civil life again, in a land which was supposed to be 'fit for heroes', but, in fact, was far from being so.

To begin again, where I left off on that fateful day when my father took his first unconscious step towards meeting my mother, deviating from his walk to have a chat with my grandfather. My Dad's easy social manner soon put my pathologically shy grandfather at ease, and after the usual small talk the two men moved on to social and cultural topics. At the end of an hour or so, they discovered they had a great interest in common, namely Spiritualism. My father's story-telling ability regarding his clairvoyant experiences soon had Grandfather's interest riveted, and the two men agreed to meet up again for further talks.

Tattsie, the old housekeeper, took a shine to Dad and encouraged him to visit, making him feel welcome at any time. Dad warmed to her outgoing nature and in late summer, called in again, this time invited by Tattsie for supper. He was pleasantly surprised to meet a beautiful young lady, introduced as Mr Westlake's daughter, Margaret, who had just finished her degree course at Oxford.

Looking at photographs of my mother, then aged twenty-two, she was quite a beauty, with her long hair over her shoulders, or plaited and coiled around her head. My Dad was a well-preserved fifty-five-year-old, with a handsome, well-boned, clean-shaven face. He sported a red Paisley silk scarf, tied round his neck, and was as neat and clean as his well-mended clothes would allow. I don't know if there was any immediate chemistry between my parents, but I can guess that the supper party was quite lively, with the 'fishwick' oil lamps casting their soft yellow glow over the table, and old Tattsie fussing around.

My grandfather would dissect his fried herring wearing two pairs of Woolworth spectacles on the end of his nose to get enough magnification to see the bones! My mother used to tell us of her father's absent-mindedness. He was having his breakfast one morning and my mother passed by in her long vest on her way to have a wash. He looked vaguely in her direction, and in old Quaker parlance said: "Thou hast a nice dress on, Margaret." My mother lived on that story all her life, thinking it most amusing!

My father and grandfather got on very well together during this period. Mother didn't fall in love at first sight as she had with Mallik, but she was certainly charmed by this good-mannered, lively visitor who was such an authority on the spirit world. My father visited the hut at Godshill more and more frequently and it was not long before he had introduced Grandfather to his psychic friend, Sidney Penton, who lived in a cottage at the north end of Sandy Balls. Penton was a good trance medium, and seances were held in the upstairs annex room. My mother was overjoyed to have a chance to get in contact with the spirit world and invited Mallik to participate in one of the seances. Penton went into a deep trance and his Persian spirit guide, *Machusha*, making his presence felt by a strong distinctive Arabic perfume, delivered an inspiring sermon from 'the beyond'. Then followed some paranormal happenings; foreign coins dropped around the room from nowhere, and Penton suddenly said: "My foot has disappeared." When Grandfather asked him how he knew, he said: "I've just felt for it, and it isn't there!" At that moment, there was a 'clunk' sound at the other end of the room, which was found later to be Penton's boot, still laced up. Penton told an amazed Mallik the correct name of the Indian village of his birth, which Mallik had not given a thought to for years. Grandfather was most impressed that Penton's boot should have been removed without being unlaced, and arranged for a local photographer to take a picture of the evidence, much to the latter's amused puzzlement. On handing the print to Grandfather, he said: "The order of the boot, I presume?" As the seance took place in the semi-darkness, there was plenty of room for fakery. I only have my mother's assurance as to the complete integrity of Sidney Penton to preclude it.

Full of the new friendship with Dad, my mother communicated it to Mallik, thinking he would rejoice with and for her. Surprise, surprise, Mallik was less than impressed. All his cerebral notions of a great loving circle of humanity came to grief at the first hurdle. He replied, very ungenerously, that in no way could he accept Tom into his circle of friends as he could not feel for him as he did for my mother. Mother could not help but think that there was some inconsistency in this line of argument, as she and Mallik's long-time girlfriend, Mary, had managed to be friends without effort. She felt degrees of loving unimportant, and when Mallik delivered an ultimatum: "Either Tom, or me", she had no hesitation in choosing my father. It was a case of one rule for Mallik, another for other folks; a case of straight forward jealousy, if he had been honest enough to admit it.

So that was the end of my mother's association with Mallik. He went on to become an obscure guru of sorts, being looked after by a small group of women who loyally devoted their lives to seeing to his practical needs, and edited his obscure, dry tomes of philosophy. He was not a practical man, and was lucky to have their selfless devotion to enable him to write uninterrupted. He went back to India in 1923, travelling with his faithful retinue of female disciples, and writing, trying in some academic way to change the face of society radically enough to free it from endless conflict. He returned to Europe in 1937, first to friends in Stockholm and then to Oxford. ❦

Chapter 4
Woodland Idyll and Troubled Relationships

The dashing Tom Charman in 1923.

Grandfather invited Dad to stay with them at Godshill about this time as he had an idea that my father, as he was a man of the woods, fond of nature and good with children, would be a great help with many of the practical aspects of the Order of Woodcraft Chivalry.

Dad's brother-in-law had died by this time, so he was no longer needed in Nomansland and so, after due consideration, he agreed to the proposition. He joined the company in the little hut on The Ridge, adding joy and laughter to the usually quiet and serious mealtimes. A good communicator and entertainer, he was the perfect antidote to leaven the lump of Westlake shyness and introspection.

About this time, my father received a strange letter in the post, and with it a cheque for £400. It was a gift from a total stranger, a well-to-do spiritualist who, while attending a seance, had been instructed to bequeath a small legacy to a certain needy artist, wood carver and fellow believer, whose description fitted my father. After some detective work among the spiritualist fraternity, he had tracked down my father's whereabouts, and had much pleasure in presenting him with this small gift, which he knew would come in handy. As the fates would have it, a small, run-down old cottage in Godshill with a three-acre field behind it, part of the Hulse Estate, had just come on the market for £400. Dad, looking to the future in a realistic way for once, bought it, taking out a small mortgage.

A Czechoslovakian weaver called Bridlig was taken on as a tenant, his rental helping towards the mortgage repayments of 10/- a week. Now, my parents had even more time to get to know one another. My father, for his part, was certainly not averse to mother's obvious growing affection, indeed flattered and excited that a beautiful young woman, 32 years younger than him, should find him attractive. He expressed his concern at their age differences, but upon her assurance that it was of no significance whatever to her, he relaxed in his newly-found heaven. Having made a commitment to each other they decided to live together in the Gypsy caravan.

Realising her father might raise objections to this plan, it was with some trepidation that she informed him of their intentions. Her forebodings were fully realised. He, lulled by the supposed barrier of the age gap, had never thought of my mother and father as being anything but good friends, and the news of his daughter's intentions filled him with dread and dismay. He demanded that my father leave the house, and my mother countered it by saying that if he went, so would she. Indeed, it was a strange situation, my father only being a few years younger than his intended father-in-law; Ernest also viewed my father as an improvident artist, with no visible means of supporting his daughter.

However, my mother's dander was really aroused, and a battle royal ensued that went on for weeks. To add fuel to the misgivings of Ernest, my mother determined not to be legally married, as she considered civil law had no place in a loving union, and that a higher spiritual moral code of integrity should be the only binding element in the partnership. It must be said, also, that the laws concerning divorce were pretty draconian.

The argument continued back and forth, growing more and more acrimonious, leaving all parties emotionally exhausted. The battle of wills, in the main, was between father and daughter, with Tom being pulled in by Ernest to swear never to have anything more to do with his daughter. Then followed some very bizarre behaviour on Grandfather's part. He hired a hypnotist to give my father a session of aversion therapy. He enlisted the aid of a relation to telegraph an urgent trumped-up message to say a volunteer was needed for Voluntary Service Overseas (VSO) in Poland, a position just right for my mother. He wrote to the Quaker Elders and had her expelled from the Society for her views on non-legal marriage, and generally did all that was possible to stop my parents from setting up together. Grandfather's actions seem vindictive and unbalanced, to say the least. He must have been pretty desperate. My mother was distressed to see her father so hurt, but if his peace of mind meant her giving up her man, that she could not, and would not, do.

At the height of this embittered altercation, a certain lady of positive character called Mary Rodgers, from an experimental colony called Whiteway in the Cotswolds, hearing on the grapevine of my parents' predicament, walked and hitch-hiked to see if she could ameliorate the situation. She was a persuasive talker and good listener, and took on Ernest, allowing him to talk himself out and relieve some of the stress that had been generated. My parents were forever grateful to her for taking the sting out of the situation. Mary managed to talk Grandfather round, temporarily at least, into seeing that the situation wasn't as bad as he had come to believe. Ernest however, was always a vacillator by temperament and the arguments still continued to flare, even if thankfully, now a bit less wild and extreme than before. A type of stalemate was reached, with Ernest alternately blowing warm and cold, producing an atmosphere that my parents found difficult to contend with.

In the very wet summer of 1920 when Ernest was on a bleak, resigned phase in his attitude to my parents' union, they decided to go off into the woods of the Forest together and make a determined break from paternal authority. In effect, go off on their honeymoon. Then followed the most bizarre situation imaginable. My mother had the strong impression (and she always took note of impressions), that she should invite her father to accompany her and Tom into the woods, and she informed Tom of her inner urgings. He protested with some justification, saying that as they had only just managed to get Ernest off their backs, why court disaster by letting him in on the act, as it were. However, after receiving a psychic message from Penton that Ernest must be able to come for his sanity's sake, he happily agreed. Ernest's mood lightened immediately.

So, in the summer of 1920, the strange triangle set off into the Forest. My parents carried their few belongings in rucksacks; a billy can, old eiderdown and groundsheet, a book of poetry called *The Open Road* by E V. Lucas and *The Perfect Way* by Anna Kingsford. My father also took some paper and pencils with which to draw. Ernest loaded his bicycle with tent and other camping gear, and pushed and cycled along with his charges. They set up camp in the lovely old beech woods at Holly Hatch, about a quarter of a mile from the keeper's cottage. Ernest pitched his tent and my parents prepared themselves a bed of dry beech leaves. Towards evening it began to rain and Ernest invited them into his tent for the night. He insisted on sleeping in between them, a situation so humorous that my parents couldn't help but see the funny side! Most days (presuming his charges wouldn't get into any 'mischief' in the daytime), Ernest would ride back to Godshill to study and collate his flints. He returned to camp one day with a worthy Quaker friend, Mr Pask, who added his pennyworth of pressure against my parents' illegal liaison in the form of a homily on responsibility and looking to the future. When my father countered with: "You as a Quaker, Mr Pask, should know all about faith and letting the future take care of itself… ", Mr Pask had the wind rather taken out of his sails. At the end of the first week, when the lovers came back from one of their rambles they found, much to their relief, that Ernest had struck camp and gone home, in a final gesture of capitulation, the wet weather and common sense telling him he had no power over the situation.

Utilising a low, sloping branch of an old oak tree as a ridge pole, my parents draped the old groundsheet over the top of it to make a rough shelter which they thatched, in a rudimentary way, with bracken fronds and heather. From cavities and hollows in the old trees round about they managed to find enough dry leaves to make a comfortable, springy bed. The rain continued unabated, sometimes for 24 hours, and the run off began to seep into the interior of the shelter, making the peninsular of dry ground left to sit or lie on less and less. They kept a camp fire going day and night, to enjoy its actual drying warmth, as well as its psychological comfort. To Tom and Margaret, in the romantic flush of their new love, the situation was great fun.

My parents stayed in the woods nine weeks in all, living mostly on dried lentils, which, though pretty bland and uninteresting, were at least nutritious and had the advantage of being cheap. That, with tea, margarine and condensed milk, bought from the stores at Fritham post office two miles away, was their simple fare. They made friends with the local keeper who kept a large kitchen garden, and he sold vegetables to them. One day, in desperation for a bit of tasty protein to augment their frugal diet, they walked all the way to Ringwood and bought two bloaters. The walk, there and back, was at least 15 miles and the bloaters, cooked over the fire, were greatly enjoyed, but my parents were left wondering why in the world they hadn't bought half-a-dozen fish while they were about it. My father drew his fairy drawings and relayed his clairvoyant visions of them to my mother; they walked and read aloud to each other. A lot of time was given to getting wood for the fire, wandering further to collect it as time went on. My mother described to me how they wanted a large log to keep the fire in, and, not having a saw or axe to cut it, they built a fire of branches under it to burn it through. It took so much wood and time to burn, they wondered in the end if it was worth all the work!

They washed themselves, and their clothes, in the forest stream running by their camp. It's surprising how much time is spent in essentials with no facilities. They were blissfully happy in the moment, very damp at times, but coming out into the sun when it briefly showed itself, like lizards, to dry out and rejoice in its warmth. However, at the end of nine weeks the simple woodland life, with the August nights beginning to get a bit chilly, was starting to pall a bit, and the £30 my father had brought with him, the remainder

August 1920. Tom Charman, photographed by Margaret in their Forest camp at Holly Hatch.

of his spiritualist benefactor's gift, had now dwindled to one or two pounds. Clearly something had to be done. Providentially, Mary Rodgers, their Whiteway Colony saviour, wrote out of the blue, putting them in touch with a family by the name of Wicksteed. Mr Wicksteed, an ex-Bedales teacher, had just been appointed head of King Alfred School, Hampstead, and needed help. My parents saw this opening as part of the great scheme of life. They were soul mates in their belief that, if you followed your inner guiding impulses, which were always, of course, directed from the spirit world, everything would work out. This made them a unique, if somewhat disconcerting, couple. ❧

Chapter 5
The Wicksteed Connection

On the 11th of August Tom and Margaret burned their shelter and tidied up their camp, packing all their belongings into their two rucksacks. Sleeping the fortuitously dry last night on a heap of beech leaves under the stars, they set off at break of day for Petersfield, a distance of 45 miles. They completed the journey in two days, which was pretty good going.

My mother said she remembered the trip for the weight of the rucksack which she seemed to be carrying days after the walk finished. She also experienced the first signs of discomfort from the injury to her foot, sustained as a small child. My parent's arrived at the Wicksteed's abode at Steep, near Petersfield, an agglomeration of converted, old railway carriages, rather surprising living quarters for the headmaster of King Alfred School, Hampstead. They were greeted by an enthusiastic and warm Mrs Wicksteed, whose first remark was: "Welcome, you are the very couple I have been looking for. You are just in time for supper!"

Mrs Wicksteed was as zany as my mother, but a bit more so by all accounts. She was a Christian Scientist, a disciple of Annie Besant, the eccentric high-priestess of Theosophy, whose search for a latter-day Messiah in India led to her discovery of a young boy whom she groomed and who was to become Jiddu Krishnamurti (1895-1986), a minor Indian guru. He founded Brockwood Park School to further his own brand of philosophy, which continues to offer an education inspired by his teachings.

Mrs Wicksteed was a kind woman, but totally impractical. Her husband was away in London organising his take-over as headmaster of King Alfred's. The supper that she said my parents were 'just in time for' didn't seem to be much in evidence, but conversation flowed as the company got to know one another. At about half-past nine, Mrs Wicksteed said, as an afterthought: "Ah yes, supper!", and disappeared into the kitchen. My parents looked at each other in some anticipation of a good meal after the long last lap of their walk. Presently, Mrs Wicksteed appeared with a tin of sardines and a small loaf of bread, which turned out to be all there was. As my father remarked to my mother later: "It's a pity the good Lord wasn't there to multiply the meagre repast!"

It turned out that Mrs Wicksteed needed someone to hold the fort at home while she helped her husband settle in at Hampstead. This involved looking after three remaining children, all boys, two of whom were day pupils at Bedales School, and Ivan, the youngest of a total clutch of five. My parents joyfully took up their responsibilities, my father breaking up ground in an adjoining field for a kitchen garden. Mr Wicksteed, a silent man, came down from London to vet his zany wife's choice of work force, liked what he saw, and offered my father a job in Hampstead clearing the school grounds of brambles, a heaven-sent opportunity to earn some much needed money. My father cleared brambles all week, his expertise with a reap hook earning him the respect and lasting admiration of Mr Wicksteed who was of an academic nature. On Friday evenings, Father would catch the train to Steep for a joyful weekend reunion with my mother and the Wicksteed boys. It was a very happy period of my parents' lives at Steep as, for the first time, they felt that they were being treated as a normal couple and not in a judgemental way as they had been at Godshill.

Despairing hurt letters still arrived for my mother from her father, who was lonely living on his own. He was quite helpless domestically and asked Mother to come and stay and help him for two weeks. This she consented to do on the proviso he didn't bring up the subject of her relationship with Tom. Ernest was in a pretty bad state, and Mother seems to have spent all her time cleaning and mending his socks, shirts, and vests. In her diary she tells, so sadly, how acutely aware she is of her father's hurt, and of the seeming impossibility of doing anything to put it right. She so wishes that parents were more able to let go of their children and let them be themselves. It seemed to her that her father had swapped places with her, and become the child and dependent.

My parents stayed happily at Steep through Christmas, enjoying the Wicksteed family festivities. In the spring, they were offered another job, this time at Golders Green, again clearing ground preparatory for King Alfred's move to the new venue. Also Dad was asked to take some of the boys for wood carving classes once a week. Mother too was given a part-time teaching post. As part of the deal there was a small lodge house, rent free, to live in, on the edge of the new school grounds. A friend donated a double bed. My parents bought themselves a tin bath and with some draped wooden boxes they soon had the place snug and furnished. Old pottery honey pots did for mugs, and a large lidded kettle doubled up as a saucepan. Working full-time their joint wages came to £3 10/- a week which was more than enough for their needs. So they decided that, if permissible, my father would work part-time in order that he could spend more hours with my mother. Mr Wicksteed readily agreed and my parents happily subsisted on £2 10/- a week.

In the evenings, my father felt inspired to paint fairies. He bought a large roll of kitchen paper, laid it out across the floor, and using Indian ink and a large brush, he swiftly gave substance to his psychic visions of elementals. He always thought it strange afterwards that he should be at his most inspired to paint nature spirits in the middle of a city. Maybe it was an antidote to being divorced from the natural world. My parents had found a local medium and joined his circle, participating in seances and Spiritualist meetings, and making many friends. The lodge had two spare rooms, one of which became occupied by Connie Jackson, a maths teacher and old school friend from Sidcot days. The other room was taken by a young surviver of the 1914-1918 trench warfare, called Wilfred Sinclair, (a friend of John Gray of whom more anon). It was a happy foursome at weekends.

With all clearance work completed, the time came for Tom and Margaret to vacate the lodge cottage. It coincided with an invitation from a man called George Allen, a member of Whiteway Colony in the Cotswolds, to stay with him as his guests. Eager for new experiences they took up his offer, and with fond farewells from the Wicksteeds, made their way to the Cotswolds. 🌿

Chapter 6
Whiteway Colony: Ideal Versus Reality

Whiteway Colony was conceived in 1898 when an idealistic Quaker journalist, Samuel Veale Bracher, bought a parcel of land near Stroud in Gloucestershire. He called it God's land, and burning the title deeds, turned it into common land, inviting anyone who wished to, to come and live on it free; and of course 'anyone' did, a real mixed bag of free-thinkers and reformers.

They built their own agglomeration of shacks and houses to live in, and a community was gradually formed, with some loose idea of living together off the land, on Tolstoyan principles. George Allen, their host, was one of the leading figures, a forceful individual, a fruit grower and well-known vegetarian athlete, who at one time held the record for walking from Lands End to John o'Groats. Originally a shoe maker, George suffered from epilepsy and was reputed to having cured himself through diet and walking. My parents were seduced by the idealistic experiment in communal living and thought they would spend a summer staying in the colony to see what it was like.

Like most utopias, the diversity of people attracted to it, with all their differing beliefs (most of them totally ungrounded in the practical issues of daily living, like earning money), already had the seeds of failure in its midst. The ethos of free love, one of the Tolstoyan precepts, was the first behavioural experiment to hit the dust. Not for nothing had society's values evolved to where monogamy was considered the best formula for maintaining social equilibrium. Human nature could flirt around the edges of free love, but it couldn't handle it in reality! One can imagine the jealousies, outrage and dissension at any marital 'reorganisation'. It was an idea quickly abandoned.

George Allen may have turned himself into an athlete, but my parents, found him a very difficult character to live with because of his manic mood swings and frenetic destructive energy, usually directed at some other poor member of the commune whom he considered was not pulling their weight, sometimes justifiably. His common-law wife Emily was estranged from her partner and lived next door.

Another Tolstoyan precept frowned on money, and a kind of barter system had existed, which again had its pitfalls as it was almost impossible to evaluate the worth of goods against work exchanged. The land, having no title deeds was common to the local farmers as well as the colonists. It couldn't be fenced against the locals' cattle, and a constant battle was waged against invading stock threatening the colonists' gardens. The commune numbered about a hundred people, some practical, some not. One man more enterprising than most, made his own adobe bricks and built his substantial house from them. Others with a propensity for navel-gazing rather than building, ended up in very inferior shacks and shelters and were given short shrift by those of a more practical bent. Without a commitment to a unifying spiritual ethos and economic structure, based on the realisation that the community couldn't exist in a vacuum but had to deal with the outside world, it was doomed to remain an interesting failure.

The land of the colony was on high ground and very shallow and poor. My mother remembered it was a very hot, dry summer and the potatoes that she and my father grew were all the size of golf balls from lack of moisture. The only water supply was rain water collected in water butts, so there was never any to spare for watering the garden. Mother said that she used to boil up all the tiny potatoes in a large saucepan on the open fire, then peel off the soft skin and fry them to make them a bit more tasty. Potatoes seem to have been their main-stay that summer and autumn. It was also an exceptional year for blackberries, my parents picking a two-gallon bucketful without having to move more than a few yards, the bushes were so loaded.

My parents stuck colony life for six months, giving of their practical best, but soon began to realise that the personality of their host was too abrasive for comfort. George Allen forbade them to speak to any of the other commune members as he had fallen out with all of them over the years. As they were his guests, Mother and Father reluctantly bowed to their tetchy host's wishes, and more or less kept to themselves. But they did go over to visit George's wife, a sweet kind lady, and enjoyed her company in the evenings. George was very annoyed that my parents should prefer his ex-wife's company to his, grew very jealous and turned them out of his house. His wife invited them to stay with her, which state of affairs added fuel to George's paranoia. In the end, he accused my father of alcoholism and having sexual relations with his wife. He transmitted such tangible aggression my father began to feel quite ill 'with the atmosphere of hate in the air'. Finally, fearing assault, Mother and Father quietly packed and left without saying anything to anyone, for fear George would pursue them.

Whiteway Colony suffered the inevitable problems over the years with the law, rates, squatters rights and so on. It still exists, but not as a commune, more a hamlet or small village of individuals leading their own separate lives.

Meanwhile, Aubrey Westlake, my uncle, was studying at Cambridge University from 1913 to 1916. He qualified as a general practitioner from St. Bartholomew's Hospital, London, in 1918 and joined a general practice in Bermondsey, a slummy run-down borough of East London. He worked under the auspices of the original and imaginative Dr. Albert Salter, who was to change the general health of the area radically, for the better, by improving housing and water supplies and getting the borough to provide public baths. The incidence of TB and other bronchial disorders was dramatically cut.

Uncle Aubrey was married in 1923 to Marjorie Harrod and they had five children, Keith, Jean, Martin, Carol and Richard.

Aubrey Westlake and his friend Kitty Trevelyan dancing in a Woodcraft Chivalry event outside Fordingbridge Church.

Chapter 7
Back to Godshill and Paranoia

My parents went back to Golders Green for a month, staying with a friend. Then in mid-December, with six-year-old Ivan Wicksteed in tow, they took a train back to Godshill. Mrs Wicksteed had asked them if they would foster Ivan for a year or so, and she would pay them 17/6d a week for his keep. Providence had provided once again to reinforce a sense that all was well!

One may ask, justifiably, at this point how two responsible adults could take on the fostering of a child without any real prospect of a house to live in on their return to Godshill. This was typical of my mother's attitude to life. It was typical too of the blind faith of Ivan's mother, who let her son go without ever questioning that the two adults in charge of him had a place to live. To give him his due, my father had written to Bridlig, the tenant of his cottage, to see if he was agreeable to sharing the cottage with them, and had received an answer in the affirmative.

On a cold winter evening, just before Christmas 1921, my parents and little Ivan arrived at Fordingbridge railway station, all their worldly goods packed in a tea chest, one old tin bath, and a couple of rucksacks. Bridlig, who was supposed to meet them with his donkey and cart, didn't turn up. So, leaving the chest and bath at the station, they walked the three and a half miles to Godshill and knocked on the door of the cottage. A slightly shifty Bridlig answered the door. He had obviously been 'got at' by my grandfather, and refused the trio entry. Nothing daunted, my parents made their way to the woodsman's cottage at the north end of Sandy Balls where my father's good psychic friend Sid Penton and associates lived. There they were made most welcome, staying two nights and sleeping in front of the cottage's open fire. During the evening of the second night, Penton received a psychic message from *Machusha*, to warn my parents to vacate the cottage as Ernest Westlake had informed the welfare officers they should inspect the house to ensure that there was no over-crowding. It seems that my grandfather was determined that my parents should gain no toe-hold in the area.

They vacated the cottage and put up a make-shift shelter with an old tarpaulin, in the lee of a nearby hedge, and awaited developments. Sure enough, the same day the welfare officers came, but they found only Penton and his friend at the cottage, and they left somewhat puzzled. After a few nights in their 'bender', my mother made inquiries as to where her father was, and found he had moved the Gypsy caravan to Oaklands, and was living in it in the grounds, using the old summer house to study and collate and label his vast collection of flint implements. He was leading a poverty-stricken and reclusive life at this point. His dismay at my mother's continued stand on rejecting legalised marriage was turning to paranoia and resulted in the outrageous and offensive attempt to destroy my parents' union, although Mother assured him that her relationship with Tom was only as brother and sister at that time. She told Grandfather she thought their love for each other was far too much of a sacrament to consummate until such time as the fates decreed that it felt propitious. This self-imposed chastity was further proof to Grandfather of my mother's unbalance, only adding fuel to his antagonism.

The 'upstairs room' that Ernest had built for his private study on The Ridge was vacant at the time and Mother appealed to her father to let her have the key so she, Tom and Ivan could have a roof over their heads. Her father adamantly refused, saying she had made her own bed, so she could lie on it. So my parents continued to squat in Sandy Balls while considering the next plan of action. Christmas came and luckily the weather was mild. The three of them celebrated with a tin of peaches and condensed milk.

My mother appealed to Uncle Clarence Rutter, Ernest's brother-in-law, solicitor and financial adviser through all his monetary muddles and disasters over the years, to come and negotiate some sort of peace between her and her father. A meeting was arranged between the parties and a parley took place, at which Clarence managed to steer Ernest into realising that he couldn't, in all Christian decency, refuse his own daughter a roof over her head. "Give her the keys, Ernest, " said Clarence, appealing to my grandfather's better nature and he, to his credit, did so. It was quite a break-through!

In a sense, it was a relief to Ernest that my parents left Sandy Balls as he saw their presence there as a threat to his estate, hinting that their immoral liaison would incite the villagers to primitive reprisals, such as setting fire to the woods or his cottages at the north and south end of the estate. It is extreme, but true to say that he regarded my parents' presence in Sandy Balls as a 'moral contamination' to his vision of the wood as a centre for the Woodcraft movement and Forest School. In his eyes, what decent-minded person would want to come and participate in a movement so tainted. At least now the culprits, the source of his distress, were one removed from the scene by living on The Ridge. It is doubtful, however, that my parents non-legal status with regard to marriage ever much bothered the villagers. They certainly never experienced any open hostility and soon became very much part of the local scenery. When, later, infant children from Forest School swam naked in the river, that was of far more interest to the villagers, who to this day swear that Sandy Balls was once a nudist camp. Grandfather's ideas about communal morality and its cleansing of individuals who didn't conform was rather 17th century and extreme, to say the least, if not a bit unbalanced!

Ernest Westlake had rented out the bungalow on the Forest when he had returned to Oaklands to be near his flint collection. It was let to a Mr Smith, a partner to a Mr Edwards, who jointly kept a small radio shop at the west end of Fordingbridge High Street. Mr Smith was a bachelor, a sparky little man with a waxed moustache like the Kaiser's, who exuded energy and confidence to his customers, far in excess of his technical know-how when it came to repairing electrical gadgets.

The radios of the time were large, full of valves, and required three power sources, a large 'high tension' battery, a medium-sized 'grid bias', and a dry or wet cell accumulator. The latter had to be taken down to Smith and Edward's shop each week, where it was put on charge and exchanged for another. The workshop at the back of the premises had an old acid-eaten bench table on which all the accumulators of the district were connected to a trickle charger and fizzed and hummed in rows, amid a sea of hydrogen.

Mr Smith had a small photographic studio at the back of the shop too, with a faded Arcadian backdrop against which he would take portraits or family groups with an old 'Watch The Birdy' plate camera, complete with synchronised magnesium flare, later on superseded with flash bulb. Smith was the perky 'fixer', and Edwards, the solid, rather melancholy, minder of the shop, selling batteries, torches, electric light bulbs and the occasional 'wireless'. I think the partners stayed together through habit rather than any mutual compatibility. In the six months or so since my parents had been away from The Ridge, the bungalow, left to the rather slummy bachelor life-style of Mr Smith, had begun to look rather uncared for. Mr Smith was keeping ducks who were using the outside rainwater tank as a pond and these had reduced the outside of the premises to a muddy mess. A row of woollen socks graced an improvised clothes line, their toes burnt out from where Mr Smith had over-toasted his feet on the fender. A disconsolate goat bleated plaintively on its tether among the gorse bushes.

It was with elation that the itinerant trio finally arrived at the hut on The Ridge and my mother thrust her hard-won key into the door of the available annex-upstairs room. Oh joy, they at last had a home in which she and Tom and little Ivan could set up house together!

"Don't send Ivan to school unless he asks to go," had been Mrs Wicksteed's brief to my parents, and of course he never did 'ask', living an enviably free existence as a result. He spent long hours with the local Gypsies round their camp fires and grew quickly into a resourceful, independent youngster. To a young boy it must have been heaven. He quickly made friends with the local villagers who took to his pleasant ways.

Looking through my mother's diary of that time, she says of Ivan: "He always looked on the bright side of things and brought sunshine with his happy presence. Although only seven, he would go off for bread and milk to the village, singing. He was wise for his age and a real companion, an uncomplaining, willing and helpful, bright spirit."

Ivan adored my parents, as they him, and he stayed a year or so with them before returning home to Steep, and belatedly taking up his schooling at Bedales, where he never really mastered the Three Rs, which remained a handicap to an aspect of his self-confidence all his life. Later on, as a teenager, he rebuked his mother for not having made him attend school during those vital first years. ✥

Ivan Wicksteed in later life visiting Godshill Ridge.

Chapter 8
Tragedy and the Legacy of Forest School

With Mother and Father launched on their self-contained life at Godshill, all would have seemed wonderful but for Ernest Westlake's estrangement. It grieved my mother particularly, not to be on good terms with her much loved father. She and my father determined to make one last attempt to heal the rift, and to this end decided to ask him to come and live with them.

Dad wrote a warm letter putting forward the suggestion. Ernest, who always needed someone else against whom to test decisions, happened to call on a mutual friend at the same time as my parents were visiting. Taken aback at seeing them there, he muttered a few excuses, and was just about to back out of the door when my father went to him, and with a welcoming smile, held out his hand saying: "Can't we be friends? Please come and live with us."

To quote from my mother's diary: "My father hesitated a moment and then he too shot out his hand, and he and Tom shook hands in friendship. It was a wonderful moment, one I shall never forget and for which I have ever been thankful."

In a spirit of happy anticipation, my grandfather went up to London to visit Aubrey the next day. It was there that tragedy struck. Aubrey had a motorcycle and side car at that time. While taking his father from the railway station, one of his wheels got stuck in a tram line and he went out of control momentarily, mounting the pavement with the sidecar and throwing his father out onto the pavement, hitting his head. Ernest was knocked out and never regained consciousness, dying of a brain haemorrhage. My uncle Aubrey must have been traumatised with grief and a sense of guilt for many years after.

My grandfather was not yet 70, but he had left behind the seeds of what was to become a thriving Order of Woodcraft Chivalry and, a little further into the future, the formation of Forest School, a most interesting educational experiment, run by my mother's favourite cousin, Cuthbert Rutter.

I have to retrace events back a year or so before the terrible tragedy, to encompass my grandfather's other notable visionary experiment, that of the formation of Forest School.

In 1921, living on his own in the caravan at Oaklands, Ernest Westlake was contacted by his nephew Cuthbert Rutter, youngest son of the Wincanton Rutters. He had a BA Cantab., and as a young and aspiring teacher he was looking for an alternative to the formal educational systems of the time. His meeting with Uncle Ernest was fortuitous. There was an instant rapport between the younger and older man, the older having the vision, and the younger the imagination and practical will. Ernest knew, that in his nephew he had met the right man to become the headmaster of Forest School, sadly not to be inaugurated until 1928, six years after his tragic death.

The first half of the 20th century spawned a large number of alternative educational movements, from Bertrand Russell's venture, A.S. Neils Summerhill, which is still going, as is Rudolf Steiner. Forest School was to add, in its own modest way, a vein of rich educational experience to a tiny nucleus of children during the 'thirties. My cousins, Keith and Jean, had a very enjoyable two years at Forest School. Jean was the authority on the school and wrote at length of her unique experiences, so I won't attempt to say anything about it, apart from a few personal or anecdotal observations gleaned from my mother. Cuthbert undoubtedly had a rapport with children. I remember him as a lovely, gentle, kindly man, someone I could have adored as a father. Forest School was always run on a shoe string, and inevitably attracted quite a few otherwise unplaceable 'difficult' children.

Cuthbert, when the School first started, was even doing the school wash each week as he was so short of staff. He gradually surrounded himself with a group of dedicated teachers who shared his idealism, for whom teaching was a vocation, and who were prepared to work for love, and a pittance of a salary.

The School was housed in three blocks of wooden buildings, the children living simply with consciousness of the natural world very much a part of their education. It was up to the teachers to make the classes for basic learning interesting enough for the children to want to attend them, as formal attendance wasn't compulsory. The School was small enough to resemble a large family, with the staff and children as equals, living within a few basic ground rules. Uncle Aubrey was the school doctor, appointed to look after the children's health.

My mother was to teach pottery and weaving at Forest School in the mid-thirties when it was stationed at Sandy Balls. As far as I can remember, the classes were held in the huts at the entrance to the wood. Mother gave a potter's wheel to the School, and I have memories, as a small boy, of some of the older boys having a go at producing pots. One of the lads was called Peter Hedger, and he used to take great delight in modelling giant heads out of clay, onto which he sowed mustard and cress which sprouted into mops of green hair! Mother taught weaving in her custom-made weaving shed - I jump ahead of the narrative here - having made a present of a loom (made for her by Bridlig, the Czechoslovakian weaver), to the school.

Cuthbert married a Yorkshire woman called Helen, a qualified nurse and ex-matron. Sadly, I think he married her for her qualifications rather than a genuine love, thinking she would be a tremendous asset to the School. In fact, it was, in many ways, a disastrous match, but Cuthbert, being who he was, made the very best of a bad piece of misjudgment. Helen was a dominant, down-to-earth lady, with a strong will and a naturally formidable persona, hardened by climbing the hospital ladder of promotion to matron status. She did not suffer well-meaning idealists gladly, who she perceived as ineffectual and out of touch with the practical aspects of running a school. The children found her aseptic, stern discipline frightening and irksome, while the adults felt her out of touch with the school ethos. Cuthbert found himself becoming mediator and public relations man, trying to ameliorate the resultant clashes of a personality out of kilter with the key innovatory educational concepts of the school. It was a difficult balance, avoiding marital friction, while at the same time keeping a working harmony in the School.

My mother and Cuthbert were very close as cousins, and many years later he admitted his dishonesty and conscience in having married Helen for practical reasons regarding the School, rather than for love. If he paid for it, he never complained. He was a man who would have dearly loved to have had children, but after Helen had numerous miscarriages they gave up trying. Just as well, as he could never have tolerated Helen's strict regime of discipline concerning children. "Helen was a very powerful broadcaster..." he used to say of his wife, if she was expressing her disapproval.

In the 'thirties, there was a lovely music teacher working at the school, a South African called Elsa Boyd, who had the children making recorders out of bamboo. She was an intense, sensitive, creative woman and a fully-trained, dedicated teacher. She and Cuthbert were very much on the same wavelength, and fell in love, but were never able to make any intimate relationship as a jealous Helen was always in the background, and Cuthbert, honourable man that he was, would do nothing to deliberately hurt the wife he had married more for expediency than love. Elsa followed the school when it moved up to Norfolk at the start of the Second World War, to take the pupils away from the immediate danger, as it seemed then, of a German invasion in the south of the country. Although she and Cuthbert remained dear friends, she eventually felt compelled to leave the School because of the tensions involved, and she went to work in a remedial school using music as a therapeutic tool.

Cuthbert was never a completely well man. He had the misfortune to be born with a leaky heart valve. In his early years, in common with many men, he smoked a pipe, but gave it up as his health deteriorated. He used to get out of breath very easily. Nowadays, with the surgical expertise available, he could have had an artificial valve fitted and he would have lived his full span. But surgery was not advanced enough in the 1940s and he died a sick man, prematurely, at the age of 42.

Cuthbert's early death left Elsa with regrets for the rest of her life that she hadn't been able to join him in a committed relationship as his partner. If they had married I think that they would have been very happy together, but as neither of them had any particular practical bent, it's hard to imagine them as equal to the task of running a school.

In her early seventies, Elsa called in at the pottery out of the blue and I fell in love with her still brightly burning passion and concern for life. Kate and I used to visit her in her little house by the Kennet and Avon canal in Devizes, sometimes taking her in our canoe on the canal, which she loved. Her eccentricities, which I guess had always been a part of her nature, had, by this time, become fairly pronounced. She drank neither tea or coffee. All her tap water was put through a rather unhygienic filter, and her veg and fruit had to have the Henry Doubleday organic seal on it before she would buy them. I can remember her once watching us with scandalised eyes as we purchased a couple of pounds of tomatoes in a Devizes supermarket; you would have thought from her expression that we were buying poison! To ease her loneliness she had a Pekinese dog called Roggy, on whom she had lavished her love and devotion. When he died, her love had been transferred to a last crusade against the use of animals in vivisection.

Elsa was a convinced Quaker and spent her time trying to galvanise the worthies in her local meeting into some sort of action on behalf of her dumb friends. Their apparent lethargy and indifference to her crusade, caused her much distress. She saw the way that man treats the animal kingdom as part and parcel of man's inhumanity to man, and it cast a shadow over her world at times. Elsa had been quite a good pianist and had a huge grand piano in her tiny living room. I dug out some old songs from my school days, including one of Rossetti's poems set to music by Vaughan Williams called *Silent Noon*. It's a supremely evocative song of tender affection, fixed in a moment in time, in the lazy summer pastoral that is forever so English. It was a difficult setting, and I had not sung it with any discipline for years, but we both gave of our best and while watching Elsa, this old lady at the piano, suddenly a light came into her eyes so that she seemed transformed and full of youth and life again. The years seemed irrelevant in our unity and friendship.

Elsa's mother had been a nurse at the Siege of Mafeking, and had written a diary from which Elsa was busy writing a family history. Her father was Scottish and she had been raised on the Cape. Sadly and ironically, for all her care - or was it because of her obsession with pure food - Elsa developed stomach cancer. Not having heard from her for some time, we phoned to be told that she was not long for this world but would like a visit. One of her sisters had come to see her through her last days. When Kate and I arrived, we found Elsa in bed, like a frail little sparrow, all her life in her eyes, un-sedated, in no pain, and mind as sharp as it had always been. "I have my mind still," she said, "and with it I can view, in a kind of detached way, this rather interesting process my body has to go through on its way to dissolution."

She gave me Cuthbert's copy of James Stephens' *The Crock Of Gold* as a memento of herself and him. We drank a toast to eternal friendship with a glass of wine, she just moistening her lips with a small sponge. We all embraced and she said: "Stay Well," and we said "Go Well", and with a squeeze of the hand we parted. Although almost unbearably sad, it was an exalted moment from which Kate and I learnt a lot about the process of dying and the indomitability of the human spirit.

Cuthbert was a good man, who even now is remembered with affection by old pupils for the contribution he made to their happiness at Forest School, where he often gathered the children around him at a camp fire and told them stories, or read from *The Crock Of Gold*. I remember picking blackberries with him when I was a child and he used to visit us, and the infectious pleasure he would give out when he had them stewed up for supper dessert. I remember refusing to say "thank you" for something at table one day and making an issue of it, and he with a disarming smile, saying to me: "If you can't say thanks, have you ever tried saying "Honks?", which brilliantly broke the impasse, and we all said "Honks" instead of "Thanks" for years afterwards! Susan, a niece of Helen's that she and Cuthbert fostered for a while as a tiny tot of two, used to call Cuthbert 'Coggy'. That name also stuck to this kind man for years.

Interestingly, Cuthbert owned The White House next to the village school during the 'thirties, and let it out to the Youth Hostelling Association. As war broke out, it was squatted in by a Gypsy family called the Pidgleys. They racketed around in it during the five war years, during which time most of the windows were smashed and replaced by sacking. The whole place was in a total state of dilapidation when Helen, now a widow, decided to renovate it and take in paying guests. The house was saved structurally, but Helen's foray into running a guest house was short lived, owing to her fanatically high standards of tidiness not matching her dwindling energies. The house management was too much for her. She sold up and went to live with her sister. They fell out and, in desperation, Helen wrote to me to ask if she could live in a caravan in our garden. I said she was as welcome "as the flowers in May", very much feeling that Cuthbert was on my shoulder, asking me to do my best by her. My welcome touched her deeply, and so it was she settled in our garden and became part of Ridge life. It must be said that Helen, at the time, was not a happy or well woman; she was overweight and chain-smoking to the point where her fingers and upper lip were permanently stained yellow with nicotine. I got on well with her, and she shared with me many of the more positive memories of her relationship with Cuthbert who, in her loneliness, she had come to idealise.

In retrospect, I think she sincerely appreciated how much her husband had broadened her awareness of all the joyful cultural possibilities life had to offer, that she would never have been aware of had she not known him. On one of her visits to the doctor she discovered that she had a thrombosis wandering around her system, and became terrified of the implications. Increasingly depressed and arthritic, she closed all the windows of her caravan one night, turned on the gas, lay down on her bed and was found dead the next day. Poor Helen, she had expressed a wish to be 'reunited' with Cuthbert, and he, kind soul, if another life awaits us, probably did his best for her troubled spirit. But he and Helen were never meant for each other. ⚘

Chapter 9
The Simple Life

I must retrace my narrative, once more, to the time some months before Grandfather's demise, soon after my parents had gained access to the room on The Ridge at Godshill.

My father had fallen foul, in particular, of George Allen from Whiteway, who kept up a hate campaign against him for weeks after he and my mother left the Colony, sending vituperative letters slandering my father to my grandfather that were so extreme, that even he gave their contents no credence. My father, to whom hate mail was far more distressing than physical violence, became quite ill with the onslaught. In desperation, he enlisted the help of one of his psychic friend Penton's many 'controls', in this case a hefty, jolly Scotsman, inevitably called 'Jock'. "Not to worry," boomed Jock. "I will see what I can do." Amazingly, a few hours later, my father suddenly experienced a sensation of relief, as though a great weight had suddenly been lifted off his shoulders and all was, once again, light and laughter. The hate mail ceased, and my parents never heard of George Allen again.

They experienced much joy and spiritual uplift from their frequent seances with Sid Penton, until he finally moved to Sussex, where they lost touch with him. My mother strangely never attended a seance again, and had to rely on her own intuition to guide her through life. Intuition for her was always deemed to be inspired from 'the other side' and must, therefore, be right. Although she made many good decisions, she could be 'certain' to the point of arrogance, or pig-headedness, at times, which was difficult to live with on occasions.

With Grandfather's death, one chapter ended and another began. My parents became materially secure. My mother inherited the Godshill Ridge property and her brother Aubrey, Sandy Balls Wood. She also acquired a small income of three pounds a week from her father's estate, which was enough for her and my father to live on if they were frugal and lived simply, to which both parties were accustomed.

The now busy B3078 passing in front of the house, was then a gravel track winding its way along the ridges toward Southampton, with the very occasional car bumping along in a cloud of dust to disturb the Arcadian tranquillity of the area. My mother and father were the first of the 'simple lifers', practicing near self-sufficiency. With the aid of the contents of an outdoor privy, Father started a small kitchen garden in the gravelly, unpromising, peaty forest soil. He was a good gardener, having had considerable experience of it in Nomansland, working his sister and brother-in-law's large kitchen garden behind their cottage.

Firewood was collected each day off the Forest, usually old black gorse stumps left after the traditional annual rotational burn in March, and carried home, faggot-like, on the back in a loop of rope. These he started to carve into the most original imaginary creatures. My mother, always a pragmatic person behind all her spiritual moonshine and romanticism, suggested that Dad might try making a few carvings to sell, and towards that end, make a few practical things like toasting forks, paper weights, paper knives, and so on. Dad thought it a good idea, and it became his way to help earn a living. When he went for a walk he would take a small pruning saw tucked inside his waistcoat (in case he met the local keeper), and if he saw a promising distorted piece of wood that lent itself to his creative imagination, he would cut it and bring it home. An old holly copse and natural piece of woodland on the north edge of Pitts Wood enclosure was my father's happy hunting ground. The old holly trees, browsed by cattle and ponies, bent and broken by winds and time, gave a wonderful variety of shapes to carve, its close grain making it a joy to work with rasp and chisel. Most of the initial rough work was done while the pieces were still green, as the wood was softer to cut. Bill hooks, rasps, files and pokers, with a few small wood carving tools for detail, were the tools of his craft. Pokers were heated up to burn out eyes and give definition to form. Often the natural colour of the wood would be enhanced by the subtle use of coloured stains, polished and burnished for hours by my father's hands as he sat by the fire on a winter's evening. The first outlet for my Dad's work was in a shop in Christchurch that used to take the work on sale or return, and every now and then a welcome postal order would arrive for 7/6d or 12/6d. Heady days, indeed!

The Czech weaver, Bridlig, stayed on as tenant of my father's cottage. He earned his living by market gardening in its three-acre field. He possessed a donkey, a small cart and light cultivating equipment, growing the usual potatoes, peas, beans and kale. I have it on authority from one of the villagers that the donkey, when slow to obey orders to back into the shafts of the cart, would be picked up bodily by an irate Bridlig and placed in the shafts, and by way of reprimand, he would bite its ear! "Come to me!", "Go from me!" and "Whoa!", were the three commands he used to control it while at work. Bridlig was so strong he was witnessed one day lifting the whole section of a roof into place on a large shed he was building.

On the ground to the side of the cottage, Mother had a weaving shed built, thatched with heather. It held a copper where she dyed her wool. Bridlig made her a sturdy, but primitive, cloth loom and taught her the rudiments of weaving in exchange for his rent. After a while, however, Mother found that Bridlig's attention wandered away from warp and weft, to her person, and he became so licentious and infatuated with her that it became impossible to continue the working relationship. He just would not take 'No' for an answer, believing that he was irresistible; my parents had to reluctantly resort to cutting him dead whenever they saw him as he was too thick-skinned to take any other hint. Bridlig was not a very good market gardener, and the enterprise folded in due course. He upped sticks and moved to Wales, where he worked looms in one of the many small cloth mills of that country.

My mother finally bought herself a Swedish, full-sized floor loom, spinning wheel and warping mill from the weaving suppliers' Dryad, and taught herself to spin, dye, thread up the loom and weave. In a labour of love, she made my father a cloth length for a suit, spinning both warp and weft, dying the wool with vegetable dyes. As a beginner at spinning, it was a mistake to use hand-spun wool for the warp as the yarn tended to be too uneven and full of slubs to run through the heddles and reed. It was constantly having to be coaxed and repaired as the weaving progressed. However, it got done and my father proudly wore his suit, a jacket, waistcoat and plus-fours, to all the craft exhibitions where he sold his carvings each summer.

With Bridlig no longer in occupation of the cottage, coinciding with a small windfall legacy, my parents were able to do some much needed repairs and alterations to the cottage, as well as getting it re-thatched. They put in dormer windows to increase the light, had the open fireplace blanked off, apart from a small grate, and installed a small, enclosed stove in the living room. They spent about £380, quite an outlay for those days.

The next tenants for the cottage were the Pask family. Mr Pask, the Quaker friend of Ernest Westlake was a retired bank clerk, a small man who always wore a black beret, and was a keen amateur photographer. Mr Pask had one of those lovely rosewood plate cameras, mounted on a tripod. He built a dark room to do his own processing next to the cottage. When his daughter Elsie died many years later, we discovered many of her father's photographic plates that offer a notable pictorial history of an Edwardian family. I remember one of the plate negatives, showing the three Pask children as close infant siblings, posing in a giant 'Old Mother Hubbard' shoe that a London studio must have made available for novel child family groups. Mr Pask was also keen on fruit trees and, wherever he had moved to in his life, he had always planted up the garden with apple, pear and plum trees. He did the same at Godshill, and many of the trees he put in are bearing fruit to this day.

A much-told story concerning Mr Pask related to his teeth, which into his old age were perfect except for one extraction. He went for the first and last time to a dentist, complaining of toothache. Pointing to the offending tooth, he asked the dentist to pull it out. To his dismay, the practitioner pulled out the wrong tooth, a perfectly sound one, and Mr Pask angrily told him to place it back in the socket from which it had been pulled. This was done, and on a second attempt the decayed molar was located and successfully pulled. Amazingly, the replaced tooth stayed in place, firmed up and never gave any further trouble.

I only vaguely remember Mrs Pask, with her long grey hair, when she was an invalid with advancing cancer, confined to bed and looking out of the bedroom window. There were three grown-up children, Roland, who was bursar at Sidcot and lived next to the school, Mary who escaped to live and work in Oxford, and Elsie who nursed her mother and lived in the cottage all her life, a sitting tenant for 2/6d a week. She made a frugal living, running a morning Dame school in the cottage, to which a handful of 'too sensitive' children for the rough and tumble of the village school were sent, myself included. This was much later, of course, in the next decade.

The renovated cottage was named 'Craft Cottage' by my parents, and in exchange for a low rent, the Pasks sold my father's carvings from a display laid out in one of the new dormer windows. From an account book of the period, one can see there was only a trickle of sales, owing to the relative immobility of the population then, and the fact that most people only had enough money for the essentials of life.

At home on The Ridge, my mother had her bicycle which she would ride to the village shop and bakery for bread and basic groceries. (It was always advisable to cycle in those days with a full repair kit as the gravelly, potholed road was a constant source of punctures.) The shop was owned by Mr Church, a survivor of the 1914-18 Great War and the horrors of a gas attack, which left his respiratory system permanently disabled. His face was always very florid as a direct result of the effects of mustard gas on his skin, poor man.

The local pub was, and still is, The Fighting Cocks. At that time, it was a thatched, rectangular building with its entrance facing towards Fordingbridge, owned by Strong's Brewery of Romsey. For many years the pub landlords were a family called Grigg. Old man Grigg, by all accounts, was a bit of a boozer, and quite aggressive when in his cups. The licence was passed on to his widow when he died, who relinquished it eventually to her son Jim, who took the pub on with his wife Barbara (née Cutler) after coming out of the Navy at the end of the Second World War. I have an old, faded photograph of my father, standing in front of the original Fighting Cocks. In the 'twenties, the old pub was pulled down and a large mock Tudor 'road house' went up in its place, built by the Brewery.

Besides weaving, my mother took up sandal-making, being commissioned to make a pair by Mrs Church, the wife of the village baker. Mrs Church suffered from bad bunions, and she always said of the sandals that Mother made her, that they were the most comfortable footwear she had ever worn. Mother found sandal-making very hard work, without much

Above: Tom and Margaret outside the goat shed along The Ridge at Godshill.

Left: Margaret spinning on the roof of the 'bungalow' on The Ridge.

Below: Craft (now Croft) Cottage, then occupied by the Pask Family. The cottage was renovated by Margaret and Tom and from here Elsie Pask ran a Dame School and Tom sold his carvings.

profit and didn't pursue the craft for long.

My parents bought themselves two Forest ponies from the money my mother received from the sale of her mother's piano, and her own violin. The ponies were called Juno and Sappho and Mother and Father taught themselves to ride. I have photos of my father as a North American Indian brave, sporting a genuine wig with many wiry plaits, astride Sappho, bareback in a rope halter, obviously enjoying the play acting. They bought themselves a second-hand governess cart and trap and as both ponies were broken to harness, used them as their method of transport for several years.

The original bungalow on The Ridge drawn by Elsie Pask and...

...the original Fighting Cocks pub with Tom Charman standing outside, second from the right.

Chapter 10
Horse Drawn Caravanning

Eventually, they purchased a large horse-drawn caravan made by a firm of coachbuilders in Winchester called Hutchings. With it came a superb set of double harness (made by apprentices for their final leather work exam - sixteen stitches to the inch), sporting the Eyre and Spottiswoode crest in silver.

With it, the ponies could be harnessed to the van either side of a central pole, and with a goat to provide them with milk, riding in a cage between the rear wheels under the van, they set off for an idyllic summer on the open road. The goat, bought from the Pentons when they moved to Sussex, was tethered at night, getting its fill of whatever leafy herbage was available. It so grew to love the regime that it used to get into its cage of its own accord each day, ready for the off!

The late 1920s offered the last opportunity to indulge in this sort of life style, before the noise, stench and general dominance of the motor car made horse-drawn caravanning an endurance test rather than a pleasure.

The Hutchings caravan was a bit on the heavy side, but with two good-sized ponies of 14 hands in tandem to pull it, taking their time they could tackle most hills. The van had the traditional braking system of the 'skid pan', an iron shoe that fitted under the rim of the wheel, attached to a stout chain fastened to the chassis of the vehicle. On coming to a downhill stretch you ran one of the back wheels onto the shoe which, when it was brought up short on the chain, brought the wheel to a dead stop, locking it on the shoe and effectively braking it. The wheel, so stopped, would be dragged down on the shoe or 'skid pan'. Usually only one wheel was required thus to be immobilised, but sometimes, if the hills were severe, both wheels could be locked. The disadvantage of this technique was, that if the hill was very long, the iron skid pans became hot enough to scorch the wooden 'fellows' or rims of the wheels, so one had to watch out and take breaks in the descent, allowing time for the skid pans to cool down. The caravan also had a system of rods connected to brake shoes that you could activate from the driving platform by a small wheel. These had rubber linings so could only be used to immobilise the van when at rest.

Mother and Father travelled many miles in the caravan, all over the south-east of England, either making use of the generous hospitality of farmers, staying overnight in their fields, or just pulling up at the roadside and tethering the ponies and goat on the verges. The ponies grew very adept at managing their tethering chains, nudging them forward with a flick of the head as they advanced, over the sward, lulling my parents to sleep with peaceful munching noise through the night. The pressures of population and life style, as we know them today, were far less pronounced in the 1920s and, as a result, there was far more tolerance shown to Gypsies and their middle-class imitators.

Tom and the Bertram Hutchings wagon on the road during the idyllic summer of 1927.

Sometimes an unpromising situation would resolve itself in the most unusual way. Typical of the many experiences they had on the road, Mother and Father found themselves on the boundaries of a large estate. It was late in the day, so they decided to ask for a pitch for the night from the big house, which they approached down a long, aristocratic avenue of trees, through a Capability Brown landscape. My mother, who took the initiative on these occasions, undaunted by the splendour of the aristocratic pile, rang the front door bell. After what seemed an eternity, echoing footsteps could be heard coming down a corridor, and a butler in tails haughtily opened the door. He did a double take of disapproval at the sight of two sandalled bohemians, plus Gypsy caravan, on his doorstep. My mother blithely asked if she and Father could have permission to park the van, ponies, and themselves somewhere on the estate for the night. To which request the butler replied stiffly, when he had gathered his wits, in the negative, and that moreover, they must get their caravan and animals off his master's estate pronto, or he would call the police! This last remark raised my mother's fighting dander, and an argument ensued, in which she said something like: "Do you mean to say that with all these thousands of acres of land at his disposal, your employer wouldn't allow two honest people to camp for just one night? Surely with all this evidence of wealth he could make an exception. Can we ask you if it is possible to contact him?"

The butler remained obdurate, and my parents were just about to accept failure, when a friendly voice hailed them from an upstairs window, and Lord so and so asked his butler to admit my parents into the grand house. There they met his lordship, whose romantic nature had been tickled by the sight of a horse-drawn caravan coming up the drive. The overheard conversation between the butler and my mother had appealed to his socialist leanings of fair do's for the proletariat. Not only were they allowed to stay the night, they were invited into the big house for an evening meal. My father's prowess as a raconteur came into its own and the evening's conversation flowed easily.

Of course, it was not long before the subject of Spiritualism came up, and his Lordship paid close attention, as it turned out that that his only son and heir had been tragically killed in the Great War. The poor man was desperate to latch on to some faith that suggested that this life was not the black end of everything. Happily, my father was able to offer very positive help towards the rehabilitation of this bereaved man's outlook.

When my parents left next morning, they were thanked effusively for coming. "You have made such a difference to my life, I cannot thank you enough," were the parting words of his lordship. I cannot remember the aristocratic gentleman's name, but you can guess that such happenings and contacts were looked on not just as chance by my parents, but as meant or guided to by "guardian angels" or higher Spiritual Beings, bringing joy to those who sorrow in this world. ✦

Chapter 11
Self Sufficiency and Goats

So passed the first few years of my parents' life together, one might say in a fairly hedonistic way, with no one to please except themselves. They built up a herd of Saanen goats, white with dainty tassels on their necks, and had the 48 acres of 'rough' fenced.

The goats were allowed to roam freely, coming home in the evening to their stalled shed below the house to be milked. Mother thought she would go into butter and cheese production and, to that end, acquired all the necessary utensils. The scheme rather fell through, owing to the goats not producing enough milk for butter. The cream content, although plentiful in goat's milk, takes 48 hours to rise fully, by which time, without refrigeration, the milk had gone sour. The churns took half a gallon of cream, and the small amounts my mother managed to extract with great labour, didn't reach up to the level of the churn's paddles. So, apart from a bit of cream cheese that tasted more often than not like a Billy goat smells, the logistics of cheese and butter from goat's milk was a non-starter. However, the goats were kept on right up to the end of the Second World War in 1945, playing a large part in the home economy of the time.

Mother became a member of The British Goat Society and exhibited some of her goats and kids at the New Forest Show in Brockenhurst. She and Father would go across the Forest with two or three goats in the well of the governess cart, with Juno in the shafts. Juno was a bit slow and sulky on his own unless you rattled a chain, which for some reason got him going at a fair old clip.

Mother's moment of glory came one year when she won a medal for the best Nanny kid in the show. It turned out to be a very undistinguished creature we called Brownie whose maximum yield, even in the first flush of her lactation, only gave half a pint of milk. So much for expert assessment of potential! ❦

Chapter 12
The Coming of Hilda Sass to The Ridge

Fraulein Anna Sass, after finishing her service with my grandfather, had for a time, acted as governess to a French family.

With the political situation in Russia becoming more and more unstable as the revolutionary elements became more organised, she heard that her niece Hilda, in Estonia, was now an orphan. By a series of cruel fates, her mother had been struck by lightning and her father had died of starvation in the advancing Russian famine. So Anna Sass went post-haste back to Russia to look after her niece. They survived together, under increasingly hard conditions, until 1920, or thereabouts. Anna, with her health failing, and as a last desperate gamble, put Hilda in the hands of the Norwegian Consul, asking them to look after her until such time as a boat could be found to take her to England. She informed Grandfather of what she had done, making a plea that someone in the family would adopt Hilda. Weakened by malnutrition, Anna Sass succumbed to dysentery and died, and so became one of the countless Russians to perish in those troubled times. In 1922, a notification came to my Uncle Aubrey that the great-niece of Fraulein Anna Sass had arrived at Southampton by boat, and would someone pick her up!

Hilda Sass, Fraulein's great niece, rescued as an orphan from Estonia, pictured in later life with the young Chris and Danae.

My uncle, by now fully committed with his family and their first two children, passed the notification on to my parents, saying: "You take this girl on, seeing as you have no children." My parents readily agreed, and so it was, one winter's day, my father took the pony and trap into Southampton docks, and picked up the twelve-year-old Hilda. Imagine the trauma of a young girl who had just lost both her parents, survived typhus and cholera, been looked after by her one surviving relative, and then, suddenly uprooted from her famine-struck, revolution-torn, native land. To leave all this and be shipped out to a totally alien culture, to speak not a word of English, and you just about have the picture. Imagine her clip-clopping across the Forest in the dark with my father, the only illumination a couple of carriage lamps powered by candles each side of the governess cart. Then her arrival at the primitive bungalow where my parents tried to make her feel at home in a language she could not understand. Her misery and sense of isolation must have been complete.

So ended one phase of life on The Ridge and my parents' total self-sufficiency unto themselves. Hilda turned out to be able to understand a smattering of French, so gradually some sort of communication was established. Hilda was soon assimilated into Ridge life, quickly learning English and making lifelong friends of a family who had bought a strip of land from my parents and built a charming brick house on it called 'Four Winds'. The family, Harry and Gertrude Collins, had two daughters, Margaret and Kathleen, just about Hilda's age, providing valuable companionship for her. Gertrude, or Gerty as we called her, was a niece of my father's. My parents did their best by Hilda, sending her to a good Quaker co-educational boarding school called Sibford, where she received a fair education. From there she moved on to obtain catering and housekeeping management qualifications which she used to great effect, earning her living in various schools as cook and housekeeper, a job in which she excelled.

Although a brilliant cook, she was incapable of imparting any information on the subject, and when my mother asked her advice on how to cook something, all she usually had in reply was an irritated: "Well, I mean, you know! Don't you know how to do that, Margaret?" To which my mother would reply, mildly but wearily: "I wouldn't have asked, Hilda, had I known." At this, Hilda would swiftly and deftly take over, without a word, whatever cooking project had been under discussion.

Hilda got on fine with my father, sharing his sense of humour and fun. It was a strange fostering that the fates had brought my parents. Hilda had very little in common with life in the Forest, or them. Fate had brought them together and they rubbed along but not more than that. Apart from a few negative references regarding 'Auntie', Hilda never mentioned her past. I guess the only way the human spirit can cope with pain sometimes, is to deny and block it totally. This she did all her life, but paid a very great price for it in the end, willing herself into dying in a state of utter depression and withdrawal from the world. ❧

Chapter 13
Visitors to the Ridge

Mother and Father's lifestyle attracted many odd and interesting characters who enjoyed their open house hospitality.

One character from Golders Green days, by the name of Wilfred Sinclair, a young survivor of the 1914-18 slaughter, arrived one day. Sinclair was a pacifist at heart, and when the order had been given to charge up and over the parapet he had fired his rifle high over the heads of the enemy. How he survived the inevitable hand-to-hand fighting was a mystery, but survive he did, and without a scratch. He had already met my parents when he had stayed with them in the small lodge house at Golders Green, and came to Godshill hoping to find balm for his disturbed psyche. He built himself a tiny hut to meditate in amongst the gorse. To sustain himself he bought a sack, (yes, a whole sack) of wheat, to turn into 'frumenty', a sort of porridge with the grain boiled in milk. His navel-gazing on such a bland, monotonous diet only lasted a little over two weeks, I am told, after which he got tired of his own company and, after a brief flirt with Hilda, disappeared from my parents' lives for ever.

Another interesting character from the 'twenties, who came to visit and rhapsodise over my parents' life style, was the itinerant puppeteer and author Walter Wilkinson, whose wanderings brought him into the New Forest with his 'Old Encumbrance' and unique 'Peep Show'. This was a specially designed show booth, mounted on bicycle wheels, containing all his own handmade puppets, tent, food and cooking utensils which he pulled from village to village, using the legs of the booth as shafts. In each village he stopped, organised a puppet show and, from the pennies he took in his cap, he kept himself for whole summers at a time. To survive over the winters he wrote about his experiences in a series of delightful books, the first of which was the wonderfully evocative *The Peep Show*. The book is the story of the conception of the show through to its realisation and happy success as he wandered through the Devon and Cornish seaside resorts and villages. All this took place in the era of the first open charabancs, whose noise and smell he could not abide; the innocent time of Pierrots and donkeys on the sands. It's a delightful book, full of youthful and romantic enthusiasm. My parents are mentioned in Walter Wilkinson's second book *Vagabonds and Puppets*. When he got married, he and his wife continued to travel all over, producing many books of their experiences. They even went to America with the Peep Show. Although the later books are very interesting, none compared with the freshness of writing of the first one.

Many years later, I was privileged to see one of Walter Wilkinson's puppet shows when he visited Sidcot school where I was a pupil. He and his wife were an elderly couple by then, but they put on a wonderful performance, he working the puppets with great dexterity while his wife supplied the music on recorder. The show lasted a good two hours and brought the house down with its universal appeal. In the traditional three-finger puppet tradition, as with Punch and Judy, Wilkinson carved all his own characters and wrote his own plays for them, developing a simple philosophy about the fun and joy of life that centred around his 'Woodenheads', as he affectionately called them. No children or adults were immune to their sense of fun, he claimed, with some justification!

Mr Smith, of the radio shop, went back to live in Fordingbridge, and so the whole house became available to my parents. As they saved a little money, so they improved the house a little. The open fireplace was the first thing to go. It had always proved useless, and the glass plumbing for the back boiler had long since burst in one of the winter frosts. So a gap was made through the old inglenook, through to the wood shed, which was converted into a lean-to kitchen area. The roof pitch was too shallow for a proper run-off, so they had the roof sheeted with corrugated iron sheeting which they then, stupidly, had taken off again in favour of a layer of more aesthetically pleasing bituminous felt. The result was to have a leaky roof for many decades which was only relieved by the strategic placing of many buckets under the drips! The space under the pile supports of the upstairs room was boarded in, so making a spare bedroom. The main living room was divided in two, and a back-to-back pair of moderate-sized fireplaces built for the resulting couple of rooms.

The story of the building of the fireplaces has become part of family folk memory. My father engaged a brickie who turned out to be a total cowboy, and he made the mistake of paying him at piece-work rates. My mother could remember him running with the hods of bricks and literally slapping the chimney up like a donkey's hind leg. He built the hearth straight onto the floorboards without any visible insulation against fire, assuring my concerned parents that all was safe and under control. When my father commented that he thought that the chimney was a bit crooked, the builder replied: "Oh, you want it straight, do you?" and proceeded to nudge and push the wobbly structure into some semblance of order with his shoulder. Amazingly the chimney stayed up and the fires worked. All was fine, until one day smoke started to come up through the floor boards, and the floor joists and planking surrounding the hearth were discovered to be on fire. My mother rushed down to Alfred Chalk, the local carpenter, and asked him for help. In the meantime, my father had been pouring water onto the fire and the surrounds of the hearth, to not much effect. Mr Chalk arrived with a pick-axe and hacked up the floor boards round the fire to expose the joists, and with the aid of buckets of water they eventually got the blaze under control. It was a near thing!

Alf Chalk was a decent man and he knew the cowboy builder my parents had employed. When he saw him in Fordingbridge High Street one day he accosted him and tore him off a strip saying: "You crazy fool, do you know your slipshod work nearly cost the Charmans their house?" "There," said the cowboy, quick as a flash, "I told them 'tweren't safe to build it straight on the floor, but they would have it!" A few days later, there was a knock on the door, and upon my father answering it, who should be there but the guilty builder. With a flourish he produced a large bunch of flowers from behind his back saying: "For the Missis!", which my father accepted graciously as being as much of an apology as he was ever likely to get! Alf Chalk subsequently put in a brick foundation under the hearth.

Alf was not a true native of Godshill. His family had their roots in Wiltshire. He left school at eleven and eventually married and settled in Godshill. He was a natural, self-taught carpenter, earning his living with all sorts of odd jobs. He had two sons, Sid, who was in the navy in the Second World War, and Len, who served in the army. Together they started a small building venture after the war ended in the 1940s. The first building work Alf Chalk ever did was for my parents when they asked him to build them a stable, feed room, trap, governess cart and caravan shed. Oak posts were dug into the ground and an L-shaped frame was erected from 4 x 2 timber, and clad in 10 inch planks with a simple, single pitch roof. The unit, with its stable doors and double doors for the trap and caravan storage, looked very smart with its coat of creosote. Alf was a scrupulously honest workman, keeping account of all the materials used in the construction of the building, down to the last pound of nails. He charged 9d an hour for his labour, and the whole building only came to £40. Such was the value of money in the 'twenties. Like Lem Putt, the privy builder of literary fame (*The Specialist* by Charles Sale (1930)), Alf was so pleased and proud of his handiwork, he brought his wife up one Sunday to look at it. To quote Lem Putt, my parents had 'certainly got themselves a mighty fine stable block'! It stayed up for sixty years and did us proud.

Alf was exempted from military service in the First World War as he had a bad hernia and wore a truss to keep his gut in place all his working life. He never had it repaired, and lived without it seeming to give him the least bit of trouble. Having a hernia saved Alf's life in all probability, but working on the land was no easy alternative to the army. His war years were spent working in agricultural gangs, harvesting hundreds of acres of corn, baling up and carting wheat, barley and oats. The gangs more or less lived off the land, sleeping in rough shelters under the hedges or in barns. Alf said the gang would have a communal stew pot that they would keep on the go all week, adding whatever rabbit, hare or illegal pheasant their lurchers, ferrets, or expertise with the catapult, bagged in the way of game. In the winter, the gangs worked at root-pulling and clamping, hedge-laying and ditch and drain maintenance. My parents gave Alf permission to hunt for rabbits on our land with lurcher dog, ferrets and shot gun. It was a spare-time sport he hugely enjoyed, as well as giving him meat for the pot. I remember the only time the lurcher was let off its leash was to chase a rabbit or help flush one out of a clump of gorse bushes. When I asked why he didn't let his dog go free all the time, he said it would get muscle-bound and lose the edge off its speed.

My mother told me of the time Alf shot a rabbit just after it had run under our boundary fence and out into the open Forest. Alf's adrenaline was flowing and it was just too good a shot to miss. The problem was that at the moment he shot the rabbit, the local keeper happened to be passing on his bicycle and witnessed Alf shoot and pick up his kill. The keeper, Slightam, was rather a sour, over-conscientious man who prided himself on prosecuting misdemeanours, however trivial. As shooting a rabbit on the Forest without a licence was illegal, in spite of the fact that it had been on our land a moment before, he reported the incident. Alf was summoned to appear before the magistrate in Winchester in a month's time, for poaching on Crown land. Poor Alf went through a month's hell, anticipating all sorts of extreme penalties, while waiting for the appointed day of his 'trial'. My mother remembered he would visit her and my father, spending long hours morosely discussing his dire predicament. "I says to the missus, I says, it t'aint like murder...is it?" Clearly a frightened and troubled man. Of course, when it came to the day of the magistrate's hearing, his name was called out, and when he went trembling into the court room, all that happened was that his trivial offence was stated, Alf pleaded guilty and was fined 10/-. "Case dismissed!" And that was to his amazed relief!

Not that Alf was beyond a bit of poaching, mind you. He used to tell me tales of going home on moonlit nights from work. Passing through the large estates where he worked, he would spy out the rows of roosting pheasants in the trees, their silhouettes black and sharp against the light of the full moon. Thus seen, they were an easy target for his expertise with a home-made catapult, and a justifiable perk against the pittance of the 12/- a week agricultural wage of the day, which didn't go far with a growing family.

In his later years, Alf suffered from bad bouts of lumbago, which he referred to as "a touch of the screws". It was very debilitating, but a spot of ferreting worked wonders on his condition! A villager told me he coaxed a crippled, disconsolate Alf on many occasions from his armchair for a spot of ferreting. They would peg out the nets, put the ferrets into the burrows and, for a few minutes, silence would rein. Then a few muffled thumps of alarm would come from underground, and suddenly a rabbit would shoot into one of the nets. Alf, who had hardly been able to move before, would suddenly come alive, staggering across to dispatch the rabbit as all hell broke loose in the subterranean depths of the warren. Alf was so busy giving the entangled rabbits the chop and resetting the nets, his lumbago was forgotten, and indeed disappeared, to the point where his wife used to regard him with suspicion at his sprightly return home, and accuse him of having been a malingerer.

I have mentioned already my grandfather's action in getting my mother expelled from the Quakers, or Society of Friends. Well, there was rather an amusing sequel to this. After my mother and father had been together for a few years, Mother wrote to the Society and applied to rejoin. The Quakers responded by sending along two Elders, long-term, fully-committed, senior members of the Society appointed to look after its interests. They were to vet my mother, and assess whether or not she was now a suitable candidate, morally and spiritually, for reinstatement. My parents were very welcoming and hospitable and the four of them got on like a house on fire, so much so that the Quaker worthies completely forgot the original purpose of their visit. By the time of their departure, none of the questions they had been instructed to ask my mother had been broached, to their own, it must be said, as well as my mother's amusement! A further meeting was arranged, at which, without my mother having to compromise her beliefs in any way, she was fully reinstated as a Quaker, and, in later years, was even asked to be an Elder. ⚘

Chapter 14
The Coming of the Car and Mettled Roads

Sometime in the mid-twenties, a survey of motor traffic on the Forest roads was taken. A sentry box was placed beside the gravel track (now the B3078), and a man posted to note the number of cars going by in 24 hours.

My mother, passing by on her bicycle, was asked, jokingly, to go up and down a few times to swell the traffic numbers. Her efforts obviously bore fruit as the road was mettled during the decade. And so began a revolution in mobility and a transport system of which our forbears never dreamed.

My mother was not slow to take advantage of the new mettled road, and the advances of the early mass manufacture of motor cars. She bought one of the first family cars to appear on the market, a brand new Austin Seven, for £150. It was a tiny little car, with a folding hood and floppy side-panel windows. It arrived from Southampton complete with instructor, who gave Mother an hour's driving instruction, then asked her to drive him back to Southampton. This she eventually did, expressing many reservations as to her competence, once on her own, to drive back to Godshill. "Oh, you will manage, there is nothing to it," said the instructor gaily, dismissing her fears - and, remarkably she did!

There was no driving test in those early days of motoring, but then there were very few cars. The Austin had a complex set of levers on the steering wheel, which either advanced or retarded the spark to facilitate easy starting. The engine was turned over by means of a brass crank handle in front of the car; no self-starter in those days! The fuel system had no filter so the fuel jet was constantly blocked up by the early dirty petrol. My mother became a dab hand at unblocking the jet, with a fine sewing needle. The filter came as a design refinement a few years later, as did a self-starter. My father, now in his sixties, for some reason never learnt to drive, leaving all mechanics to my mother. Nevertheless she said he was always a competitive back seat driver, constantly urging her to take risks and go faster, exhortations she easily resisted, being of a cautious nature. She never had an accident, it must be said.

Building the road from Godshill to Fordingbridge.   *Photo:Fordingbridge Museum.*

The little Austin soldiered on, progressively getting more of a rattle trap. The side screens cracked and the hood developed holes, so that one had to dress up to avoid a stiff neck from the draughts on a long run. The pull up Fordingbridge hill would cause the engine to boil, and the radiator cap, which had been lost and replaced by an old thermos flask cork, used to blow out, accompanied by a gush of steam. Very occasionally, Mother could be prevailed upon, if the road was straight and there were no other cars, to put her foot down on the accelerator, and the old Austin would struggle and shake its way up to its maximum speed of forty miles an hour - and didn't it feel like it! Having a car must have made it much easier for my parents to get about and socialise, and also for transporting my father's carvings to the various exhibitions. These were by far and away his best outlet for sales, as his personality made him an excellent salesman.

In those days there was a small garage business on the right-hand corner going into Fordingbridge near the Victoria Rooms, owned by a Mr Jeffrey and son. Mr Jeffrey was an honest trader and mechanic, and my mother trusted all the maintenance and mechanical problems of the Austin to him over the years. I can remember the hand-cranked petrol pumps and the way Mr Jeffrey would tilt the hose at the end of fuel delivery so that the last drop went into the tank. One formed friendships with garage proprietors in those days that, somehow, one doesn't today. Mr Jeffrey's son's expertise went so far as to be able to strip an engine and rebore the block. He was the 'hands-on' mechanic, either under a car in their tiny workshop, or fabricating some part on his lathe in a sea of oil and swarf. His father did the paper work in the office, and with his air of affable confidence was the public relations man for the business. ◀

The strange wooden carvings of Tom Charman fascinated Sir Arthur Conan Doyle. The two became close friends.

Chapter 15
Conan Doyle and Paranormal Matters

CURIO CARVER

TOM CHARMAN

GODSHILL
FORDINGBRIDGE
H A N T S

Among my father's many friends was the former doctor turned successful author, Sir Arthur Conan Doyle of Sherlock Holmes fame.

He lived, at that time, near Cadnam in the New Forest, in a property called Bignell Wood. Now in his latter years, he too had become interested in Spiritualism, which formed the common bond between the two men. Conan Doyle had met my father in London at one of the annual Artist Craftsman's exhibitions in Kingston. Initially attracted by my father's strange carvings, he quickly discovered Tom's interest in the paranormal and his attention was held at the mention of fairies, as he had just written a convincing preface to his book *The Coming of the Fairies*.

This book, published in 1922, described how two North Country lassies had actually seen fairies and photographed them with a simple box camera. Examples of their visions, the Cottingley Fairies, captured on film, illustrated the book. At the time the book caused a sensation, making the girls celebrities for several months, and inundating their home village with the curious and credulous, Conan Doyle among them, as well as reporters eager for a sensational 'scoop'. He had all the negatives of the images taken by the girls subjected to rigorous tests by 'experts', and they pronounced them genuine. *(The girls, Elsie Wright and Frances Griffiths admitted in the 1980s that the photographs were faked using cardboard cut-outs, but Frances still maintained that one was genuine.)* To Conan Doyle, simple Watson that he was, this photographic proof of elementals was exciting stuff, and he began to lend his name and prestige to matters paranormal. Through him my father had articles printed, complete with illustrations in the *Psychic Gazette*, organ of the Psychical Research Society, recounting his psychic visions of elementals and theories as to their place in the scheme of creation.

Conan Doyle was a frequent visitor to our little bungalow. A large affable man of simple tastes, he enjoyed my parents' life style with its rich vein of the improbable. I recall visiting Bignell Wood House as a child, a huge rambling place in the woods at Cadnam. It had a large sweep of lawn in front of it leading down to a Forest stream that flowed through the grounds. On this lawn there was a bronze heron that, in the twilight, my imagination turned into some terrifying predatory creature. But this was all in the future, of course. Lady Doyle, a be-furred, sophisticated individual, in comparison to her friendly bear of a husband, accompanied him on his many travels, and they were often away from Bignell Wood for weeks at a time. A family called the Bickles acted as caretakers. They also became part of my parents' circle of friends. ✦

Chapter 16
The Beginnings of Godshill Pottery

With the decade of the twenties nearing its end and my father reaching his late sixties, he was beginning to find woodcarving a bit hard work, and my mother, always innovative, decided to take up pottery, with the idea that she would throw the pots and my father decorate them with his birds, animals and fairies.

The annual Artist Craftsman exhibition had developed from the Knox Guild shows held in the art gallery above the library in Kingston-upon-Thames, later moving to Central Hall, Westminster in London. The idea was conceived and organised by the husband and wife team of potters in Oxshott, Surrey, Denise and Henry Wren and was now well established, attracting creative talent from many different parts of the country including such famous names as the Dolmeche family, responsible for the manufacture and revival of the recorder.

Denise and Henry Wren established what was arguably the first studio pottery in England, in the small village of Oxshott, designing and building their own house and coke-fired kiln. My parents often met up with the Wrens at their pottery stall, and recognising their expertise, my mother enlisted their help in setting up her own pottery.

Alf Chalk was employed to build a small workshop and throwing room and, recommended by the Wrens, a very experienced master potter from Kingston's Norbiton Potteries, Mr Mercer (who had taught Denise Wren), came and constructed a potter's wheel and a large up-draught, coal-fired muffle kiln with two stoke holes. Mr Mercer was an expert flower pot and vase thrower, and demonstrated his expertise, complete with bowler hat and pipe in the corner of his mouth; he fired my mother's enthusiasm as to the possibilities of the craft. Mother bought in all the necessary equipment and glaze materials from Wengers, Stoke-on-Trent, and again, on the recommendation of the Wrens, contacted a Miss Gillesby to teach her the basics of the craft. Over a long weekend Miss Gillesby gave my mother a crash course on all the rudiments of pot making, and after that it was a question of trial and error and using one's common sense. Talk about being thrown in at the deep end!

My mother struggled to learn to throw with the local yellow earthenware clay that she dug from a clay pit beside the workshop. Her technique of clay preparation was laborious in the extreme. A bucketful would be dug up as cleanly as possible, and after being wetted up, it was turned out on a stout wedging table and beaten to a homogeneous consistency. This process took a whole afternoon and yielded about 20lb of clay.

The kiln was vast; two men could get inside its muffle. If my mother had had more knowledge, she would never have chosen such a large kiln. But Mr Mercer, a fast, productive big ware thrower all his life, was only building a kiln to the specifications his style and rate of production demanded. Indeed, he knew no other. Anyway, over several months, my mother struggled to master the clay on the wheel, gradually becoming less lumpen and more fluent. Eventually, my parents amassed enough for a kiln load of what must have been very heavy, formless, beginner's pots. No matter! The kiln was packed, its wicket sealed, and the excitement of the first biscuit firing commenced. It was a twenty-four hour job firing the kiln, gradually building the fire up, keeping the fire bars clear of clinker, and raking out the ash from the ash pit to maintain a good air flow.

Neither of my parents had any knowledge of how to fire the kiln. It was grossly inefficient anyway, as being up-draught, the flames only heated the muffle in passing as they roared away up the chimney into the open air, using about five per cent of the total heat produced by the fire. Eventually, as the energy and endurance of the stokers began to

© Photopress. Fleet St. London EC4. Image (OXP/63) kindly provided by the Crafts Study Centre, University for the Creative Arts

Denise Wren demonstrating the Mercer kiln at Oxshott Pottery. This was the type of kiln that was installed by Margaret and Tom in the Godshill Pottery.

flag, a pink glow began to show itself at the spy hole; over the next two hours this became a cherry red, and individual pots became visible, and eventually, *Hurrah!* the pyrometric cone indicating the temperature inside the kiln had started to bend. It was a moment of triumph. Stoking over, there followed a frustrating two days to wait while the kiln cooled down. Then with hearts thumping with anticipation, they began the chipping away of the clay smeared over the wicket. One brick, two bricks prized out; a pot just visible. Quick, fish it out with stick or gloved hand, and witness the never-to-be forgotten alchemy of fire on earth, ochre to terracotta. Ceramics, so much part of man's cultural evolution.

My parents, total amateurs in the craft, were filled with wonder at the transformation. 800°C was hard enough to achieve with the kiln for the biscuit firing, but the glaze glost (or first) firing required a temperature of around about 1,000°C. The pots were glazed carefully and repacked in the kiln on ceramic stilts to keep them off the shelves, and the firing cycle started again. 800°C was reached, but try as they would the kiln obstinately refused to go any higher. My parents piled on the coal, and smoke and flames poured out of the chimney into the night sky, but the 980°C pyrometric cone continued to sit smugly upright refusing to keel over. My parents gave up eventually through sheer exhaustion, hoping that the cone they had used was of the wrong formulation, but, of course, it wasn't. After a frustrating wait, a pot was eventually fished out of the hot kiln, and its glaze was found to be in the larval pitted stage, on its way to fluxing, but still very under-fired. Two months' work appeared to be down the drain.

My parents decided that they needed more help, so they contacted Roger Carter, an old Sidcotian, who owned Poole Pottery in Dorset. He kindly sent down one of his old stokers to take my parents through a firing cycle. The stoker was an expert in his field, and without any apparent effort, he coaxed the kiln up to temperature in record time, towards the end maintaining a strict balance between keeping the level of heat output up with the least possible coal. Too much coal doused the fire temporarily, and thus the heat output, only producing smoke. He maintained a balance by feeding the odd lump by hand. It was a revelation! And so my parents learning curve progressed.

They never produced great pots, partly through lack of expertise. They were fired too low to be chip or breakage resistant. My mother concocted various green and blue slips which she poured over the pots, mingling the colours dribble-fashion, in vogue with the times. When the pots were leather-hard, my father cut his designs of birds, animals and elementals, through the coloured slips to the red clay behind, incising with knife or linocut tool. He also painted his designs, with brush and underglaze colour, onto the pots. Mother then applied a transparent glaze to the pots so the design showed through.

These amateur efforts were sold at Craft Cottage along with my father's carvings, but it is doubtful if their sale did more than cover expenses. Of course, my mother had to have a go at that ultimate challenge for the potter, namely, a tea pot! Her efforts, with my father's decoration turning the handles into snakes and the spout into a bird, looked highly original. However, when you picked them up they weighed a ton, and with tea in could hardly be held with one hand, pouring like uncontrolled drains! The friendly local policeman, on the Godshill beat, saw my mother's collection of wonderful teapots, and expressed great interest and admiration. So my parents gave him one, which he carted home as though it were the crown jewels!

Denise Wren was instrumental in helping both Margaret and Chris set up the Godshill Pottery. She is pictured in 1966-7 with a pot for the Commonwealth Institute Exhibition.

In the 1920s, at Oxshott Pottery. Denise and Henry Wren are pictured right taking tea amongst the clay, with Mr. Finsler, a six month apprentice and an unknown woman.

Among the various artists and crafts people who became friends of my parents were a young couple, Charles and Hilda Leek, who exhibited leather work and pewter.

Charles was an artist and taught in Christchurch, where he and Hilda lived in a large caravan that he had designed and constructed himself. They owned two beautiful hunters called Jorrocks and Twinkle and enjoyed riding. As the friendship grew, Charles and Hilda asked if they could move the caravan to Godshill Ridge, and on my parents' agreement they found a pitch next to the budding pottery. It was not long after that the Leeks asked if they could put up a stable and bring their horses too, as the Forest offered such good riding. So a stable went up below the pottery, and along with the Collins' family home, Four Winds, added to the early development on The Ridge.

Charles used to ride to Christchurch to teach, staying in digs during the week and riding home at weekends. He was a gifted, if awkward man. His painting ability was attributable to a well-observed and absorbed art school training, as much as to natural talent. It was competent, predictable, and of its time; even sort after nowadays, which irony would please him as he always used to say: "An artist is never famous until he is dead."

I guess when my parents first knew the Leeks, Charles and Hilda's marriage was at its best, but Charles was a difficult man to live with. His inferiority complex, hidden by a veneer of self-deprecating charm to his friends, was replaced by an increasing chauvinistic arrogance and rudeness towards Hilda as the years went by. She was then quite a good-looking woman in a thin, 'twenties fashion, pragmatically bending to the wind of her husband's frequent philistine behaviour. My father got on well with Charles, indeed was on good enough terms to rebuke his rudeness towards Hilda on occasions by interjecting with: "Now, what do good boys say?" when a basic 'please' or 'thank you' had been omitted from an irritated demand. Charles seems to have been able to accept it from the older man. More of the Leeks later on.

Chapter 17
Apple Orchards

My grandfather had bought one-and-a-half acres in the bottom eastern end corner of the Purlieu at the same time as he bought the rough, and he planted it with many different varieties of apple tree.

I still have my grandfather's original plan of the orchard, with the rows of trees marked and their varieties; Worcester Pearmain, Allington Pippin, King Pippin, Coxes Orange Pippin, Russet, Bramley, and so on. All round the boundary of the orchard my grandfather had a hedge of Cherry Plum trees planted, to provide a further crop of fruit besides apples.

In its early stages, it was quite productive, and among the other host of enterprises of my parents, they had an apple room constructed, thatched with heather. It had an interior full of shallow racks for storing the varieties of apple the orchard produced, with a view to selling them, if and when the market was propitious. Without proper temperature control, or indeed much insulation from frost, the apples didn't keep too well. So apart from a limited domestic consumption, there wasn't enough of a market to make the enterprise worth the effort.

Mr Collins, from Four Winds, took over the orchard for a while to see if he could make an economic success of producing fruit, adding to the selection by growing red and black currant bushes between the then bush apple trees. Disastrously, the orchard had been planted in a hollow that turned out to be a frost pocket, the frost striking as often as not when the apple blossom was in full flower and decimating a potential crop. Harry Collins, who was a trained engineer rather than a market gardener, found the labour involved was not equal to the meagre return made on the fruit. What the frost did not get, the birds raided, leaving him very disillusioned, and after one season he gave up.

One of the villagers also had a go at working the orchard, to no effect, and my parents left it to go wild. Alf Chalk mowed the grass under the trees with a scythe each June, which they made into hay for their two ponies. Over the years, the apple trees grew into large standards and the Cherry Plum hedge into a tangled thicket, yielding but two freak bumper crops in the 80 years since it was established. ⚘

Margaret, John Coltman, Tom and Mrs Coltman, known as Aunt Alice and a psychic medium.

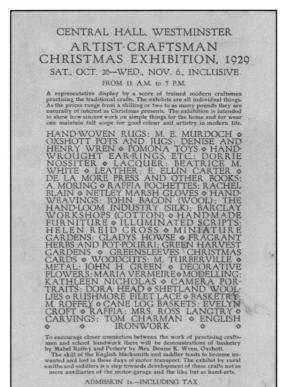

CENTRAL HALL, WESTMINSTER
ARTIST·CRAFTSMAN
CHRISTMAS EXHIBITION, 1929
SAT., OCT. 26—WED., NOV. 6., INCLUSIVE.
FROM 11 A.M. to 7 P.M.

A representative display by a score of trained modern craftsmen practising the traditional crafts. The exhibits are all individual things. As the prices range from a shilling or two to as many pounds they are naturally of interest as Christmas presents. The exhibition is intended to show how sincere work on simple things for the home and for wear can maintain full scope for good colour and artistry in modern life.

HAND·WOVEN RUGS: M. E. MURDOCH ◇ OXSHOTT POTS AND JUGS: DENISE AND HENRY WREN ◇ POMONA TOYS ◇ HAND·WROUGHT EAR·RINGS, ETC.: DORRIE NOSSITER ◇ LACQUER: BEATRICE M. WHITE ◇ LEATHER: E. ELLIN CARTER ◇ DE LA MORE PRESS AND OTHER BOOKS: A. MORING ◇ RAFFIA POCHETTES: RACHEL BLAIN ◇ NETLEY MARSH GLOVES ◇ HAND·WEAVINGS: JOHN BACON (WOOL); THE HAND·LOOM INDUSTRY (SILK); BARCLAY WORKSHOPS (COTTON) ◇ HAND·MADE FURNITURE ◇ ILLUMINATED SCRIPTS: HELEN REID CROSS ◇ MINIATURE GARDENS: GLADYS HOWSE ◇ FRAGRANT HERBS AND POT·POURRI: GREEN HARVEST GARDENS ◇ GREENSLEEVES CHRISTMAS CARDS ◇ WOODCUTS: M. TURBERVILLE ◇ METAL: JOHN H. GREEN ◇ DECORATIVE FLOWERS: MARIA VERMEIRE ◇ MODELLING: KATHLEEN NICHOLAS ◇ CAMERA POR·TRAITS: DORA HEAD ◇ SHETLAND WOOL·LIES ◇ RUSHMORE FILET LACE ◇ BASKETRY: M. ROFFEY ◇ CANE LOG BASKETS: EVELYN CROFT ◇ RAFFIA: MRS. ROSS LANGTRY ◇ CARVINGS: TOM CHARMAN ◇ ENGLISH
◇ IRONWORK ◇ ◇ ◇

To encourage closer connection between the work of practising crafts·men and school handwork there will be demonstrations of basketry by Mabel Roffey and Pottery by Mrs. Denise K. Wren, Oxshott.

The skill of the English blacksmith and saddler tends to become un·wanted and lost in these days of motor transport. The exhibit by rural smiths and saddlers is a step towards development of these crafts not as mere auxiliaries of the motor-garage and the like but as hand-arts.

ADMISSION 1s.—INCLUDING TAX

Credit: OXP/Christmas Exhibition 1929, kindly provided by the Crafts Study Centre, University for the Creative Arts

Chapter 18
Friends from Burley

Other good friends over the years were the Doncasters, a middle-aged couple who lived at Burley in a beautiful thatched house called Byways.

Ted Doncaster was a retired engineer with a lot of restless energy he had used to create a magnificent, limestone rock garden around the house, full of hidden irrigation systems. It was open to the public in the summer and was a joy to wander round. Mrs Doncaster was a lovely gracious lady who always wore home spun and woven clothes, her prematurely grey hair in coiled plaits round her head; she looked as though she had come straight out of a Rossetti painting.

Again, it was through craft exhibitions that my parents had made the initial contact. The Doncasters had a beautiful daughter called Kitty, who lived with her parents and had her own small hand-loom weaving business in premises at the back of the main house. She was a superb mistress of her craft, with a great colour sense. Like many women of her generation after the 1914-18 war, Kitty sadly never married. Her brother had been killed in Flanders Fields and her mother, almost mad with grief, had sought consolation from an Irish lady called Mrs Coltman, who was a psychic medium. Mrs Coltman, or Aunt Alice as I was to know her, was able to give enough evidence to the grieving mother to convince her of her son's survival in the spirit world, a revelation that transformed Mrs Doncaster's life and outlook, and the two women became life-long friends.

Aunt Alice was a charming, animated little lady in her seventies when I knew her. Her husband had been well off and had left her enough money to buy a small farm in Burley, opposite Byways. She had one son, John. Her mediumship was, to an outsider, comic in the extreme. Linking hands around a table in the classic manner, Aunt Alice would close her eyes and go into a twittery, trance-like state with much heavy breathing. A small black girl called 'Curly Tops', her control, would start to speak through her in halting pidgin English, giving messages of comfort from the dead to the living sitters round the table. Aunt Alice, eyes shut, breathing heavily, her face full of concentration, always seemed to find it very laborious being the deciphering channel for her infant control's effort at communication. The fact that her 'control' was a personality that could only speak in rudimentary English only seemed to add to the confusion and comedy of her seances, which resembled the wonderful spoof seance shown on *Steptoe and Son*, the television sitcom, with a very young Patricia Routledge as the medium. I don't know if Aunt Alice was aware of the comic side of her seances. Deluded she may have been, but charlatan she was certainly not! And if she was able to convince lonely people their loved ones were still around and make them happy, that was no bad thing.

Another friend was Mrs Large, a remarkable lady who had served as a young nurse under Florence Nightingale in Scutari in the Crimea, and worked her way up to become head matron at Great Ormond Street Hospital for children. Mrs Large lived in Brighton, and I have a hazy memory of visiting her there, mainly because of a parrot she had in a cage in her sitting room that could speak, which seemed magical. She was a small, energetic woman, slightly imperious in manner, maybe acquired from her position of eminence in the medical hierarchy. She was also a visitor to The Ridge.

"Make sure my bed is aired properly, I do like a well-aired bed!" she wrote prior to a visit. My mother took out all the sheets the day before her arrival, and aired them carefully on a clothes horse in front of the fire, before making the bed up. Mrs Large duly arrived in a taxi, a dead fox fur, complete with head and legs, dangling round her neck in the macabre fashion of the times.

The three of them had a convivial supper and when bedtime came Mrs Large asked my mother if the bed was aired. My mother assured her it was.

"Better be on the safe side," said her visitor. "Do you mind running the warming pan between the sheets?" The warming pan was a deep, cast-iron pan with a hinged copper lid with ventilator holes, and a long pole handle. One filled the pan with hot embers, closed the lid and slid its warm mass up and down the length of the bed between the sheets. This my mother did, confident that the previous day's airing would prove her conscientiousness in the matter. Imagine her dismay, however, when the warming pan produced a cloud of steam. She could only apologise abjectly and say she had done her best the day before, but obviously to no avail. Mrs Large was gracious enough to accept her apology and said it must be the weather.

My father had natural good manners, and was outgoing and gallant in his courtesy. On his first meeting with the formidable Mrs Large, his attentions were not appreciated. Thinking his manner was theatrical and insincere, she brushed him off with the dismissive remark: "I don't care for fancy men…" My father's assurance that he was genuine and sincere in his welcome, mollified her somewhat, but she remained suspicious until she got to know him better, when she unreservedly apologised for her initial prejudice.

A certain Lady Lizzy Lind of Hageby, an early animal rights activist and proselytiser for the Anti Vivisection Society, called in one day for dinner. My mother apologised for the menu that happened to be chicken, saying that if she had known that her visitor was coming she would have had vegetarian fare.

"Oh, not to worry," came the hearty reply. "What I say to my public often doesn't bear any relation to what I do in private. I'd enjoy some chicken!" She ate her dinner with relish! 🌾

Kitty Doncaster with Chris, or 'Pandy' as he became known in the family, and the Fritham iron spring water which runs into Fritham Lake.

Chapter 19
Greece: A Change of Gear

The 'roaring twenties' finally came to an end without having caused so much as a ripple in most rural areas, and the 'thirties began quietly enough with not much hint of the depression to come or the political tensions leading up to the Second World War.

My parents decided to go to Greece. Or rather my mother had 'an urge' to visit the birthplace of civilisation, the source of so much of her philosophical education. My father was only too happy to participate in whatever adventure was going. They bought themselves a new Camtors 'Alaskan' tent, and as mosquitoes were forecast, Mother constructed netting to keep them out. It was arranged that they share the journey with Mrs

Kitty Doncaster, John Coltman, Margaret and Tom waiting for the train at Beaulieu Station en route to Greece in August 1929.

Coltman, her son John, and Kitty Doncaster. Third class tickets were bought and the party set off. My mother wrote a diary of her trip, so I won't attempt to describe their journey here. Suffice it to say it marked a new phase in their life and relationship.

My mother's inner promptings to visit Greece, looking at the journey in retrospect, were (even if she didn't consciously formulate any reason), largely to be able to find some symbolic arena from which she could fulfil her longings to have children. Ideally this would be some sacred temple, imbued with all its ancient association with prediction, that would free her from her vow of sexual abstinence, and at the same time transform the physical expression of love into something sacred, rather than profane. If the ancient gods decreed that the moment was propitious for her child to be conceived, then it would be no ordinary child waiting to be plucked from the great pool of reincarnating spirits, but one on a similar spiritual plane of evolution as herself. It would be a soul mate and also contribute great things to mankind's spiritual awareness.

Sexual union was inextricably linked with the sacredness of procreation in my mother's eyes. That it could be viewed in the context of an exciting and pleasurable bonding mechanism in its own right degraded the act and ran down the spiritual batteries of a union, thus reducing the vital spark of the marriage partnership to one of commonplace habit. Such was my mother's thinking, I truly believe, as I ponder it all these years later.

Where was my father in all this plethora of anticipated, propitious symbolism? He was not an intellectual; in fact, he shied away from too much abstract chewing of the cud. "Enough said!" he would finally interject if an intellectual conversation got bogged down in too much abstraction. Although he connived at my mother's self-imposed chastity, she said he had admitted to her that if he had been a younger man, he would have found it very hard, if not impossible, to conform to her vision of self denial. He must have wondered privately many times during his advancing years, if he was ever going to produce a flesh and blood child with my mother. However, with his ethos largely complementary to hers, and because he loved her dearly, he was content to wait on her inner dictates.

The 'thirties were comparatively quiet times in Greece and the country was largely unspoilt. The ancient archaeological treasures had only a trickle of curious visitors, and were free of the vast hoards of tourists that now come to view such places as the Parthenon. Where else but at the Oracle at Delphi, in the temple of Apollo, the sun god and giver of life, should my mother come to the quiet, but glorious realisation that the time was right for her and my father to conceive a child. There, on the large stone slabs covering the vault-like chamber from which the once famous Delphic oracle delivered its momentous predictions concerning the future, they at last consummated their union and became man and wife, sleeping naked through the warm night under the stars. It was, undoubtedly, a wonderfully intense, joyous moment for them both in all ways, though my mother, in later years tended to intimate in unguarded moments, that sexual love wasn't all that it was cracked up to be. My somewhat irritated rejoinder had been: "How do you know? You never gave yourselves much practice did you?"

My mother was aged 35 and my father 68 at this time. Life did not work out in quite the perfect way that my mother had expected the gods to order it. Although she conceived, she had a miscarriage soon after arriving back in England. After two more miscarriages and heavy menstrual bleeding, she realised there was something wrong, and after medical examination it was discovered she had a large ovarian cyst, making the carrying of a foetus for more than a few weeks impossible. Typical of the duality of my mother's outlook and character, she refused surgery, and went on a quest for healing among all the wacky, eccentric, fringe practitioners that abounded within the spiritualist fraternity. Among those contacted was a certain Madame Skarnie, an eminent spiritual healer of her day, and mother travelled all the way to Paris to an appointment with this rather pompous lady, all to no avail.

Having run the gamut of the alternatives, she switched to her sensible, pragmatic mode, accepting surgery was the only solution. Her aunt found a sympathetic elderly woman surgeon, a Miss Maud Chadburn, who skilfully removed a large, benign fibroid tumour from mother's uterus, in the South London Hospital for Women in London. She remembered her time in hospital, over the Christmas period, for the complete lack of fresh vegetables in the menus. My father used to smuggle in cold cooked sprouts to her on his daily visits. She had memories also of the lady surgeon's expertise at carving the turkey on the ward during the festivities!

Her faith that she would eventually have children was rewarded barely four months later in the spring of 1932 with my conception. My parents were over the moon with joy and anticipation, as were all their friends. Psychics were consulted and crazy predictions were made as to my future. It was a heavy loading to be born into, and now that I have got over my anger, I can only laugh in incredulity and wonder at my mother's crazy manipulations, engineered with such obstinate and sincere certainty that she was "being led"! Who led her with such blind conviction, I ask myself? Her imagined spirit world has a lot to answer for.

Christopher Pan Charman at 8 months with joyful Margaret.

I entered this world on the evening of 12 January 1933, at 8.30pm, the first of a new generation to be born on The Ridge. It was a home birth on my mother's insistence, in spite of reservations on the doctor's part because of a remote possibility of complications resulting from the earlier surgery. Mother was attended by Doctor Vickery, who must have been at the arrival of many generations of the local inhabitants in the Fordingbridge area. He and my father sat in front of a good fire discussing spiritualism, and generally yarning, while my mother got on with her labour. The birth was reasonably easy, with no complications, and there was much rejoicing.

The 1930s saw the first comprehensive book on child care, written by an eminent obstetrician of the day called Frederick Truby King. Baby and infant mortality rates were a lot higher in the 'thirties than they are now, and it was time something in the way of medical and practical guidance was published to help mothers. I believe that Truby King was the first person to accurately evaluate the differences between human breast milk and cow's milk, and suggest ways to make the latter up to the same formulation as the mother's own, if the mother herself hadn't enough. To judge if your child had fed enough to sustain it, you weighed it before and after a meal and compared the difference with a chart of average intake against weeks old. A system that on the surface seemed admirable, but in practice didn't take into account a babe's propensity, in the early days, to burp up, or spontaneously vomit, all the food it has just consumed. To a young mother who has just breast-fed her babe all the milk she has for the time being, it lead to bouts of acute anxiety as to whether her babe had absorbed enough. Truby King, in his academic wisdom, advocated a strict regime of feeding at certain hours only, exhorting the mother to ignore her babe's plaintive howls if it did not conform to the laid-down routine. If you 'gave in', he warned, your child would soon become a demanding little tyrant, and you knew what behavioural problems that would lead to.

In the first few weeks following my birth, my father employed a lovely lady of his acquaintance from Nomansland to assist my mother in launching me into life. Mrs Mussle was of Anglo-Indian descent, married to a native Forest man. With her own family grown into adulthood, she generously gave of her natural common sense and maternal expertise, soon dismissing Truby King's dictates with the remark: "What for you want to bring up a baby from a book? If him cry, he'm hungry and need a cuddle and a titty!" My mother was only too happy to comply with what her instincts already told her, taking me into her bed and feeding me on demand. With warmth, maternal contact and food, from then on I would sleep contentedly, she told me. Mrs Large pronounced me: "…a good specimen, and not too fat", a great compliment from such an expert mother, I thought. ⚶

Picnic at Fritham Lake in 1934. Chris is a year old. Cuthbert Rutter is standing far right, next to Margaret. Dorothy Rutter is seated on the lap of her husband to be, William Guest, and Tom with Chris is seated left.

Chapter 20
1933 Childhood Memories

My earliest infant recollections, before my sister Danae arrived on the scene, are very few. One memory stands out though, of being carried on my father's shoulders on a walk to the holly copses bordering Pitts Wood.

He placed me on the horizontal limb of an old yew tree, and taking a small, bone-handled penknife from his pocket, he peeled and sliced an apple, which he then fed to me. Why that fairly inconsequential happening should remain so clearly in my memory sixty-five years on, I don't know. On another occasion, I remember my mother holding me up with great excitement to witness Father Christmas striding along the track in front of our house in his classic red costume trimmed with white, sporting a bushy beard and sack of presents over his shoulder. We waved wildly, and he smiled and waved a cheery acknowledgement and disappeared in the softly falling snow. That experience was the single biggest contribution to my sense of excitement and wonder over Christmases to come for the next twelve years. Even at boarding school, when I was faced with the jibes and cynicism of my peers, I clung stubbornly to my fantasy of Father Christmas, the essence of all that was magical at that festive time. The pure impossibility of trying to get to sleep on Christmas Eve because of the almost uncontrollable excitement and anticipation of the festive morn; the waking at midnight, the furtive, explorative, inquisitive pinch and feel of a bulging, mysterious stocking at the foot of the bed.

"How does Father Christmas get down the chimney without getting covered in soot?" my sister and I would ask our mother. "Doesn't he get stuck with such a large tummy? Won't he burn his feet when he comes down and lands in the hot ashes?" Her explanation was always brief and unassailable. "Well, you see, he's magic!" she would say. That was good enough as far as I was concerned.

I have a dim recollection of a sense of 'bounty' from those first Christmases. My mother said that presents for me from their friends simply flooded in; there were so many that my parents rationed them, a few each day so as not to get satiated, enabling them to keep track of the givers and thank them.

Among the quasi-fringe sciences my parents embraced, was the dubious art of predicting people's character from the shape of their cranium, namely phrenology. One of its practitioners, Joseph Millott Severn, was a friend of my father's, and inevitably as an infant, I was taken along to the eminent, elderly, bearded man to have my bumps read to assess my potential. From my mother's memory of the event I learned that a flat area at the back of my head denoted a distinct lack of ability to concentrate that I must guard against. All I can say as to the accuracy of the assessment is that I have always been able to concentrate on anything I have been interested in, and am bad at keeping my mind on anything that disinterests me, which must be true of many people.

Sunlight, a cornucopia of fruit and a feeling of complete contentment pervades my memory. I have visions of apples, all red and luscious in their autumn colours, piled in boxes; there are ladders at the foot of apple trees, myself on the lower rungs sampling an apple and gazing up at my father's plus-four clad legs as he picks the fruit into an open rucksack on his chest, his shoulders and head masked by branches and the dappled sunlight of an early autumn day. Dad had a small light wheelbarrow, its superstructure made of woven willow. This he used to push me around, a substitute for a push chair and much more fun. After his death, when it had disintegrated from being left out in the rain, the only thing that remained was the front wheel and integral wooden axle. My sister and I used to bend over and grasp the axle ends in both our hands and push the wheel along

Tom handing down apples to a young Chris.
"...a feeling of complete contentment pervades my memory."

the ground in front of us until the friction and heat produced forced us to stop. We called it our 'hand warmer'!

Mother and Father had a dog when I was tiny. He was called Mike, a red-haired Irish terrier and quite a character. I remember experimenting with his temperament by putting a clothes peg on his tail and getting bitten for my pains. It was an early lesson not to take liberties. Mike had the habit of ambling about in a nonchalant manner among our loose ponies. Suddenly picking a horse, he would launch himself at its rear end, grasping the tail just below the dock, and hang on with his teeth as the startled pony galloped off down the hillside. Mike would hang there, swinging, for a few hundred yards or so, drop off in mid-gallop, and as nonchalantly as he had begun, give one or two proprietorial scuffs with his back legs on the sward and then stroll off, stiff-legged.

Some of the old ladies in the village were afraid of Mike, and he knew it. He used to lie in wait for one old dear in particular, and when she came out of the village shop with a loaf of bread, he immediately started to stalk her in a menacing stiff-legged manner. On becoming aware of his presence, the old lady would give a little scream, drop the loaf and run, which was the whole point of the offensive as far as Mike was concerned. He would make a bee line for the loaf, and eat it. This practice didn't, it must be said, endear Mike to the villagers, and my parents were forever apologising for his anti-social behaviour and paying for spoilt loaves. We used to have a cigarette box in the house with a picture of Mike on its lid, done in marquetry. Although Father only smoked one cigarette a day, (two, if in London), the box was always kept full to offer to visitors.

Mike, already of an uncertain temperament in his youth, became more and more unreliable and bad-tempered in his old age, and I had to keep away from him for fear of being snapped at. When he became incontinent, Mother had him 'put to sleep', and his absence left a hole in the household. He was replaced by a mongrel, a black and tan, short-haired, half-Dutch barge dog. He was called 'Dutchy' and, like his father's ancestors, he carried his tail curled up over his back. He was the first of the many and varied 'Heinz' dogs to live either long or short lives with us, depending on whether or not they were run over by the increasing motor traffic. ❧

Tom, 'Pandy' and Mike, a dog of uncertain temperament.

Chris, Danae and Margaret, and the summer house. The platform was constructed from a brougham coach.

Chapter 21
My Father's Last Years

Two years nine months later, on 6 November, 1935, Danae was born, a solid, ten pound baby. Our father was nearly 73 by then, and soon after my sister's birth began to show the first signs of a form of dementia, arterial sclerosis of the brain, or 'hardening of the arteries' as my mother used to always refer to it.

It began with Dad just feeling out of sorts, anxious and unable to put up with us noisy children. I had been conceived early enough to have appreciated his warmth as a father, and felt the change in atmosphere from outgoing love to withdrawal and irritability on his part. Our mother was determined to keep Dad at home and lead as normal a life as possible. He struggled on with his carving in the upstairs workshop, and we were told not to get in his way or make a noise. I can recollect my sister and I being shouted at, and Mother rushing up to fetch us and ameliorate the situation.

It was not an easy time for her, having to cope with two lively children and an ageing, confused and anxious husband. We still had no running water or any form of plumbing.

The young Chris, mother Margaret and Danae with their dog Duchy, a Dutch barge dog.

Dad took to going out into the Forest in the middle of the night, in his pyjamas, regardless of the weather, getting disorientated, lost and chilled. After a year and a half of trying to cope with his deteriorating condition, the final straw came when he started to exhibit violent tendencies towards us children. With great sorrow, because she loved him so much, Mother finally came to the decision that the only way to save the situation was to have my father 'sectioned' and put into care in a mental home.

So my father was 'certified' and placed in a home for the mentally-disabled in Fareham. My mother used to visit him each week in the Austin Seven. At first he recognised her, and his dementia exhibited itself in worry and anxiety about us and how we would be able to cope without him. Later, he ceased to know her and just stared into space. This involuntary rejection she found unbearably painful as it marked the end - at least in this life - of their relationship.

To witness the disintegration of the vital, generous personality with whom she had shared her life and beliefs for nearly twenty years, must have been almost unsustainable at times. Sometimes, out of the blue, she would receive a letter from him in which he would be completely lucid and his old happy self, urging her to visit and let him know how we children were getting on. These windows of lucidity would fill our mother with a desperate hope that some miracle had occurred, and she would rush to Fareham, only to be greeted by a blank, uncomprehending face. These moments of clarity, when the remaining ganglions in my poor father's brain made enough contact to fire properly, gradually petered out. He still got up and washed and dressed himself carefully. "He was always such a clean old gentleman," the nurses told my mother after his death. Our Dad 'endured', trapped behind his malfunctioning brain for three years in all, mercifully dying in his sleep on 11 January 1939. By a strange twist of timing, my son Tom was born on 11 January 1963, one hundred years after my father's birth.

Mother, although sad of course at the loss of her beloved Tom, in a sense, had already done her grieving, witnessing the disintegration of Dad's personality. They both believed that the body is a temporary abode of the spirit, or life force, while on this earth and, that on its disintegration, this spirit is exchanged for an ethereal body with an after-life. This belief now sustained her; her man, she believed, was even more alive and looking after her. Again, she was having to convince herself, as she had done in her lonely childhood, that the 'guardian angels' of her mother, father, and now dear husband were as close, loving and concerned for her welfare as ever.

I attended my Dad's cremation, going into Southampton with my mother in the old Austin. Danae must have been left behind with one of the loving Swiss au-pairs. I find the situation, writing about it now, much more poignant than I did at the time. Mother and I were the only people there on that cold January day in that civilised, impersonal conveyor-belt emporium of sanitised body disposal. We sat together in Quaker silence looking at my father's coffin, and Mother whispered to me that Daddy wasn't in that box, only his worn-out old body, and that the real Daddy was free at last and beside us, bidding us be of good cheer and not sad. While we sat in silence, some schmaltzy music was played on an electric organ, the curtains parted and my father's earthly remains theatrically slid on silent runners to be consigned to the furnace. To a small boy it was too theatrical to be real, but now at sixty-six, I find it all too final.

My mother exhibited a genuine joy at Dad's release from his travail, and our journey home was filled with her stories of their happy times together, and what a good Dad he was, how he was nearer to us than he had ever been, and so on. I, too, cannot remember feeling sad at that point. After all, I hadn't seen my father for three years, and as is the way with children, had accepted that he had to go away because he was ill. In a sense, I had forgotten his existence and any nasty memories of what his illness had done to his character and his attitude to my sister and I. It was not until years later that my anger and distress surfaced in niggling resentment, that my mother, through her self-centred and obstinate adherence to an ideal which had delayed my conception, had deprived me of a father with whom I could share love and companionship as I grew up.

Just below the surface, throughout my teenage years and into adulthood, there was always a constant, unexplained irritation with my mother. Throughout her life she exerted a benign, almost unconscious, pressure. I was brainwashed in a sense by her ethos and, at the same time, conscious that I needed to ditch most of what she had loaded me with in order to find my own identity. She was convinced that because she had played out her own life to certain spiritual strictures, I must be on the same wavelength. To outsiders she was a respected, inspiring and wise liberal lady. That she loved my sister and myself unconditionally there can be no doubt, but as the first born, she had invested in me something that I could not, and finally, would not deliver.

Danae, to a large degree escaped the intensity of being groomed into a pre-ordained mould, but like me experienced much irritated exasperation with Mother on occasions. She never knew a loving Dad as he was too ill to appreciate his little daughter. Deep down, I am sure, she feels she missed out on that special relationship.

As we grew into our late teenage years there is no doubt that we were lumbered with concepts that didn't add up in the real world and were at odds with our burgeoning sexuality. It was all most confusing and painful. To the very end, my mother, although saddened and puzzled by my dissension from a large part of her ethos, convinced herself that I would always 'come round' to her way of looking at things, and that my present rebellion 'was only a phase', a term she used to persuade herself out of many, very deep-seated, problems.

After Dad's cremation, Mother collected his ashes, and as a last ritual scattered them in the Forest as a libation to his life. As she writes so movingly in her diary of that time: "As I scattered your ashes, the strong blowing wind caught them up and whirled them away, so that they swiftly merged into the misty air. So the old garment which once clothed your spirit, has once more become part of the elements which nourished it. I saw all that was left of your earthly remains, vanish as smoke in the air. I felt how insignificant are the things of this world, compared to the things of the spirit." ⚘

Danae and Chris in the garden outside The Pottery, looking across the valley towards Burgate.

Chapter 22
The Coming of Trudy into our Lives

I have already said that a family called the Pasks were living in Craft Cottage, originally my father's house. Just as my father began to show signs of his illness in mid-1936, the Pasks took in a young Swiss lass called Trudy Christen.

In exchange for domestic help (old Mrs Pask being an invalid in the early stages of cancer at the time), Trudy was to receive instruction in English. The Pasks were rather a dry, frugal Quaker family who didn't speak much, so Trudy did not get much practice in conversational English. She was desperately hungry all the time as the Pasks had bird-like appetites. They made lemon barley water, and used to feed the exhausted grains to their few chickens. Trudy was so hungry on occasion that she used to stuff herself on the left-over barley instead of feeding it to the chickens! The Pasks were vegetarians, but they did not seem to cook many vegetables, and Trudy longed for a break from semolina and the endless round of sweet milk puddings which she hated. They had porridge for breakfast, followed either by a boiled egg or kippers. Fish heads were procured from the fishmonger and were boiled up on the open fire for the Pasks' cats, filling the house with a fishy smell. Trudy found the Pasks stiff and boring to live with, and very demanding of her time domestically. Elsie taught her English grammar for a short, uninspiring while each day, but the whole arrangement was very unsatisfactory.

Trudy was very home sick. She was just 21, and very naïve by today's standards. Many years later she told me she had found great emotional strength in the natural world. She recalled a visit to Bournemouth, her first view of the sea, and the wonder of the waves crashing on the shore. She grew to love the English countryside and its churches, and marvelled at Salisbury Cathedral. She stayed, for a memorable three days, with the more independent-minded Mary Pask in Oxford and visited no less than twenty-three Colleges. She found them all beautiful, especially Christchurch, All Souls, and Maudlin. Of the churches, she found the Anglican the most beautiful.

Mother, visiting the Pasks one day in the Austin to see if she could run some errands for them, happened to meet Trudy and, speaking German, they got into conversation. She invited Trudy for tea. As it meant giving up her free afternoon Trudy was not terribly pleased. However, she reluctantly agreed, and my mother duly picked her up and introduced her to my sister and I, and to my sick father. Trudy found The Ridge very primitive and dirty, my mother only just being able to cope with the work and conditions.

Mother was desperately lonely, in need of an adult companion and some intellectual stimulus apart from us children. It was one thing, the simple life without children, but with two infants to bring up at the age of 42, it was a bit daunting. Trudy visited The Ridge once or twice a week and developed a great attachment to my sister and myself, giving my mother a much needed break from child minding. She quickly acquired skills in colloquial English as my mother talked to her non-stop about anything and everything. Trudy always averred that: "All my English is your mother's, her vocabulary and expressions." It was all so different from living with the reserved Pasks, who kept their distance. My mother was loving and outgoing towards Trudy, and she found herself looking forward to the afternoons she visited The Ridge.

Elsie Pask was jealous and annoyed at Trudy's increasing pleasure at her visits to see us, and made a few derogatory comments about my mother's non-marital status, saying: "We must pray for her redemption", adding how her children, although very charming were: "Oh, so spoiled!" which may well have been a bit of sour grapes on her part.

*Trudy Christen with young Danae and Chris.
Trudy and Margaret became close and she was
a regular visitor to The Ridge.*

Trudy came from Zurich in Switzerland. Her mother, whom she loved greatly, had died of cancer, and Trudy had nursed her, a traumatic period in her life. Her father was a paraplegic, an early victim of polio, paralysed from the waist down. He had earned his living as a peddler, hawking his wares around the countryside from his wheelchair. He had tremendous strength in his arms and shoulders and used to propel himself over the most difficult terrain to get to some of his customers. He was an excellent swimmer, powering himself across the mile or so of Lake Zurich with his arms, trailing his useless, withered legs behind him. With single-minded determination he saved enough money to become a supplier of merchandise for other pedlars and thus moved up a rung in the battle for financial security. He did so well as a supplier he was able to buy a block of flats on the outskirts of Zurich and became modestly well off, and even able to own one of the first motor cars of the time.

Trudy's mother was a woman of great sensibility, whereas her father, for all his determination and drive, was rather insensitive to his wife's needs. However, they made the best of their life together. Maybe the sheer effort of getting through each day forced Trudy's father into presenting a front of insensitivity. There was a lot of social prejudice directed at people with physical disabilities at the beginning of the century, and Trudy's father had his share. One day, having completed a hard morning's work he decided to take a break and change his position. With great effort he managed to lever himself out of his invalid chair onto a park bench, laying out full length along it. He was just dozing off to sleep when a policeman prodded him in the ribs and told him to "Move on" as the seat he was resting on was reserved for "real people" and not for the likes of him. Attitudes have thankfully changed a bit since those times. ⚘

Chapter 23
Childhood and Mrs G

Life on Godshill Ridge was hard work. It was only one step away from camping. There was no running water, no drains, and no electricity. We had Aladdin oil lamps and Primus stoves to cook by. In the chimney of the fireplace, the kettle was suspended from a bar and a chain with an adjustable hook. Most of the hot water, for tea, washing-up of dishes and ourselves, was heated over the fire in this manner. The lavatory was an outside earth closet with two buckets; one for excrement and the other for urine. Instead of toilet paper we had old railway time-tables, cut-up newspapers or magazines, which if ruffled up a bit became soft enough to use on one's nether regions!

After Dad's death, Mother needed some assistance. With the war clouds looming and Trudy and all the other young ladies departed for their homeland, Mother enlisted the aid of an old Forest friend of my father's called Mrs Gardener, or Mrs G as we were to know her in later years. She visited one winter and helped my mother with all the many practical chores involved in keeping life going in the cold weather. Mrs G was a wiry, severe, little lady that Danae and I didn't much like as she was stricter than our mother, and used to slap us regularly for our minor misdemeanours. Mother made it a policy never to interfere with Mrs G's methods of disciplining us. If we complained to her of our treatment or a perceived injustice, she just said: "Well, don't do that again and you won't get into trouble." Mrs G seemed to have eyes in the back of her head and always managed to pounce on us when we least expected it.

By this time, we had rather an unusual summer house on a platform, added to the end of the upstairs room. How it got there requires me to go back a few years. Mother and Father had decided, after several caravanning trips in the Hutchings van, that it was a bit heavy, even with two horses to pull it. So after looking round for something lighter, they discovered an old brougham stashed away in a coach house in Southampton. It was a very light carriage with a four-seater compartment, complete with doors, slung on a light, sprung, steel chassis on metal-spoked and rimmed, rubber-shod wheels. The vehicle had a swivelling front turn-table section, making it very manoeuvrable. My parents had the pill-box passenger compartment detached from the chassis and utilised it as a neat little summer house. On the chassis, they had a local carpenter construct a very light caravan, using tar paper reinforced with horse-hair as the walls, stretched over a skeletal ash frame and topped with a plywood canvas-covered roof. It was very simple, furnished inside with a few cupboards with sliding panel doors, and a well compartment in the floor. The open end, where one sat to drive, could be closed off with a tailor-made canvas sheet. It was light enough for an adult to pull it on the level, and a tribute to my mother's practical design sense.

The summer house was a delight of Victorian craftsmanship. The coachwork was superb with a lot of teak going into its construction. The windows were of plate glass and slid up and down like those in old railway carriages. The doors had brass hinges and the catches had bone handles. The twin opposing seats had upholstery filled with horse-hair. If the brougham had been looked after in its original state, it would be worth a fortune now, instead of the £15 my parents paid for it. It was reached by some steep wooden steps leading up to the open platform on which it was bolted. Danae and I were soon going up there and playing on the unguarded platform which was about nine foot off the ground. Danae, although only two and a bit, was mighty athletic and used to whizz up and down the stairs with great dexterity. However, came the day when, not concentrating, she stepped backwards into space and fell off the platform and dislocated her shoulder. Charles Leek came to the rescue and drove us into hospital in Salisbury. I remember Danae being placed on a table and her attention being distracted by a coloured, fluffy piece of rope, just long enough for the expert doctor to click the offending shoulder back into place. It was done before she realised it and only yelled when it was all over.

Mother had a wooden barrier put round the platform after the accident, but the stairs were left open. One of our pranks was to take the cat up on the platform of the summer house, and lower it down over the guard rail to the ground in a bucket. Sometimes the cat jumped out, but it easily coped with the few feet it had to jump down to the ground. It wasn't really cruel, but it got Mrs G's dander up and she used to climb the steep stairs to the platform to administer retribution. "You naughty, naughty children", she used to scream shrilly at us as she administered slaps on our hands or the backs of our legs. On occasion we managed to escape her wrath by dodging in and out of the cab and slamming the doors behind us, trapping her inside momentarily, so giving us the chance of shinning down the stairs and away into the gorse thickets. It only put off the evil hour however, and we got our just deserts in the end, knowing it was no good to complain to Mother.

Mrs G with Danae and Chris on their favourite rocking horse. Mrs Gardener 'had eyes in the back of her head' and was 'a great practical help to Mother'.

Under the summer house platform, Mother had fixed two leather-clad iron rings, suspended on ropes, for us to swing on and perform gymnastics. Danae was too small to reach the rings and she used to stand on a box or I would be prevailed upon to give her a bunk up. Once on the rings, she was an adventurous athlete, much better than me as she had no fear at that age.

There was no doubt that Mrs G was a great practical help to Mother over the cold winter months. The pair of them used to cut logs together with a cross-cut saw and sawing horse. It was a slow job, taking five minutes to make each cut - a warming task in itself; today it would have taken a few seconds with a power saw. Mrs G had known a hard life, and was dedicated to the work ethic. She and her mother, Forest-bred, had spent some time in America during her youth, an experience that was memorable in a subsequent life that was dominated by constant penny-pinching poverty. In America, she met and married a man called Arthur Gardener, a Californian bee keeper. He had a vast apiary, one of many run in conjunction with the pollination of thousands of acres of fruit trees grown in that state. The Gardeners arrived in the Forest and scratched a living of sorts from a tiny smallholding at Stoney Cross. Their lives were dominated by hard work, Arthur often incapacitated by stomach ulcers, from which he eventually died prematurely.

Mrs G's grandfather was the landlord of The Compton Arms at Stoney Cross, a one-time staging post for the mail coach. During his time as landlord there was a lot of smuggling in the area, and often the mail coach would arrive to find that the change of horses waiting at the inn, instead of being fresh, were lathered up and exhausted from a night spent hauling brandy inland from the coast near Lymington. The loan of the horses was often paid for with a cask of brandy - *nudge nudge, wink wink, say no more*! Mrs G's grandfather, as a lad, was once put in charge of a waggon-load of brandy hidden in some dense woodland near Rufus Stone. He fell asleep from the alcoholic fumes given off by the spirit. Luckily, no excise men were abroad on that occasion!

Mrs Gardener developed crippling osteoarthritis in her old age and she came to live the last decade of her life in a little chalet at the end of our garden. She was a valiant old lady, bearing her affliction with Christian fortitude. She tried many different diets and cures for her affliction, but none to much effect. Drinking copious amounts of water, laced with soda bicarbonate that made her burp lustily, salads of chickweed and dandelion leaves, cortisone injections that eased her limbs temporarily and miraculously turned her old long grey hair black, as in her youth.

The radio was her life line and she loved to sing along with the hymns in the religious broadcasts. Many was the time, while working in the garden, I heard her shrill, cracked old voice courageously singing out in praise of the Lord, in spite of her nearly constant pain. I made the mistake once of telling her that her radio batteries could be made to produce a few more hours of power by heating them. This appealed to her acquired sense of frugality and I found myself re-energising fleets of her batteries in front of the fire to extract the last amp of power from them, before she would agree to indulge herself in some new ones.

She had a tiny patch of garden for some flowers in front of her chalet which she used to determinedly weed, using a pair of wooden tongs to reach the offending interlopers and pull them out. She also had a pair of kitchen scissors with a couple of canes lashed to the handles so she could operate them without having to bend. You could hear the ball joints grinding in their sockets as she moved, her hips were so badly affected by arthritis. A hip replacement was never mentioned as being an option. Looking back, it would have transformed her life.

Mrs G was full of classic, wise old saws like: "More haste, less speed.", "Patience is a virtue."and "Measure twice, cut once." If she received a parcel tied up with string that was hard to untie, it would drive her to growls of impatience and frustration. Then would be our chance to get our revenge by quoting her proverbs back at her! She was not without humour and with an explosive *HA!* she would hand over the package for us to open, and cackle with merriment when we too found it difficult! She kept her hair long, brushing it for hours each day, before winding it in a severe bun held in place by many spiky hairpins. She always maintained that it was a mistake to ever wash hair, as it denatured the scalp of its natural oils.

Her one vice, if it could be called that, was the taking of snuff, to which she was addicted. She would sniff it off the back of her hand, making her nostrils brown and causing sneezing fits of great magnitude, which she seemed to enjoy, wiping the tears away with beatific satisfaction. She also had a tiny tot of whisky after supper each day (for medicinal purposes only); a bottle lasted at least a month. To pass the time, she knitted countless pairs of socks for myself, and other members of the household, on four fine steel knitting needles, 'turning' the heels in the classic manner.

I got on vey well with Mrs G as a young adult and she was always deeply grateful for anything that I could do for her. She had a wonderfully well-fitting pair of dentures which enabled her to eat anything, including blackberries, figs and grapes, and never suffered from sore gums. While she was with us, the garden was more free of weeds than at any other time. Her eagle eye soon spotted any that dared to show its face, and I was sent to hoe it out, with the admonition: "One year's seed, ten years weed." I must say, although I found her pessimism justifiable on occasions, it was a bit over the top; but then I didn't suffer the constant pain of worn out joints. When my Dad had visited the Gardeners' holding in later years and inquired of the tired, semi-invalid Arthur how "Jenny" was doing, Arthur would reply wearily: "Oh working, you know, working…"

The woman, the work ethic, the poverty, seemed to have finally combined and conspired to afflict her poor old body with a disease as appropriate as it was cruel. She was a brave soul, who never once gave in to self pity. She was attracted to my father at one stage in her youth, but he had sheared off as soon as he became aware of her attachment. She was too much of a pauper in spirit for his gay, (in the original meaning), lively, free-wheeling nature, and he didn't fancy being trapped in her joyless web. Mrs G finally had to go into the local hospital, brave to the last, and her death must have come as a welcome release. I visited Minstead churchyard later and found her and Arthur's gravestone. It's strange to think that is all that remains of two human lives, loves and struggles. ❦

Chapter 24
The Last of Infancy and the Beginning of School

As infants, Danae and I wore open Clark's sandals with crepe soles in the summer. Danae, however, much preferred bare feet and was forever abandoning her footwear and clothes as the fancy took her.

Mother could follow the line of a walk she had taken from the discarded shoes and clothing en route. Danae acquired exceedingly tough skin on the soles of her feet as a result of going barefoot, and she could run over gravel with no sign of discomfort. If she did get a thorn or prickle in the sole of her foot, she simply stopped in mid-gallop, inspected the afflicted limb, and with a deft tweak picked the offending thorn out and carried on running. If it was too small to pick out with her fingers, she bent her foot round to her mouth and used her teeth as tweezers. She was independent-minded, resenting help, saying: "Do it mine self!" If she had a new idea for a game she used to say: "I've got a good I-plan", a phrase the whole family adopted, as it combined 'Idea' and 'Plan' so neatly and logically.

Danae and I were so lucky in our childhood freedom. In summer we only wore clothes if it was cold or visitors were coming whose sensibilities would have been offended by our nakedness, which wasn't often. After the clothes had been washed and rinsed, we used to play happily in the tub of rinsing water for an hour at a time, pouring it over ourselves and each other, using an old tin mug or saucepan as a dipper. Sometimes a visitor would turn up at at the gate and Mother, noting our grubby appearance, would perform a fire-engine clean up of our dirty faces with a smelly dish cloth grabbed hastily out of the sink. We hated this and would wriggle and squirm and yell: "*Ugh, ugh, horrible, it's horrible!*" behaving rather like kittens when they are forcibly washed by their mother. Mother was a great believer in eating lots of fruit and she used to buy quantities of huge Jaffa oranges for a penny each, delivered from Edwin Jones' store in Southampton every week. Danae and I shared a lovely rocking horse bought from the same store for the bargain price of 10/-.

My school days started at Elsie Pask's Dame School in Craft Cottage, where lessons were held each morning. It was a traumatic day for me and I cried lustily when my mother left, but soon got over the shock. My mother thought I was too sensitive to join the infants' class in the village school, as she considered the village children too rough. Miss Pask's class consisted of some other 'sensitive souls' like myself, and a backward village lad of 14 called Lionel Harris, who was still finding the challenge of reading almost beyond him. Stan Lawrence, the son of the local policeman, and a few others made up a class of eight or so.

We did our lessons on a slate using a scribe to scratch our simple sums on them, and a sponge attached by a piece of string to erase any mistake. Names of objects in French were taught by sticking the appropriate sticker on objects around the room, and chanting the name when it was pointed to with a cue. Fifty years later, a yellowing label was still sticking on the ceiling saying "Le Plafond". There was no corporal punishment in the way of slaps, or the traditional caning on the hands. Discipline wasn't too strict, but I remember one always got a good telling-off for chewing the end of one's pencil. Miss Pask aways had a pot of bitter aloe, a vile concoction, that she used to dip the ends of pencils in to deter those who had the chewing habit. It stopped most pencil eaters, apart from Stan Lawrence, who seemed to positively enjoy the flavour.

Painting in watercolours passed me by, but I quite enjoyed papier-maché and making raffia tea cosies which involved rigging up a half-circle of radiating warp on a cardboard former on which to weave the length of raffia which was attached to a safety pin.

After my first term, Mother gave me a tricycle and I was able to cycle to school on my own. The only problem was that I had to run the gauntlet of the village school which I had to pass on my way to Miss Pask's each day. It was a thing I dreaded, as the village children used to throw stones and put sticks through the spokes of my tricycle wheels, running along taunting me for not being one of them. I found it very daunting and I always used to try and make a sprint for it in the hope that I wouldn't be noticed. I used to try and enlist the good-natured Lionel, the hefty 14-year-old with a mental age of six. His large presence was enough to deter the worst of the attacks, but I could see that it embarrassed him to be seen to be defending me too strongly as, after all, he was a true native of Godshill, going back many generations, and needed to be accepted by his peers.

I don't know what I would have done without Lionel; he learnt to read, married, and became the local postman, cycling his rounds every day, fair weather or foul, always cheerful and with a predictable sense of humour. The poor man developed Parkinson's disease in his fifties, and his wife, unable to handle his deteriorating condition, left him and went back to her roots in Southampton, taking their two children with her. Lionel was still driving his Mini with hair-raising abandon well into the stage where his co-ordination was badly impaired. I can remember him chasing across the village green in his tiny red car, after his terrier dog that had escaped to do a bit of rabbiting. How he hoped to control his dog from the car I don't know. Lionel is sadly no longer with us, but I shall always be grateful to him for his reluctant, protective presence in running the gauntlet of the village school.

I envied Danae not having to go to school but, eventually of course, she did. Always more adventurous physically and mentally, particularly at that stage of our lives, she mastered a small two-wheel bicycle, and at four-and-a-half was cycling to school with total confidence and aplomb! By this time I had graduated to my own two-wheeler which, to my embarrassment when it arrived from the Edwin Jones store, was an outsized, step-through girl's bicycle which my mother thought would be easier for me to mount and, with economy in mind, would also give room for future growth. Blocks were fitted to the pedals and the saddle put right down to enable me to reach them. With Mother running up and down behind, holding on to the saddle to begin with, I soon mastered the elation of balance and joy of riding a proper bicycle. On two wheels we had much more speed to run the gauntlet of the village school. I used to kid myself that I was protecting Danae but, if the truth be known, my tough little sister was protecting me; she seemed totally impervious to the taunts of the village children. Looking back, it shows just how empty the roads must have been at the tail end of the 'thirties and early 'forties for our mother to allow us to cycle to school on the road. There was no hysteria over possible molestation either, so the amount of freedom we had bears no comparison to the children of today. How times have changed. ❦

Chapter 25
Our Goats

The goats were very much part of our childhood. They were a mixed bunch when I knew them as Mother hadn't been fussy about keeping her line of Saanen pure bred, taking what ever local Billy goat she found available for the nannies when they came in season.

It was a noisy business, taking an in-season nanny to the local Billy goat in the well of our small governess cart. She bleated her need plaintively all the way to her perfunctory, smelly stud. Eventually Mother did keep one of our male kids to rear for stud purposes for a season or two. From a dear little playful kid 'Billy' soon developed into a gross, sexual athlete that you could smell a mile off! Born white, he was stained a dirty yellow from self-administered, well-directed, copious squirts of pungent urine. Thus anointed he would be impatiently restless, inspecting the apparently disinterested, neat and clean nannies, to see if they were in an interesting condition. Now and again, he would raise his bearded head high, and curling his upper lip back in a comical leer, give vent to a snickering bleat of frustrated lust, sidling up to harass yet another of his harem.

Mother never taught us about sex. We were supposed to have extrapolated that aspect of life from the goat's behaviour, so she informed us years later. At the time neither my sister or I connected their biological behaviour with humans in any way, albeit somewhat puzzling and intriguing. Without the smelly Billy we did know that kids would not be born, but nothing more crossed our minds. As for sex being in any way connected with an aspect of love, goats were not much of a role model. Billy could be quite aggressive, especially in the mating season. I remember tending a bonfire in the dusk of an autumn day when I caught a glimpse of a pair of impersonal eyes. Moments later I received a well-aimed butt from Billy who suddenly appeared out of the gathering dusk, sending me flying, fortunately not into the fire. Mother always managed to control him by grabbing his collar and giving it a twist, so inducing a strangle hold to which he succumbed. His sexual influences went beyond procreation. His presence seemed to stimulate the production of a hormone in the nannies that caused their milk to become tainted, so that it began to taste much like he smelt. The day came when Alf Chalk had him for meat in exchange for his pelt, which my mother had cured and turned into a bedside rug, a hint of yellow staining always remaining along with the inescapable memory of his odour.

Danae and I had hours of fun playing with the new kids when they arrived each spring. We would struggle up the hill from the goat shed with them in our arms, unresisting, and then, letting them go, run down the hillside and watch with joyous amusement as they skipped and skittered after us. We inevitably appropriated one as our favourite and loved it for its soft perfection and almost human little grunts and bleats. Although Mother was quite realistic and surprisingly unsentimental regarding the husbanding of animals in our charge, she made sure we were protected as far as possible from the traumas of their demise. We were never faced with having to eat the little animals with whom we had so ardently fallen in love. Alf Chalk used to take them away after a month or so, while we were at school, and kill them for the pot, returning the skins to our mother for curing and the manufacture of nice warm gloves. I always used to grieve for my little friends for days afterwards, only to be told by Mother that they had 'gone to heaven' a place which seemed very remote. Occasionally, a nanny kid would be kept back to replace an old stager, which helped to ameliorate my sense of loss.

Danae and I quickly learnt to milk the goats, one-handedly at first, into a tin mug or two-pound jam jar. As our fingers got stronger, so we graduated to two hands. Goats were good animals to learn the technique of milking as they had generous udders and teats that one could grasp easily. Unlike cows, they didn't hold their milk up, so it was much easier to extract, although I do remember Mother using a fine knitting needle sometimes to poke out the nipple of one particular goat.

Chris, armed with jug, hoping to milk the Nanny goat.

The only drawback to milking goats was their maddening propensity to kick, usually just as you were getting to the end of a session, which generally meant that the entire container of milk extracted went flying - or a dung-covered foot ended up in it. There followed much swearing at the wasted effort and picking out of bits of dry goat dung in the remaining milk. The only way to stop the 'kickers' from knocking your milk pail over, was to ram them up in a corner with your shoulder and intimidate them sufficiently with a background of swearing if they threatened to raise a hoof, while you hastily extracted the milk! We never threw away the contaminated milk. If too dirty we fed it to the dog, but otherwise it was simply strained through a muslin cloth. Our immune systems seem to have coped well with the pecks of dirt that we must have imbibed.

The milk yield was small and seasonal, six to eight goats at their best in the spring flush, giving between them just a gallon. The animals loved May time when the gorse was in full blossom, eating quantities of the yellow flowers which seemed to make the milk really flow. After the first flush, the yield dropped off and we were lucky to get a quart a day by the autumn, but it was enough for our needs. Mother discovered that if she kept up the milking right through the winter, once spring arrived, their yield, though not as great as when stimulated by the birth of a kid, increased enough for our needs. It was certainly a standby during the war years and we consumed quantities of bread and milk for our supper each day - simple, enjoyable and nourishing.

There was an anarchic 'element' in Godshill village which at intervals through our childhood set fire to our rough, especially at night when there had been a dry spell in the month of March. It was a dramatic spectacle watching the conflagration, the old gorse bushes blazing up like giant torches into the night sky and wrecking our fences. As children, we were often roped in to mend holes in the three-quarter mile boundary fence of our domain. The goats had the freedom to roam the 48 acres of rough heathland from which they largely obtained their nourishment. They were notorious for breaking the fire-

Goats and their kids were all part of growing up. They quickly learned the technique of milking and, Mother faintly hoped, about sex.

weakened fences down and getting into the smallholders' fields and spoiling their market garden produce. Goats are browsing animals and if they see a titbit they fancy on the other side of a fence they stand up on their hind legs and, resting their feet on the topmost strand of wire, they reach for it. Our animals soon made holes in the fence line, and the enterprising mischievous creatures had many a moving feast, spoiling rows of peas, turnips, cabbages and other crops that the hardworking villagers had painstakingly grown. Spoilt rows of vegetables didn't make for good relations and Mother spent a good deal of her time apologising and remunerating them for their losses. Danae and I used to help Mother cut pegs from six-inch lengths of holly which, when sharpened, she drove into the ground, pinning down the frail wire netting into the gaps. Some of the goats were fitted with bells Trudy had brought with her from Switzerland, their mellow tonkle indicating where the herd was at any one time, enabling us to drive them out of a neighbour's crop before too much damage was done.

Mother used to make a bit of hay each June from the grass that grew round the apple trees and an acre patch just above the stream. Alf Chalk would cut it for her by hand with a scythe and Mother turned it with a wooden rake. When it was fit, she put it into 'pooks', and one of the villagers, Able Chalk, was contracted to cart it to a tiny Dutch barn in the same field, where it was stored for the winter to feed the goats and ponies. Hay-making for us children was a wonderful pastoral picnic, and Danae and I had great fun playing in the heaps of sweet-smelling meadow grass. When the hay in the barn reached the roof level it was fed in through a little door in the gable ends and we had a rare old time pushing the hay into the far corners of the roof space until there was only room for ourselves in the last snug little pocket.

Chapter 26
The Beginnings of Mod. Conveniences

In 1938, Mother had a bathroom built onto the house. Alf Chalk and his sons did the building work and more or less learnt the plumbing as they went.

As we still had no water supply apart from the well and rain water, a one thousand gallon underground tank was dug and cement-lined to collect all the rain water off the roof of the house. A semi-rotary hand pump was installed to pump the stored water to a header tank on top of the bathroom roof, which in turn supplied an indirect hot water system and, for the first time, a running cold water tap to an inside kitchen sink with a drainage pipe to take away the washing-up water into a soak-away. Luxury indeed, which must have made so much difference to our mother's work load. Cast iron radiators were fitted into every room and a coke-fired Ideal boiler installed to heat the system.

Unfortunately, Mother underestimated the cost of running a central heating system, and she never had enough money to fire the boiler more than once a week; it turned out to be far less 'ideal' than its advertisement claimed. It used twice as much coke as it should have done and wouldn't stay in all night, however much one fiddled with the damper. The circulatory system was faulty, owing to amateur plumbing, and some of the radiators refused to get more than tepid. However, we could get a hot bath once in a while and wash in a hand basin with a plug and drain. Inevitably, in one of the hard winters, the radiators froze and, being cast iron, they all cracked and became useless so had to be disconnected from the system.

Part of our daily chores was for each of us to put in 250 strokes of the pump to raise water to the header tank in order to give us continuity of supply to the taps. I wonder what toxic elements we imbibed with our unpurified rain water coming off a tar-felted roof over the years. It must have been very lacking in essential trace elements. Maybe our immune system benefited from not being molly-coddled by too much early hygiene; Mother lived until she was 89 so she didn't do too badly.

Chris and Danae in the wash day rinsing water.

Charles and Hilda Leek, Mother's friends from craft days, bought two acres of land from her in 1938 and came to live permanently on The Ridge, converting the old apple room into a house.

They still had their two hunters, Jorrocks and Twinkle, for whom, by agreement, they had built a stable on our land. Charles taught art at Bournemouth Art School and commuted on his motorcycle and side car each day. The sale of land meant a small amount of much needed extra capital for our mother. As children, we never went hungry or felt deprived, and it is a tribute to her economic management that she made our life together so rich, united and secure on such slim finances.

Charles was a very good neighbour if you kept on the right side of him, but a bad enemy if you disagreed with him. Mother, when she sold him the land, had an agreement drawn up to the effect that Charles would be responsible for maintaining fences against our goats, thus absolving herself, in theory, from any liability for any damage they might cause. In reality, she soon found that an agreement is only as good as the morality of the person with whom one has entered it.

Charles just would not fulfil his part of the deal, erected an inadequate fence, and our goats were forever getting into his produce. Short-tempered, he fell out with my mother, saying it was impossible to fence against her animals. He sent her nasty letters threatening legal action, although legally he had no leg to stand on, making life very unpleasant for Mother who was already at full stretch keeping the family together. Charles took to hiding behind a bush by a gap in his boundary and taking swipes at the goats with a large fencing mallet, which if it had found its mark would have killed them. As it was, they were too agile and dodged his attacks, and on one occasion, in missing them, he hit his own shins a glancing blow that partially disabled him for a week. The air turned blue and terse letters full of accusations and legal threats came thick and fast. Finally, Charles cut off all social contact and didn't speak to Mother for some ten years.

Fortunately, Hilda, his long-suffering wife, always remained a friendly neighbour, calling in most days for a chat. There wasn't much of a pretence at a loving relationship between her and Charles by this time; in fact, he treated her shabbily, swearing openly at her when his demands were not met to his satisfaction. One cold winter evening, coming home from teaching on his motor cycle, he skidded on some black ice and had a bad accident, fracturing his skull. On leaving hospital he was even more irrational and unbalanced in his behaviour. Hilda would often unburden herself to Mother who was a good, sympathetic listener. Luckily, Hilda had a good sense of humour that helped to ease her really rather dreadful marriage. Not surprisingly, I think she was too afraid of her malevolent husband to leave him. When she threatened to do so, she told us with nervous humour that Charles had countered her threat by walking around the place with a noose around his neck!

Chapter 27
Further Childhood Memories

When Danae and I were infants our mother used to bake her own wholemeal bread with flour ground locally at Bickton Mill on the Avon outside Fordingbridge.

When baking she would give us children a small piece of dough each, which we had great fun kneading into a lifeless grey lump before putting it in a small bun tin, which Mother placed in the oven with the main loaves. In summer, the bread was left out in the sunshine to rise, and I can still remember the smell of the yeast when I think back. In due course, the results of our efforts were taken from the oven, and the unleavened, indigestible-looking buns, with a bit of butter or jam spread on them, were eaten with relish!

In the valley below us, bordering the Forest, was a cottage occupied by a local family called the Brewers. Old Mr Brewer kept chickens, a cow, and a few heifers on six or so acres next to the cottage. He earned his living wheeling and dealing in everything from second-hand bicycles to poultry, eggs and butter, going into Ringwood Market each week and buying 'on spec', items that he thought might make a few bob if resold. He was very deaf, probably as a defence mechanism against his loud, talkative wife, who used to call him in from the fields for his lunch with shrill blasts on an A.R.P. whistle.

The couple had raised six children in the little cottage, and had had a late-comer, a lad called Dennis, a year or two older than myself. Danae and I would be invited to tea at the cottage, which had a stream running beside it inhabited by newts and frogs, which we would catch and put in jam jars and observe. Coming home in the dusk across the fields, Dennis would accompany us part of the way, mischievously planting the possibility that a dark spot in the hedge on the other side of the field just might be a wolf! My fertile imagination would begin to work overtime, building up all sorts of unknown dangers lurking in the hedgerows. I would engineer it so that Danae who always seemed totally unconcerned, walked ahead of me as a buffer against the imagined, but oh, so real, terrors that might jump out at us. I was not at all brave, in fact rather a coward, at such times compared to my phlegmatic sister.

Dolls were of no interest to Danae whatsoever. Mother had a wondrous Victorian doll with voluminous skirts and petticoats and delicate porcelain head with real hair. Her eyes rolled and shut when you laid her down, and when sat up she wheezed "*Ma Ma*". Its sophistication raised no flicker of interest from my sister, mainly because it was not alive. Cats took the place of dolls. They were dressed up and put in a dolly pram, and pushed around like real babies. Sometimes the cat submitted to this treatment and went to sleep, but most of the time it lay in the pram, one baleful eye glaring out from under the bonnet, waiting its chance to make a flying escape into the gorse bushes. However, the long skirts it was dressed in acted as a hobble and it was soon caught, forcibly put back in the pram, and tucked well in with a blanket!

Out on the Forest there were lots of gorse bushes with intimate little grassy clearings which we made into our personal dens, indulging in imaginary picnics of gorse blossom, washed down with diluted grape juice procured from 'Heath and Heather' by Mother as a healthy drink. The B3078 had so little traffic then and we were never supervised while crossing the road, free to come and go as we pleased.

A tragedy occurred while playing in the caravan with a new kitten. Danae had tethered it inside with a piece of string and we had gone to dinner quite forgetting it was there. When we remembered it was to find the kitten had jumped out of the van, and the string, not being long enough for it to reach the ground, had become a noose. I can still recollect my horror when I found it hanging there in the gloom with a droplet of congealed blood in the corner of its mouth. Mother was really angry and forbade Danae to treat cats as dolls from then on.

In the early days when the hillside was covered in old gorse, apart from a green sward that ran down from the house to the goat shed, we enjoyed baking potatoes. Cutting a small circle of turf out of the sward, we made a shallow depression in which we built a little fire of twigs gleaned from amongst the gorse. When the glowing embers had filled the depression they were raked back and a few potatoes were placed in the middle and covered over with the embers. After an impatient wait of twenty minutes to half an hour, the blackened spuds would be hooked out and eaten with great relish, charcoal and all. Making, and being entrusted with fire was a freedom we experienced from a very early age, and we were always very careful not to have an accident.

We never looked forward to clothes-washing day as Mother enlisted our reluctant help in rinsing and mangling. Mother placed the dirty linen in a large galvanised bath in the washroom, set on bricks to give enough clearance to put two Primus stoves underneath. Soap was bought in blocks and cut up into slithers, and added to the bath with enough water to cover the clothes. With the two Primus stoves roaring away, the bath soon heated up and was allowed to boil for half an hour. Some of the hot water was then baled into a corrugated 'dolly tub' with a few of the clothes. These were pumped up and down with a copper-headed plunger, its action designed to induce a certain amount of suction to extract the dirt. This was Mother's work, then my sister and I took over. Outside was another galvanised bath on blocks, which we filled with water from the rectangular rain water tank installed by my grandfather. Being open, in the summer it was a good breeding ground for mosquito larvae which we had to strain out by pouring the water through a piece of muslin. To the bath full of water we added a cube of 'Reckitt's Blue' dispensed from a little muslin bag and agitated, until the deemed colour was reached. The 'Blue' was supposed to make the clothes whiter. The washed soapy clothes were pumped about for a bit in the rinsing water to get the soap out, and I turned the rubber roller of the mangle while Danae fed the clothes into it. It was boring work and we used to relieve the tedium by filling up the pillow cases with water. By feeding in the open end first we could trap the water and then by winding the mangle fast, it was possible to split the seams of the pillow case, or at least get jets of water spurting out of minor holes. This, while entertaining for us little vandals, was maddening for our poor hard-working parent who had to re-stitch all the broken seams.

For all her major sewing tasks Mother had an old Wilcox and Gibbs chain-stitch sewing machine. Chain stitch was great if you made a mistake, as it was easy to undo and there were no bobbins to load, but one had to make sure that one finished off each piece of sewing by hand to prevent unravelling. Our clothes were mended and darned, and mended again. Mother was an expert at refurbishing clothes; money was so short she had to be. I am afraid that Danae, being the younger, got rather more 'hand-me-downs' than I did, which sometimes led to a justifiable feeling of grievance on her part. ❧

Chapter 28
Illness

Mother didn't have Danae or myself immunised against the usual childhood illnesses of diphtheria, hooping cough or measles. I don't know why. Maybe it was because of some inner conviction that she could keep our bodies healthy through life style and good diet.

For whatever reason, we were never protected and Danae developed diphtheria when she was five. She was rushed into Old Sarum isolation hospital where she stayed for five traumatic weeks, Mother trailing out by bus to visit her and, in the initial stages, busy preparing herself for my sister's possible demise. It was touch and go for a while, but medicine had advanced enough for drugs to be available to clear the deadly mucus membrane blocking Danae's airways. She was spared a tracheotomy and survived. The hospital lived up to its name, with mothers visiting their offspring in a prison-like setting, windows separating the two parties. Poor Danae, it must have seemed like some impersonal hell hole. She remembers the nurses, dragons who made her sit in front of her cold rice pudding for a whole afternoon if she wouldn't eat it. Small as she was, she never gave in to their tyranny.

The original Rupert Bear adventures in hardback were Danae's favourite books at that period, and I can remember Mother having to sterilise them by putting them in the oven. They came out brown and very brittle! A medical officer was called in as diphtheria was a notifiable disease, and he taped up all the planking of the walls of our bedroom and fumigated it with sulphur candles. It was all quite a to-do one way and another. Danae had a dearly loved teddy bear; he had to be disinfected too. His worn pads went brittle and disintegrated and Mother replaced them beautifully with soft goat skin. She lovingly made him a suit of clothes out of goat fleece, trousers with braces, and a jacket with hood, and this she would show to Danae from behind the windows separating them at the hospital. It must have been terrible for mother and child not to be able to touch each other during those five weeks.

Initially, when Mother visited Danae she would leave me at home. At that time we had an acquaintance living in the upstairs room, a woman called Olive Potter. She was a neurotic type and was recuperating from a broken leg. Our playroom, below her room, had a gramophone in it, and I used to bate Olive by playing *Land of Hope and Glory* on it, a tune she detested. I would put the record on and beat a hasty retreat on hearing a vexed Olive stomp down the stairs on her crutches, listening with amusement as she ripped the pick-up head off the record. Of course, as soon as she was safely upstairs, I gleefully put it on again. Olive eventually hit on the obvious ploy of confiscating the record and complained to my mother. From then on Mother insisted that I accompany her to Old Sarum where she left me on the boundary of a wartime aerodrome, where I filled in the hour of my mother's visit by watching Lysanders and other aircraft take off and land. I became quite an expert on aircraft of the RAF during my enforced hours of observation.

Diphtheria really took it out of Danae and she arrived back from isolation hospital looking like a little waif; it was some time before she was back to her old self. We both weathered measles and escaped hooping cough. Then at seven I caught scarlet fever, another notifiable disease, and was in bed for seven weeks. All visitors were barred entry to the house. I don't remember much about the illness apart from running a high fever and getting very thin. Convalescing, Danae used to play draughts with me, rather to the dismay of our mother. Danae insisted that 'everything was OK' as she was handling the pieces with a dish cloth to avoid contamination, an idea of her own that tickled my mother's sense of humour in spite of her apprehension. I got so thin, my Uncle Aubrey recommended I consume half a pint of cream each day. Mother used to beat up an egg in a pint of hot milk that I loved, especially the froth. Danae was a loyal companion during those long days of recuperation, playing card games and Snakes and Ladders. So we both survived fairly serious illnesses, life went on, and our strength returned.

Mother had a seriously sweet tooth which translated itself into sending us to bed on a wine gum! It was a brilliant recipe for acquiring dental cavities. Oh, the agony of toothache, with Mother pushing little balls of cotton wool soaked in oil of cloves into the cavity to try and stop the pain. There was a long agonising night to get through, and then off early on a train, all the way to London to visit a high class dentist, a gentle operator recommended by Uncle Aubrey. The local dentist, a Mr Brown, was considered to be too much of a butcher, insensitive to children and sporting a primitive treadle drill. With apprehension at the prospect of the dreaded drill, we reluctantly seated ourselves in the dentist's chair, the large shallow spittoon next door with its irrigating swirl of water coursing round with a faint gurgle. "Open wide please, this won't hurt," came the smooth, false reassurance from the dentist. With every muscle tense as a drum, one waited for the stabbing pain, more anticipated than ever felt and only for a fleeting moment. At last, the vibrating buzzing drill was put down and "Rinse your mouth please," came the command. With relief you took a mouth full of pink wash, produced by a pill in a glass of water that fizzed exuberantly, and spat into the swirling spittoon.

It was the policy in the 'thirties to put fillings in milk teeth. Fear giving way to curiosity, I would watch the dentist weigh out his mercury and mix his amalgam in a tiny pestle and mortar, finally rolling up the resultant silver lump into a ball. A rubber squeegee would be depressed and filled with warm air from a spirit burner, then blown into the cleaned cavity to dry it out, prior to filling it with amalgam which was pushed and compressed into place with tiny clinical tools. As a reward for being good we were given a blob of mercury to play with! *Oh*, miraculous element, *oh*, how dangerous with hindsight. "Good children," Mother would say, and give us two wine gums as a special treat on going to bed that night.

I remember one disastrous journey all the way to London to see the dentist when Danae had tooth problems. On sitting down in the dentist's chair, Danae, usually a calm sort of person, this time just flipped and yelled blue murder, and wouldn't let the dentist anywhere near her, let alone treat her tooth. With the dentist increasingly irritated, Danae wouldn't give in and back home we had to go without treatment. Mother was really angry at the wasted day and expensive journey. Danae, normally phlegmatic, from that day detested dentists. We both had bad teeth, probably owing to the amount of sugar we ate with everything, and the fact that we drank rain water with no trace elements. Mother seemed oblivious to the connection between sugar and dental decay. ❦

Chapter 29
Education

Mother took our spiritual and religious education in hand by reading us rehashes of bible stories each day from little illustrated books that were in print in the 'thirties.

She also bought a huge, illustrated copy of the *New Testament* with a picture on each page. She would read the text and we would listen and look at the pictures, sometimes asking questions. And then we would sit still for two minutes, and think of Daddy or what she had told us about the picture. The illustrations were realistic and pre-Raphaelite in feeling and style. I can still recollect my morbid fascination at the pictures of Christ being whipped bloody by Pilot's minions, and later hanging on the cross between the two thieves, a cruel crown of thorns sending the blood streaming down his agonised face. It was, and is, an image of cruelty that still mirrors man's continuing inhumanity to man. Impossible to equate as a child, though I did find the images sad and disturbing.

Mother used to read a lot to us from a variety of books. Some were like *The King Of The Golden River*, a thinly disguised morality tale, dressed as a fairy story. Others, such as the adventures of Ulysses, from adaptations of the Greek legends of Homer, made very exciting listening, as did Hans Anderson fairy stories. In the early years we adored *The Tale of Peter Rabbit* and all the other Beatrix Potter books. I could never get enough of JM Barrie's *Peter Pan*, which Mother read to me every night, or even twice a night for six months or more. She must have been so fed up with the story, as eventually I knew it all by heart and would correct her if she made a mistake or did a bit of sly editing! She bought the Hans Anderson stories in several large volumes, the evocative period illustrations, graphic in their portrayal of pathos, through to the supernatural and demoniac. The pictures accompanying a story called *Auntie Toothache* appeared in the margins, and took the form of gargoyle-like demons boring into large molars with a hammer and chisel, brace and bit, very evocative of the pain of toothache. The fairy tales were deliciously frightening when snuggled up to Mother, but, if I am honest, they did feed an already overactive imagination and help stoke up an irrational fear of the dark when alone.

We also had the twelve volumes of the children's encyclopaedia edited by Arthur Mee, a great standby when we were ill in bed. The Arthur Mee encyclopaedias are very much inspired by the colonial and social mores of the 'thirties, full of inclusions like *The Picture Story of Oil, The Marvel of Hearing, The Story of Where Power Comes From, what it does and how it works*. There was a section called *Wonder: Plain answers to the questions of the children of the world*, and illustrations like *The dying Capernicus feels the pages of his new book*, or *The march of man from the age of barbarism to the League of Nations*, and so on. All so English, so full of the national pride of that time at our industrial and colonial might. They were designed to portray a patronising exclusivity of knowledge to the youth of our nation, to fill us with pride at our superior place in the world, coupled with a patronising tolerance of "our coloured friends". This perhaps cynical assessment of the Arthur Mee ethos comes with hindsight, of course. At the time it was accepted as part and parcel of how we viewed ourselves and the rest of the world in the 1930s.

Miss Pask's school offered a rather poor education, and Mother determined to teach us herself for two hours in the afternoons. We learnt to read and spell with *Beacon Readers*, a series of graded books with interesting stories like *The Cock, The Mouse, and The Little Red Hen, Billy Goat Gruff*, and other such traditional tales. Reading was fun, arithmetic boring. Most of our education for the first five years we inculcated from our mother.

Mother used to try and make it fun. She used flash cards to teach us mental arithmetic and would go over and over them each day until we became fluent. One thing we did learn at Miss Pask's was our times tables which we chanted each day and never ever forgot as a result. They have been most useful throughout my life and there is a lot to be said for rote learning of certain things.

We were initially introduced to writing via a script designed by Mary Richardson. Mother mongrelised it by introducing a Greek E into my version of the script and for some reason my writing never matured, nor was it ever very legible except when I wrote with an oblique italic nib. Learning at home wasn't altogether satisfactory as we equated home with freedom, and as a result were often bolshie and uncooperative in the face of Mother's determination. We stretched her patience to its limits on many occasions with our grumbles and lack of concentration. Nevertheless, we acquired a good wide vocabulary just by living with her, but our ability to spell with certainty and accuracy has remained abysmal, owing to laziness and lack of application at a time when one was of an age to acquire and retain knowledge.

In the early days of the war Mother got to know a Canadian woman called Mrs Munroe who had two children, Robin and Elspeth, slightly older than Danae and I. She was a qualified teacher and rented the cottage at the north end of Sandy Balls. Danae and I used to be invited to tea there. Coming back home through the woods we used to scare each other pointing out the tree that Sid Sparks was supposed to have hung himself from. Before Mrs Munroe, the previous tenants of the cottage had been the Spark family, an elderly mother and her two adult sons, Sid and Maxwell, the latter employed to do the cleaning at Miss Pask's. Sydney was a fairly wild young man who suffered from mild epilepsy; he was a brilliant footballer in spite of this disability, playing for 'The Turks' in Fordingbridge. A story circulating at the time concerned a deer poaching incident in which Sid had been apprehended by the local Forest Keeper Slightam, but had escaped from his clutches and run off into the woods. I don't know if it is true, but apparently the poaching laws stated that if you could evade capture for one month, you were free at the end of that period to re-enter society and the law could not touch you. Sid apparently managed this, living off the land and appearing as bold as brass at the end of the appointed month, none the worse for his period of deprivation. As well as being an epileptic, Sid was also a manic depressive and during one of his depressions he sadly hung himself in the woods near the cottage. The exact location of his tragic demise has gone into the realms of legend, but to Danae and myself it became a certain hoary old oak in the gloomy north end of Sandy Balls.

Miss Pask's school expanded with the War and we acquired another teacher called Miss Cooper who had been doing missionary work in Morocco. She took us for basic Geography where we learnt the counties of England from a jigsaw puzzle, chanting their capitals and manufactured products by rote. I remember only the first two: "Northumberland, Newcastle-on-Tyne, noted for coal, iron and ship building" and "Durham, Durham-on-the-Weir, noted for coal, iron, ship building and mustard." She also taught us Scripture about which I remember nothing. I do know that Miss Cooper was a lot more fun than Miss Pask, and because of her travels and experiences abroad, she was much more liberal and less spinsterly than her employer.

The Ministry of Education was starting to take an interest in dame schools at this time, and inspectors came and visited our little school and found it 'sub-standard'. The fact that neither of the teachers were qualified in any way did not help, although the inspectors had to admit that the two women were performing a valuable job with the slower children. Mrs Monroe hired one of the larger huts in Sandy Balls and set up an infant school of her own. So it was that Danae and I, and a large percentage of our peers, moved into Mrs Monroe's classes, which we found much more stimulating and fun. Being young and professional, she brought a freshness to her teaching that grabbed our attention, along with the novelty of her soft Canadian accent. Quite a troop of us would gather each day with our satchels full of pencils, rubbers and exercise books. I still remember a cherished pencil box with a roll top lid that, when you slid it back, seemed to disappear like magic. It was Japanese and had an almond tree painted on it in the formal brush work style of the Orient. Later on, during the War, Mother sold Mrs Monroe the Hutchings caravan which became her home until hostilities ceased. It ended its days in Sandy Balls, acting as home for many different people, but with little maintenance it slowly rotted away.

Danae and Chris - the adventure that is childhood.

With Mother's connections to the various branches of the Rutter family we often visited each other. One family kept Angora rabbits. Mother was given some of the rabbits' fine soft hair, and mixing it with wool, spun it and knitted us little warm pullovers. Sadly, she didn't bargain on the affect of washing them in too hot water which turned them to felt and shrunk them to half their original size. The same Rutter cousins had a railway track laid around their garden and an open waggon to ride in. The track was laid on a slight incline. You pushed the waggon to the top and gravity took you all round the garden to some buffers which brought you to a gentle halt. Wow! The excitement of riding that railway, how I loved it!

Once, I stayed for a week at Kingsley and Ethel Rutter's home in Shaftesbury. Kingsley Rutter was a related solicitor who, in Quaker tradition, saw to all Mother's legal matters without charge. I quite enjoyed my stay, apart from not being allowed to mow the lawn on a Sunday. Never having seen a lawn mower before, I was intrigued by the Rutter's machine and determined to run it over my host's lawn. It never occurred to me that mowing a lawn on a Sunday was a sin against the Lord as it came under the heading of work. To me, mowing a lawn and seeing all the clippings spraying into the grass box was just good fun. But *NO!* I was told in no uncertain terms to desist by an outraged Ethel.

What a strange rule, I thought, and how different from home.

By this time, the Collins family had moved from 'Four Winds' and taken up residence in Bournemouth. The parents, Dad's niece, Aunt Gertrude (or Gerts as she was known) and Uncle Harry were always very welcoming, along with their beautiful daughters Margaret and Kathleen. We would have wonderful days at the seaside when Danae and I would ride piggyback on the girls' shoulders and have mock fights trying to unseat each other. We participated in all the usual fleeting sandcastle building, waiting for the tide to come in and fill our moat, which it did, too fast, sweeping away the walls and ramparts of several engrossing hours work in minutes. Seaweed, razor shells, ice cream cones and sand in the cucumber sandwiches, all the gamut of sunny seaside experiences common to youngsters on English beaches the country over.

I stayed for a week in Bournemouth in the Collins household, and was spoilt so much, had such a good time, and fell so in love with the two young women, that on coming home, I moped about the place for days. It was such an anticlimax, like a malaise, and Mother was quite concerned as I was unable to articulate my distress. Kathleen had several boy friends and one of them, called Max, stayed in Sandy Balls with her. They

Kathleen Collins, Hilda Sass, Hilda Leek, Danae, Margaret and at the back, Charles Leek and Christopher.

invited us to a special tea party held in a garage-like hut. When we arrived we could not believe our eyes at the sumptuous spread laid out before us on trestle tables. There were stacks of Danish pastries, the cream and jam oozing out of them, trifles, jellies and goodies designed to fit a child's vision of cornucopia! We had a wonderful feast, coming away as tight as ticks, and thinking what a great pair Max and Kathleen were to know so much about children's taste as to preclude from the menu boring things like sandwiches, salads and savoury items! ❦

Chapter 30
Religion

Early in our lives we were taken to Quaker Meeting which was held once a month in a log cabin in Sandy Balls, overlooking the Avon Valley.

Lots of elderly worthies attended, including a Mr Thompson who rode from his house in the village on a tricycle, which although it was novel, always puzzled me as to why an adult should choose to ride a tricycle when one normally graduated to a two-wheeler as soon as possible. Mother said it might be something to do with a defect in Mr Thompson's sense of balance. Another 'Friend' used to come from Hale with his wife on a tandem, a builder called Douglas Deer, a real 1930s Cycling Tourist Club (CTC) member, in plus-fours and highly polished brown brogues with decorative leather work on the uppers. Later on his daughter came too. Usually some of the Pasks attended and, sometimes, Hilda Leek. Our Uncle Aubrey came very occasionally. We youngsters were allowed to leave the meeting half way through so we didn't have time to get too bored counting knot holes in the log cabin, or studying the more eccentric faces and figures of the adult assembly.

Silent worship is a difficult discipline for a child as it has no ritual or peg from which to hang or to stimulate one's inner senses. Meeting was the discipline of sitting still, but the spiritual element didn't come into it at that stage. As well as Quaker Meeting once a month, we went regularly to Sunday School, taken by two elderly spinster ladies called Miss Howell and Miss Richardson. They were Congregationalists and belonged to a movement called the Scripture Union, into which we were willingly conscripted as it made you eligible for a book prize each year. Sunday School was held in the local chapel in Godshill every Sunday afternoon, where we would meet many other village children and sing such hymns as *Crown him, crown him, All ye little children* and *He is love*. Miss Howell would play an antiquated harmonium with mouse holes in the bellows so she had to pedal it very fast in order to produce enough air to sustain the notes. As it wheezed into action an older villager, a tiny woman called Edie Chalk who always used to attend for the singing, would come in flat, half a beat behind the organ, and we children, with giggles, followed her lustily behind, in our high-pitched trebles. As Edie started first, she always ended last, still flat, not ever having picked up the true pitch en route.

Sometimes, on a red letter day, Mr Bains, the peripatetic Congregational minister, would attend our Sunday school. He was a tall, vigorous man in his seventies, with white hair and beard, and very kind. We looked forward to his coming. He generally arrived on his fifty-year-old bicycle with his violin strapped to the top tube. Taking the instrument out of its case, he would rosin the bow and lovingly tune it. This accomplished to his satisfaction, he would tip a signal to Miss Howell, and, with a beaming smile, launch into *Crown him, Crown him*, or whatever hymn was set for that Sunday. It was lively playing, and you felt Mr Bains was sincerely happy in his vocation of "making a joyful noise unto the Lord". He would deliver a little Christian homily half way through the proceedings and then let rip with another hymn. Miss Richardson would relay to us what some faceless Bishop was doing by way of spreading the gospel 'to our coloured friends in the Colonies' then, with a final hymn, we would all troop out. Mr Bains stood at the door, smiling in benediction, and either patted our heads or shook hands with us, depending on how old we were. And so a session ended.

At the end of each year, we had a prize-giving day in which the children participated with a song, reading or recitation. I had been given a ukulele, and laboriously learning three chords, I sang *Old Folks At Home* in my piping treble. Unfortunately stage fright overcame me with the pressure of performing in public, and I forgot my second verse. I just dried up, going red with embarrassment. I smiled weakly and retired defeated, while everyone generously clapped with enthusiasm and sympathy, so it didn't seem to matter too much.

We were always presented with quite a good book on these occasions, usually written in the ripping yarn, GA Henty, Boy's Own, adventure style. I remember the title of one; it was called *The Lonely Pyramid*, all about the adventures of a boy who finds himself abandoned and lost in the desert. That Prize book each year was a well thought out psychological ploy by the Congregational church as it gave us a good incentive to attend Sunday school, and we never contemplated playing hooky from it. Every year, a child in the Scripture Union was given a nice marker and a diary with listed Bible readings for each day. Mother gave me a good Bible that even had a few pictures in it. For a month of each new year I became quite pious, and religiously read the passages from the Bible as instructed, using my new book mark. As I had very little idea of what I was reading about and so could only go through the motions of my daily task, it was a duty that soon palled. I'd forget for a few days, and then make up for it by reading the back verses, inevitably in an increasingly perfunctory way. No one ever asked us how the readings were going or if we understood them, so, inevitably, human nature being what it is, Bible study was soon forgotten in the active adventure of living for another year.

As a sort of postscript to the Sunday School period, I remember being given a toy violin which had rather poor wire strings. I told Mr Bains about it, and he, kind man, said he would come to our home and put some proper strings on it for me. He duly arrived on his trusty, immaculate bicycle, with three speed and chain that ran in an oil bath. He must have travelled thousands of miles on that cycle during the course of his ministry. Anyway, he took a look at my fiddle and, digging out some old strings from a music case, he strung my little toy instrument and taking his own bow, as mine was slack and had no tensioner, he launched into quite a passable rendering of *Crown him*, in spite of the neck of the fiddle seeming far too tiny for his broad old fingers. I thought him an absolute wizard to get a tune out of a toy fiddle at all, and shall always remember that old man's kindness in going out of his way to help me and share his enthusiasm for the violin. ❦

Chapter 31
Cubs and Men of the Trees

I was a sucker for badges at six and seven and expressed a wish to join the Cubs. Mother knew of a family called the Lennards who lived opposite Sandy Balls entrance. Their red-haired son, David, was a Cub and I envied him his uniform cap and woggle.

He was a bit older than me and therefore a bit patronising, but he condescended to take me to a Pack meeting and meet his 'Akela' (as the Pack leader is known). So greatly excited, I went to Fordingbridge Cub House where dozens of small boys of my age were horsing about in total anarchy like a lot of puppies. Into this chaos stepped a formidable elderly lady. "*PACKS!*" she screamed irritably at us, and clapped her hands, and as if by magic the bedlam ceased. The boys were sorted out into their Packs and, as I wasn't yet enrolled, I had to stand on the edge of the group and watch the rest playing competitive games. As each one finished, 'Akela' would scream "*PACKS*" again, and all would gather round her for their next instructions. I never became a Cub, I didn't go overboard for 'Akela', she was too much like a more athletic version of old Mrs Gardener, strict and without humour. Nor did I feel socially at ease with all that number of boys. The whole thing was too autocratically organised for my nature.

Although I didn't become a Cub, I did become a Twig, in a society called *Men of the Trees*, a movement initiated by a man of vision called St Barbe-Baker. There lived in Godshill at this time, in a property in Newgrounds, a strikingly odd lady by the name of Miss Goodman. She was a tall, imposing and excitable woman, red of face and with large 'Carmen Miranda' style earrings. The advancing years had not been kind to her neck line which sagged in red folds rather like a turkey wattle. She was a great disciple of Barbe-Baker and enrolled us all into becoming 'Men of the Trees'. We were given a green felt oak leaf as a badge to pin on our lapels, and Miss Goodman would stride out with her platoon of 'Twiglets' across the Forest, and armed with our little hatchets we would do battle with the ivy growing on the mature oaks in Pitts Wood. We loved our felt oak leaf badges, but even better, was a small enamel badge I managed to obtain, that had an oak depicted on it and was inscribed *Men of the Trees*, and the obscure motto *Twehomwi*, its meaning forever a mystery.

Miss Goodman wrote doggerel poetry rather in the style of Patience Strong, and had a crazy Red Setter called Paddy who chased all our pregnant goats, causing them to abort or have difficult births. To Miss Goodman, Paddy could do no wrong, and as she hadn't seen him chase our goats, of course, he was innocent! That Paddy escaped on his own and went on the rampage she wouldn't acknowledge. She was highly offended at our mother's mild insistence that Paddy was the culprit and fell out with her. Paddy was subject to fits which got worse as he got older and he eventually died of a seizure. Of course, Miss Goodman was devastated. Mother consoled her with the thought that even dogs have souls, and that if she could imagine her Paddy in a Doggy Valhalla, in time his demise might not seem so bad. Miss Goodman was comforted and the two women resumed their friendship. ❦

Chapter 32
Toys and Games of Childhood

On winter evenings, when we were small and had loads of energy to expend, Mother used to let us play 'Keep the kettle boiling', a game which consisted of leaping over the back of an old and sagging, dusty armchair, doing a forward roll and somersault into the seat and over onto the floor.

We followed hard on the heels of each other, round and round until we were exhausted. It was noisy and boisterous, but as the noise was happy Mother remained tolerant.

Remembered toys are little lead horse and carts, delicately made and painted, and all sorts of farm animals with which we could play our make-believe games in farmyards made of bricks. We had a very good toy shop at the far end of Fordingbridge High Street, which formed the other half of Geddes, the chemist. He sold Hornby train sets which were my delight, except the locomotives would derail on the corners of the track that I laid out under the chairs and table of our living room. If I had laid the track with the right camber (an engineering law of which I was ignorant), I would have had far fewer derailments. Danae used to bring 'Goods' to the railway station in her horse and cart and I would load and deliver them by train to their destination in another part of the room. We played for hours at this.

The one recurring problem with anything clockwork was the loss of the key to wind it up. In vain did Mother try and avoid the misery of this situation by making us wear the key round our necks on a piece of string. Sooner or later, I would take the key off in the excitement of play and forget where I had put it. During our childhood, toys were still made in tin plate, and the only plastic was celluloid that was used for cheap dolls. Some of the clockwork toys were very ingenious, like the German-made Schuco scale model cars that came complete with tiny gear stick and three-speed gear box. They had a steering wheel that you could activate via a long fine cable. This sophisticated little toy, like everything else, was powered by a clockwork motor. I never acquired one of these much desired little cars - they were too expensive for Mother's purse - but I had a friend who had one and how I envied him. It was more fun, somehow, playing with a clockwork toy than the battery-operated toys of today, having to wind them up to achieve a new surge of power. Mr Geddes sold cowboy outfits mounted on a card consisting of a hat, a neckerchief, a sheriff's star, and a gun belt complete with cap gun revolver. Caps were tuppence a hundred, bought in a tiny pill box. Mother gave us pocket money, a half penny for every year of our age, so at six I had 3d a week to burn holes in my pocket. In those days, you could buy a slim bar of Nestles milk chocolate for a penny, or a balsa wood catapult glider for 2½d.

Sometimes at Christmas, Santa would include in our stockings a hairy black clockwork spider which, when wound, would zip around the room bouncing off table legs to dart off again in a different direction. Great fun. In the days before Charles Leek fell out with Mother, he made a wooden horse and cart for Danae and a tractor and trailer for me. They were robust and simple and we loved them, playing many inventive games around them. My friend Lionel gave me a water pistol once, again made out of tin plate. It had an internal copper barrel with a slide under it that worked a plunger. You pulled the slide toward the trigger guard with the muzzle immersed in water to fill it. When you pulled the trigger it ratcheted the plunger forward in increments of a quarter of an inch, expelling a squirt of water. One had six shots before having to reload. How much more fun than the modern plastic water gun with its back pack of half a gallon of water.

As the War got going, tin plate toys became scarce. I used to buy a cardboard pistol from Mr Geddes, made of three layers, with the trigger sandwiched in the middle. A rubber band passed through the end of the muzzle and was stretched back the length of the barrel and looped over the breach. With the gun came the ammunition, consisting of stiff little cardboard discs that you slipped behind the elastic band at the point of the breach. Pulling the trigger pushed the loop of elastic up over the end of the breach, thus releasing it to catapult the disc, planing on its way like a tiny frisbee, if you were lucky. At 4d, these cardboard weapons were quite a bargain, and with them we fought many mock battles amongst the gorse bushes. Eventually, the rubber band would snap or the cardboard trigger get tired and floppy, and we would have to wait another week to get a new one.

To and from school in the winter we would slide on the ice on the village pond with the other village children. In those days (before the epic summer drought of the 'seventies, when the centuries-old, clay-puddled bottom cracked), it never seemed to dry up. On windy, mild days we would throw sticks in the water and have competitions to see whose stick would be first to reach the other side on the miniature waves produced by the wind. At weekends or holiday times, if it were wet, we passed the time with a tea party, getting out our tiny Japanese tea sets consisting of tea pot, sugar bowl, milk jug and six cups, saucers and plates which we laid out with much care on a small table.

Danae had a tea set with yellow and gold banding, with roses round the side of each piece. My set had blue banding and Japanese calligraphic-style decoration. We made ourselves miniature jam sandwiches, and although Mother would not let us have tea (too stimulating!), she let us have cocoa in our teapots. The tea party started very decorously and Danae's teddy bear was offered the first jam sandwich. As the tea party progressed, our delicate finesse, subconsciously adopted to be in tune with the delicacy of the tea sets, tended to disappear along with our manners to our other imaginary guests. The last of the dregs of the cocoa would be tipped unceremoniously into the sugar bowl, and the tiny sandwiches, instead of being nibbled went down our gullets at a gulp. Tea parties never lived up to their promise, especially when it came to having to wash up our tea sets at the end of the meal, when the whole game had begun to pall anyway. In spite of this, tea parties were a frequent diversion.

We each had a doll's house. Danae's was a modern, sectional cream bungalow with lattice windows that opened. Mine had belonged to Mother and was like a small cupboard with three shelves representing the three floors, wallpapered inside. The house had an outward façade styled vaguely in the Victorian manner, with a door and painted windows matching the heights of the various storeys. Animals inhabited Danae's bungalow. I don't recollect who inhabited mine, but I do remember lots of miniature furniture, along with tiny, grey-enamelled cooking pots and pans, I used to set up on the various floors. It was good, in retrospect, to have a mother who took it for granted that boys should like playing with doll's houses and tea sets, and who never questioned what the rest of the world might have considered to be 'sissy' pursuits for a boy.

A toy I still have today, as I really looked after it, is a model, stationary steam engine. It is beautifully engineered and that it still runs is a tribute to that fact. Mother bought it for me for my 7th birthday, paying, I believe, the large sum of fifteen shillings for it. I was allowed to run the engine on a tin tray on the dining table. The brass boiler held about half a pint of water which was heated by a meths burner with two wicks that poked up underneath it. With the piston top dead centre, one waited for the water to boil and the first wisps of steam and drops of moisture to escape from the safety valve. Then, with a flick of the fly wheel, off she went, the piston a blur of movement. It was absolute magic for me to see the power of steam in microcosm. To this day I can empathise with the fascination that steam power has for grown men when they refurbish an old traction or showman's engine. I always had a can of oil handy, and every time the engine slowed I would put a drop on the piston cam and there would be immediate response as the engine picked up speed again. My liberal oiling probably accounts for it being a runner still. The steam engine had a drive pulley and, using cotton as a drive belt, I rigged it up to a cotton reel on a knitting needle in a box, making it spin merrily. Tearing bits of paper, I 'manufactured' sweets, by flipping them off the spinning cotton reel into an old match tray, which Danae delivered stacked neatly on her horse-drawn cart to the depot where they were fed to her teddy bear. When he was satiated they went to light the fire. It was such fun tending to the needs of that little living machine, with the smell of meths, steam and hot oil.

Eventually I tired of making sweets and moved on to butter production. Using two cotton reels side by side and an old Watermark's ink bottle which I filled with cream, I placed it between them, and by driving one of the cotton reels I was able to turn the cream in its tiny churn until such time as the agitation turned it to butter. The operation was just within the scope of the power of the model, but it made it puff a bit! I would churn for what seemed like an eternity, only once turning the cream to butter. With hindsight, I guess the heat of the engine made everything too hot for the cream to turn. Later, my son Tom had a mobile traction engine model that trundled around the floor. Though I don't think he played as much with his machine as I did mine.

Picnicking on Mother's tomato and egg sandwiches down by the Forest stream that flowed through our fields, we would while away the time plaiting the pithy green rushes that grew on the banks. Sometimes we would make swans out of them. Starting at the fat end, we would coil the rush into a small lozenge-shaped little raft, which we pinned together with long gorse prickles. Leaving a few spare inches of rush pinned at an angle from one of the pointed ends of the lozenge to make the swan's neck, the final quarter inch of rushes was bent over and pinned, again with a gorse prickle, to make the swan's head and beak. We used to have great fun racing our swans on the current of the stream, rather like 'Pooh sticks'.

It was very boggy the other side of the stream and we used to throw off all our clothes and go charging into the lovely, quaking, muddy morass until we got so bogged down we could go no further, or deliberately fell flat on our faces, bellies in the mud. Then, shrieking with glee, we would dash to the stream and plunge in, the mud floating off our bodies and away downstream in an instant. Then it was out of the water to rush laughing into the bog again. I don't think I have known such heaven again! Oh, youth and innocence, where have you gone? Later, we grew friendly with some village children and took them for a mud bath, but when we took our clothes off they said it was "rude", and insisted on wearing their knickers and pants. 'What was rude?' we wondered, and the first self-conscious seed of awareness was sown in our Adam's garden of innocence, even if we were only dimly aware of it at the time. ❧

Chapter 33
Catherine Street, our Evacuee

The German offensive against Britain was gaining momentum in 1940/41, with the enemy bombers coming over in droves to blitz our major towns and cities. Southampton and its docks received a terrible roasting, and the sky on the horizon was lit up each night with burning buildings and the beams of search lights probing the night sky for raiders. We could feel the ground tremble from the blast of the bombs, even from fifteen miles away.

Children were being evacuated to the countryside from Southampton and a batch were allocated to the Godshill area. Volunteers were called for to offer a billet for these children for as long as it took for the worst of the bombing to abate. Much to our selfish fury, Mother volunteered to take in a child. We didn't want a stranger in our house, we moaned, and Mother gave us a homily about how children were being injured and killed in Southampton from the German bombing and how we should all do our bit by giving them a safe home away from the town. Danae and I skulked about the house planning all sorts of nasty receptions for the stranger who was going to invade our space.

The evacuee turned out to be a tough, streetwise, fair-haired girl called Catherine Street from Shirley, a deprived area of Southampton. She was a year older than me and bigger and stronger. We pragmatically abandoned our intended violent reception on the spot and settled down to make the best of the new situation. At dinner times, no matter what we had on the menu, Catherine would mash up all the ingredients into a round sculptural lump before eating it. She was noisy, abrasive, and definitely the dominant party of us three, quite tough enough to go to the village school where Mother was instructed to send her. She palled up with Danae, and I felt most aggrieved at being pushed out of the action; there was a lot of squabbling.

From Mother's diary of the time she was manifestly ill-prepared, in her gentle middle-class innocence, for coping with a child from a real working class background. Catherine exploded Mother's pre-conception of childhood innocence and loving order and was jolly well going to hold her end up. She had a hard, harsh voice and an accent that made Mother wince. Mother noted primly in her diary: "Such things do count, however much one may try to rise above them", and as if slightly conscience-stricken at her judgmental stance: "But in spite of it all, she has much good in her and many possibilities."

Catherine was with us from July 1940 until December 1941. In November 1940 her mother paid a fleeting visit to see how her daughter was getting on. I don't suppose she had ever been out of Southampton before, and the bus ride across the Forest in the gloom of a winter evening must have made her wonder what awful godforsaken dump her daughter had ended up in. For the duration of the War we had to have thick, blackout curtains on the windows so no light showed. Occasionally, our friendly copper, PC Dove, would tap on our door to tell us we had a chink of light showing, and warn us to pull the curtains properly. Imagine a fearful, town-bred Mrs Street getting off the bus into what must have seemed a black wasteland apart from the just discernible outline of our apparently lifeless bungalow. I remember we were all having supper around the table in the light of the Aladdin lamp, when this scared little woman tentatively entered the room to catch the first glimpse of our family and her healthy daughter who was consuming a large plate of bread and milk. Mother welcomed her and sat her down with a cup of tea in front of the fire and we surveyed each other.

Mrs Street can't have been more than in her early thirties but she looked a work-worn sixty. Her hands shook slightly as she drank her tea and apprehensively looked about her.

"Are you all right, Catherine love?" she asked hesitantly. "Yes, Mum," replied Catherine shortly, as she shovelled in the last of her bread and milk. Mrs Street relaxed a bit, realising that her daughter seemed happy in this back of beyond abode, then tensing up again as another disturbing thought struck her, she addressed my mother: "For God's sake, where are the shops?" she asked, almost in despair. I think Mother was able to reassure the worried mother that her daughter was in good hands. She stayed the night and caught the double-decker bus back to Southampton the next morning, a good deal more easy in her mind than when she came.

Margaret holding Danae, Mrs Street, evacuee girl Catherine Street, Chris, Mrs Watson and 'two shy boys'. One is probably Cedric Rose.

Mother tolerated Catherine's sojourn with us; I cannot say she did more than that. I think she found Catherine too disruptive and irreverent while she was trying to influence the spiritual aspects of life for Danae and myself. We ceased to have quiet times together after breakfast; the outside world was making itself felt, and Mother was uneasy as she was no longer the only influence in our lives. In December 1941, Mother decided that she had completed her stint of looking after Catherine and asked around the village to see if any other family would be prepared to take her. A family called Marks agreed and Catherine cheerfully decamped and appeared to integrate very well with her new foster family. The Marks lived in a little thatched cottage opposite Miss Pask's. All continued reasonably well until one night the parents returned home from the local cinema to find that the children, encouraged by ringleader Catherine, had made a fire in a wastepaper basket under the stair well. If the adults had come back a minute or so later the whole cottage would have gone up in flames. Mrs Marks told Mother she couldn't possibly have Catherine in the house another day as she was too much of a handful. So Mother contacted the evacuee agency and Catherine was packed off back to Shirley to take her chances with the bombs.

As a sequel to this, 50 years later, a plump, middle-aged lady paid a visit to the pottery and announced: "I am looking for a Mrs Charman. I don't suppose you remember me, but I stayed here once when I was a youngster during the war. I'm Catherine Street, and I just thought I would call in and see if anyone was still around." Mother had died by this time, but after my initial surprise I told her that I remembered her and her stay with us very well. I introduced myself and we had a good old chat about the past and present. She was happily married with grown-up children and many grandchildren, and life for her seemed to have worked out very well. I gave her a piece of pottery for old times sake which she appreciated, and we parted, wishing each other well.

With the war on, food rationing was introduced, and each member of the family had their own ration book. Mother bought her rations from the Co-op. We were allowed 8oz of fat, 2oz of tea, 8oz of sugar, 1oz of cheese. The man at the counter would open the ration books and snip out the relevant coupons with a pair of scissors, assessing what we were allowed. Up to the war we had been vegetarian, but Mother, always pragmatic, now thought it best to get hold of whatever protein was available, even though it was only the occasional sausage, chop or rasher of bacon. Bread wasn't rationed until the end of the war, and we bought that from Mr Church, the village baker, who used to deliver twice a week. A standing order of groceries was also delivered to the door. We certainly had good service in the days before we all became so mobile.

Photo: Fordingbridge Museum

Mr Harold Church, the baker, delivered twice a week in Godshill. He is pictured, circa 1920, with Archie Horsburgh and his staff, outside Crowdean (Croadene) a reference to the chickens he kept. The house became the post office, but is now a residence renamed The Old Bakehouse.

Soon after the start of the war, the War Office issued the civil population with gas masks as it was feared that the Germans, who had used gas in the First World War, might do so again. At the Village Hall, each person was given their mask in its regulation cardboard box, with a string so that you could carry it over your shoulder. Instructed how to put the masks on, we hugely enjoyed the novelty of viewing our compatriots resembling weird-looking visitors from Mars. I remember an official changing the filters on the masks, presumably designed to improve resistance to whatever gas the Germans decided to attack us with. In the event, gas was never used in the Second World War. The memory of the terrible effects of gas on all parties during the First World War must have been too much alive for its use even to be considered. ✛

Chapter 34
Other Wartime Guests

We began to acquire various characters in the house. First to arrive was Olive Potter, the neurotic wife of a Communist sandal-maker and second-hand book seller called Stanley Potter, a kind, absent-minded man who lived in Kingston-upon-Thames.

Mother had written to him many years before to get some information on the craft of sandal-making. Olive had a daughter called Hazel a year younger than me. She was a pretty girl with dark curly hair, but seemed disturbed and lacking in practical common sense. Although eight years old she could not open a door. We used to watch her in amazement as she screamed and rattled the door knob until it was opened for her. She was also unable to tie her shoe laces or dress herself. Olive had had an affair with Stanley, who had left his infertile wife to live with her because he wanted a child. Hazel was the result of their short-lived union and her birth was a traumatic event for Olive whose pain threshold was zero. She was put into a state called Twilight Sleep, a morphine-induced condition that left her scarcely aware of giving birth. Olive was pathologically incapable of mothering her child and never bonded with her.

Hazel survived somehow, only to be sent at the insanely tender age of three and a half years to a nursery boarding school. Stanley, experiencing the full misery of living with a woman who was so impractical she could hardly boil an egg, swiftly decamped and went back to his first wife who was loving and broadminded enough to accept him back into the fold. Neither party were equipped to cope with the practical realities of parenthood. What that first boarding school was like for Hazel, who knows. We took no notice of her shrieks, nor were we too tolerant of her other shortcomings; she either sank or swam.

To give a bit of intellectual stimulus to an otherwise child-orientated life, Mother organised, amongst her friends, a 'French afternoon' once a week. She would make one of her famous sponge cakes, baked in a biscuit tin oven over an oil stove, and a group of adults would assemble in the living room for a couple of hours of social conversation in French, interspersed with tea and cake. An elderly couple, ex-Order of Woodcraft Chivalry 'Great Bear' and his large wife Ama, used to turn up from Sandy Balls. These, with Mother, Olive Potter, and Hilda Leek made up the hard core of the weekly get-together. It was adult 'prime time' and Danae, Hazel and I were banished to our own devices for the afternoon. Mother retained the French that she had learnt as a child, and she always sounded very fluent compared to everyone else. Olive Potter was excellent grammatically, but she had no ear for the music and pronunciation of the language. The rest of the party hovered on the edges of the conversation. The event was much looked forward to each week.

Olive had joined the Women's Land Army (of all things foreign to her nature), and had been allocated a job by the Forestry Commission, marking and counting pit props for the mines. She rented our upstairs room for two shillings a week and cycled to Fritham each day to work. One day she fell off her bike, broke her leg and was laid up for a few months. She was not the easiest of patients, tending to put on the 'moaning minny', helpless act, so that our good-natured mother was forever seeing to her needs.

I have already narrated the incident that had me banished to the windy boundary of Old Sarum air field when Mother was visiting Danae in hospital. The old wind-up gramophone with which I annoyed Olive was played frequently. Mother had bought us a job lot of secondhand 78 rpm records that covered a wide spectrum of music and sketches. My favourites were the Gracie Fields songs ranging from *Sally*, sung straight, in her glorious natural voice with just that touch of the Lancashire mill girl, to her really funny character songs like *We've Got To Keep Up With The Joneses* or *Turn Erburts Face to the Wall, Mother*, in which she so cleverly distorted her voice you would hardly know it was the same woman. Other songs were sung by celebrities of the day such as Owen Brannigan, like *The Old Rugged Cross* or, a real tear jerker, *Don't go down in the mine, Daddy*; real sentimental dirges those two. *Dick Turpin's Ride to York* and *The Man on the Fying Trapeze* we played and played. A comedian of the day, Sandy Powell, recorded such sketches as *Sandy's Honeymoon* where a man nearly misses his honeymoon because of his obsession with football. Another sketch, *Sandy, the Fireman*, had a little song at the end of it that went like this: *"When the fires put out, to the Missus back I roam, and though I've been putting out fires all night, I've to light em when I get home!"* The humour was all very unsophisticated and innocent by today's standards.

Olive had a friend called Lyn Smith, an infant teacher from Ruislip, Middlesex. Her husband, Sidney, owned a small garage business that had been turned over to producing parts for armaments in the war effort. Lyn, I guess, was fleeing the constant threat of bombs. She belonged to the Land Army for a while, sharing the upstairs room with Olive and accompanying her to the woods each day to mark out pit props. They wore cord britches and brown boots with regulation light khaki shirts, and had blue marker sticks which they used to put a cross on the ends of each pit prop as they counted them off.

I was much more interested in the bright yellow Caterpillar tractors that were employed in hauling out the timber from the woods. Each tractor had a tiny donkey engine that was employed to start the main diesel engine which, when it caught, came to life with a shuddering roar that for us spelt infinite power. The Caterpillar tracks seemed to make the machine capable of going almost anywhere as they spun and swivelled their way across the most impossible looking terrain.

With oil supplies being used up for the war effort, petrol rationing was introduced, it only being available in very limited quantities for those civilians whose job depended on it such as doctors, teachers and farmers. So the old Austin was laid up in its garage until later on in the war, when Lyn, having taken up teaching again, bought it from Mother for £30 and used it to drive to school each day. 1940-41 passed and the intensity of the bombing reduced as the Allied Forces began their own bombing offensives. Lyn returned to London to teach in her home county once more. She and Sydney bought a neat little caravan and, with Mother's permission, put it at the end of the garden for weekend visits.

Olive Schaffer entered our lives at this point. Blitzed out of London, she had been editor of *Healthy Life*, a fringe medicine magazine. Yet another weird eccentric, she was a bit younger than Mother and a disciple and practitioner of Dr Bach, known for his 'Bach' remedies, a rarefied form of homeopathy which still has its practitioners. The fact that Dr Bach is supposed to have succumbed and died from his 'potencies', didn't deter her from collecting the dew off a rose at full moon and putting it in a tiny glass phial with a drop of brandy to stop it going mouldy, and selling it in all sincerity to a string of patients with various ailments. Mother used to smile cynically sometimes, and say that she thought that the brandy tot did more for one than the dew off the rose! The various 'potencies' collected from nature were called 'Remedies' and they were labelled with whatever condition they were supposed to alleviate. For example, 'Rescue Remedy', or, 'Hypertension Remedy', 'Insomnia Remedy' and so on.

At that time Olive lived in a large hut in Sandy Balls with her small son, Julian, and Paul, a few months younger than me. Her husband was in the army and away on active service. I saw him once or twice; he was Jewish, thick-set and short with rather an unattractive florid face. Apart from fathering Julian, I don't think that he and Olive had anything in common. His visits were brief and neither party showed any interest in the other. Olive, who must have been quite attractive in her youth as she was still quite handsome in her early forties, was, I am certain, ambivalent in her sexual orientation. She was certainly an advocate of free love. Besides Julian and Paul, she had had another son, Tony (held in sacred memory), who was tragically killed while serving as a fighter pilot in the Battle of Britain. Paul hadn't a clue who his father was, and I guess neither had Tony. Olive had never bonded with Paul or shown him any love, allowing a lesbian couple to bring him up at the point when I met him as an eight-year-old. I knew them as René and Gretta McKeogh. René was a chain-smoking, fat, slightly sleazy, moustached little lady with a voice like old leather. Gretta was an upright and forthright tin soldier of a woman who wore her hair in an Eton crop, sporting slacks and a black beret. Whatever upbringing Paul had with those two ladies, he was always a good-natured fellow and we became great buddies.

Mother, desperate for adult company, fell for Olive's veneer of loving response to her intellectual need, mistaking it as belonging to the same spiritual wavelength as her own. With her usual magnanimity, she invited Olive to move from Sandy Balls and come and live with her on The Ridge. So Olive, Julian and Paul became the next occupants of the upstairs room. It was fine with me, as I had a new playmate in Paul, but for my mother, the whole experiment in living together soon soured. Olive's attraction to my mother was more than 'just good friends'; she wanted more than a cuddle. So straight away the two women found that their wires of expectation were inextricably crossed. My mother's attachments were passionate, as they were for Trudy, but they consistently had their roots in a spiritual companionship. The chemistry between the two women quickly deteriorated, and there was often a destructive tension in the air that was palpable, even to us children. Mother, who hated discord, did her best to keep life harmonious, but found it increasingly hard work, and began to wonder how she could have made such an error of judgment in her assessment of Olive's character.

Olive, who had never bonded with her two eldest sons, was besotted with her third, Julian, or 'Mammies little sausage', as she used to call him fondly. 'Sausage' could do no wrong, and as he grew bigger and more mobile, so he became more destructive. Poor Paul was set to act as nursemaid and nanny, and made to mind his small terror of a little brother. On one occasion, Julian cut the rush seats of all our dining chairs, and Paul, on reporting it to his mother, was beaten for his brother's misdemeanour.

It was always happening. When I say beaten, I mean beaten, with a riding crop that ironically Mother had given Olive in friendship, carved by my father when she had expressed a vague wish to ride. My Dad would have been appalled that it should have been used on an innocent child. I wince at the memory of the scene now, of Paul being dragged whimpering with fear into the bedroom, his demoniac mother with riding crop raised to strike him. The door would slam and screams would come from the bedroom. It was the one time in my life that I saw my mother really angry. Her sense of justice was outraged, and on several occasions she waded into the violence to rescue poor Paul.

'Little Sausage' sat and lapped up the transferred retribution with silent, almost malicious, satisfaction. Julian was fly enough not to engage in any of his vandalism when Mother was around, as he got a good smack and reprimand. If we witnessed anything, we told Mother; it was no good telling Olive her 'treasure' was up to something, she just vented her spleen on us.

Sometimes there would be days when Olive was gentle and peaceful. She made friends easily and abandoned them as easily, to their bewilderment, seeming to need the constant stimulus of pastures new. The only really consistent friendship Olive had was with my Uncle Aubrey, who as a medical practitioner was avidly exploring the possibilities of alternative medicine, Bach remedies among them. They would often confer together on their respective patients and the right treatment to deploy. Olive spent long hours upstairs in front of a little smouldering fire, concocting her Bach remedies and sending them off to her patients with advice on treatment in a neat tiny hand, always in purple ink. She smoked Black Russian Sobranie cigarettes in a long cigarette holder, all part and parcel of a delusional affectation to bohemian gentility

I only saw Olive on a horse once. She was so nervous and out of rapport with the animal it was painful to watch. It was a romantic notion that palled in its practical reality, and she never went riding again. Paul continued to be errand boy and general dogsbody for his mother, collecting groceries, the daily paper and so on, which he always did good-naturedly. He had a trusty Enfield bicycle with a hub brake and the inscription 'Built Like A Gun' on its frame.

Olive Potter was in her own caravan by this time, parked on The Ridge next to our stable. Mother took on Hazel and looked after her as Olive was totally useless. To avoid the problem of having two Olives in The Ridge community, Olive Potter adopted an old nickname of hers, Robin, and Robin she remained until her death.

Our meal times were a bit of a battle ground as Olive, Julian, Paul and Hazel ate their meals with us. 'Sausage' was always the problem as he was never disciplined by his mother for his misdemeanours at table, which ranged from emptying the jam pot over the tablecloth, to sawing the edge of our old dining table with the bread knife. Danae remembers Hazel bringing Julian's anti-social behaviour to Olive's attention, only to receive a slap across the face for her pains. Hazel, of course, howled and Mother expostulated with Olive, asking her not to be so unjust and blind to what was happening. And so the arguments would rage. Danae said she used to listen to Mother and Olive arguing for hours at night when she was in bed trying to sleep. Ironically, it was only when Robin called in that a certain amount of harmony was restored. A third party being present seemed to diffuse the tension.

When the daffodils came up in the spring, Julian pulled them all up; his mother had after all, given him carte blanche to pursue his anti-social anarchic vandalism. Even the demise of our rush-bottomed dining chairs slashed with a kitchen knife, was a destructive act that only called forth the mildest of rebukes from his mother and certainly no apology for the damage caused. This pattern of behaviour established itself when Julian was between three and four years old. It didn't bode well for the future.

I remember, with great clarity, one occasion when 'Little Sausage' got his just deserts. We had a sparky young repertory actress, Olive Lush, staying for the weekend, who witnessed Julian's behaviour pretty quickly. He discovered her handbag, turning out all her make-up, powder and lipstick and so on. She caught him at it, and without more ado she picked him up and, before he had time to think, she dumped him in a gorse bush. "There," she said, "I'll give you 'Mammy's little sausage!'" There was quite a lot of justifiable glee as you can imagine, that Julian should at last get his comeuppance; he had after all made our lives a misery for some time. Olive was furious, of course, but Miss Lush was more than a match for her, both in spirit and youthful strength. "If he gets at my property and you won't discipline him, I surely will," she said with spirit!

On another occasion, when Julian had been left in joint charge of Paul and Danae, he fell over on some hard ground and bit through his lower lip. There was blood everywhere. Paul was thrashed and Danae severely reprimanded for her culpability in allowing Julian to fall. Her gross negligence, she was told, would be reported to Mother, who was out at the time. So Danae lit a diversionary fire in the gorse below the house, which she showed great initiative in putting out. Olive, who was scared witless by fires, praised Danae for her courage, and told her that she was no longer to be reported for her negligence in looking after her son! Danae's diversion had paid off splendidly.

Mother was a good gardener and always managed to keep the plots free enough of weeds to produce all the vegetables we needed for the house, most useful during the war years. Every year we cleaned out the goat shed below the house; its accumulation of dung had built up to a layer eighteen inches deep. Mother brought it up to the garden on a wheelbarrow, with Danae and I hauling on the front with ropes to help her pull each load up the hill. Goat dung grew fantastic vegetables, and we used to get cauliflowers the size of a frying pan.

Olive fancied herself as a gardener, so Mother foolishly gave her a piece of the main garden in which to grow her own vegetables. Her gardening expertise, like so much else in her life, turned out to be all in the mind, and her part of the garden went wild with chickweed and nettles which she wouldn't pull out as she maintained they were very good for salads. The nettles and chickweed may have been all right when they were young, but Olive allowed them to go to seed. Mother, knowing the job it was going to be to keep the land clear of these dominant weeds in future years, implored Olive to fulfil her side of the bargain and at least try and keep the garden weeded. It was a plea that fell on deaf ears, and if Mother attempted to do any judicious weeding, Olive would fly at her and there would be another row. It was not a happy time for Mother, having to live for the foreseeable future with the results of her misjudgment of Olive's stability. ❦

Chapter 35
Swimming

Again I have to marvel at the freedom Mother gave us. She used to take us for picnics down by the river in Sandy Balls, where Paul and I learnt to swim in a lovely little side creek.

There was a plank bench on piles mid-stream that one could grasp for reassurance or as a place to sit or dive from. The creek was about three foot six deep and just right for gaining confidence. Mother had one rule concerning the digestion of food before swimming which we obeyed without argument. Uncle Aubrey had told us the probability of getting stomach cramp was much greater if one went swimming straight after an intake of food, and it was best to leave a time lag of about one hour for a hearty picnic lunch, and half an hour for a jam sandwich tea. Several tales of drownings circulated at the time, of young men getting stomach cramps and becoming tangled in river weeds which, embellished by our own imaginations, acted as a strong deterrent both to swimming in the main river or entering the water before the allotted time span.

We learnt to swim well. I adopted the side stroke with a scissor kick of the legs, which has always remained my strongest long haul stroke, while Paul had a good, if somewhat ragged, crawl. Mother let us swim in the main river where although the current was stronger, it was still safe. The whole river was deeper in those days and moved more slowly, brushing the top of its banks. The tranquillity was enhanced by the gently waving skeins of water weed in its mysterious depths, the calls and scurryings of coots and moorhens skittering across its surface, and the rainbow blur of skimming dragonflies. The bathing area had a ten foot high diving board which we eventually summoned up enough courage to dive from, plunging down into the green depths of the river and just managing to surface again before a slight panic took over that one might not make it in time! We had come a long way since tentatively hanging on to Mother's back while she kicked out with an immaculate breast stroke.

At the bottom of Fordingbridge hill, by the weir where the river loops in close to the road, one used to be able to hire rowing skiffs from a silent little man called Mr Rake. He was a real craftsman and made all the boats himself. They were lovely slim little craft, beautifully constructed and varnished, with a seat in the stern where the cox of the day sat and operated the rudder with two cords. There were single and double sculled skiffs at their moorings opposite the weir. If there were four of us, Mother hired the larger double-sculled boat. We had a natural healthy respect for the weir, being terrified of going over it, although it was rather irrational as the depth of water over the sill of the weir was deep enough to take the boat's draught. Mother would take the rudder, and Paul and I a set of oars each, and after gingerly negotiating the weir, we relaxed and began our uncoordinated way up river with much splashing, laughter, and catching of 'crabs'.

Not only did Mother scull well, having learnt the skill of rowing during her days at Oxford, but she added the refinement of turning and feathering the flats of the oars across the water and back for the next stroke in a lovely stuttering glide, all to the rhythmic creak of the rowlocks. The skiffs had an adjustable board in the bottom of the hull against which one braced one's feet when rowing. We quickly mastered straight sculling and the added sophistication of feathering soon after. I can't remember Danae ever rowing, but I guess she had her turn even if only to keep her end up. It was a lovely way to spend a lazy summer's afternoon, just messing about in boats, nibbling sandwiches, trailing one's hands in the moving water, gazing down through the weeds at the shoals of little fish. In those days before riparian rights became an issue, we had a good mile of navigable river to play around in, and nobody warned us off. We were as quiet as the tolerant fishermen we passed on the banks.

So, we could row, we could swim, and we were sensible enough to obey the ground rules of safety, and from then on Mother let us take out boats on our own. We spent all our pocket money and more, generously donated by Mother who often used to sub what she considered a worthwhile activity. The cost of boat hire was 1/- an hour for the single scull and 2/- an hour for the double. Sometimes, we would hire a single each and race eachother. Paul and I were pretty even at sculling but very soon realised that a race could be won by tactics deployed by the cox. Whoever persuaded Danae to act as cox for them stood a fair chance of winning as she had a competitive spirit and knew how to take the shortest line on the river and avoid the strong currents. Who ever had Hazel as cox heard a lot of screaming (until she learnt to swim) and was lucky not to end up ramming the bank! We, as her peers, I am ashamed to say, were never very supportive of poor Hazel's shortcomings.

The consumption of bottles of ginger beer or lemonade purchased from a twinkling Grandpa Harrod's camp stores at Sandy Balls, with maybe a slice of Dundee cake, were always part and parcel of a visit to the river. Grandpa Harrod was quite a linguist and used to address us in obscure Urdu, and chuckle with amusement at our nonplussed faces. The ritual of shaking up the bottle and spraying each other, thumb over bottle end, with the fizzy sweet sticky contents was always irresistible, followed by diving into the river to wash it all off. Oh, halcyon days, rushing around the water meadows, playing tag to get dry after a swim. Olive seldom braved a boating trip. I don't think she could swim and was fearful of the river as a consequence. ❧

RAF Ground Crew working on a range of bombs being tested, including the Grand Slam which created a vast crater in Godshill. (see following page). Crown Copyright: IWM CH 15856.

Chapter 36
The Bombing Range

Soon after the war started, twelve square miles of the Forest was fenced off as a bombing range with an eight foot high chain link fence.

Checkerboard targets were placed on the hill across the valley to the south of us for strafing practice by Hurricanes and Spitfires. We often had army manoeuvres in front of the house, mortars being set up on the verge of the road, and piles of mortar bombs beside them. At a given command to fire, the gunners, with unhurried discipline, would post the bombs down the mortar tubes and with a dull crump they hurtled in a slow arc across the valley to explode near or against the reinforced concrete targets. We were enthralled, as our presence was tolerated even though we were only ten or so yards away from the action. Danae, always with an eye to the main chance, used to pinch newly laid eggs from our nesting boxes and sell them to the good-natured soldiers for the black market price of 3d each! After the soldiers had gone, we used to collect up all the percussion caps from the mortar bombs as souvenirs.

On the first day of bombing practice in the range, half the village turned up in front of our house to witness it. We had been warned to criss-cross our window panes with sticky paper to prevent them breaking from the explosive shock that the bombs were supposed to produce. We waited in expectation…and we waited. Eventually a bomber droned high overhead, a speck in the sky. It made a circuit of the area and then, as we watched, a tiny object dropped out of it, and we all waited for the explosion with baited breath. There was the sound of a dull thud and that was all, the bomber droning off into the distance leaving us all with a sense of anticlimax! In the months and years to come, when we had all become blasé, some tremendous explosions occurred when we least expected them, making the whole house shudder. As it was made of wood, the vibration didn't matter, but we were very glad our house wasn't made of brick or cob as it would have sustained some cracks from those mighty explosions.

Besides the tall targets opposite us, there was another flatter, round target made of reinforced concrete, placed on the open plain just above Pitts Wood. It was indestructible and Italian prisoners of war were employed to earth it over with bulldozers after the war ended. It stands there for eternity like some 20th century tumulus, covered in heather and gorse. To the west of it, along Hampton Ridge, a dummy aerodrome was assembled with some horseshoe-shaped banks of gravel thrown up to house shot-up Hurricanes and Spitfires. It was built, supposedly, as a decoy for enemy aircraft, diverting them away from the many bomber command RAF airfields dotted around the area. In actual fact, none of them were attacked locally for the whole duration of the war, so we were lucky. The Barnes-Wallis bomb of Dambuster legend was tested on our range; it may well have been these that caused our house to shudder on occasions. On 6 November 1941, Danae's sixth birthday, a German bomber fleeing from a raid (either on Bristol or Coventry), and carrying a load of bombs, jettisoned them as it flew over The Ridge.

We heard the whine of the bombs and the dull crump of them detonating. The ground shook, and Mother said "Quick! Get under the table!" Quaking with excitement, we did so. The noise of the bomber droned away into silence and we carried on with the birthday party, wondering just where the bombs had fallen. Next morning we were out early, looking in the rough, and found a great crater in our track at the foot of the hill. It had exploded in yellow clay sending lumps everywhere. The area is known as 'the bomb hole' to this day.

The RAF had built billets on the village green, as far as the Fighting Cocks, for all the staff managing the bombing range. At the entrance to the Ashley Walk track there were large padlocked gates through which the RAF personnel lorry used to trundle most days, on its way to inspect targets and to keep a lookout for unexploded ordnance. On the brow of The Ridge two rough landing strips were made by bulldozing off the top layer of gorse and heather to expose the white gravel. RAF personnel flew in once or twice in light spotter aircraft called Austers, to confer with the bombing range staff. It took many years for the gorse and heather to re-establish itself in the sterile pure gravel.

We had a young horse that Mother was breaking in to harness. We called him March as he had been born in that month, and he was quite a handful. One afternoon, we took him out for a practice spin in the old governess cart along The Ridge to the Telegraph Post and back. Just as we were approaching home, a Hurricane fighter aircraft roared over and deliberately buzzed us. It came in so low we could see the pilot's face as he glanced across at us. When he was dead over our heads he deliberately and gleefully fired his cannon. March, scared out of his wits, took off at a flat-out gallop, the breeching strap on our old harness broke, and as most of us were sitting at the back of the cart, up went the shafts, and before we knew what was happening we were all gently tipped out onto the road. With us gone, the shafts flopped forward again into position, and we were left lying in the middle of the road watching, with some alarm, cart and horse clattering off into the distance towards home.

To our horror, the four o'clock double-decker bus to Southampton was coming up the road on its way back from Fordingbridge, and with our hearts in our mouths we watched the two vehicles converge. By a stroke of good fortune, March, scared even further by the approaching bus, veered off the road just in time to avoid a collision. We had by this time picked ourselves up, and we ran home as fast as we could to find our cart in pieces with a fiercely kicking March trying to free himself from a tangle of broken harness. At least the horse was unhurt, apart from a few nicks sustained in his struggles to get free. We calmed him down, and with a few muttered imprecations directed toward the Hurricane pilot for his misplaced sense of humour, we tidied up, thanking our lucky stars there were no broken bones.

Crown Copyright. (From the Frank Myerscough collection.)

The first ever Grand Slam bomb, dropped over Godshill 13 March 1945. The River Avon is below.

Mother had lent her Bertram Hutchings van to the Home Guard as a shelter and lookout post, and it was parked next to the road, fifty yards from the start of Ashley Walk track. A second bomb had landed right in the road, five yards from the van, blowing a crater big enough for a car. Strangely, not one pane of glass in the van was broken or even cracked by the blast. The Home Guard contingent, fortuitously, were half an hour late coming on duty that evening, having been tempted by an extra few jars at *The Fighting Cocks* before walking up to the van. It was just as well they were late, as the bomb had fallen on the exact spot where the sentry on duty would have been standing. A sentry was posted over the crater, and in the early winter morning fog, a lone motorist, seeing a dim figure with a rifle, thought it was a German soldier and drove straight at him. The sentry, who was standing at the side of the crater, just managed to dive into it and escape injury, and the alarmed motorist gunned his car for Fordingbridge saying that the Jerries had arrived, only to be told later that he had nearly run down one of the local defence corps!

There was a mounted section of the Home Guard made up of local worthies, many of them in their late fifties or early sixties, and veterans from the 1914 War. They formed a motley crew, supplying their own pony and weaponry, at first often an antiquated hammer-activated shotgun or Lee Enfield rifle. It was rumoured that, at the start of the War, they had only half a dozen rounds of ammunition each. The real fear of invasion receded as the Home Guard platoons became more organised.

With the petrol shortage, steam lorries began to operate again for heavy haulage work. They often chuffed past our house at about thirty miles an hour, their smoke stack over the cab and looking like an enlarged cauldron, exuding that unforgettable smell of coal steam. The main drive of these heavy and imposing vehicles was transmitted by a huge linked chain to a giant sprocket on the back axle, which hummed in a powerful, comforting way. With the boiler of the steam engine beside him in the cab, the driver must have been kept nice and warm in the winter months, and boiled alive in the summer. To us, these giant, steam-driven, leviathans were an exciting novelty not to be missed. ◄╫►

Photo by Frank Myerscough.

The top of the Grand Slam crater, looking towards South Ashley Walk and the rest of the bombing range on the horizon.

Chapter 37
Cousins

At the time of Mother and Father getting together, there had been a period of estrangement between my mother and her brother Aubrey, who took his father's side in disapproving of the liaison, and there wasn't much contact between the two families.

Fortunately, after the Westlake clan came to live in Sandy Balls, Marjorie, Aubrey's wife, and my mother got together and made a determined effort to get relationships going again. With the death of both my father and grandfather, the two main protagonists had left the equation and things were a lot easier. An annual summer picnic was organised, each family acting alternately as hosts. It worked very well and became an institution.

When we were hosts we would go to Millersford Bottom and dam the Forest stream, frolic in the bog, and play hide and seek and rounders. We made a large fire and boiled the water from the brook to make the tea; our uncle always refused to drink the tea for fear of parasitic worm infestation from the Gypsy camp, Tin Town, half a mile up the valley. We would boil the water for a quarter of an hour before making the tea, and no one seemed to come to any harm. Mother made egg and tomato sandwiches, a filling that was all her own invention and that everybody seemed to like. She also made a biscuit that was rectangular and had hazel nuts in it which she referred to as 'Fire Lighters' for some unknown reason.

When it was our cousins' turn to host the picnic they took us down to the river where we swam and ate fish paste sandwiches and Madeira cake and drank pop. In the security of a group we could swim downstream for a quarter of a mile to the south end of Sandy Balls to an area known as the 'Deep Bathing Spot', and then swim back again against the current, which although strong, was possible in those days when the river was lazy and high. Later, when I reached my teens and had had enough of living with crowds at boarding school, I was bloody-minded and moody and refused to attend the annual picnics, much to Mother's perplexed distress. I needed to be on my own, and if the only way I could achieve this was to be arrogant, selfish and anti-social then that was the way it was.

At Christmas, we would sometimes be invited to our cousins at Woodcott, which was always very cosy. In the part of the house they called the 'Long Room', we would play party games, like passing a match box from nose to nose, or an orange under one's chin down the line of party-goers without using one's hands, which led to some complicated embraces. The game that had us rolling about in uncontrollable laughter though was 'Poor Pussy', in which a blindfolded party member had to pass down a well-shuffled row of people and stroke them in turn, saying 'Poor Pussy', at which the recipient of the stroking was obliged to utter a well disguised 'Meow!!' The person blindfolded then had to make an intelligent guess as to the identity of the 'Poor Pussy' he had just stroked. If he guessed correctly, he changed places with the person he had rumbled. The Westlakes were inveterate gigglers and my uncle Aubrey was never able to sustain a silence when being stroked, or able to utter 'Meow' without immediately being identified by his infectious laughter, during which the helpless tears used to stream down his face. Aunt Marjorie was just the same, as was Martin. We laughed until our sides ached. ❦

Chapter 38
House Maintenance

The disadvantage of having a wooden house was, and is, the rot factor.

With the terrific work load that Mother had with outsiders coming into the family, she didn't have much time for maintenance, bar a lick of hot tar.

She determined one day to tar around the base of the stable as the planking was getting a bit the worse for wear. So, drawing off a bucket full of viscous tar from a 40-gallon barrel she had bought, she placed it on her brand new kitchen stove, a Valor oil-fired, double burner, with the object of heating it up good and hot to make it thin enough to brush onto, and be absorbed by, the boards.

Diverted by another demand from some quarter, by the time she remembered the tar, it had boiled up and all over her stove. It must have been heartbreaking. I was posted to keep Danae who was only a toddler at the time, from wading into the hot molten mass and scalding herself, while Mother, in what must have been despair, scraped up the solidifying tar off the stove and floor surfaces. It took hours, and the stove never regained its look of pristine splendour. ❧

Constant maintenance over the years to prevent rot has involved the regular application of hot tar.

Chapter 39
Landreth Leper

The sheer hard graft of Mother's life precluded time or energy for any sort of inward life, so letter writing was a great outlet for her spiritual needs.

Mother made the acquaintance, through Olive Schaffer, of an interesting young serviceman called Landreth Leaper, a Captain in the Royal Electrical and Mechanical Engineers (REME). From his correspondence, kept by Mother, he appears to have been a good linguist and an accomplished classical scholar; his obscure letters are littered with references and Latin asides. They are full of a weird mixture of romanticism and Jewish angst. Born in 1919, he was about twenty-two, and Mother, forty-six. He paid us several visits and grew very fond of my mother to the point of falling in love with her. She in her turn was a 'passionate friend'. His need, in spite of the age difference, demanded more in the form of a physical intimacy which she, ever so gently, denied him, saying he should save the ultimate physical expression of love for his future wife when he met her. Their friendship survived this rebuff to both their credits. Their joint classical education united their spirits and they wove a complex intimacy that was almost a recap of Mother's relationship with Mallik, guru of her Oxford days, except that Landreth was flesh and blood as well as an academic scholar.

When Landreth visited our home in his uniform, I used to find myself mildly resentful for some inexplicable reason. He was very aware of the fact, and was most circumspect and although friendly, gave me space to make my assessment of this male stranger who had suddenly arrived. Maybe I sensed that in his presence my Mother lit up and became preoccupied with him, and I felt excluded. Not that she was conscious of the fact and would have been mortified had she been made aware.

Landreth was very attracted to the youthful innocence of small children and rather like the Reverend Dodson, author of *Alice In Wonderland*, he was greatly enamoured with my small sister whom he idealised and to whom he dedicated poems. In effect, she became his muse, much to her puzzlement, and later, when she was a teenager at Sidcot, he would write to her much as he used to write to Mother. They were introspective intellectual musings, which she hardly understood, as well as obscure poetry. In a way, Landreth was trying to preserve Danae in amber, projecting onto her his idealised image of innocent youth, and a life unsullied by the process of growing up. It was slightly creepy and made Danae very uncomfortable, as intuitively she knew that she was being given an identity that in no way was comparable with how she saw herself.

Landreth was posted all over England and to Stirling in Scotland, and as the war ended and the tension of its presence abated, so the correspondence between Mother and Landreth gradually petered out. He became a teacher, married a lovely lass and had two children. However, the marriage was not altogether a success for him on an intellectual level. Running true to the patterns he had shown in his dealings with our family, Landreth sort solace in the company of one of his young students. He wrote to my mother in 1962 and paid her a visit. My guess is he came to ask my mother her opinion of his proposed liaison and possible marriage to his student friend. I don't know for certain what transpired, but I don't think she gave him the advice he was looking for. As well as teaching, Landreth was by then writing pot-boiler romances for women's magazines, under an assumed pen name. He sent mother various writing styles, à la Barbara Cartland to straight eroticism and porn, which Mother gently rebuked him for as being 'inartistic'. The last we heard of him was in a sad letter to say he was overweight and suffering from heart trouble and diabetes. Old age was horrible, the poor man said. ❧

Chapter 40
Last Summer at Home before Boarding School

In the summer of 1942, Mother, who had such fond memories of Sidcot, resolved to send me there too, as offering the best chance of a good education.

Apart from the unsatisfactory village school, whose pupils left at fifteen, the only decent education at the time was offered by Bishop Wordsworth's grammar school in Salisbury, and I certainly was not grammar school material!

So Mother and I cycled to Sidcot, taking two days, and breaking the journey at Dewes House at Mere to stay with Aunt Alice Rutter, my mother's godmother. I enjoyed the cycle ride; we did about forty miles a day and stayed at a hotel outside Winscombe, named after the school. It must be a mark of how little enthusiasm I had for going to Sidcot, that apart from my dismayed wonder at the impersonal size of the place and its institutional feel, I remember nothing of the visit. I sat the entrance examination, I well remember, at Charles and Hilda Leek's house, Hilda acting as a kind invigilator. The questions were fairly rudimentary and I made a pathetic attempt at drawing a horse's bridle and came away feeling a complete idiot. However, I was accepted as being of average intelligence, and got a place in the lower third form to start in the autumn term of 1943.

In the summer holidays of 1943, Mother let Paul, Danae and I camp for three weeks on our own in Sandy Balls, giving us our ration books and money to buy our own groceries. Paul had an old army tent and Danae and I had Woodcraft tents, gifts from Aunt Marjorie, that were open at the front, with no mosquito netting. To buy tinned food a points system of rationing was in force, the more exotic the food the more points per tin. The cheapest protein, money and points wise, was pilchards in tomato sauce which, fools that we were, we spent all our points on. So for three weeks we had nothing but pilchards...and didn't we live to regret it! I can hardly look at a pilchard fifty years later.

Apart from swimming in the river there wasn't much washing of one's person, and Danae to whom, unfairly, all the washing up of camp utensils had fallen because we boys were too lazy, decamped off home in justifiable protest at our chauvinistic refusal to wield a dish mop. Paul and I stuck it out for the full three weeks, getting heartily bitten by mosquitoes and the large wood ants which invaded our tents attracted by the many food scraps. We spent our days rushing round the water meadows by the river, flicking at Cabbage White butterflies with our towels. I hope, in retrospect, that they were Cabbage Whites and not Brimstones as, little savages that we were, we killed very many of them. With all the insect bites and little washing, the itchy sores round our mouths and faces turned to impetigo and I contracted Pink Eye (conjunctivitis). Nowadays, a few antibiotic creams and drops would clear these conditions in no time, but the ointments and lotions then available took weeks to take effect and I would wake each morning with eyes totally bunged up. As a postscript to this holiday, when Paul and I decamped and took down his tent we discovered a very squashed adder under the ground sheet that we must have killed inadvertently when sleeping on top of it! A lucky escape. 🐛

Chapter 41
Sidcot

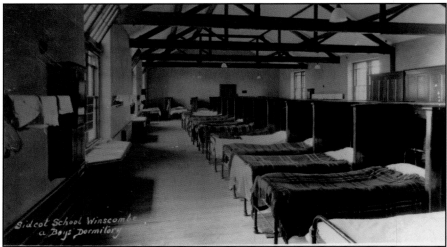

The Boys' dormitory at Sidcot Quaker School in the Mendip Hills, near Winscombe, Somerset. On the reverse of this card is a message from Chris dated May1945, addressed to his mother which reads: **Dear Mum I have got here safely but dont feal to good. Please will you send me my Ration book, and others. Please send a nice long letter and a bit of something. I wish I could get out of this of feeling bad Much love Pandy**

The time approached for me to bid farewell to home and enter the unknown and alien territory of a boarding school, and I was not looking forward to it.

I stalled by picking my impetigo scabs and making my eyes water each morning to enhance the illusion that they were still bunged up with conjunctivitis. I managed to pull the wool over Mother's eyes for three weeks, but finally the day came when she accompanied me on the train to Somerset, with my trunk of new school clothes, each article complete with my school number and name, written out neatly by my mother in indelible ink.

I entered Sidcot Quaker co-educational school at the end of September 1943. I was ten and three-quarters and lonely and frightened by the prospect of being parted from my mother and my roots. Fees at Sidcot for a well-off boarder were £120 per term. The Quakers had bursary funds which they awarded to less wealthy Quaker families to enable their children to attend such schools, and my mother had applied for financial help; my fees had accordingly been reduced to a sum, unimaginable now, of £25 a term.

Owing to my malingering, I began life at Sidcot nearly a month late, which was a disaster for me. Unwittingly I had forfeited my first chances of integration with my peers. By the time I arrived in their midst, they had palled up and shaken down into their various groups and pecking orders. I came from such a different background I think I would have had a job to integrate anyway. Entering the oak-panelled splendour of Newcombe House, with its highly polished parquet flooring and atmosphere of institutional conformity, was much more intimidating to me than the other boys. Their more conventional upbringing, I am sure, made it easier for them to accept the social status quo.

Newcombe House was run by a Mr Thomas Tregear, a strict but kind man who was also the school's geography master. He was helped by his plump, homely wife Norah. There was also a young and friendly housekeeper. I had always addressed everybody by their Christian names up to this point in my life and it was a shock to be disabused and told that from now on I was to address members of staff as Sir, or Miss. For the first time in my life I had to wear a uniform as grey as my enthusiasm for it. House shoes had to be worn inside and we were severely reprimanded if caught sliding on the superb parquet floor. In the lower third we led an almost separate life from the rest of the school, sleeping and eating at Newcombe, and being taught mostly by an elderly lady called Miss Rolands in part of the school known as The Wing. Miss Rolands was form mistress for the lower third girls who lived in The Wing.

My sense of desolation at this period in my life was complete. After each day spent hiding behind a mask of normality, it was with relief that I could go to bed and cry myself silently to sleep. My pillowcase, on going to the wash, was stiff with the salt from my tears, and I used to fold it carefully before placing it in the linen basket so that no one would notice and taunt me for being a cry baby.

A much more embarrassing factor was my bladder capacity. No way was I able to go through the twelve-hour night without a trip to the lavatory. This meant having to run the gauntlet of one of the nastier members of my form in the bed next to mine, a boy who was a very light sleeper. No matter how quiet I tried to be, he always woke up and thumped me. I became so frightened of his aggression I used to try and hang on all night, my bladder bursting, and when the agony became too much, to relieve myself in controlled small amounts; it was just enough to bring some relief, so I could last till morning. It was pure hell, lying in a damp bed, as night after night I had to go through the same agony. Of course, every two weeks came the time to change our sheets. I managed to hide my dreadful secret for a month, but one day, inevitably it was discovered and I was baited unmercifully. "Charman's peed his bed!" went up the derisory cry of the mob.

Alerted by all the noise in the dormitory, Mr Tregear poked his head in through the door, and quickly assessing that I was the recipient of all the hurtful mirth, he called for silence in which you could hear a pin drop. Quietly he called me outside and asked me what was going on. It had already been drummed into my consciousness that one of the unspoken rules was that one never sneaked or informed on each other's misdemeanours. So I was forced to admit to my shame that: "Well Sir, please Sir, they are laughing because I wet my bed." Mr Tregear, to his everlasting credit, could see my agony and was quiet, kind, and non-judgemental. Under his authoritative discipline the baiting ceased, and with a bit of confidence restored, nights, after this, lost their dread.

We boys ate in Newcombe Hall with Mr and Mrs Tregear and the housekeeper, each at the head of three tables. Breakfast would consist of porridge followed by a tiny rasher of bacon or a sausage on a small bit of fried bread, and to finish off we had a round of bread and a small level teaspoonful of golden syrup, our allowance each breakfast. The staff had toast and marmalade. Dinner was brought on trolleys up the drive from the main school kitchens in large metal tureens, and as a result was never very warm. It seemed quite reasonable fare to me, ranging from meat and two veg, mince pie with pastry (that we referred to as 'dead baby'), to Shepherd's pie, boiled cod or rabbit stew. There were usually just about enough spuds, but the cabbage always seemed to be doctored with soda and overcooked. I enjoyed it never the less, and was sorry there was not more. Memorable second course puddings ranged from jam tart to boiled suet puddings with custard that we called 'Stodge'. These came in various types. There was apple, most people's favourite, followed by jam, chocolate, and Spotted Dick filled with raisins. Tapiocas and Creamola puddings were our least favourite. Tea time was ad-lib bread, making a spoonful of jam go as far as you were able, with either a glass of milk or a cup of tea. In the evenings we had three quarters of an hour's homework, or prep.

Arriving at the Quaker Sidcot School's main building was daunting enough (above). Chris's residence in Newcombe House, with its 'oak panelled splendour' was 'much more intimidating to me than the other boys...'

Knowing that if I drank a full glass of milk, or worse still a full cup of tea, I would be unable to last out prep without having to ask to 'be excused', I tried to get away with drinking nothing beforehand. This, to my dismay, was not allowed and I had to consume the regulation intake. Having expelled as much of my fluid intake as I could before prep by haunting the loos till the last minute, I began my endurance test, waiting until I could bear it no longer. The staff on duty always queried the regular request to relieve myself, hinting that if it continued they would report me to the school doctor. In the end I waited too long of course, and dashed from the form room, leaving shame in the form of a puddle behind me. A puzzled, slightly contrite master hurried after me to ask if 'this sort of thing was a common occurrence'. "No Sir, not often," I blurted out in misery. Fear and rigid rules conspired to make certain aspects of life hell!

Chapter 42
Early Days at Sidcot

Our form master was a handsome young student teacher called Hugh Maw who took us for natural history, physical training (PT) and games. We boys hero-worshipped him for his charismatic and athletic prowess.

Several times a week he would supervise us getting to bed and woe betide anyone who stepped out of line as they got one of his 'trade marks', a resounding slap on the thigh as retribution. The definition of the imprints of the administrator's hand were eagerly compared.

Our pocket money was £1 per term and Mr Tregear doled out our money, either 3d or 6d a week, each Saturday morning. Saturday was a good day as we had the freedom to go as far as the games field in the afternoon and watch the First XV rugger match against a visiting school. Our first port of call, however, was to Seymour's tuck shop on the corner of the games field. Here we purchased from old Mrs Seymour (who had also sold sweets to my mother's generation), a threepenny Mars Bar, a quarter of a pound of Foxes Glacier Mints or some equivalent confectionary, to suck with relish while we watched the match and cheered on our school team.

Saturday evening was roller skating evening in the boys' shed and a privileged few had skates in our form. How the 'have nots' envied those whose parents were rich enough to buy their children a pair. One day after breakfast at Newcombe, Mr Tregear said to Garth Reynolds and myself: "I have something that might interest you two boys. I have two pairs of roller skates. One has cushioning and toe clips and the other pair only has fixed wheels and straps. I want 5/- for the best pair and 2/6d for the other. To make things fair I am going to toss a coin. You elect who is going to call and if the caller gets it right he has first choice of the skates. If he gets it wrong, the other boy has priority, OK?" I can remember Garth and I willing the coin in our favour, and my jubilant exultation at winning the superior pair of skates.

I lived for skating in the boys' shed at every opportunity, but Saturday evenings were best of all when we had two hours uninterrupted play before Mr Tregear or Hugh Maw rounded us up and shepherded us back to Newcombe House and bed. We became very proficient at skating a circuit from right to left as this was the easiest direction for right handers. We learnt to corner at speed by crossing the right leg over the left and, in a second, could spin into a halt, facing the way that we had been travelling. I never became fluent at skating anti-clockwise or backwards, unlike a certain Basil Conns, a thin whiplash of an athletic skater who, when we played skate hockey with a chuck, was capable of dribbling the chuck backwards single-handedly, defending it by using his whole body as a shield. Then with a final quick spin he would flash the chuck into the goal before you had time to blink. He was the master skater, no doubt about it!

Sundays were a bit of a bore because of Quaker meeting. In the afternoons we always went for a walk in the local hills, girls and boys together led by two members of staff, remembered by generations of Sidcotians as Pig Drives. Hugh Maw was the most popular leader as he told us stories, but Pig Drives, it must be said, were not our favourite way of taking a walk. The boys kept in a clique, as did the girls, with the occasional bit of bravado and horse play from the boys, usually to the girls' justifiable outrage and whining complaint. I found a friend in a lad called John Ransome and so became more integrated, but like Lionel from Miss Pask's days, he could not be seen to identify too closely with me for fear of losing his own place in the form group. By ourselves he was generous, and I was eternally grateful to him for putting himself out on a limb to do things with me. I was on the way to being 'accepted'.

Mother had visited me at half term and been most impressed at staff reports of my good behaviour and how well I was integrating into school life. How little adults see, or choose to see, deluding themselves that their schooldays were the happiest days of their lives and must be, therefore, for their own youngsters.

Mother stayed in bed and breakfast accommodation below Wavering Down, and I was granted leave to go out to meals with her - breakfast, dinner and supper. Oh, how I lapped up my mother's ready love. All the hell of the previous weeks dissolved in her secure maternal arms. She knew next to nothing of my traumas. I hid them all as children do, and only told her in later years, when it was too late for either of us to properly clean the slate. I shall never forget the final Sunday evening, before going back to the school, when I clung to her in tears and gut-wrenching despair at a further separation. Through ignorance we missed evening meeting and I was late for bed, arriving at Newcombe to be confronted by an irate, worried Mr Tregear, who asked me why I hadn't been to the meeting; did I not realise it was obligatory? I guess he could see I was pretty fraught and genuinely ignorant of school rules, and so he let me off with a firm reprimand. I felt so bad at Mother's departure, I almost wished she had not come to visit me at all.

Time stood still as I waited for term to end, and I ticked off the dwindling days to the Christmas holiday with mounting excitement. In the last two days, lessons wound down and we packed our trunks with the help of the young housekeeper. Roped and labelled, they were loaded on to old Mr Hembrey's cart and pulled by Bess to Winscombe railway station ahead of our departure, travelling PLA (Passenger Luggage in Advance) to their destination.

Finally the great day arrived, a six o'clock start when all the dormitories erupted in a great pillow fight. Mr Tregear let it go as being part of a traditional schoolboy exhibition of celebratory high spirits! After breakfast, all coated, gloved and scarved, we went to the main school to line up by the Headmaster's study and file past George Hutchinson, the Headmaster, and the Headmistress of the time (whose name escapes me), shaking hands with them and then out into the cold dawn to walk down to the railway station at the far end of Winscombe village. Then onto the little train that ran on the Cheddar Valley line through the Mendip hills on the first step of our return home for Christmas. Oh, blessed departure!

The Christmas holidays went all too fast. Father Christmas still managed to fill our stockings full to the brim with the most exciting things, in spite of the war. But then, he was magic, and my belief in his reality never wavered, even in the face of the derisory scorn that my peers had poured on my conviction. The home fire burned brightly and the ceiling of the living room was almost hidden by our ancient, but much loved, and now slightly tatty, coloured paper decorations, along with the still beautiful pre-war Japanese lanterns, lit inside by candles. Even Olive Schaffer seemed mellowed by the festive occasion, her tiny, silver-haired mother paying us a visit, frail as a porcelain tea cup, and her skin almost translucent. Olive's mother made wonderful Christmas puddings that always contained, instead of the usual silver trinkets, the traditional silver threepenny pieces wrapped in greaseproof paper.

I just squeezed in my 11th birthday on 12 January 1944, then back I went to Sidcot for the spring term. I was tearful and hated the leave-taking, but at least I now had some idea of what boarding school was like, and had begun to cope with its life style. The year passed and I joined the Scouts. George Hutchinson, the Head, was a keen Scout and ran the Sidcot troop. My first introduction to scouting was a simple knot-tying competition with penalties for those who could not tie theirs correctly. Asked to make a simple reef knot, I tied a granny. As a penalty I had to dive into the icy swimming pool, (it was February and unheated), and act as though I was drowning so that one of the patrol leaders could rescue me as part of his life-saving proficiency badge test. I can remember to this day diving into that freezing water with all the troop looking on. I surfaced with a holler and a yell, and flapped about gasping with the intense cold, feeling I really would drown if my rescuer did not come quickly. Nicholas Wadsworth was my rescuer and very competent he was, floating me on my back and kicking strongly for the pool side, and I was soon hauled out and towelled down. I cannot have been in the water for more than a minute, but it felt like an eternity. George Hutchinson was fulsome in his praise for my courage, I remember, and perhaps for the first time I felt a glow of confidence and pride.

I learnt the Scout promise, and one Friday afternoon in front of the Scout hut, behind the laundry and woodwork shop, wearing my too long khaki shorts, Baden-Powell hat, and neckerchief complete with woggle, I repeated the Scout promise in front of the troop, while saluting the Union Jack. George Hutchinson gave the order: "Scout Christopher Charman, right about turn, quick march..." and back I strode to join the 'Sea Gull' patrol. I think the other two patrols were called 'Pewits' and 'Owls'. We learnt to tie various useful knots, starting with the common reef knot, bowfin. sheep shank, sheetbend and so on. We learnt how to shorten a rope without cutting it, how to splice a rope and to whip the ends. All good stuff! I used to covet the colourful proficiency badges acquired along with a particular skill, and earned a few of them myself for the sleeve of my shirt. For some reason the Seagulls didn't show as much initiative as the Owls and Pewits, and always came bottom in number of proficiency badges or competitive games. Our patrol leader was an easy, sleepy, casual type called Bennett and maybe his non-competitiveness rubbed off on his patrol.

We learnt how to make the obligatory spiral 'damper', an indigestible affair made from self-raising flour and water mixed to a dough, a long sausage of it being wrapped around a green stick and baked over a fire. Most of the Scouts did not seem to realise that trying to cook the bread in the flames of the fire just burnt it and covered it in soot. My practical experience of roasting spuds in an open fire with embers stood me in good stead, and I took great pride in baking my 'damper' to a lovely golden brown, while others of a less patient turn of mind ate theirs black and hard on the outside, with gooey dough inside. If we were lucky, we were given some syrup to put on our indigestible creations.

One memorable Saturday, George, as we daringly called him amongst ourselves, took us out at night for a 'wide game', in an area of the Mendips called locally Humpty Dumpty land. This was a district that had been worked by the Romans as open-cast mining for lead, not far from the village of Shipham. It was a game that involved a lot of stalking and crawling about on one's belly to reach a certain vantage point without getting caught. I loved it for its adrenalin-charged excitement and for the fact that we were going to go to bed at nine rather than seven-thirty. Ransome and I were eventually caught before we could make our objective, but not before experiencing the frisson of trying to move silently and unobserved over the humpy landscape, knowing other eyes were on the look out for you. When we finally got back to the school, George made cocoa in the physics lab on a bunsen burner, and while we drank it and sat around on the lab benches, he took out his exquisitely made concertina, with filigree work at each end and ivory buttons, and we had a sing-song of all the tried and cherished camp fire songs of the time, like *Ten Green Bottles* or the interminable *Green Grow the Rushes O*. There was a certain simplicity, an innocence about that evening that has fixed it in my memory for ever.

After a year I grew disillusioned with Scouts. The highlight of each scouting year was to go camping with a trek cart for a weekend to the other side of Crooks Peak, by a river. Being a Sea Gull I never showed enough initiative to master the art of lashing, and gain my Second Class qualifications. Lashing was a prerequisite to going on a camp, in order to make plate drying racks and build bridges across rivers. My extensive experience of camping before I went to Sidcot of course counted for nothing, and I was too lazy to learn the additional skills deemed necessary.

So I left the patrol and took up Natural History. That gave me the freedom to explore the ponds of the 'combe' (or valley), and collect frogspawn, tadpoles, stickleback and weeds to make an aquarium of pond life. Hugh Maw took us for our first chemistry lessons, and we learnt the wonders of growing copper sulphate crystals in a concentrated solution of the oxide by dangling a tiny particle in it from a piece of thin cotton. He taught us to write up our experiment in an ordered way, namely Aim, Method, Result. Looking at my work, Hugh Maw would look up with assumed exasperation, tempered with a bit of a weary smile. "You dissolve, not melt some copper sulphate," he would bark. "Charman, what do you do with copper sulphate?" and both I and the rest of the class would have to repeat after him the correct method and learn the difference between dissolve and melt. I have never forgotten it, I must admit.

Sports Day came at the end of spring term, when the school playing field was marked out with a 440 yard, or quarter-mile, oval running track. Hugh Maw and the Upper Fifth and Sixth boys, whom all we 'brats' hero worshipped, used to compete with each other in sprints, just for the hell of it. Those involved had vastly differing physiques. First, Martin Westlake, my cousin (or Tubby Westlake as he was called), was powerful and thick set, his buddy Peter Fox, a small, fleet, wiry fellow, Garth Kew was of classic middle distance running physique and Hugh Maw himself, a powerhouse sprinter with upper body strength to match his legs. We 'brats' used to watch fascinated as the four young men battled it out. Hugh Maw used to win more often than not by a whisker, but then he had the advantage of spiked shoes, whilst Martin ran in bare feet. If he had the loan of some spikes, he often used to pip Hugh Maw. There wasn't really very much in it and the average time for the 100 yards was something in the region of 10.8 seconds. A lean tall boy called Paul Nash was the long distance runner of that time, a leggy six foot lath of a young man with very light upper body development, but with great stride and stamina. George Hutchinson was a great advocate of exercise, and at break time the whole of the boys' side would gather on the boys' playground to be marshalled by Hugh Maw into a squad and marched up and down, wheeling and turning. This was followed by stride jumping and other physical jerks. During one of the first spring terms we had a very hard winter with big snow falls, and there was a lot of sledging in the 'combe'. Hugh Maw, I remember, got out an old pair of Hickory skis, waxed them up and slalomed down the steep 'combe' hill slopes.

Hugh was rather attracted to a beautiful girl from Martin's form, a honey blonde called Daphne Southall. When she and her form mates came out of gym class late, in their blouses and gym knickers, and walked back to the girls' side across the boys' playground, Hugh Maw used to bark at us: "Eyes right!" As one, the matching phalanx of school boys' faces would be turned toward Daphne, who not surprisingly would go red to the roots of her hair, poor girl. After PT in the playground, at the command of "Dismissed", there would be one mad dash for the dining room to queue for dry bread and watery cocoa, first come, first served. The prefects doled out the cocoa and had the privilege of not having to queue. It was amazing how much bread we got through, dunked into our meagre cups of cocoa. After break, it was back to two more classes before dinner, followed by half an hour's compulsory siesta, taken lying on one's stomach on one's bed, reading a book. After I had been at Sidcot a year, Hugh Maw left the school to serve in the Friends Ambulance Unit for the remainder of the war. He and Daphne Southall married, very happily, later and Hugh became Headmaster of Sibford Quaker school, where our refugee Hilda Sass had her schooling years before.

Tuesday and Thursday afternoons were devoted to games. In our case it was soccer in the top field by the observatory, just off the school island. The top field was a rough sloping piece of ground on which we marked out our goal posts with our white sweaters thrown on the ground. Mr Tregear took us for these sessions, and looking down the hill I used to watch the older boys playing rugby and envy them, longing to play scrum half in the school team like my cousin Martin, who wore his colours on his blue rugger shirt. Soccer was so boring! I think most of us felt the same, as we hacked away at the stupid football in the tufted grass of that unkempt field, amongst old sheep turds that stained our games clothes when we fell on them. In spite of the thousands of washings my games shorts lasted me the entirety of my playing life, into my late twenties. When first they were supplied from the school, Mother turned them up six inches and they still came to my knees. By the time I reached the Sixth form they were just right. The match shorts that we used to wear for best often ripped in a game, and then we would all form a protective circle round the player who had lost his pants, while he divested himself of their tattered remains to derisory cheers, and put on a new pair.

I loved the swimming pool, as being the only boy able to swim I had a flying start on the rest of my form, as did Sally Stanton, the only girl. We could dive too, and at the end of my first school year, it was mooted that I enter for the Southall diving competition. So, greatly daring, I entered, and found myself competing against Sixth form girls. I think I got good points for my dives but part of the competition involved a plunge. Being skinny and small, my feet sank fairly quickly and there was no way that I was going to hold my breath for any length of time, so I only managed a few yards. The well built, mature Sixth form girls, on the other hand, had much more buoyancy and bigger lung capacity and seemed to float for ages, adding valuable last inches to the distance of their plunge; they won that part of the competition hands down. A set of ten tin plates were thrown into the deep end at random, and we had to 'duck dive' for as many of these as we could pick up, before lack of air forced us to the surface. I stayed down too long and got the first head ache in my life, a real migraine which lasted for days. This event went in favour of the older boys. To my gratification, my dives were good enough to win me third place, the girls taking the first two places. Although I went in for the Southall each year after that, I never made third again. Competitive diving is a cold business; getting wet and then waiting about for one's next dive left us shivering and goose-pimpled by the end of an evening's competition.

Having the surname Charman inevitably meant that I was called 'Charwoman', and when my other Christian (or should I say, pagan) name was wheedled out of me as being Pan, the general hilarity knew no bounds. "What is he doing, the Great God Pan, down in the reeds by the river?" and other such quips were the flavour of the day for a while. I was fast learning to survive, part of which strategy involved not rising to the attempts to bait me. So I passed my first year, for better or worse. ✤

Aero modelling days at Sidcot. Christopher is on the right, with his friend, John Ransome. John's friendship helped Chris become 'accepted' at the boarding school.

Chapter 43
Sidcot: Second Year

In my second year at Sidcot, our form made the transition to the main school for all our activities. We slept in a large dormitory, being woken at seven each morning by the school bell and the Prefect in charge, who yanked the sheets and blankets off the more tardy risers.

We clattered down the stairs to visit the subterranean loos (known as the Bog), then back into the boys' washrooms to get away with as little washing as possible under the cold taps. Then, back up the stairs to run the gauntlet of a Prefect, who craftily felt the napes of our neck and ears to check if they had seen water that morning. We quickly put on our clothes and rushed down to the boys' shed for 'collect', where we assembled in our various forms, prior to wending our way in an orderly fashion to the dining hall for breakfast.

At the end of the dining hall, nearest the girls' side, was 'Top Table', where either the Headmaster or Mistress, or lesser members of staff sat on duty and ate their meal. They rang a small bell when all were assembled for a moment's silent grace for the meal, then we all tucked into our simple fare. Tea or milk was available, the tea served from large two gallon urns. The porridge was made overnight from oat meal as opposed to oat flakes. On occasions it had lumps in it and sometimes the odd weevil or, not so nice, a cockroach! The kitchens were the happy hunting grounds of the biology teacher for the latter, later to be used for dissection in the lab at the end of the boys' playground.

At Newcombe, the ration of golden syrup, while meagre, had at least been thick. In the main school it was watered down to the point when it was a major feat to keep any of it on one's slice of bread. Boiled eggs were usually very hardboiled. Fried eggs, bacon or kippers, accompanied the porridge on different days. On the signal of a second bell, a moment's grace marked the end of the meal and we all trooped out to make our beds, take up our brooms and dusters and clean whatever portion of the school we had been allocated. Being wartime, all pupils were expected to pull their weight with keeping the school clean. To this end, there was a duty rota for chores like sweeping the gym and dusting the wall bars. Each job was inspected by a Prefect to see that it was up to standard before we trooped over to the school hall for the obligatory assembly. We sang a hymn accompanied by the music master on the piano, then either the Head gave a short reading of an 'uplifting nature', or one of the music teachers played an instrumental piece or sang. There was a few moments silence and then the Head would make announcements concerning school affairs and we would walk out in an orderly fashion to our lessons in different parts of the school.

We had our own form room and our form master in the Upper Third was Barry Davies, ex-Sidcotian, art master and woodwork teacher. I never got the measure of Barry, as we called him amongst ourselves. He was as encouraging in his teaching as he was autocratic in his discipline, and one felt psychologically in a 'catch twenty-two' situation; a kind of intimidating limbo. I liked him but I was somewhat frightened by his barking manner. Accounting, in our account books, for every last farthing spent of our meagre pocket money drove me spare, but we had to balance the books to his exacting standard as though we were handling thousands of pounds instead of pence, before we could withdraw our meagre threepence or sixpence each Saturday.

On the positive side, Barry Davies used to acquire eight or so large framed prints each term, usually of Impressionist paintings. These would be hung all round the school for the first week or two of each new term, and Barry would treat each class to a lecture on

the history of each painting and analyse the influences that had gone into its creation.
I enjoyed these sessions and gained a lasting fascination for the Impressionist period.
Later, the paintings would be removed and hung for the duration of the term around the
dining room for our delectation.

George Hutchinson was a great stickler for the 'short back and sides' hair cut which
we had every three weeks. It was a bit like sheep shearing. The only good thing about
it, perhaps, was being pulled out of a lesson to queue up in the boys' washroom to wait
in the 'shearing' line until one's time came for the obligatory 'sherp up'. One of the four
hairdressers, younger than the rest, had a brill-creamed mop of hair with a large quiff
plastered back over his head in greasy splendour. Unlike the others, he could sometimes
be prevailed upon to exercise a compromise in how much he took off. I hated having my
hair constantly hacked off just as it was beginning to recover from the last onslaught and
would do my best to engineer getting my hair cut by this man. There wasn't much finesse
employed in the cutting, which was mostly done with electric clippers, using a comb as
a gauge. This had the advantage of speed of operation, and ninety boys were got through
in the course of a morning. To be fair, George Hutchinson used to submit himself to the
same shearing gang along with us as a democratic gesture.

Friday afternoon was hobby afternoon, but as it was war time the Head decreed that
we should spend the first part of the afternoon doing 'voluntary' land work in the market
gardens below Shute Shelf that were growing their 'bit' for the war effort. So along we all
trooped to weed and hoe and do the seasonal jobs such as harvesting potatoes as they
were spun out of the ground. I don't know if the owners of the market gardens thought
much of the various squads of unenthusiastic juvenile helpers they received from the
school, but from our point of view it ruined any real chance to indulge in the hobby of
one's choice.

We had a student master who took us for English, Mr Richard Brayshaw, who was a
great Shakespeare enthusiast. I remember him bringing a model into class that he had
made of the Globe Theatre, with all the actors cleverly made by him, their costumes
fashioned in exquisite detail out of coloured wax. It was fascinating to look at and
educational in the best sense of the word. Mr Brayshaw formed an attachment with the
housekeeper which was somewhat frowned upon by the establishment, so the word went.
He left rather suddenly without explanation. We learnt he married her later and rose in
the teaching world to take on several Headships, the last of which was notably, Sidcot,
showing how daft are social mores in the face of love and true commitment.

At the turn of the century, the school had produced its own coal gas, and the tar, as a
by-product, had been utilised to make the extremely good asphalt surface of the boys and
girls' playground. We boys played many games on it in any spare moment that presented
itself. Some of the Fifth formers made trolleys out of an old pair of skates and held hair-
raising slalom races down the playgrounds' natural slope from the science lab to the boys'
shed. Old rugby balls would be hoofed around, some of the Sixth formers endeavouring
to hoist one over the art school behind the clock tower, to bounce on the science lab tiles.
This, although spectacular, was frowned upon, inducing a reprimand if witnessed by the
MOD (Master On Duty), but it was always happening.

Another, and lethal, game was 'Hot Rice', a kind of sadistic French cricket. Why it
should have been called 'Hot Rice' I have no idea. It involved throwing a tennis ball at
the body of another boy who wielded an old cricket bat to defend his person for as long
as he was able. He could move about but the ball could be thrown from any distance,
which was often point blank and hard, delivered with malicious glee! As soon as a hit

was scored, the recipient dropped his bat and the scorer became the target. It was fast and furious and could be very painful, partly its attraction. Several walls adjoining the playground had been rendered and a black line drawn across them at net height, enabling one, if one possessed a racquet, to play a lone game of tennis, slamming the ball against the wall to hit it on the rebound. We also played a variation of base ball called 'soft ball', with a baseball bat and large leather-bound ball. It was possible with a good 'strike' to drive the ball a good eighty yards onto the swimming pool roof, and make an easy home run then with no trouble.

There was a strong aero-modelling club in the school that had its headquarters in the old natural history room on the way to the gym. Some of the aero modellers used to fly their elastic-powered, tissue-clad aeroplanes, with inches to spare, over the scullery walls into the girls' playground. I watched fascinated and resolved to take up aero-modelling as a hobby, as natural history was fast losing its attraction.

Considering the age ranges and different forms participating in this hobby, we were a very harmonious democratic lot, united by the smell of dope and the fascination of flight. No member of staff ever interfered with us and we enjoyed almost complete autonomy. One's skills were acquired by watching the best of the senior modellers at work. John Ransome started to model at the same time as myself, and we both made a simple glider called a Vander which we towed up on a line on the games field. The models always seemed to have an attraction for trees and both of us were forever, it seemed, climbing up into the branches and poking them out, all ripped and broken. Effecting repairs seemed to take up a large part of an aero-modellers life.

In winter months, the playground became our sliding ground. The senior boys would go out last thing before going to bed on a frosty night with buckets of water with which they would carefully lay down a long sheet of ice for sliding on the next day. At break time all ages would queue for a chance to slide full tilt down the slope to the boys' shed. It was dangerous stuff, and after two boys had gone into the brick wall and sustained concussion, it was made a rule that a senior must be placed at the bottom of the slide as 'catcher' to prevent further accidents.

Between the two walls dividing the girls' side from the boys was an alleyway backing onto the school kitchens and scullery, through which all food, garbage and laundry passed. At the upper end of the alleyway was a wonderful antiquated coal gas engine. It sported a huge flywheel with a belt drive linked to an overhead shaft that ran the length of the old school laundry, and from which subsidiary belts were linked to drive all the clothes washing equipment. The engine and the laundry would be an industrial archaeologist's dream find today! On wash days one could hear the immortal engine firing on its one cylinder every five or so revolutions of the giant flywheel: *PHUFF-phuff-phuff-phuff-phuff-PHUFF-phuff-phuff-phuff-phuff…*

The school was frozen in time when I was there. Nothing much had changed since Mother's time in the early days of the century. Jimmy Ware, the school handyman, who cynically mended and refurbished desks and chairs and other abused school property that we inconsiderate, unthinking youngsters had vandalised, had worked the school gas retorts as a young man. In his mid-seventies, old Mr Hembery (Ted), with his pipe and walrus moustache, was still quietly and leisurely carting coal and coke for the school boilers, dung for the school gardens, laundry baskets to and from the laundry, our trunks to and from the station; his cart was pulled by Bess, the latest in the long line of school horses, and almost as old as her master. Then there was the old fellow in charge of the boilers, nicknamed 'Squinty Oxide' on account of one glass eye; another devoted servant of the school. Teaching staff stayed on too in those days, long beyond their 'sell by' date. Dick Harman was one, our dry old scripture master who was to become our form master in the Lower Fifth. Another, John Russell, history master in the 'thirties, Quartermaster in the army during the war, came back and was teaching way into his sixties, retaining intimate associations, although bent like a sickle with arthritis, until his death. Mr Hinton, physics master, was another stalwart, who worked the whole of his teaching life at Sidcot. He retained a link with the school, a kind man with a memory for old scholars that would rival an elephant. ✥

Chris and Danae, with mother Margaret and, pictured above, with Trudy.

The staff at Sidcot School in 1950
Back row from left: John Haddon, Geography; Arthur Bains, music; Anne Hobbs, Games; Richard Hinton, Physics; John Newick, Art; Sister Gregory; ?. Second row, ? Needlework Mistress; ? Mr Aubrey Hopes, Chemistry; Elvina Trinder, French; Michael Mates, Latin; Bernard Banner, Maths.; Vera Martin, violoin teacher, Miss Watts, Maths; staff, staff. Front row, Games master, Bernard Langdon; ? Roland Pask, the Bursar; Hilda Bodman (staff); Ivan Gray, English; Mary Hooper, English/ head mistress; David Murray Rust, head master and his wife Frances; Evelyn Phillips, French; John Russell, History; Rosemary Blomfield, Girls Music; Margaret Rastrick, Biology.

Teenage years - engaging in life at Sidcot included music, theatre, gardening and, of course, girls.

Chapter 44
School life - Masters and Students

Once a week we went to the school hall for a music class taken by a sensitive teacher called Edward Davis, inevitably known as 'Teddy' or 'The Bear'. There we learnt two songs in spite of ourselves: *Cargoes*, a setting of John F Masefield's poem, and *John Mouldy* by Walter De La Mere.

I can sing them to this day, they were drilled into us so thoroughly. Edward Davis was a good pianist and musical purist. His sensibilities must have been sorely tested by our philistine attitude to music. He was a hopeless disciplinarian, and didn't we know it; we gave the poor man a hell of a time! Sometimes in despair at our deliberate sabotage of the songs, and other rowdy, disruptive, diversionary tactics, he would add to the bedlam by slumping with his head on the keyboard of the piano, producing a violent discord, which only fuelled our laughter. I apologise, Edward Davis, for being one of that unruly pack of small barbarians that made classes such hell for you.

George Hutchinson, who knew his staff very well, would sometimes insinuate himself quietly into the back of the hall in the middle of our music classes. Woe betide us if we didn't notice in time for him to pick out some dominant miscreant and take him off to his study for a severe reprimand or a 'twanking', if the offender was deemed persistent. The Head had only to enter the room and instantly you could hear a pin drop, which I don't suppose did much for the self-confidence of Edward Davis, even if well intended.

In the 'forties, a squad of gardeners were employed, probably at subsistence rates, to tend the two and a half acres or so of school garden. In charge of operations was Mr John Lindsay, head gardener of many years standing, a small man, kindly, quiet and contemplative, a pipe-smoking master of his profession. There was no mechanical tilling of the soil, all the beds being dug over by hand with liberal applications of well-rotted sheep's manure. The fertility of that garden was remarkable; its small acreage supplied most of the needs of the school in vegetables and even the occasional luxuries like strawberries and green peas. Both, though lovely, were crazily extravagant in space and labour for two hundred people.

John Lindsay had a tranquil greenhouse at the top end of the garden in which he used to grow his exotic flowers. There was always a tap dripping at the far end of that warm humid retreat which, like the homely tick of a grandfather clock, lent a comforting sense of peace difficult to find anywhere else in the school grounds. I remember Mr Lindsay raising some rare, exotic cacti which only bloomed once every seven years. The year it bloomed we were told all about it in assembly, resulting in a pilgrimage to the greenhouse the following week. John Russell, the history master, even took a colour slide of the elusive bloom. Each autumn term when the school play was performed, John Lindsay produced, without fail, the most wonderful display of chrysanthemums to decorate the wings and apron of the hall stage; they were truly magnificent.

Along the outer edge of the garden, Mr Lindsay grew cordon apple and pear trees, carefully grafted, pruned and trained. Currants and gooseberries were turned into jam and tarts in the school kitchen. It was the senior girls' job to pick these, a task they found rather a bore, and in the case of the gooseberries mighty prickly! The whole garden was an economic triumph perhaps not appreciated by most people. I know one cannot turn the clock back, but it is sad to see that most of the garden and John Lindsay's little paradise of a greenhouse is now under an Olympic-sized swimming pool and sports complex. The cordon fruit trees have gone with the gardeners, and what land is left is now lawn and planted with labour-saving shrubs. The school meals, I understand, are now served cafeteria fashion. I cannot help but feel we are missing something.

Barry Davies, our form master, was keen I become form representative for the Upper Third and I, poor fool, was flattered and put my name forward. As I was the only one stupid enough to do so, I was voted on. George Hutchinson ran a supposedly democratic School Council which met every two weeks to discuss matters relating to the school; events, questions of discipline, or the running of the school generally. I felt a very small fish in a very large pool and only had the vaguest idea what most of the senior council members were talking about in their discussions with the Head. I was supposed to take notes on all that was said and occurred, and make a report to take back to my form, but in the event made a pretty good hash of it. Barry Davies was full of scorn at my ineptitude and barked his disappointment that I should let him down as he had put great trust in me. I felt very small and hopeless.

An almost impossible duty in my capacity as 'rep' was to be put in charge of preparation each night. I had the power to send 'disruptive elements' in my peer group to the Master On Duty (MOD) but, if I did so, I also had to bear the anger and dislike of my peers after 'prep' was over. It was an invidious position in which to be placed and I became very unpopular for a time, as well as having to do overtime on my own homework to make up for time lost to disruption. If everyone knew that Barry was MOD I had no trouble, as all were aware of his strict reputation. He backed me up unreservedly but I never had the imagination to be able to see my 'no win' dilemma in having to discipline my peers. I resigned from my duties at the end of a term, and shortly after, the lower echelons of the school ceased to be represented.

Children with flu-like symptoms, running a temperature, or with other more serious maladies, were sent to the school sanatorium to recuperate. The school employed a matron and several helpers to run the 'San' and the daily surgery, where either genuinely ill people went, or malingerers, hoping to get out of school work or a test that was coming up. Spring term was usually the time when school epidemics occurred. I spent time at the San on several occasions, trying to spin out my stay for as long as possible with others of like mind. I remember putting my thermometer in my cup of tea once, in order to boost my temperature to life-threatening proportions. Of course, the tea was far too hot and it blew up the thermometer in no uncertain fashion; there was mercury and glass everywhere! The matron of the time was none too pleased when I handed her the stub of my thermometer which was all that remained. "Your Father shall hear of your conduct," she snapped at me, to which I rather cheekily replied: "He has been dead for four years!"

In the San with tonsillitis we were the recipients of some of the first antibiotics, in the form of large lozenges, which we sucked to amazing effect. Bath nights in the San were always rather embarrassing as our nudity was often viewed by the young matron who even, on occasion, invigilated our ablutions to the extent of scrubbing our backs. We were just approaching puberty with the first fuzz of pubic hair and were alarmed that we might get an erection in her presence. This had been the case, anecdotal evidence suggested, with one of the more sexually mature youngsters, with the matron, on noticing it, expostulating: "Down, you naughty boy!" It was a situation that made the mind boggle and was probably total fiction, but such scandal was fascinating to us youngsters.

During the war years so many fit young men were in the armed services it was a job to find a games master after Hugh Maw left to work with the Friends' Relief Service. We had two in fairly quick succession. First was a Navy man called Mr Brisco, who was reported to have survived being torpedoed and had to swim for four hours before being picked up. If true, this made him a remarkably tough man. He had double-jointed elbows, I remember, which were noticeable when he was doing stride jumping. His sport, not surprisingly, was swimming, and he coached a new arrival in our form, Edward (Teddy) Moar from America, to great effect.

This young man, at only twelve, was a mature, if somewhat spotty adult, a head taller than us, and a black stubble of a beard by each afternoon. Just back from the States to where he had been evacuated, he came loaded with candy which he dispensed with casual largess and so became instantly popular! Teddy was a good crawl swimmer, having had superb facilities in the USA, but he was lazy. However, Mr Brisco saw his potential and managed to motivate him, coaching him to become a very powerful swimmer for his age. I remember Teddy plowing up and down the pool, pushing a board ahead of him to strengthen his leg thrash. His dedication paid off and Teddy won all the junior swimming events in record times, becoming 'Champ' for that year.

When Mr Brisco left, his place was taken by an RAF pilot officer recovering from the stress of too many sorties. While drilling us in the playground one day, Ian Trott, a lad a form above me, put one finger under his nose in jest, and gave the Nazi salute. In a flash, the PT instructor had dodged in amongst the marching ranks and grabbed the startled Trott by the throat and, shaking him like a rat, yelled: "How dare you make that gesture! Don't you EVER think of doing it again, or I will knock your back teeth down your throat, is that clear? What do you think I have been fighting for these last few years? It's certainly not to see that obscene gesture repeat itself here." We were left in no doubt that he meant it, as was an ashen-faced Trott.

George Hutchinson was a headmaster of the old school, and the social values he brought were much in the Bevan Lean tradition under whose headship he had passed his school days, at the same time as my mother. He used the cane, but mainly as a deterrent against bullying, he told my mother, as it seemed to be the only punishment a bully understood. This argument seems very suspect in the light of today's knowledge of human behaviour. To be called to George's study for a misdemeanour was an intimidating business in itself, as I can vouch from my one experience of it. I cannot remember exactly what I had been sent to him for. Maybe it was for the thankless baiting of our French mistress Miss Jackson one time too many. I can remember when I arrived at the door of the Head's study there was one other apprehensive boy waiting his turn to brave the inner sanctum and a possible 'twanking'. The study door opened and a slightly strained youth emerged looking relieved. "What was it like, did you get a twanking?" we asked him. "Oh, it wasn't too bad" was the reply. "I wore an extra pair of pants so I didn't feel the cane very much. George gave me 'four'."

When my turn came I knocked, with heart beating, on the study door and was commanded to enter. George was sitting behind his desk, stern and forbidding. I was asked why I had been sent, and then how many strokes of the cane I deserved. I tentatively suggested two, expecting to get more. I was commanded to bend over and the Head, taking a whippy cane from his desk, delivered two smart cuts with it across my backside. The whole event was not so much painful as intimidating in its deterrent value. George advised me sternly not to repeat my misdemeanour and dismissed me back to class. George Hutchinson was the last of the 'twanking' headmasters.

In my early days at Sidcot some of the fifth formers would capture us and lock us in remote parts of the school. I remember being a victim of this horseplay along with a mild, good-natured fellow called Andrew Rutter. We were kidnapped and locked up in a garden shed at the bottom of the girls' playground. Fortunately, or we would have been there all night, some girls sleeping in the wing adjoining the Head's residence, heard our shouts that evening and alerted the 'Master On Duty' to our plight. We were released a good two hours after our official bedtime. We were, of course, silent as to who the perpetrators of the prank were, and the MOD didn't press us for information, knowing the school code.

Like Bevan Lean before him, George Hutchinson, was only too human and fallible and tended to act precipitously in certain situations concerning school discipline, getting events out of proportion and compounding them. One Sunday evening, some sixth formers, my cousin Martin among them, and most of themPrefects, arrived back a quarter of an hour late for evening meeting.

Their entry into the hall seemed a bit noisy, and unknown to us, they had partaken (oh, wicked sin) of a glass of cider at The Star Inn on their way back from a caving expedition. Next day in assembly, George harangued the school on the evils of drink, naming all those who had fallen from grace, and expelling them for the remainder of the term. It was an ill-considered action from the point of view of discipline in the school, as the Prefects involved had effectively lost credibility when trying to keep order the next term. The saving grace was that most of them had been voted on democratically by us, largely, and inevitably, for their sporting prowess on the rugby field, so they soon regained our respect and the episode was forgotten.

The Head, in his dark blue pinstripe suit, always wore a red carnation in his buttonhole, in honour of his mentor Bevan Lean, supplied fresh each day by Mr Lindsay. George continued as Headmaster until the end of the war, just overlapping with the new Headmistress Mary Hooper, a tall stately lady, born to the vocation, with a great dignity and poise that hid a lovely sense of humour and humanity, which inspired friendly respect from the pupils. I don't think she found GWH too easy to get on with, but she certainly got on well with the new Head, David Murray-Rust who joined Sidcot in 1946 just after the war ended. Although his physical appearance and mannerisms evoked a certain amount of mirth, his psychological approach to discipline problems came as a breath of fresh air and worked far better than George's 'twanking' regime, even if on first experiencing its techniques or ploys we may have derided it as a soft option. I didn't appreciate his qualities at the time, but he was a wise man.

Mary Hooper taught us current affairs and history, inspiring stimulating debate in her classes. Later on she was to be my lifeline, coaching me in history for my school certificate exams. I had been floundering under the disinterest of John Russell and his regurgitated notes and had been given 0% by him for my mock exams. Mary Hooper's sympathetic tutelage gave me enough knowledge and self-confidence to get a credit in the actual exam. I remember giving her a pottery bowl I had made as a 'thank you', which she received with her customary intake of breath and the warm grace that was her hallmark. Mary Hooper provided the platform for good social interaction essential to humanity. She used to hold coffee evenings for the sixth formers each Friday in the school drawing room next to the Headmaster's study, which always included the most scrumptious doughnuts. We used to take great delight in offering her one, just to see her try and eat it without getting particles of sugar over her immaculately made up face and chin! She always managed the impossible, retaining her cool dignity and quite aware of our mischievous ploy, I am sure!

When we were older and had graduated from junior meeting, held in the library, to the large meeting in the school hall, Mary Hooper, her gloved hands folded in tranquil repose, would sometimes fix us with her hawk-like stare, knowing full well our minds were wandering into regions temporal, and try and will us back into the spiritual fold.

We challenged her in our turn, and gradually her stern gaze would melt at the corners into the faintest hint of a smile, and we knew that the temporal and the spiritual had met! Sometimes a daft, but irresistible and infectious giggling fit would seize us, and Mary Hooper, trying to stare us into serious silence, would herself be infected by the wave of laughter and visibly break down herself, and the tension would be broken. If you came across Mary Hooper anywhere in school, you could always have a chat with her, and no matter how naïve, prejudiced, arrogant or idealistic your argument might be, she, with a deep breath would consider your opinion and discuss it with you as an equal. With great gentleness, she would often suggest some more realistic or tolerant amendment to your view, without being at all judgmental. She made you feel you were of value in your own right, which did wonders for one's self-confidence when it was most needed. All this was much later in my school life, of course.

Early in 1944, two sixth form art students, Beth Harris and Joan Hawks, utilised the west end wall of the dining room to paint a mural of the school and grounds, taken from an aerial photograph. It took about a month to complete and was painted in powder colours. We had great fun picking out and identifying all the tiny figures in the mural going about their work in the school grounds. They were all recognisable by their occupation. Each day a little bit more appeared on the wall to be looked at and talked over; it gave endless pleasure throughout our school days.

During the war, the school had its own mobile fire pumps manned by eager sixth formers. They used to drill in the school playground, rolling out the fire hoses with speedy expertise to connect to the pumps and fire hydrants. Long ladders were run up the walls of the school buildings and the youthful firemen would wrestle with the hoses and nozzles that had suddenly become alive under the pressure of water delivered by the powerful pumps. It was exciting to witness the jets of water spouting from the nozzles in a thirty-foot arc over the playground and onto the swimming pool roof. How we brats envied the school's National Fire Service team and their slick disciplined expertise.

I, along with others, joined the Junior Literary Society and took part in a nativity play at the end of the autumn term, taking the role of one of the Three Kings and singing the verse relating to my gift of frankincense. Garth Reynolds was the giver of Gold and John Ransome, the myrrh. Mary was played by Sally Stanton and John Norman became a reluctant Joseph. In the spring, we produced *Toad of Toad Hall* and I took the part of Ratty. It was great for one's ego and self-confidence to act in front of the whole school. The school hall had a very good stage and there was a lot of rivalry to get the backstage jobs such as lighting and stage manager. The workforce behind the scenes were always very dedicated and efficient. The school play that made the most impression on me was *The Barretts of Wimpole Street*. David Trott, a handsome sixth former, took the part of Robert Browning and Meg Graty, a girl friend of Martin's at one stage, took the part of Elizabeth Barrett. She was lovely, with a pallid countenance in keeping with her part, and I think we were all in love with her after watching the play. Michael Van Blankenstein, a vast, six foot plus young man took the part of the overbearing and possessive Papa Barrett. He acted so well and was so intimidating, I was quite frightened by him. How we all rooted for the two young lovers, especially as it was rumoured that David Trott and Meg Graty were a 'couple' anyway. It was all most romantic.

John Ransome and I became romantically attached to two young girls in the form below us. The object of my affections was a dusky, curly black-haired girl called Marion Smith, and Ransome was enamoured of a small spitfire of a girl called dramatically, Eleanor Von Schweinitz. Greatly daring, by mutual consent, we blacked out our form room and feeling for our chosen girl we tasted the first thrill of a shared kiss and, oh boy, was it heaven! Marion and I, Ransome and Eleanor, used to take self-conscious walks together and hold hands, snatching the occasional kiss and embrace, and liked to think of ourselves as couples. It did not last long, however, as the two girls soon grew tired of our immature horsing about while trying to impress them, and they 'chucked' us without ceremony. We, on our part, had little regret!

Taking local walks, it was not long before we were attracted by the railway and tunnel at Shute Shelf. The tunnel ran a quarter of a mile through the hillside where Wavering runs out to the Bristol Bridgewater road. It was dark and mysterious, with alcoves you could dart into when the vibration in the rails signalled the train was coming. It was exciting to slip in, just as the little locomotive, whistle blowing, blackened the tunnel entrance with its swaying bulk. As we waited, a column of air was pushed towards us by the approaching train. There followed a crescendo of noise, a thunder of wheels, the glow of the firebox glimpsed for a moment, steam, smoke confusion, and the strobe effect of the lighted passing carriages. A rush of air was sucked past us as the receding train burst out of the upper end of the tunnel and disappeared, a black silhouette on its way to the next stop, Axbridge, around the corner of Callow Hill. Looking back it was a dangerous exercise messing about in the tunnel, but I don't ever remember being told that the tunnel was out of bounds. Putting a penny piece on the railway line for the train to run over was another diversion. To see the flattened result from the great pressure of the locomotive was awesome.

For some reason the tunnel seemed to be the place where local women used to abandon their sanitary towels, or even the occasional pair of knickers. These objects, connected with the mysterious workings of a woman's body, held a certain fascination for small gangs of boys on the edge of puberty, and it was known and talked about by the lower male echelons of the school that the Southall family were sent to Sidcot on the proceeds of the sale of 'Southall's Sanitary Towels'. Such is the mentality of young boys at a certain moment in their lives!

The Physics master in my first years at the school was a tubby red-faced man called Mr Fitton - 'Bunter' to us boys. Of indeterminate temper, when roused his face would turn even redder than its normal shade, and he would clip the offending boy round the ears, first on one side, following up as he reeled sideways, with a smart clip on the other side. "So you think you are clever, Sonny, do you? Well, take a clip from Bunter!" he would shout, while delivering the accurate blows. He would sometimes supervise our prep. We rigged up an ingenious system with a piece of card on which was drawn a caricature of Bunter. This card slid down behind the blackboard and could be raised and lowered with a piece of string, cunningly worked by one of the boys from his desk. On previous occasions, we sourced much entertainment and mirth from baiting other members of staff, raising the card behind their backs and, anticipating their reactions, making it disappear behind the blackboard again before they could look round to see what all the merriment was about. One of our form was clever at caricature and we had a different mug shot of each master on prep duty. On the occasion of Bunter taking charge, there was a buzz of anticipation before he arrived. A look-out mouthed 'KV!' ('beware!' or 'Sir's coming' in Latin i.e.*cave*), from the top of the stairs, and we all waited in the form room in electric suspense. Bunter arrived, placed his books on his desk in front of the blackboard and taking a large pair of scissors from his coat pocket, he deftly cut the cotton thread holding our strategically-placed card, and with a muttered "Snip from Bunter", he sat down to his work. We, flabbergasted at his powers of observation, short-circuiting our fun, were so silent you could hear a pin drop. At the end of our allotted time Bunter said quietly:"I think we all deserve an extra half-hour's work this evening, don't you boys?" We acquiesced without a murmur, Bunter had us licked!

A new French teacher arrived, a Miss Jackson, who with her shrill, affected voice and nervous manner, had no chance of keeping order. She must have approached our classes in trepidation. Text books would be placed on top of the classroom door, strategically placed so that they would fall on her head when she entered the classroom, to roars of sadistic merriment. It was pure bedlam and the poor woman's only recourse was to send us to the Headmaster, who worked overtime 'twanking' the ringleaders to little effect, as they took to stuffing their pants with newspaper. In so many ways, the classroom was a jungle in which only the strongest survived. You got hell, and in your turn, gave hell to someone else. Thoughtful consideration was a quality that came later in life.

Half term was marked by a free Monday off, collecting a packed lunch made up by Birds Bakery and Temperance Hotel in the village, and going off on long walks in the lovely surrounding Mendip Hills, to places like Dolbury, Wavering and Crooks Peak. The packed lunches never varied; a fish paste sandwich, a jam sandwich, a jam tart and a shortbread biscuit. One walk of note was to Dolbury. It was a wet summer's day and a group of five of us boys found ourselves up a rocky combe, getting rather damp and miserable. One of our number discovered he had a red match in his pocket, so we resolved to make a fire. As we only had one chance to light it, we took infinite care with our preparations and, with baited breath, gathered round, our coats held out to make sure the strong wind didn't blow our single match out. The match fizzed, nearly went out, then held and grew in strength, and it was quickly put amongst the dry twigs and grasses we had scavenged to start the fire. The fire came to life and building it up to a good healthy blaze, we steamed out and warmed our backsides, heating up cans of baked beans to supplement our meagre picnic lunches. After eating, we climbed to the rocky summit of the combe and spent the whole afternoon prising large boulders out of the hillside to send them crashing and bouncing dramatically down the steep slopes into the valley below. We were lucky there were no walkers other than ourselves on the combe that day.

Half term would usually end with a film being shown on the antiquated school projector. The film shown would have been democratically voted for a few weeks previously. The school hall had a projection room at the back of the hall that was never short of enthusiasts to man it. Passing through the aged 16-millimetre machine, the film often jammed and, over-heated by the high wattage bulb, it would melt in viscous folds across the screen and everyone would groan with frustration. It happened so frequently that the projectionists would try and inject a little humour into the situation by putting up a slide onto the screen with the apology: "Sorry, Hechnical Tich" while they struggled with their spools of film to re-thread the projector. To get through a full-length film such as *A Tale Of Two Cities*, without half-a-dozen breakdowns was quite a feat. Watching Sidney Carton go to his brave death with the little seamstress, and hearing him declaim: "It is a far, far better thing I do...", left most of the girls, and secretly myself, feeling very tearful!

Eventually the projector got so bad, it was mooted in assembly that we raise the £200 or so needed to buy a brand new one. We made a large symbolic thermometer to register how the funds were progressing, and the whole school pitched into various enterprises to raise the money. I remember spending weekend afternoon walks picking bucketfuls of rosehips from the hedgerows, that were sold to Delrosa to make their rosehip syrup, a good source of vitamin C. The money for the new projector was raised in a little over six weeks, and we enjoyed trouble-free films from then on. It was a nice change to listen to a sound track without the massive 'wowing' from the constantly changing frequency that dominated the old machine. Films of note have to be such classics as *Men Of Aran*,

Drifters, and *Nanook of the North*, all documentaries made by that great Irish director Robert J. Flaherty. Two others that were memorable were Italian films, *Vivre Im Pache* and *Bicycle Thieves*. The film club, not surprisingly, was the most popular club in the school. I believe the late David Conns, who made films while still at Sidcot, went on to work in the film industry.

Half way through the Upper Third in 1945, the Germans were finally defeated by the Allied Forces and the school celebrated VE Day by having a day off and baked beans for supper, a treat usually reserved for half term. Later came the victory in the Pacific arena, when the Japanese surrendered to the obscene suns of the first atomic bombs dropped on Nagasaki and Hiroshima, and we had another holiday known as VJ Day. ⚘

Mr Ted Hembery, who sported a walrus moustache, and Tom, one of many school horses used to cart coke, coal, dung, laundry and pupils...

The cycle shed and Tom's stable at Sidcot (from a painting by Tim Holding, 1972).

Chapter 45
Into the Fourth Form

In the Fourth Form we organised several get-togethers with the girls, centred around food, known as 'Binges'. Each of us contributed a shilling or so to a kitty and democratically decided what we wanted, broadly, to eat and drink.

On a Saturday afternoon we would troop down to the village and stock up with goodies for our evening 'Blowout'. Tizer was the favourite fizzy drink of the time and we would back it up with iced buns, chocolate eclairs, custard cream slices, baked beans, Smiths Crisps and sausage rolls, all good balanced stuff!

It was the custom to invite the form master and mistress to these 'Binges', which we held in our form room, pushing our desks to the side of the room and stacking the feast on the top desk. Some of the boys exhibited a greed that was embarrassing to watch, stuffing their faces with everything until they nearly choked, making sure they didn't miss out on anything. The girls put us to shame with their civilised behaviour; we boys were still little savages.

The first Latin master of my Sidcot days was Mr Peters. The lower forms did not take Latin, so I never experienced him as teacher in his chosen subject. He was, however, a great Rugby enthusiast as well as Classics master, and when in the Lower Fourth we were allowed (Oh! blessed day) to go to the big games field to play rugger for the first time, he was our mentor. I can still feel the thrill of grabbing that ovoid ball and battling forward in glorious ego-centric isolation until ground into the mud by my irate peers, angry I had not passed the ball in true team fashion. In those days you had to play the ball with your feet after being tackled, before gathering it up again. I remember Mr Peters blowing his whistle with an amused, but not discouraging smile, and while praising my green determination, impressed on me the fact that rugby was a team game, and that there were rules of play that I must follow. In the years to come I don't think many of us ever looked at a rule book. We just absorbed the rules by a kind of osmosis. I was never quite sure of the offside rule from first to last.

I lived for games afternoons in the spring and misty autumn; the mud and glory of tackling your adversary low and bringing him crashing down in mid-sprint. The red Somerset marl clung to our boots and games kit like glue. I loved the physicality of the game and aspired to be as good as those so out-of-reach seniors in the First XV. At the end of the Lower Fourth, John Ransome left Sidcot to go to Bootham, a boys' Quaker school, where no rugby was played. Ransome, in a letter back from that school, nostalgically reported that he played in goal in their soccer matches, as being able to handle the ball was the nearest that he could get to rugby.

The last gym lesson of term was, by tradition, given over to an exciting game called 'Pirates'. Utilising all the gym apparatus, we were free to move around, providing we did not touch the floor. In a form of tag, a selected boy had to try and touch the others one by one, or force them by sheer pressure to touch the floor. In either case they would be out. If the catcher touched the floor, all those previously tagged could rejoin the game. We all turned into pocket Tarzans swinging from ropes to wall bars to mats to box to pommel horse, in our endeavour to avoid our fleet pursuer. It was great fun and a wonderful precursor to holiday time.

Although the worst of the homesickness was now over and adaptation to school life as complete as it was ever going to be, I still loved home with a fierce loyalty. Olive had moved out and Mother was able to get back some of her old tranquillity. Thankfully, now that the two women lived apart they seemed able to return to a reasonable amicability.

Her visits to Sidcot at General Meeting in the summer term were much looked forward to as, unlike other mothers, she brought a tent and camped in one of the fields on the way to the combe. I was secretly proud of her unconventionality, and was settled enough not to be sad at her leave-takings as I had been in the past. As I began to reach adolescence and put on a spurt of growth, Mother was hard put to find enough ration coupons for my clothes, especially shoes.

I was never much good at mathematics, and its mysteries were compounded when we started to do algebra and trigonometry. If I had been able to have the luxury of one-to-one teaching from a sympathetic teacher I might have got somewhere. As it was, I had Francis Armitage, a brilliant mathematician for bright scholars, but totally lacking imagination and patience when it came to perplexed duffers like myself. With computerised speed he would work out his convoluted equations and come up with an answer in a flash, leaving me floundering in his wake.

Catching sight of my bewildered face, he would inquire sharply: "What's up, Charman? Why are you making that face?"

"I don't understand, sir," I would reply.

"Oh, he doesn't know his logarithms," Mr Armitage would announce sarcastically to the class at large. "Charman, stand on your desk and repeat the expression that was on your face just now…well, GO ON, BOY!"

I would stand reluctantly, seething, on my desk, hating the man for making me a scapegoat for his lousy teaching. In the end, I wrote home to Mother telling her of my predicament and she wrote back to the Head and I was allowed to drop maths at the age of fourteen.

Francis Armitage had been an invasion glider pilot instructor, and had survived a fairly bad crash in which he had sustained a head injury, which may have accounted in part for his irritability in coping with apparent idiots. But it had certainly not taken away his mental agility with figures. He still had a dent in his skull as a legacy from the accident. This, coupled with his Christian name, inevitably earned him the nickname of Fanny Kink or just Kink! He was our form master in the Upper Fourth and the antipathy between us was mutual. His report on my conduct for each term was always scathing and ran along such lines as: "Charman's insolence and uncooperative attitude make him a liability to his form. If he does not mend his ways, I do not hold out much hope for him out in the world later on." Fortunately, Mother, who was aware of our destructive interaction, was more amused by the character report than dismayed.

Miss Rolands, another natural mathematician, told me she regretted that I had given up maths as she considered it was a subject that was vital to getting on in life. As I had always wanted to be a potter, I told her I hoped I might just get away with the basic maths I had already learnt. A few weeks later, Miss Rolands, to my lasting delight and appreciation, took me to see Clevedon Pottery where William Fishley-Holland, one of the famous Devon potter dynasty, practiced his craft. She took me one Friday, introduced me and left me for a whole fascinating afternoon. Mr Holland and I chatted while he made mugs from the well-known Fremington clay, as red as the Somerset marl with its iron content. I watched his bearded, elderly father unpack a glost setting of slipware from the large coal-fired muffle kiln out in the yard, and marvelled. All the school's butter dishes were made at Clevedon Pottery and came in many colours. The butter ration was limited to four ounces a week, and put into the butter dishes with our school number on the side. The children used to abuse these lovely little handmade bowls much to my sadness, scudding them along the tables to crash and chip against each other at the end of each meal. That visit to a traditional pottery decided me on my life's occupation. Thank you, Miss Rolands, for your imaginative gesture, it was more important to me than you will ever know.

Besides art, Barry Davies taught woodwork. Although I was an expert aero-modeller and won prizes for my constructions, I was no great shakes at woodwork. I never got beyond making a pin tray and a pair of bookends, items which were invariably given to the less able to keep them out of mischief. Barry was always giving us precise lessons on how to use and maintain tools, watching us with an eagle eye for any deviation from his instructions to the point of intimidation. The class was frequently stopped in its tracks by Barry barking: "Stop work, gather round!" and we would all crowd round the latest miscreant that Barry had managed to spy sharpening his chisel at the wrong angle, or who had put his plane blade in back to front, or sawn his tenon joint on the wrong side of the scribed line. "Now show us what you were doing, Bennett," Barry would bark, and the unfortunate Bennett would begin to demonstrate his criminal mistake, only to have Barry yell: "NO! NO! not like that, you idiot. What is this idiot doing wrong?" Barry would ask of the class, while Bennett, pink and sheepish with embarrassment, hung his head. Then, some of the more confident woodworkers would be asked to demonstrate the right method, and we would be told to mark, look and learn!

The gifted woodworkers made cabinets and coffee tables with complex dovetailing and were Barry's privileged elite, trusted with the expensive, more exotic hardwoods to work on. During one memorable woodworking class in the severe winter of 1947 when the Mendips were covered in snow, Barry suddenly said: "Right, you lads, we are going to produce eight toboggans before dinner", and under his dynamic supervision we did just that, using good simple woodworking techniques, saws, hammers and nails. We sledged later with the rest of the school in the snow-clad combe, a doubly satisfying experience because we could enjoy what we had made. Barry Davies taught me manuscript writing which I have always found useful in sign writing and pottery. He taught me how to paint trees too. In later years, when he was principal of Reading's Teacher Training college and my Kate went for an interview as a student, he showed her some of my paintings he had kept all those years! Barry's bark was worse than his bite. In retrospect I have to admit he was OK! ✸

Chapter 46
Sustenance for Mind and Body

When George W Hutchinson was Head, we all sat in our separate forms in the dining room to eat our meals, and quite enjoyed it as we could talk to our mates.

When David Murray Rust arrived he introduced a regime where all the forms were tumbled together, supposedly an exercise in social democratisation. Although it was not a popular move at first, age differences at school being naturally divisional, it forced us into a socially more integrated, homogenous community. Staff and prefects manned the heads of the tables to dish out the various courses. When second course was served, if it was jam tart or stodge, a second helping from the slide in the kitchens was very often a case of first come, first served. To facilitate a fast return by the waiters seated either side of the server, he or she was encouraged to cut the pudding into pieces as fast as possible. I remember being waiter and scuttling up to the slide with my tray for a dollop of extra stodge, to be met by the experienced cynical gaze of our long established cook Violet Trickey, who was thoroughly conversant with our greedy ploys down the years. I may well have barged in front of some equally resourceful girl already in the queue for seconds, and Violet spotted my cheating and demanded my name which I gave her. "I knew your name spelt trouble," she announced. "Go to the back of the queue." You didn't argue with a cook of Violet Trickey's standing.

At breakfast, our new Music master, Mr Bains, would dole out the porridge like an automaton, half asleep still, and while engaging him in conversation we would move the bowls away and he would slop a dollop of porridge onto the table. "Mind out, sir," we would say. "You have missed the bowl." It took him a long time to twig our devilment.

The housekeeper was a short dumpy woman, a little lady with a hair lip and not much sense of humour, called Miss Elvin. Because of her hair lip she had a speech impediment that the schoolboy mentality latched onto with gusto, producing wicked impersonations of the unfortunate woman's more memorable utterances. Cremola pudding, a kind of processed tapioca, yellow and with a vanilla flavouring, was universally disliked, much to the fury of Miss Elvin, who, when doling it out, met with almost blanket strike action in consuming it. "Ich luvly hremola hudding, ich very nutrihus, yu mus eat ih!", she used to irritably whine, her face going red with fury. "I will tell uh hedmathter ich yu don eat ih!" Gallons of the stuff went back to the kitchens on the day when it was part of the menu.

We used to annoy Miss Elvin by insisting on eating our stodge with a spoon, which seemed to us the obvious choice of utensil. To her it was *de-trop*, and I can still see her confiscating all our spoons in a fury and substituting forks. From then on, we all knew when stodge was going to be our pudding because only forks would be laid throughout the dining room.

A new Latin master arrived to take the place of Mr Peters, a Mr Thompson, nicknamed Thatch because of his unruly hair. Try as he might to plaster it down first thing in the morning in time for breakfast, it was very wiry and forever springing away from his scalp at a stiff angle, ringing his head like a fringe of badly-laid thatch. A good friend of mine, Alan McCombie (known as Hank), had a shorthand drawing he used to do of Thatch that was instantly recognisable. When we started to learn Latin, it was obvious that I, amongst others, wasn't going to be a very apt pupil. Thatch made our class rise on his entering the classroom, and raising his arm in a perfunctory manner, he would greet us with a Roman senator's *Salvete Omnes* (Hail, all), to which we students had to reply in chorus *Salve, Magister* (Hail, Sir). Thatch who had a sardonic and sarcastic turn of humour, gave us all names, according to how he rated our IQ. Mine inevitably was Lepidae, the swift one! Apart from being able to declaim *Amo, Amas, Amat* (I love, you love, he/she loves), I never really learnt much Latin.

Thatch, alias Hess, or Lamp Post, also took us for English literature. I remember a poem we talked over in class called *Pylons* by Stephen Spender. I recall Thatch going into ecstasies over its imagery, in which the poet likened pylons to "nude giant girls that have no secrets", an image that did nothing for the majority of us and seemed totally inappropriate, although it did make the girls blush.

One day Thatch asked us to extemporise for five minutes in front of the class on a subject of our own choosing. Each speaker was introduced with a theatrical flourish by Thatch. On one memorable occasion he excelled himself with his flowery introduction: "Martin Rutter, that well known authority on the craft of woodwork, who has come to impart to us this morning some of his great knowledge and expertise on the subject. Ladies and Gentlemen, Mr Martin Rutter!" To amused clapping, Martin, a good-natured member of our form from a farming background and with a delightful Somerset burr, shuffled self-consciously to the front of the class, a small piece of paper in his hands. Smiling uncertainly, he stammered into his address. "Well, er, woodwork , well, er, it takes up a great deal of time, er, yes, a great deal of time." That was it, Martin got no further. In vain he stared at his notes for further inspiration, and finding none reiterated: "Yes, well er, a great deal of time." In hysterics at Martin's audacity we all clapped satirically, and Martin just stood there and smiled until Thatch dismissed him in disgusted ignominy back to his desk with some sarcastic comment. My contribution was to describe a horse-drawn caravan holiday that Danae, Mother and I took one summer school holiday. It went down well, mainly because of the novelty factor. Even Thatch was appreciative for once.

Thatch became romantically entangled with one of the domestic staff, a woman who looked like the deceased wife who comes back to haunt her husband in Noel Coward's play *Blithe Spirit*. So she was nicknamed Alvera, a tall, slim, palely interesting figure. She and Thatch made a strange couple. The staff put on a comic ballet in a review show at the end of one term, in which the male dancers had to lift their female partners high in the air. Everyone managed the athletic sequence apart from Thatch, who hadn't sufficient muscle to lift his Alvera more than six inches off the floor. However, it all added to the comedy. Later, the pair were married and left the school.

After the war ended we acquired a new and more permanent games master, Mr T W Langdon, a small, muscular man with public school attitudes. He instigated a house system within the school to inspire internal sporting competitiveness. The four houses were named after explorers, Nanson, Shackleton, Rhodes and Scott. Langdon's greatest contribution to school sport in my eyes, was to harness the up-and-coming seniors' enthusiasm for rugby, and form a B team to play inter-school matches. The dedication we of the 2nd team put into our play was, I am sure, greater than the 1st team. We won more matches and gave not a fig for our safety in the rucks, tackles and mauls. In the end, I broke my collar bone from tackling too high, and was off games for a whole term, much to my misery and frustration.

I teamed up with Michael Cox, an artist with a commercial style, and together in the art room on Friday evenings, we combined to produce a large banner in poster colour, lampooning the other school side in caricature, with slogans like: "Go it, the Wasps", our school colours being yellow and navy hoops. We would rush up and down the touch line with this banner, yelling encouragement to our team until our vocal chords were shredded. If we could not play, being a spectator was next best thing. All went well until Mr Newick, our replacement art master for Barry Davis, new and revolutionary in his "Be brave, be bold, be free" approach to painting, accosted Michael Cox and myself, and said he could not possibly let us continue with our vulgar, cartoon-inspired banners, as we were letting down the school art standards. We were to be refined and reserved in our approach from now on, and submit all our efforts to him to pass as suitable for display on the rugby pitch. Michael and I were furious at this unwarranted censorship, as we considered our propagandist posters just that and nothing to do with artistic expression. I think we had one more go, using dreary stippled silhouettes of rugby players, but they lacked the bite of our deadly cartoons and so we gave up.

T W Langdon was a complicated little man. Light of lower body, he was very powerful in the arms; a perfect weight-muscle ratio for going up and down gym ropes without using his legs and feet, though the effort did make him go very red in the face. He was very scathing of our efforts and used to sneer: "You couldn't knock the skin off a rice pudding. could you lads?" Although Langdon endeared himself to us initially by forming the 2nd team, as we got into the Sixth form we became more cocky and began to question his decisions. Langdon could not cope with his authority being questioned in any way. As long as we had been subservient, things had been OK, but sensing he was losing authority our relationship quickly deteriorated. The new chemistry master was a young man called Aubrey Hopes, a Welsh rugby player who, in his time, had played for Cardiff. Watching the 2nd team at play he offered to coach Ian Dixon and myself as a potentially good half-back partnership. We were only too happy to do anything to improve our play and greatly enjoyed the voluntary help from our new mentor. Langdon however, when he got wind of the fact that Hopes was helping us, was unable to cope with the situation and created such an atmosphere, it was with apologies to us that Hopes backed off to keep the peace with his prickly colleague.

Chris's 'deadly and vulgar' cartoons were frowned upon!

Cross country runs over the local Mendips were organised instead of games sometimes, if the weather was too bad. These were universally hated and we did everything in our power to avoid them. Langdon used to place markers round the course and, armed with lists of the runners, they were instructed to tick them off as they went by. On one occasion several runners took a short cut, leaving out one of the markers, a callow youth who stayed loyally at his post in full expectancy the missing runners would eventually pass him. Back at school, all the runners had returned several hours, showered and changed ready for tea, and still no Richard Corkhill. It began to get dark and Langdon went on a hunt to find him, still at his post in the dark, faithful to the end. The runners who had taken the short cut swore blind they had passed the marker and that he must have missed seeing them in the mist and rain. It was a situation in which nothing could be proven and Langdon, however much he fumed and had his suspicions, could do little.

On another run we were in a group and decided to march the course; when Langdon, on a bicycle, came to see why we were taking so long and ordered us all to run, no one took any notice of him. With his face a lurid red with impotent fury, he rode off muttering dire warnings at our insubordination. Murray Rust was aware of the destructive cycle that we had got ourselves into with Langdon and gave us advice on the right psychological approach in dealing with the more extreme elements of our games master's character. It was a revolutionary ploy on the Head's part to even indicate that he found TW Langdon difficult. A positive move instigated by Langdon was to get some of us trials for schoolboy rugby at County level. David Crocker, a natural winger with a wonderful jinking run, came to play for Somerset as did Peter Weeks. I got to play twice for Hampshire school boys against Sussex. I think we lost on both occasions, but to play for one's County was heady stuff.

One spring term, when I was in the Fifth form, there was an outbreak of chickenpox. The San was full to bursting. I eventually acquired one or two spots but never felt at all ill. However, I was deemed to have the disease and along with five other boys we were billeted somewhere at the top of the school in an attic room, in splendid isolation for a few weeks. I never felt ill or experienced the terrible itching inconvenience of my peers, so life in the attic room was a great holiday from school work. We were very much left to our own devices.

We devised a game called Houdini, in which we took it in turns to be tied securely to a chair from which we had to free ourselves without help. Stuart Linney was trying to free himself for over an hour one day and grew quite upset. However, he wouldn't give in and eventually, chafed and bruised and lathered in sweat, he fought free. There was a gas jet and tap in the wall and we had a couple of old, two-pound baked bean cans in the base of which we punched a small hole. Turning on the gas tap, we filled the cans with coal gas, and deftly turning the open ends of the cans down on the hearth of the fireplace to trap the gas collected, we lit it at the small hole we had punched. A tiny yellow flame burned for two or three minutes until an explosive gas-air mix was achieved inside the can, followed by a small explosion, and the can would jump a foot in the air!

From the kitchens to the attic rooms there was a lift shaft with a small lift, or Dumb Waiter, that took food, laundry, and other items to the various levels of the old school buildings. The beautifully made ropes that worked the lift were over an inch in diameter and must have been there for over a hundred years. Our meals were sent up to us on this lift. To relieve the tedium of our enforced isolation, we would propel each other down in the lift to the kitchens to make a raid on whatever food was left about. We had some narrow shaves with the ever watchful Violet Trickey, (aptly named), but we were never caught in the act and added a few tasty morsels to our meagre rations. ❦

Chapter 47
Mother and Danae go off to France
Colourful Tenants on the Ridge

What of life at home during these times? Danae attended the village school and fought her battles with some of the latest intake that included an East End family of girls from London called Constantine.

Their father had been involved with my uncle in furthering a political movement in the late 'thirties called Social Credit. Danae's desk was next to one of the older sisters, a powerful girl. The desks were so arranged that each pair of children shared the same lid, and Danae's rival took great delight in slamming it shut whenever my sister wanted anything from it, causing much bad feeling and black and blue finger tips. It was a constant fight, but Danae held her own in the tough jungle of the village school. With the war at an end, Mother decided she needed a break from Ridge life and, as my grandfather had done, she decided to go to France with Hazel and Danae.

The idea was to find work and try and place the two girls with a French family so that they could gain a good grasp of conversational French before sending Danae to Sidcot. In the autumn of 1946, through the auspices of Dorothy Rutter, one of her cousins, Mother found a position as housekeeper and general factotum in a French school, the Ecole Normal d'Institutrices in Auxerre. The school was run by a Madame Santucci, a severe lady and something of a martinet. Mother found her domestic standards rather exacting but, by using tact and diplomacy, she managed to rub along with her employer. By good fortune she had taken her diploma in anthropology with her to France, which when submitted to the French Ministry of Education, qualified her for the job of Repetitatrice. She took the opportunity to teach English with enthusiasm, if a trifle apprehensively. For the first time in her life, aged fifty, she was free of domestic chores and able to exercise her academic and intellectual capabilities. She was earning a salary, paying £11 a month for her keep, and living in a free room at the school. It was all most satisfactory.

Meanwhile she had rented our home out to a Mrs Burn and her teenage daughter, for 10/6d a week. Her daughter, Jennifer, had an ancient and reluctant horse called Tommy. The rent was low, in lieu of the couple looking after our goats and chickens. Mrs Burn, who was sweetness and light itself before taking up the tenancy, turned out to be a sour, scheming old skinflint. She got behind very quickly with the modest rent, which in the end they refused to pay, as they considered that the work they put into looking after the animals more than paid for their tenancy. In the face of Mother's mild protests, Mrs Burns veneer of politeness disappeared and she was extremely rude. Eventually they left in high dudgeon, taking Tommy with them, and we all heaved a sigh of relief!

We gave the upstairs room to a young artist friend called Adrian Lees, an ex-Forest School pupil, free in exchange for doing a bit of maintenance to the house. Mother's name was good for credit with the local traders and she gave Adrian permission to buy the materials necessary in her name, such as nails and wood for repairs. When Danae, Mother and I returned for the Christmas holidays, it was to find Adrian had run up bills with the local traders all over Fordingbridge, and then disappeared into the blue with no attempt at repairs. The worst debt was for a new pigskin saddle costing £20, a small fortune in those days. He bought it from Thorn, the local saddler, saying it was for an Arab stallion that my mother had just purchased. Mr Thorn had felt at the time there was something fishy about the transaction, but as he had mended Mother's harness for years and she was totally trustworthy, he let Adrian have the saddle on tick. So Mother's first job that holiday, apart from 'mucking' out our upstairs room, was to pay off all the creditors.

Adrian Lees had drifted into our lives, coming to visit Cuthbert when he was staying with us one summer in the early 'forties. He was a gifted young artist, with great charm and plausibility. Just out of the army, he was travelling about with nothing particular to do, and Danae and I quickly warmed to his friendly generosity and began to see a lot of him. He wore faded army fatigues and sported an old American Ford V8 army truck which he drove everywhere.

"I will teach you how to drive it army style," he offered one day, taking me out on the now deserted aerodrome at Fritham. I readily agreed; this was too good an opportunity to miss. Naïve youngster that I was, little did I know what I was letting myself in for. The friendly Adrian disappeared entirely, to be replaced by a rasping bully of a sergeant major instructor, yelling directions and abuse at me for over an hour, while I banged and crashed the gears and stalled the engine in my attempts to master the rudiments of how to drive. What little clutch control I had at the start of the so-called lesson was forgotten, and all coordination left me. The army style of training seemed to me to be designed to reduce your confidence to nil. It certainly had that affect on me and I ended up collapsing in tears.

"Well, you did say it was all right for me to teach you how to become a truck driver, in the army style," said Adrian. "You may feel muddled now but it will all come back to you next time we go out." It was all too much for a twelve-year-old, and I didn't give Adrian another chance to addle my brain, and refused further so-called driving lessons.

Danae at 10. A pastel portrait by artist Adrian Lees.

One memorable day, Adrian took Danae, Mother and myself, up to London, to Lewisham to visit an ailing Cuthbert who, with his wife Helen, were fostering her two-year-old niece, Susan Garrod. It had been very wet weather, with terrific overnight storms, and the ford over the brook on our way to Woodgreen was well up, to a depth of 2ft 6″. We suggested going around it via Fordingbridge, but Adrian, macho-minded with his rugged 'go-anywhere Ford V8', insisted his vehicle would manage to get through the flooded ford with ease. Halfway across, the truck's engine sputtered to a halt. Adrian cursed, we opened the doors to get out and water swilled through the cab of the truck, in one side, and out the other. The magneto was submerged and all the electrical circuits waterlogged. A local farmer pulled us out with a cart horse and trace chains, and we waited three hours while the magneto and distributor were dried out and exhaust system drained, Adrian muttering implications the while. With a fading battery, the V8 sputtered to life again and, crammed into the small cab with sodden feet, we made our disrupted journey to Lewisham and dear old Cuthbert. He was obviously enjoying Susan, his tiny charge, when she could escape the overzealous attentions of Helen, who was continually wiping non-existent dirt off her person.

I remember Adrian taking Danae and I on an expedition to Hamleys toy shop in Regent Street, a mecca for children, and saying we could choose anything we liked. Wow! Seeing our eyes wandering over impossibly expensive toys, he hastily amended his offer to: "Well, you choose and I will buy it if I have enough money…" I don't remember what Danae chose, but I plumped for a pair of headphones to use on a crystal set, all the rage at Sidcot where we ran the earth wire along cracks in the floor boards to attach it to radiators, and slung the aerials under the beds.

Lying in bed at night, a single headphone under one's ear, you could clandestinely listen to all sorts of programmes. I remember listening to the boxing match where Freddy Mills became the middle-weight champ of the world, and relaying the results of the rounds to the rest of the dormitory in a loud whisper as Barrington Dalby delivered his verdicts. It was a nice gesture of Adrian's to buy us presents and we came to regard him as some sort of benevolent uncle. He made an excellent pastel portrait of Danae that we have to this day, aged ten or so, with her bobbed fair hair and the fringe she wore in those days. So when Mother went to France, and Adrian seemed to have nowhere else to go, she let him have the upstairs room; a magnanimous gesture that, as I have already described, he abused and she came to regret.

In the summer holidays, Mother, Danae and I had some memorable picnics, going for walks to Holly Hatch and visiting the site where our parents had built their 'bender' and had their 'honeymoon' in the beech woods. The overhead branch that had supported the ridge of their shelter was still there, even if now dead and weathered. We made a fire and fried some eggs on a Roman tile from the brook, using the crust from a slice of bread to retain it, and boiled up some water for tea in Cuthbert's old kettle. Danae and I lazed away the afternoon, guddling for the small trout in the Forest stream, while Mother dozed in the sunny clearing by the camp fire. It was idyllic and our mother was more relaxed since taking up the teaching post in France. "The job is more like a paid holiday…" she says in her diary of that period.

Our old Forest mare, Daphne, an offspring of our parent's first pony Sappho, took naturally to harness and Mother resolved to introduce Danae and myself to horse caravanning, which we greeted with enthusiasm! So, one summer holiday, we trundled out the lightweight caravan and, harnessing up Daphne, we set off in the evening sun for our first camp at Eyeworth Pond, near Fritham. The driving bridle of our old Eyre and Spottiswoode harness had the conventional blinkers to shield the horse's eyes from viewing the bulk of the caravan behind her. We reached Eyeworth at dusk, and tethering Daphne nearby with an iron stake and swivel chain, we brewed a cup of cocoa on a small camp fire and went to bed to the comforting and soporific sound of Daphne grazing the sward, deftly nudging her tethering chain ahead of her. On our second day out Daphne started to hesitate in her stride, finally coming to a grinding halt and refusing to move. I got down from the caravan and, holding her bridle, led her forward without trouble. As soon as I got back on the caravan, however, she refused to budge. We found that if she could see one of us she pulled willingly, so for the rest of the week's trip each of us took it in turns to walk in front, which was a bit of a nuisance to say the least.

Our journey took us to New Milton where we managed to find a field to stop over with grazing for Daphne, while we enjoyed a day on the beach. Apart from the already increasing number of cars it was a wonderful trip. On our last day, coming back from Ringwood we still hadn't sorted out Daphne's problem, when Mother said: "Why don't we take off her blinkers? If she bolts, at least here on a big road we will have a chance of getting her under control again." So with great trepidation we took off Daphne's blinkers. She just shook her head, looked about her and trotted off as good as gold, totally unconcerned by the caravan behind her. How we wished we had experimented a few days earlier.

A year or two later we were to go on another trip using a different horse. We had acquired a Welsh cross, New Forest gelding from Forester John Chalk, in exchange for Daphne and ten pounds. He was a beautiful, stocky thirteen hands, dark dappled grey and we called him Joey. He was definitely Danae's horse and she took endless pleasure in riding him. He was supposed to have been broken for trap work and so we decided to try him in the lightweight caravan. Having had the experience over blinkers with Daphne, we foolishly put Joey into the shafts without them. Pulling forward, Joey sensed and saw the van moving behind him and, panicking, took off at a flat-out gallop, the van swaying behind him. We watched in some alarm as horse and van receded down the yard until it hit a hollow, and bouncing up in the air, it crashed down on its side, ripping all the tar paper covering.

Joey was not hurt, fortunately, but as usual the harness was in tatters and had to be repaired by our long-suffering saddler, Mr Thorn. Charles Leek who hadn't spoken to us for ten years, turned out to be a tower of strength on this occasion, and helped us right the caravan and repair it. He could not have been nicer. It was almost worth having the accident to have him communicate again. We pulled the caravan round to his house, and he and I stripped all the ripped sisal paper off, down to its frame, and replaced it with new cladding of the same material. To make it taut and waterproof we painted it with green cellulose paint, rather in the same way as tissue on a model aircraft. Although we painted in the open air, I developed a splitting headache from the cellulose fumes and was quite ill and disorientated for a few days. Charles seemed unaffected.

In a week, the van was back on the road. The thin metal-spoked wheels had solid rubber tyres that had been on their last legs on our previous trip, and Mother had managed to find a firm to replace them with new, so the van was now well shod. With great care and some apprehension, Joey was reintroduced to the van, this time with blinkers, and he seemed fine. So off we set, only to find the new hot-rolled tarmacadam surfaces on some of the roads were like an ice rink for a steel-shod horse; poor Joey just could not keep his feet, let alone hold the weight of the van back on an incline. So back home we had to go and ask the local blacksmith to tap and screw in some hardened steel studs on Joey's shoes to enable him to get a grip on the new surfaces. It made all the difference. At Eyeworth camp, Danae offered to get water from the iron well on Joey, and was bucked off on her way back. Mother and I, back at camp, heard a sudden clatter of hooves and Joey arrived full tilt, without Danae. Alarmed we dashed down the track to look for her, and found a rather subdued, slightly concussed Danae, all gory from gravel cuts where she had hit her head on the hard track. Being ignorant then of possible problems arising from blows to the head, we just hoped that a good night's rest would restore Danae to normal, which indeed it did, fortunately! This was probably the last time we went out together as a threesome.

Our next tenants, during the time my mother taught in France, were a young couple called Ricki and Muriel Santi. He was a brash, flash, handsome man of Italian extraction, with a gold-toothed smile, and she was a pretty red head. With them came a young man called Sid Finch, a Whitechapel secular Jew. When the threesome first arrived, they determined to make their living from a woodwork business. To this end the upstairs room became the workshop. It soon became apparent that Sid was the craftsman, Ricki's role being to speculate on the fortune they were going to make on the business, and sandpaper a few items now and again in a desultory way. Sid made a run of two dozen bookends as a starter, and Ricki tried unrealistically to sell them door-to-door locally, going round on my mother's old bicycle. He managed to sell a couple of pairs at most, and the whole project, ill-conceived in the first place, came to a grinding halt.

Ricki eventually got a job in the local garage and whiled away his time strumming his guitar and painting large oil canvasses of a pregnant Muriel in the nude. Muriel, whom we later discovered had a diploma in domestic science, swanned about the house in a negligée or dressing gown, getting away with the minimum domesticity possible, without the house becoming a total tip. Sid, who in the first few weeks realised that as long as he was about he would be skivvy for all of them, soon decamped to Olive's house on The Ridge, where for a honeymoon period he became her toy boy, then her handyman partner for several years.

The Santis stayed on through the summer, and all the goats, at first milked in a haphazard manner, were soon left to their own devices. The chickens too, either dying of starvation or fox attack. Ricki, inclined to have a hot temper, lost his job, and he and Muriel, living on the dole, growing disillusioned with the simple life, just upped and left in mid-supper. When Mother, Danae and I met up for the Christmas holidays and entered the house, it was like going on board the *Marie Celeste*. The dining table was covered in dishes and pots and pans from a half-finished meal, mould and decay covering every dish. It reminded me of Dickens' description of Miss Faversham's wedding feast, left for decades to decomposition, rats and spiders. The Santis had taken on a puppy and the evidence of his occupation was everywhere, under tables, on carpets, under and on beds. The whole place stank to high heaven and we had to have a bonfire of many of the furnishings. For months afterwards, an odour peculiar to the Santis remained, to remind us of their notorious occupation. They left behind most of Ricki's oil paintings and a Brownie box camera, and had the nerve later on to bill my mother for them when they still owed six months rent.

The Santis reneged on all their promises. The old goats had died of neglect and the remainder Mother, with our help, rounded up and had humanely killed. On opening the chicken house we found dead starved skeletons. It was a strange home coming, and quite an eye opener into human callousness and moral irresponsibility. Mother had only charged the couple 2/6d a week of which she might have seen 10/- for all the months they were there. The only positive aspect about our home-coming was being able to take charge again of our tatty old home, and for myself to have Mother and Danae back again in the country.

There was an amusing sequel to the Santi episode. Mother used to take a Sunday tabloid newspaper, *The People* of all publications, mainly because one of its contributors to a weekly column was a man called Hannen Swaffer, who was a Spiritualist - surprise, surprise! Five years later, looking at the large newspaper, there was a bold spread, an article headed: *"BARROW BOY MAKES GOOD! Barrow boy Ricki Santi has painting accepted by Royal Academy. For forty-two year old Ricki, for five years a barrow vendor and self-trained amateur artist, it's a dream come true. "I was gob smacked when the selectors gave me the news," said Ricki modestly. "I always had faith that my Ricki would hit the jackpot one day," said his wife, petite, red-haired 32-year-old Muriel. "I am so pleased for him." The couple plan to celebrate in a modest way, but fame is not going to their heads. "I could never leave the Barrow and me mates," said Ricki, "Its a way of life, you see," he added philosophically."* We read all this with great merriment, knowing what we did of the couple and I still smile when I think of it. ❧

Chapter 48
Paul, Olive and Romany Tan
Danae enters Sidcot

About the same time as I went to Sidcot, Olive's son Paul, who had an exceptional treble voice, won a singing scholarship to Westminster Cathedral Choir School.

René and Gretta McKeogh, his long-time guardians, were instrumental in getting him there. The two women had a recording made of Paul singing the boy's treble classic made famous by Ernest Lush, *Oh, For The Wings Of A Dove*, and Paul's rendition of it was almost as good. Olive, who had shown no interest in Paul as her child, fell in love with his recording enjoying the reflected kudos. This expressed itself in a sudden honey sweetness to Paul, who was totally nonplussed, but thankful not to be on the receiving end of the cruel side of her nature for once. I think it was with a certain amount of relief that he left a home in which there was precious little love and took up the life of a chorister.

The domestic situation between my mother and Olive continued to be pretty scratchy, so that when Olive expressed a wish to buy a piece of land and put up her own house on The Ridge, Mother jumped at the idea and, for £100, sold her a couple of acres along the road, a few hundred yards from us. A sectional wooden building was bought that had been a large, deep litter chicken house, and Alf Chalk was employed to put it up. The land on which the house was to be built was an old gravel pit, and it fell away rather sharply, so the house had to be supported on tall cement pillars on the lower side. Alf Chalk made all the pillars by hand from gravel on the site, mixing the cement with a shovel and tamping it down into hand-made shuttering. This was just pre-1947 before the first building restrictions came into force, so more or less any building could erected.

Olive had the interior of the house divided into six or so poky bedrooms, each with their own tiny open fireplace. The intention was to take paying patients for treatment with her flower remedies. A four thousand gallon underground tank was constructed for rainwater storage, no mains supply having arrived yet. A flush lavatory was installed that used four gallons of water to flush it. As all water had to be pumped up by hand to a header tank for household use as well as flushing the lavatory, Olive, or any patients she had in the house, had to put in an hour's pumping each day to keep up with demand. To add to her difficulties, the interior of the underground tank had not been rendered with a strong enough mix of cement to make it leak proof, so in spite of its size, Olive was always running short of water.

Olive always had impractical pretensions to grandeur that her constantly precarious financial situation could never realise or sustain. She was going to build stables and a coach house, and God knows what else, but the house took all her spare cash, and her dream never materialised. She called the house, typically enough, Romany Tan (today it is known as Saltings). Strange, neurotic women came to stay there, seeking cures for various maladies, mostly psychological cases, who drifted around like lost Ophelias or Pre-Raphaelite Beatrices. Be-sandalled and often nude, long hair flowing, they wandered about in abstracted manner amongst the gorse. We children, in our play during the holidays, would sometimes come on them by chance and flush them, startled, out of their reverie. Romany Tan and its weird occupants were quite a source of entertainment and mild scandal locally.

It was a blessed relief to our mother when Olive left to live in her own home, taking her destructive son, Julian with her. The realities of Olive having to manage her own home and the practicalities it entailed, must have been a rude awakening.

We stayed at Olive's that Christmas in reasonable harmony, as Olive in her own 'manor house', a status she gave Romany Tan in her mind, put her in an expansive friendly mood. Paul, back for Christmas holidays, once again assumed the role of cheerful factotum, his choir school education making him more than ever into a polite conformer. In the summer holidays, we still hired boats together and swam. His cousins Densham and Rita Stone, and their parents, used to come from Bristol and stay for a time, sometimes picnicking with us. But we were not so close as before, so different our educations, and as we reached our mid-teens we drifted apart. Paul's education was autocratic and Catholic-based and it made him very conventional and conforming, whereas I was passing through a non-conformist phase, rebelling at all society's values and being a regular arrogant pain in the neck!

In the autumn of 1947, Danae too entered Sidcot, a much more travel-toughened worldly-wise individual than I had been. Although we did many things together at home, strangely we virtually never spoke to each other at school. It was not through lack of affection, just that the school ethos seemed to engender a studied indifference between siblings, accentuated by having a girls and boys side to the school.

1947 saw me into the Lower Fifth and beginning to enjoy school life as much as I ever would. Our form master was Dick Harman (or RAH), who had been long enough at Sidcot to become an institution. He was a gruff old fellow with a kind heart, but I found his scripture lessons very dry. He was an inveterate pipe smoker and helped give the Masters' common room its yellow tinge and distinct stale smell. His own private room and study was close to one of the main dormitories, and I remember one evening we were all called up one by one from prep to visit his study for a homily on the dangers of masturbation. Of course, each boy on his return from RAH, gave us the lowdown on what had transpired, so we had a pretty good idea of what to expect. When my turn came I knocked on his study door and RAH's gruff voice bade me enter. The room seemed extra full of smoke that evening as RAH gruffly interrogated me on my masturbatory proclivities. "Ever heard of onanism?" was his muttered opening salvo. "How many times a week?" he barked. "Once, twice, three times, how many?"

"Oh, I would say about once a month, Sir," I hastily stammered lying through my teeth as all the others had done. RAH seemed visibly relieved that I had even admitted to the unmentionable vice, and became less strained during the remainder of the brief interview which was given over to the damage I would do myself both morally and physically, if I 'over indulged', ending with a homily on dedication to the work ethic. It was, in retrospect, a fairly typical social attitude of the day that masturbation should be seen as 'self defilement or self abuse', making it an issue of which one ought to be ashamed.

Dick Harman was an excellent bat at cricket, a game I was never a fan of except when bowling. At bat I was a 'haymaker', all or nothing, usually nothing. I just couldn't master a 'straight bat'; maybe because I could never subscribe to colonial mores either! RAH used to coach us for slip fielding by throwing the ball onto the rounded surface of the pitch roller, from which it would glance off viciously in all directions, testing the speed of our reflexes. I hated this exercise as it left one with bruised and swollen fingers from mistimed catches. Fielding was catastrophic on my fingernails as, in the boredom of the occupation, I unconsciously tended to chew them. I would go into a pastoral doze in the sunshine until an anguished cry of "Charman! *BALL!*" would wake me out of my bored torpor too late to stop the flying ball from reaching the boundary, amid groans of despair from my peers.

Swimming was my sporting summer passion, from the allotted two-minute dip first thing before breakfast, to the twenty-minute session in the afternoon each day. I went in for, and gained, all the life-saving awards that were available because it gave me access to the pool. For the Silver award, one was required to swim a mile in clothes, complete with collar held on with a stud, tie and cuff links, after which, without rest, you undressed, treading water. It was a challenge I loved as it was all well within the range of my physical abilities. I even mastered the academic theory of the circulatory system of the heart and other bits of knowledge necessary for resuscitating half-drowned persons. Mouth-to-mouth resuscitation was not in the Royal Life Saving Society manual at that time. ❦

Chris, standing first from left, joined the ranks of Prefects in the Sixth Form and below, seated second row, fourth from left, had become a keen rugby player.

Chapter 49
The Fifth Form - School and Home

With Dick Harman producing, the Lower Fifth put on an end of term play called *Ambrose Applejohn's Adventure* (by Walter Hackett). It was a rather naïve three-act fantasy about an unambitious middle-class individual, who dreams himself into a pantomime piratical world.

I played the boring half of the character and Teddy Moar, the masterful dreamer pirate. Whenever he got to the point of ravishing the dusky maiden he had just captured with the opening exclamation of: "Now will I have that kiss!", Teddy would tail off with embarrassment and whine: "Oh Sir, do I have to yet?" RAH would puff on his pipe in exasperation and shout: "Go on Moar, don't hang about. Give the girl a smacker!" and the rest of us would cheer derisively. It was a strange inhibition from a member of our form whose amorous exploits were to become the stuff of school legend. To Anne Lloyd, a delightfully ample lass, who took the part of the dusky maiden and who could be made to blush at the slightest provocation, Teddy's prevarication was very unfair and made her burn with embarrassment.

At home, our Russian Estonian refugee, Hilda Sass, was still with us for holidays. Our home was her home, and we had grown up knowing her as Auntie. She was a heavy smoker getting through forty cigarettes a day, and she enjoyed alcohol. She was twenty-one years older than I, and her catering qualifications, allied to household management, had gained her entry to several schools where her expertise was highly valued. Her social life was always a bit limited to her friendship with the Collins' daughters at Four Winds, Margaret and Kay, and Freda Grover, a great niece of my father. Hilda never seemed to have any luck with her men friends, all of them turning out to be, in the parlance of the times, 'Rotters'. In 1947 she made the acquaintance of a florid-faced local farmer called Edsall; we knew him as Duncan. Hilda used to visit him each evening at his farm over the hill at Hale, and come back with large pats of homemade butter he had given her. A romance seemed to be in the offing, and just as everything looked as though it was going to be rosy, Hilda became pregnant. Duncan rapidly distanced himself from the situation, denying paternity, and leaving poor Hilda high and dry, expecting a child.

In 1947 attitudes to illegitimacy were still censorious and judgementally loaded against women. Mother, in spite of having Danae and myself technically out of wedlock, was still taken aback by Hilda's 'condition', but she did her best for her in the event. To shield Hilda from local prejudice, she sent her to London to have her child and convalesce under the competent eagle eye of Helen Rutter, Cuthbert's wife, now widowed. The babe was small, but healthy; a six-pound girl Hilda christened Jennifer. It was a traumatic time for Hilda who was terrified that the social stigma of illegitimacy might focus on her in a judgemental way back in Godshill. She would not go out to the shop locally for some time, for fear of losing face. However back amongst us on The Ridge, where we all accepted the situation without comment, Hilda soon felt at ease. She found a good job in Fordingbridge, catering in a guest house and tea shop in the High Street called St Ives Café. This gave her enough income to pay for her cigarettes and their keep.

So our mother, after experiencing her first bit of freedom, felt it incumbent upon herself, at the age of fifty-two, to take on the role of full-time child minder to little Jennifer. This task she undertook cheerfully with her usual conviction that someone somewhere out in 'the great beyond' was saying: "This is your role for the foreseeable future and all is well". Indeed, little Jenny was a happy addition to our household. In the early years, Jenny was so much with my mother she referred to her as Mum. Sometimes Mother would sing

Land of Hope and Glory in a cracked voice and Jenny would go into immediate despair, flinging her arms around her neck and plaintively wailing: "Where are you, Mum?" The persona Mother presented by her rendering of the patriotic song must have turned her into an alien being in Jenny's eyes! Hilda, coming home from work used to bring us some of her beautifully decorated little fancy cakes once a week, which made tea time extra special. As Jenny grew to secondary school age, Hilda was able to find cook and housekeeping jobs in good private boarding schools and have Jenny educated at half fees.

Hilda and Jenny in their garden. Mother had become child-minder to Jenny - 'a happy addition to our household'.

So time moved on and I found myself in the Upper Fifth at Sidcot. We were the last form in the school to take the lower school certificate exams before 'O' and 'A' levels were introduced. In these reminiscences, I am alarmed at how little I can remember of the subjects I took. English literature and language certainly, biology and zoology. I am pretty sure I had dropped physics and chemistry, certainly Latin and maths. That left history, art and French. In all, five subjects. I enjoyed English, because I always enjoyed our English master Ivan Grey, a large man, rather in the Vaughan Williams mode, who made poetry come alive for me by purchasing sets of eighteen records from the London Library of Recorded English. These contained poetry readings by such noted poets and actors as Dylan Thomas, Cecil Day Lewis, James Stephens, Cecil Trouncer, Pauline Letts, Richard Harris, to name but a few. Although they were only scratchy 78s, they brought poetry alive for me, transforming my callow, lukewarm appetite into an avid desire to hear more.

The music of language became an inspiration for me for the first time and has never left me. It is no exaggeration to say it was a revelation and I owe much to Ivan Grey for introducing me to the spoken word. I heard that after he left Sidcot in the early 'fifties he took up the headship of Bootham, the boys' Quaker school to which John Ransome, my buddy in the lower school, had been transferred. Sadly, Ivan Grey died prematurely of a heart attack while in his prime.

Zoology and biology were quite fun too, especially in the classes when we took our vasculums, a botanical box, under our arms and made forays up the combe to collect specimens of flora and fauna in the study of the ecology of the area. The time came when we learnt all about the biological aspect of reproduction, beginning with the earthworm and ending with human. It was all so clinical, it seemed totally divorced from the totality of human relationships, but I suppose it served its purpose exam-wise. We knew the basic mechanics of sex anyway from the most borrowed book in the library, *Sex And Marriage*, written by a couple named Barns who had both their children at the school. Looking back on that side of our education, I cannot help feeling we would have benefited a great deal more if we had learnt something of love and the psychology of relationships in relation to our sexuality. Some education in marriage and parenting would not have gone amiss either. I am amazed that this most crucial aspect of our lives is so left to chance. I am lucky to have such a good partner to share my life with, but we could have done with some insights into parenting rather than depend so much on trial and error, perhaps making our children victims of our own negative influences. Then, maybe, some of the repeated mistakes and patterns in all relationships could be modified or broken for the eventual benefit of society at large in its quest for balance and harmony, and thus happiness.

Unlike Danae, who had the advantage of learning colloquial French as a youngster, I was useless. I lacked motivation and that engendered laziness. I never had a hope at school certificate French and I didn't care. To give pupils a chance, there was an oral exam as well as the written, which those of dubious ability were encouraged to take. I was given a passage to read which, because I had a good ear for language, I was able to tackle with a fluency that totally belied my ignorance of the content. *"Tres bon, c'est magnifique!"*, said the cheerful little French examiner, who then proceeded to quiz me on my comprehension of the passage. He soon found out I was a complete ignoramus and we finished the interview in English talking about school life in general. History, and my relations with Mr Russell, I have already described, and my subsequent credit in the actual exam, after coaching from Mary Hooper. Art was no problem either, and I felt confident of a pass in English. We had mock exams at the end of the spring term. I can only remember passing in Art and English and getting a famous 0% for my history paper, which had great red lines and the word 'illegible' scrawled across it.

In the summer term we sat the exams proper. I failed English language but passed in literature. For art I managed a credit, a pass in biology, a credit in history, a fail in French. In those days you automatically failed to get your school certificate if you fluffed English language. So that was it. Ivan Grey was mystified. Mother, to her credit never berated me and thus never undermined my self-confidence for enjoyment of living, assuring me that there was more to life than academic status! ꕤ

Chapter 50
Ten Green Bottles in Cologne, Tamsin and the Upper Fifth

In retrospect, my fifteenth year was great fun, encompassing many new experiences. In the spring term of 1948, through the school, I arranged to join a Youth Hostelling Association work party to Cologne in Germany.

My companions, Michael Pittard, his girlfriend Tamsin Heardman and I travelled to London where we stayed in a hostel overnight, and trained and ferried our way to what remained of the once great Rhineland town. We were billeted in an old German bunker, or air raid shelter, that the German YHA were converting into a youth hostel. It was quite a job as the walls of the bunker were built of reinforced concrete, three metres thick, strong enough to survive a direct hit. With infinite patience and labour, workmen were blasting and boring holes through the walls for windows and doors, and dividing up the interior for accommodation to house 200 young people.

We were allocated to a gang digging trenches to take cables, drains and water mains, heavy but enjoyable work. We never got used to the long-handled heart-shaped shovel, but it did come in handy when the trench was six foot deep. With typical Teutonic precision, the spoil from the trenches was thrown out in separate heaps according to the strata we were working on, and it went back in the same order. Our workmates, the local Germans, were cheerful, friendly and hard-working. Part of the bunker had already been converted to accommodation when we arrived, and was up and running with a bunch of hostellers from all over the world.

Chris, front left, in Cologne working with local Germans to convert a bunker into a youth hostel.

For breakfast, we were given a roll, with jam, and a cup of acorn coffee. On this continental breakfast we did a full morning's manual work, having a substantial meal at midday, usually a vegetable pottage with lots of potatoes. The warden was an outgoing enthusiastic man in his forties. He was very musical, and played the violin with gusto each evening, when he led a sing-song in a bunker close by which had been converted into a community and concert hall. The hostel had an intercom system, and each new contingent of hostellers arriving were usually persuaded to sing a national song relating to their country, which was broadcast over the system. The Germans were noticeably the most literate musically, often singing their folk songs in four-part harmony, whereas the British, if they managed anything at all, it was usually *Ten Green Bottles*, a very meagre offering. Our German warden rehearsed and conducted the concerts of folk song himself, using his hands to indicate an imagined tonic sol-fa by pointing at different levels to indicate the notes. It was quite effective. As soon as we had the tune, he would pick up his violin and accompany us, occasionally stopping his playing to conduct us with his bow.

In the men's dormitory we had an odd, middle-aged Yorkshire man who always seemed to be 'mashing tea' of which he consumed gallons. He was a skiver when it came to work and did nothing but talk. He never washed his feet or socks, so you could always tell when he entered a room without looking up. Added to that anti-social aspect, he also snored. He seemed impervious to the close proximity of his offending 'cheeses' or our blunt allusions to it. In the end we all bedded down as far away as possible from him. He didn't seem to mind. We often worked with two Germans, Hans, a fair-haired giant who had an attractive girlfriend in the Wagner mould called Gerta, and Max, a darker, fine-boned athlete, both men over six foot. They were employed as helpers and administrators to the warden. A wild, scraggy cornstalk of an Australian called Scorsby, visiting the hostel, fancied his chances with Gerta one night. Invading her sleeping quarters he was confronted by the bulk of Hans; Scorsby beat a hasty tactical retreat, muttering that he must have got his bearings muddled!

One evening, the work party paid a visit to a bar. It was my first visit to such a place, and my introduction to alcohol and German beer. I was shocked by the bawdy population at the dimly lit counter. Naïve prude that I must have seemed to everyone else, I refused to drink and just observed, with growing disquiet, Tamsin getting very drunk, tearful and maudlin. Michael wanted to stay on with the rest of the party and asked me, as I didn't seem to be enjoying myself, to see that Tamsin got back to the hostel safely, which I did, feeling disgusted and sorry for her at the same time. She was sick several times in the street before we got back to the hostel, and was wan and contrite the next day.

Poor Tamsin. She was the younger of two Yorkshire sisters, and her sibling Belinda, a solid powerful lass, two forms above me, married a Yorkshire Dales farmer. Their mother was an expert in gynaecology and child birth, and travelled round giving lectures to schools. When Tamsin was about fifteen, her mother died of a brain haemorrhage and she was left desolate and inconsolable. At that stage of my life, under the influence of Mother, I was a believer in an afterlife, and I remember Tams talking to me of her grief and trying to hang onto that illusory concept. Nowadays I realise one cannot bypass grief and pain at bereavement. All that we know of a personality, their spirit, their warmth, their love, is transmitted through physical presence. When that decays and dies and we are left behind, part of us dies too in the face of its finality. What remains can only live as long as memory survives.

Tamsin, unstable at the best of times, never really recovered from her mother's death. She was a brilliant and natural runner; no other girl could touch her in the sprints. She was neurotic, affectionate, impulsive and wild. Leaving school at the end of the Upper Fifth, she appeared at an Old Scholars' reunion that I attended when my two children were infants. It was the same Tamsin, aged beyond her years but with the same spirit animating her now lined face. She greeted me like a long lost friend in the mêlée of the President's tea in the dining room, throwing her arms round my neck. To my everlasting shame, I momentarily stepped back in embarrassment. In that second she sensed rejection, the light went out of her face and she looked an old woman. She told me she was just recovering from a nervous breakdown and a bout of alcoholism. On my inquiry as to how she was at the moment she replied with a sad smile. "Oh, I have died a bit since you last saw me, I've died a bit."

That was the last time I saw or spoke to her, and I heard a few years later that she had died of alcohol poisoning. Poor, poor girl, poor woman. I kick out in bed at night sometimes in shame at my crass, self-centred insensitivity at Tamsin's insecurity on that day. A warm hug from me in return might have made some difference to her sense of self worth, instead of reinforcing rejection. Another part of me says, by way of ameliorating my conscience, that the seeds of her own destruction were there by that time anyway, but if I am honest that is a feeble excuse. Tamsin inspired friendship and also tried the patience of those close to her. I know Michael Pittard was pushed to the limit by her irrational behaviour. He exhibited a great patience and love in the face of her persistent neuroses. If I felt a kinship with any of the girls in our form it was with her, though I never expressed it at the time. Maybe I felt protective more than anything; she was very much a little girl lost.

Cologne was still a shell of a city, the saturation bombing had reduced most of it to rubble, apart from the cathedral which stood in magnificent isolation amongst the ruins, a testament either to God's intervention, or a result of good luck. It was said that the Allied bombers deliberately avoided the cathedral, but it is hard to believe that anything but luck was on their side, aiming from a height of 35,000 feet. On our time off at weekends, I went swimming in the Rhine, about a quarter of a mile wide at the point where it flowed through the town. The current was so strong you had to get in the river a quarter of a mile upstream from where you wished to finish up, and that was after swimming diagonally against the current. It did not do to study the river water too closely, as a number of pipes along the banks were discharging raw sewage. However, being young it did not deter me, although I must confess that I kept my mouth firmly shut as I swam across. I made the mistake of hitching a ride on one of the numerous 100-foot long barges plying the river, covering myself in the most obnoxious greasy muck while trying to obtain a toe-hold. I also remember a fair on the edge of the river. We took a ride at night on the Chair-o-Planes which spinning so fast lifted us almost horizontal to gaze in wonder at the reflections of the lights of the fair in the dark waters of the Rhine. Tamsin, just for extra kicks, deliberately twisted the slender chains supporting her chair, scaring the living daylights out of Michael and myself. She was yelled at, in a torrent of German invective, by one of the fairground 'roustabouts'.

It was a great two weeks work and sight-seeing. We visited a factory making cars and wondered how anyone could work in such a noisy environment and retain their hearing and sanity. The neon lights of the famous scent factory flashed and flickered across the river each night, in a city fast coming back to life after its near annihilation. We bought all the usual tourist rubbish; bright little felt caps to which we attached badges and baubles. I bought a tiny, single octave, harmonica and had great fun seeing how many tunes I could play without running out of notes. We browsed among the market stalls and watched a street vendor selling a patent ointment, guaranteed to get rid of hard calluses and skin on one's hands. A burly workman, with horny hands, was trying an application of the ointment and after a two-minute wait all the callus was scraped away, like magic, and he was left with soft pink hands. I wondered how he faired the next day when he went back to work with shovel and pick.

On our last evening at the hostel, the English put on a review created by Scorsby, our Aussi free-wheeler. We read it from scripts, and though funny to us, it only produced a puzzled silence from our German friends. We sang *Ten Green Bottles* for the last time, and with loads of black coffee inside us, we caught the midnight train to France. I remember Tamsin went to sleep with her head on Michael's lap with her thumb in her mouth like a small girl. I watched a newly-married couple opposite us in the carriage; he, rather a dingy young man, carrying all the copious luggage, she a lovely teutonic blond, forever looking at herself in a tiny hand mirror and touching up her already perfect make-up. He didn't smoke, but she did, he, anticipating her need for a light, diving into his coat pocket for a lighter. He clearly adored her, watching her every move. She, for her part, assumed a studied, cold indifference to his constant attentions. She looked tired of her man already. How long would their relationship last, I wondered.

I said goodbye to Michael and Tamsin at Tilbury and caught the last train to Southampton, arriving in the dark too late for the last bus back home. I walked to the other side of Totton and slept peacefully under a hayrick until dawn, walking home in the early morning sunshine. In retrospect, it was an interesting adventure, seeing at first hand the terrible whirlwind that the Germans had reaped in the war, and witnessing the indomitable spirit of the ordinary people rebuilding in the face of such total destruction.

Back at school, I had joined the choir and was taking singing lessons from Miss Bloomfield, a cheerful, good-natured lady who had a fine soprano singing voice. She sang most weeks in assembly. Her choice of songs nearly always had a high note at some point, which in the past she may well have been able to reach easily, but now was an only too obvious struggle. The whole school waited with bated breath for her to fluff the note, which she did more frequently each year.

Miss Bloomfield was, in school girl parlance, known as a 'Good Sport' and one could always appeal to her lenient nature. My sister has a recollection of 'Blommy' accosting her, and another sparky girl, after midnight in the school gardens and inquiring what they were doing out so late at night. Quick as a flash, my sister's companion had, with a cheeky smile, countered the enquiry with the rejoinder: "And what, pray might you be doing at this late hour?" Apparently the sheer effrontery of this repost tickled Miss Bloomfield's sense of humour, and after telling the two girls to return to bed, the misdemeanour was never reported.

I learned many songs from Blommy, from Lisa Lehmann's *Myself When Young* from *In a Persian garden* by Omar Khayyam, to John Ireland's setting of Masefield's *Sea Fever*, and Purcell's *If Music Be The Food Of Love*. My favourite however, though I could rarely do it full justice, was *Silent Noon*, a love poem by Dante Gabriel Rossetti, set to music by Vaughan Williams. It celebrates an unforgettable moment in time for two lovers lying in the exquisite pastoral of water meadows in high summer. Vaughan Williams is always at his best in interpreting the sacramental aspects of the natural world, and this song is no exception. It is also heart-movingly English in its essence. I love it!

The choir sang Bach's *Peasant Cantata* at a General meeting concert given by the school, in which I sang a solo. It included recitative. It was a nerve-racking ordeal to sing in front of so many people, and I added to my stress by trying to get out of wearing a tie and other formal clothing. John Russell collared me trying to sneak out to the school hall in informal garb, and frog-marched me back to change into something more formal. "Charman, you look like a rat catcher in that garb, get changed properly," he ordered. I arrived on stage fuming and found singing *Good Fellows, Be merry!* somewhat difficult, anger and natural nerves drying my throat. Nerves played havoc with any solo singing I did in public, and I was never able to give of my best on these occasions. The *Peasant Cantata* was a success in spite of my poor efforts, and the audience were not too critical. After the concert I ranted about dress and convention to my mother who was visiting and camping in the combe. She listened tolerantly until I had vented my anger and then offered me some strawberries!

When Violet Tricky, and her faithful helper, Miss Borbank, finally retired, school cooking and dinners went through a crisis. Cooks were coming and going like yo-yo's; even David Murray Rust's wife had to take charge at one point. No one knew the temperamental nature of the school steam ovens like Violet and Miss Borbank, and to get a stodge of a light consistency was a rarity. On one occasion, the puddings dished up were two inches high of uncooked suet dough. We ate the plum jam round the sides and the rest went back to the kitchen waste bins to feed the local farmer's pigs.

The school had a rota for washing up which fell mostly to the girls, while the boys were relegated to the scullery to scour all the pots, pans and trays. I remember a domestic member of staff, a tiny lady called Maggie with gaps where her front teeth used to be, being in charge of us. She was a kind, cheerful and tolerant, talkative old soul and we boys got on well with her. The sinks in the scullery were made of teak and looked a hundred years old, with sheet lead surrounds. How we didn't get lead poisoning I don't know, as much of the school plumbing was of lead also. Cleaning pans involved a lot of scouring with caustic soda that left one's hands dry, red and sore. We were always glad when our stint of scullery duty was over, and never gave a thought that for old Maggie it was a never-ending job.

Sometimes, in the summer term, we had to skin great cauldrons of beetroots for salads. This was fun as we evolved a technique for getting the skins off by squeezing the beet between our hands. The beetroot would squib out of our grasp leaving the skin behind, more often than not scudding across the scullery floor in the process! We just swilled the rogue beetroots under the cold tap and off they went to be sliced with the others. "What the eye does not see, the heart does not grieve over", as the saying goes.

Mother generously gave me a new bicycle when I reached the Upper Fifth form. It was a Raleigh roadster with hub dynamo lights and a four-speed Sturmey Archer hub gear. Having a bike transformed my weekends, as it did for many other pupils. We could get further afield, to places like Cheddar and Weston-super-Mare, and at half term, Glastonbury and Wells. Best of all, I could dispense with the train at the end of term and cycle the seventy-two miles home. Starting at seven, in the early mist of morning, passing through the sleepy little Mendip villages to the Wiltshire towns of Frome and Warminster, was magical, and when I glimpsed the spire of Salisbury Cathedral, I knew I was within striking distance of home and dinner, and my heart sang. It was, in fact, faster to cycle than to go by train.

Michael Cox and I started collecting photographs of film stars. This was the period when Hollywood glamour was at its zenith, with stars like Rita Hayworth, Betty

Grable, Ingrid Bergman, Dorothy Lamour, Jean Simmonds and many others. Michael actually wrote to Jean Simmonds saying he was a fan, and she sent him an autographed photograph of herself, or her agent did! This was much prized in our collection. Jean Simmonds played the part of Stella in the film of *David Copperfield*, shown one half-term, and we were all mad about her. We filled a whole scrap book with these glamorous, artificial beauties of the film industry, and amassed about 200 glossy photographs.
Like all crazes, it died a natural death as our interests changed. Michael enjoyed the unattainable glamour of the stars and was less critical of their manufactured artificiality than I was, so in the end I gave my shares in the album to him and the collecting stopped. Popular music of the day came from great American musicals like *Annie Get Your Gun* or *Oklahoma*. Ballads were the popular choice and 'rock' was unheard of. Danny Kaye had just made a name for himself in films, and I scandalised the classic sensibilities and priorities of my friend Alan McCombie, by buying all the Danny Kaye records I could lay my hands on in Weston's record shop. I have the records still, and now they must be something of a novelty.

In the Upper Fifth, we boys acquired a small room up a flight of stairs to the side of the gym which we used as an exclusive social centre. It had a gas ring for heating up food, a table and a few chairs, and we called it 'The Swamp'. On Saturday evenings we would heat up baked beans and other schoolboy fodder to sustain our ever-hungry selves. We tried to make up some basic ground rules for keeping the place tidy, but people like Teddy were notorious for never cleaning utensils and, for a lot of the time, the Swamp lived up to its name and was pretty slummy! Being out of the way it was also a place of privacy for current couples to indulge in a bit of heavy 'snogging', away from the MOD.

At about this time, the school received a visit from the school inspectors, to assess the quality of the teaching, and general education standards. Inspectors sat in on classes and all the extra curricular activities and the cooking and kitchens were inspected. On that particular day, sods law was in full operation. We had mince for dinner and it was 'off', no doubt about it! We could smell it as we entered the dining hall. The Headmaster, Mary Hooper, and the inspector, sat at the top table. We had silence and, contrary to the usual burst of conversation that followed, there was not a murmur. Then one by one the waiters began to take the bad meat back to the slide in the kitchen. It was an eloquent, silent protest. I am still amazed that the cooks of the time were not aware of the situation in the course of the preparation of the meal. I don't know what the outcome was, but I guess it was suggested some form of refrigeration was needed.

An inspector came and sat in on our choir practice. I think we were learning some Elgar at the time. Mr Bains was doing his best, and we were all going great guns when the inspector, a pompous little man, rapped the top of the piano and barked out rudely at Mr Bains: "Right ho, Sir Thomas, I will take over now!", and proceeded to conduct us to the end of the piece. Mr Grey was spitting with anger and indignation that the inspector should treat Mr Bains in such a cavalier fashion and I could hear him muttering: "I'll give him Sir Thomas!" Our sympathies were with Mr Bains, the arrogant rudeness of the pompous inspector was inexcusable. Whatever the report from the inspectors, it cannot have been too bad. ❦

Right: Chris with the first bread crock he made at Godshill Pottery.

Chapter 51
The Wrens

For the first three weeks of the 1948 summer holidays I was a guest of the Wrens, my mother and father's old potter friends from the Artist Craftsman exhibition days.

The Wrens founded their 'Studio Pottery' in 1912, one of the first of its kind in the country. At the house they had built in Oxshott, Surrey, Denise Wren, a large woman, with enormous vigour, drive and enthusiasm, had run pottery courses each summer with her husband, Henry. He had died, but she and her daughter Rosemary still ran the courses. Mother had written to Denise, telling her of my ambition to become a potter, and she had responded with a kind and enthusiastic letter:

"Dear Christoper P,
We would love to have you stay, and if we can offer any of our help and expertise toward you realising your ambition to be a Potter, we will be only too pleased to help. It's a vocation, so don't expect to become rich from it. There will be lean times and good times.   *With kind regards, Denise Wren."*

Oxshott was a comparatively small village then, with just the beginnings of urban development. 'Potters Croft' was in a pot-holed, gravelled side lane, Oakshade Road. Henry and Denise had designed their bungalow themselves. It had overtones of Ruskin, Morris and Sir Archibald Knox in its design and structure. The concrete floor had attractive coloured Art Nouveau patterns let in on the corners of the main living-cum-all purpose room, sadly faded by the time I saw them.

Denise had an aviary of small birds that she adored, and was also a great authority on bees. Like my mother, at one time she had kept goats. Although a meat eater, she had a Buddhist attitude to all living things, even to invading wasps, which if they entered the house, she would capture in a jam jar and carry outside, saying they were all part of life. For me, 'Potters Croft' was paradise.

Denise could not have been more welcoming, generous or encouraging, giving me almost total freedom in the pottery, which consisted of an agglomeration of disorganised sheds and lean-tos, part of which was designated as Denise's workshop and the other for her lively twenty-five-year-old daughter, Rosemary. Rosemary had just finished at Art College and was busy setting up her own workshop. Denise was employing a thrower while I was there, to make vases that she fired to stoneware temperatures in a venerable old gas kiln. She was using a rich, opaque, turquoise glaze at that time which tended to run and weld the vases to the shelves, so there was a lot of grinding and tidying up of ware and shelves after each firing.

One of the summer courses was in full swing when I arrived, and it was interesting to watch the students at work. They came from many different backgrounds and occupations. One young man normally earned his living as a wood worker. His coiled pots were a model of sound construction and design. Most of the people on the course were women teachers, wanting to acquire a basic, working knowledge of the craft to enable them to further their career. I was privileged in that Denise trusted me with the wheel, and I had many happy hours practising, making large fruit bowls with Denise giving constructive critique of my forms and throwing techniques. Her approach to teaching pottery was very much 'try it and see'. She encouraged innovation. Mixing glazes was approached a bit like cooking, with a casualness born of years of experience, bringing what is an exact science into the realms of understanding.

Some students were bold and practical, others tentative and with little self-confidence. Denise was able to inspire even those most lacking in creativity to a standard of work of which they could be proud. The only student she fell out with whilst I was there, was a rather pompous, self-opinionated man of forty or so, called John, the son of a vicar who had taken up pottery and was wanting to polish his throwing skills. The Wrens had just invested in a brand new Bolton wheel for production throwing that had a cone drive. John had prevailed upon Denise, against her better judgment, to let him use the wheel to practice making large pots. Tiny little Rosemary, who had been trained as a thrower under John Colby, could make large two gallon cider jars with ease; it became imperative that student John go one better than her. The Bolton wheel was very expensive, and Denise had laid down a few ground rules as to its careful use. John's efforts to emulate Rosemary's big ware expertise were not very successful, and he grew more and more irritated, and consequently worse and worse, collapsing pot after pot. In anger, he threw a collapsed pot on the floor of the workshop and bits of clay spattered onto the cone drive. In alarm, John tried to wipe off the lumps of clay now interfering with the wheel's smooth transmission, making it slip and bump. He picked up a piece of cloth and tried to wipe the clay off with the cones revolving, winding the cloth all round them, just avoiding getting his fingers trapped. In mounting panic he tried to burn out the rag with a cigarette lighter, and only succeeded in scorching the leather-clad face of the main drive cone, putting a slight flat on it so the wheel ran with a distinct bump. Seeing he had done major damage to the transmission, John, rather than face Mrs Wren, just upped and fled the scene, phoning later to say he had been called away suddenly to nurse his sick mother. Denise was justifiably annoyed and exasperated at his irresponsible behaviour, but was relieved the man had gone.

Denise was born in Adelaide, Australia, her father an inventor of compressed air engines, some models of which she still had in the house and showed me with great pride. He brought the family to England at the turn of the century, where Denise had gone to Kingston Art School, training in design under the strong influence of Archibald Knox, one of the great artist craftsmen of the time. She was always of an innovative nature and a superb draughtswoman, inventing a series of coke-fired kilns for schools, all built, tried and tested at Oxshott. She made comprehensive plans for these, (artistic in themselves), complete with building instructions that she sold to educational establishments and would-be potters wanting to get launched in their own business. Her own old, stand-up kick wheel, for which she had also produced working plans, was made by Mr Mercer, the same flower pot maker in Kingston who made ours. Certainly a woman of many talents.

An old family friend, Miss Scammell, was staying with the Wrens while I was there. A dear old lady, known affectionately as Scam, she had a lovely sense of humour and did not mind in the least if you pulled her leg. "Go on with you, you young rascal," she used to say, exploding with theatrical indignation and laughter at the same time, giving me a shove. She suffered a good deal from a catarrhal condition of the sinuses, for which she used to puff away inexpertly on herbal cigarettes for relief.

"They are supposed to help my complaint, but I sometimes wonder if they don't make it worse," she would complain, holding the cigarette, which smelt like a burning hayrick, at arm's length. I loved old Scam, she was a real dear, and we got on very well.

Firing the little coke-fired kiln was the pinnacle of my stay. It had a fire box that stayed in very low all night to heat the kiln slowly through, and then by judicious stoking the next day and opening of air vents, raking the fire bars to keep them free of clinker, the temperature gradually rose. I was constantly gazing through the spy hole at the pyrometric cone to see if it was starting to bend over, and almost singeing my eyebrows!

At the end of the long living room, Potters Croft had a large fireplace and inglenook. In later years I was to attend an annual Christmas party when the fire burned brightly and Denise, in her hand-woven 'twenties style dress would sail in from the kitchen like a galleon bearing traditional round Christmas puddings that had been cooked in a muslin cloth in her copper. The parties were always fancy dress and had a theme. It was a wonderful occasion, quite Dickensian in character, its warmth of atmosphere always to be remembered and adding to the rich tapestry of life's experiences.

Denise Wren was a great authority on bee-keeping, having several hives of her own. In the early years of the first landslide Labour government after the war, there was a project initiated called the Groundnut Scheme. The Labour government, in its wisdom, decided that certain areas of Kenya, then a British Protectorate, would be just the place to grow peanuts. To this end, huge resources in the way of machinery and fertiliser were shipped out to the colony and large areas of scrub country cleared of its bush, ploughed and sown with groundnuts. Denise Wren had just invented, and was trying out, a new hive for bees that enabled several colonies to live within the confines of one hive, by clever devices employed in the construction that kept the several queen bees apart.

The administrators of the government initiative were wondering how they were going to get all their thousands of acres of groundnut plants pollinated. Through the grapevine of bee-keeping journals they heard of Mrs Wren's innovative new hive, and offered her passage out to Kenya to supervise the organisation of the bee colonies for the pollination aspect of the project. Denise had a great time out in Africa, all at government expense, but in spite of her best efforts, 'the Groundnut Scheme' was destined to be a complete failure and an albatross around the neck of the Labour party. The land chosen to plant out with peanuts was very fragile ecologically and ripping out all the native scrub caused frightening erosion. In relation to the vast resources put into it, the yield of peanuts was pitiful. Like the share cropping in America, it created a dust bowl denuding the area of all its natural flora and fauna. ⚘

Chapter 52
Topsy

Coming back from the Wrens that summer, for the first time in my life I fell hopelessly in love, with a beautiful, long-legged girl with blond hair down to her waist.

I was swimming in the river when I first glimpsed her slender, brown, bikini-clad figure running round the water meadows and her attraction was overwhelming. I, greatly daring, managed to get into conversation with this lovely girl. Happy to talk, she told me her name was Topsy. She exhibited a wild naïvety, mixed with an ambivalent knowingness which, coupled with her looks, made her irresistible.

Encouraged by her smile, I asked her if she would go out horse riding in the Forest with me one evening. She was nervous of horses, but agreed to the proposition never the less, much to my delight. I put her on steady old Daphne while I rode Pixie, another of our ponies, and we went out one lovely summer's evening to Eyeworth Pond, near Fritham. Hitching our mounts to a tree, we made a fire in the surrounding beech woods and lay beside it in the gathering dusk watching the flames and sparks in the darkness of the tree canopy. With heart thumping, I tentatively put my arms round my new found love, and she, oh joy, responded to my embrace, as we exchanged our first gentle kiss. I thought I would never touch the ground again. While the fire crackled and the sparks danced on the ends of the flames, we saw heaven in each other's eyes. That first explosive awakening of the chemistry of attraction was like nothing before or since for me. Of such fragile star dust is first love made, and none the less real for all that.

We spent the rest of that summer holiday totally preoccupied with each other. There was an old Scots pine in the bottom of the rough in which I built a tree house, thatching it with heather and bracken. Topsy and I mooned away many evening and night hours in romantic bliss, listening to the soughing of the breeze in its branches.

Topsy was just sixteen, six months older than I. She had experienced rather an insecure childhood in an interesting and zany family. Her mother Pat wrote children's books, and her father was a travel writer and journalist. He had just abandoned Pat and taken up with another woman, with whom he was now expecting a child. Topsy was the eldest child of three. She had a sister, equally fey and lovely, three years younger, nicknamed Beany because of her long legs. There was also a brother, known as Tempo, who had aspirations to become an artist.

Parting from Topsy at the end of the summer holidays was a terrible wrench and I wrote reams of romantic nonsense to her, expecting reams of the same back, matching my sense of bereavement. Alas, all I got was the occasional odd line or two in her large, round child-like hand, that conveyed nothing of the trauma I felt I was going through. My commitment to a being I had unrealistically invented in my romantic, frustrated, erotic imagination, was complete. I hung on in, hoping for a bit of feedback to deny the reality of it but Topsy's responses became more and more spasmodic, giving me nothing to feed on. She was the realist. In my obsessional longings I was blind to the fact that we had little in common apart from a glorious chemistry of bodies, and that was frustrated by idealistic sexual restraints. All I know is it was agony at the time.

Topsy stayed with Mother, going to Salisbury Art School for a term, and we met again for the Christmas holidays, this time much more restrained on my part. She, well, she was just Topsy, as loving as ever in my company, but without the complications that had invaded my head. I must have appeared very pompous, self-righteous and judgemental.

At this time, Topsy's Dad asked if she would come and help out his new wife on the domestic front as they had a new babe, were expecting another and were unable to cope. So Topsy left, and with that my first passionate attachment ended. I still hold her in great affection and always will, for the memory of that first butterfly-delicate summer of exchanged passionate kisses and the embrace of young golden limbs in the years so long, long ago. ❧

Chapter 53
Sixth Form Life 1949

In the autumn of 1949 I entered the Lower Sixth Form at Sidcot. Murray Rust had asked my mother if she thought I would gain anything of value from staying on, as I seemed at odds with the ethos of the school.

I talked the situation over with Mother and we both came to the conclusion that I had a lot to gain socially from remaining, if nothing else. So I stayed, and the fact that I hadn't passed my school certificate was ignored. I moved on to the full 'A' level syllabus, taking English, biology, zoology and art, not a very onerous work load it must be said. The degree of learning was set at a much more concentrated level than previously; in English the plot of Shakespeare's *Hamlet* was dissected from every angle and precised for comprehension. Ivan Grey and Miss Watts took the classes. Miss Watts, a young new arrival to the teaching staff was easily embarrassed, and Hank (Alan McCombie) used to savour reading purple passages out loud in class from his own unexpurgated versions of Shakespeare's plays, just to watch her blush in discomfiture.

Hank was a character with many talents, sadly no longer with us. A form buddy of great academic ability, he did just enough to get by. In the lower corners of his textbooks, you could find the saga of *Sam's Roadster* in flick animation form, each drawn with painstaking care several hundred times for every back-firing smoke-belching episode. A fan of Picasso, he drew endless versions of the *Weeping Woman*. I too was an inveterate doodler, and Hank became a patron of some of my better sketches, buying them from me for a penny. Another project that demonstrated his growing interest in engineering was the construction of 'Big Dippers', made with great labour from clay. The object was to construct one to enable a marble to travel the whole length of the model. He would be at it for hours, modifying the runs to get it all just right, and prep would go out the window.

A project that attracted a lot of attention was the 'Hummul-Van Hummul and Hummul-Van Boeing' rocket project, where Hank and Richard Kern, a 'rocket technician' collaborated on a space rocket. They bought some firework rockets and installed them in a balsa wood capsule fitted with fins. Richard Kern devised a fuse system to fire the rockets in stages. It took weeks to design and prepare, but at last the launch day arrived and a large body of curious pupils assembled on the combe to witness the Blast Off. Launch coordinator Richard Kern gave us a résumé of the past projects that Hummul-Van Hummul and Boeing had been involved with, and wishing the present project good luck, the Rocket was placed on its launch pad and the touch paper lit. In suspense, we all waited for lift off. The rocket wobbled as the first rockets fired, and it hesitantly rose to a height of ten feet or so. Then a malfunction of the fuse must have occurred, and the remainder of the rockets exploded inside the casing at once, blowing the whole projectile to smoky oblivion! Hummul-Van Hummul and Hummul-Van Boeing sadly shook hands, muttering that they would have to go back to the drawing board, and as there were no more funds for rockets, the project regretfully folded!

In the Sixth Form one was allowed Church leave two or three times a term, as an alternative to Quaker meeting. I enjoyed the moments of silence in between the church ritual, but was intolerant of the rest of the service. If I am to be honest in my recording of this period of my life, my spiritual arrogance was so appalling it makes me cringe. The intolerance of my body language must have ruined the services I attended. "Why go," said my embarrassed peers, "if all you can be is critical." I had been reading of some of the more extreme Roman Catholic indoctrination of its children, with its terrifying concepts of hellfire and damnation, and my reaction had turned me into an equally destructive spiritual fascist. Chastened by my peers, I ceased to vent my arrogance on the poor old C of E, and took to holding Pantheistic Quaker meetings on top of Sidcot hill, inspired by the writings of Richard Jeffries, the nature writer, and his disciple Henry Williamson. At least this had the merit of not hurting anyone, even if against school rules.

I kept up my aero modelling as a hobby and purchased one of the first miniature diesel engines to power model aircraft in the school. A firm called Keil Craft made kits and, every other term, Mother would generously buy me one. The engine was a 1.3cc Mills Diesel, and I made an aircraft in which to fit it called a Scorpion. This I brought back home to fly in the Forest where there were less trees for it to fly into. Sid Smith, Olive Potter's garage friend, kindly spent hours with me, flicking the engine over to get it started. It ran on refined diesel oil and ether, and its power quite startled us. On the day of the first free flight, launching the Scorpion into the air, it buzzed away into the sky, climbing in large circles until it was only a speck. Then, fortunately, the fuel ran out, the engine stopped and the model glided up the valley, with me after it, head in the air, terrified that if I took my eyes off it I would lose it. Panting with exhilaration, I marked its landing point nearly two miles away and finally retrieved it. As with all model aircraft at some point, I failed to trim it adequately enough before flying it under power, and the model crashed, at full power and in ever tightening circles, into the ground. It seemed to be the lot of an aero-modeller to spend his time in reconstruction, with brief moments of elation at a good flight, and resignation when a badly-trimmed aircraft hit the deck.

Gliders were just as much fun as powered aircraft, and I, along with others, used to fly them off the top of Crooks Peak or Wavering Hills. Towing them up on a thin line, to 100 feet or so, before letting them off the tow hook, we watched them sail away over the valley, and hope they got caught up in a thermal to take them way up and out of sight. We always put our address in the cockpit of the model in case we lost it in the hope that whoever found it might be honest enough to contact us. Very rarely our models had the luck to hit a thermal, but one lad's did and his aircraft was returned from Bridgewater, twenty miles away. Quite a flight!

Indoor models were great fun, the elliptical wings being made from 3/32 balsa stringers which we covered with a film of dope. Submerging a wire frame in a bowl of water, a spoonful of dope was poured onto the surface which spread out like oil in a fine layer. By raising the wire frame, it was possible to catch and transfer the film of dope onto the wings of one's model and, after a few minutes drying, trim off the surplus. This thin, taut, transparent covering was incredibly light and strong. Powered with fine elastic, the motor driving a tiny prop and with rudder set so the model flew in circles, we would fly them in the gym, where they flitted like moths, climbing up into the high ceiling of the building.

Control line flying was another craze where solid little powered models with tail and aileron control worked by two lines, buzzed at high speeds of up to 100mph round the operator, who made them loop and tumble in complex aerobatics. It was a skilled business not to get your control lines so twisted you lost control. Miniaturised components for radio control had just come on the market by the time I left school. Free flight, with a timer to limit the run of an engine, was all we had. The timers were erratic and many a power model flew off into the unknown to be looked for in vain for weeks after. We all belonged to the NGA, The National Guild of Aero Modellers, and often bought our plans from the aero modeller plans service which sported an infinite variety of aircraft, some models very novel and bizarre in design. The aero modelling room was always warm and the company congenial. An exacting hobby, but with lots of rewards.

Edward 'Teddy' Moar was a complex character. It was his misfortune to have been sent to America as an evacuee, and on his return had arrived in our relatively physically immature midst. His father was in the navy and, therefore, hardly known to him, and his mother was an inspector in the educational system. Whereas we, at the onset of adolescence, quickly passed through our spotty phase, Teddy seemed plagued with a malignant cocktail of hormones that affected him physically in an ever present crop of boils on his poor scarred back, and testosterone-driven obsessive love affairs. His sexuality consumed him and was sublimated in reams of angst-ridden erotic poetry and Beethoven symphonies. The latter he would play for hours in the school hall, by himself, conducting an imaginary orchestra, sweeping a maverick lock of black hair back from his forehead in imitation of his square-jawed, taciturn, heroic composer. In the midst of all this sub-personality, he was also a thoroughly likeable fellow; a very good average at academic work, the captain of our rugby team, most interesting to talk to, and hopelessly ham-fisted at practical things. My Kate remembers him wandering round the games field reading AA Milne's *Winnie the Pooh* and thinking it very strange reading material for a sixth former.

A sad history has filtered back to me over the years. After doing his National Service, Teddy went to Cambridge and got a degree in psychology. The first Old Scholars weekend that I attended, he invited us to an evening meal at Sidcot Hotel, where he discussed the quality of the wines, and told us he was busy learning Russian so he could read Tolstoy in the original. Married three times, when his final marriage failed he sold his house and proceeded to drift about, living in various hotels, spending all his capital and under the illusion that he was the Tzar of Russia. Obsessed with Sidcot, he hired a taxi to see the school and linger over memories of a former girlfriend. I gathered from Hank that, after running through all his money, he was sectioned and put in an institution. How many of the seeds of his malady were already sown when we first met up with him, to erupt later in his sad demise?

My life in the Sixth Form is a jumble of memories. I enjoyed art work, apart from learning perspective which was a dreary exercise. John Newick was an innovative art teacher, introducing us to four-minute life poses, darting into the materials cupboard to come out in his bathing trunks to pose for us. He introduced us to a colour linocut technique that used one block with multiple printing, cutting away sections of the block between each print and overlaying colours. The result was very lithographic. Of course, you were limited to the number of initial prints taken as the block was recut to the point where there was virtually nothing left of the subject. I tried my hand at this and produced *Old Meg, She Was A Gypsy* from the poem *Meg Merrilies* by John Keats. Newick thought it too caricatured. He and I were always disagreeing, in a friendly fashion, over my style of painting. However, a series of academic pencil studies of my left hand, were considered good enough to put in the General meeting art exhibition, which was quite a concession.

Newick's protégé's, inevitably, it seemed, girls for whom he had a soft spot, were Nancy Davis and Jill Savage. They produced endless clay horses, nudes and heads that Newick took to the potter Fishley Holland to fire. They had the run of the art room, and all that they produced was lauded by their mentor. John Newick was an accomplished pianist and used to extemporise on classical themes on his battered old grand piano; one could often hear the music drift out of Rose Cottage near the school entrance on a summer's evening. He came by the piano by accident at an auction, the auctioneer mistaking an inadvertent nod of the head for a bid. Newick used to tell the story with great amusement as he recalled the first shock of becoming the owner of a grand piano, and then the logistics of moving it from the sale room to his house. It turned out, he said, to be quite a bargain, with a good tone, apart from the moth having got at a few of the hammer felts.

Andrew Rutter, in the form above me, enjoyed the esteem of John Newick. He was an accomplished still life painter, taking endless care with the highlights and reflections in glass or copper. His studies, done in powder colour, had a richness that belied their medium. Andrew excelled in the coloured linocuts, producing exquisite prints of orchids and other flowers, the overlaid colours giving great subtlety of tone. The 'A' level art exam included the painting of an imaginative composition, the title of which was *Street Musicians*. The time allotted for the painting was something like three hours. I had a wonderful time making a painting of a couple of buskers, using pen, coloured inks and poster paints. The buskers were old, battered and mournful, and they were playing at night outside a pub in the sodium lights of a suburban street. I was convinced I had captured something good in the painting and felt confident of a pass. Newick's remark was: "Well, Christopher, I don't hold out much hope for your imaginative composition. You will insist on this cartoon style, so I am afraid you will fail." When the results came through and I achieved a top grade for the painting, he was gracious enough to apologise for his inaccurate assessment. I was elated, as I always had a great admiration for Hogarth and Rowlandson as commentators on the social and artistic mores of their times.

Mother generously bought a potter's wheel for the school, although I was almost the only one to use it. It was housed in a small shed at the end of the girls' playground. It was a sit-down kick wheel, well-constructed, and I spent many hours on it throwing different shapes of pot. I had bought some plans for a coke-fired kiln from Mrs Wren, in the hopes of being allowed to build it as a pottery project, but the school authorities seemed loathe to let me do so, perhaps due to safety factors, or the expense. So I had to be content with green pots, a selection of which I put on display at a General meeting exhibition, getting a merit which pleased me. David Murray Rust's children were six or seven years old at that time, and were given a great deal of freedom, the little devils getting in amongst all my freshly-made pots at one stage and collapsing them, much to my fury. It took quite a bit of doing to diplomatically tell the Headmaster that you had caught his youngsters vandalising your work. The Head, to give him his due, listened attentively and must have taken appropriate action, for it never happened again.

Langdon, the games master, entered those interested from the First XV in the West Country Schoolboy 7-a-side championships held in Bristol, in the Easter holidays of 1950. Michael Cox invited me to stay overnight with him and his father. He was a kind host and we joined up with the other five players the next day at the Bristol ground. Seven's was an entirely different ball game from fifteen a side and needed specialist training, which we hadn't had. The whole game only lasted a quarter of an hour each way, but we were left gasping and trounced after the first round. We had a good meal at Michael's afterwards however, the social bonhomie making up for our early elimination from the contest.

Swimming was going through a high point at this time with the arrival of an American family called the Touchers. Paul was in our form, his striking sisters in forms below us. Paul, perhaps through some exotic blood in his ancestry, was a handsome, beautifully proportioned athlete, swimmer and diver. He proceeded to smash all the Senior records by several seconds, ploughing up and down the pool with relaxed ease, performing somersault turns, an innovation in itself that gained him yards of superiority. Along with his athletic prowess, Paul was also a proselytising born-again Christian; a clean cut young American with Jesus as his 'Personal Saviour'. We respected his simple faith because we were in awe of his swimming prowess, but we did take exception to him giving us homilies if he happened to overhear us swearing in his presence. This made him feel very sad, for he genuinely feared for our spiritual health if we "took the Lord's name in vain".

As Sixth Formers we were eligible to be elected as Prefects. This made us responsible for our own behaviour as much as for others. If you were good at games you were almost guaranteed to be elected. Inevitably there were the handful of unfortunates who didn't gain office. My good friend Hank, for example. He and John Norman were given responsibility for overseeing the juniors billeted at Combe House without the advantage of Prefect status or the perks, like Prefects' supper, as we did. The system was very unfair in many respects, and I am glad to say a thing of the past, as the Prefect system, so traditional of public schools, was abolished in the ensuing decade.

Our duties as Prefects were to take preps, keep order at 'collects' and if we observed individual pupils flouting the school rules. We had the power to administer punishment (or Punny), in the form of quarter of an hour increments. "Take a quarter, Smith", this for disrupting prep, say; and if there were any cheeky prevarication: "Take a half, Smith". This would be entered in a book and twice each week, at a time allotted for 'Prees Punny', a Prefect would be allocated to supervise the various miscreants, who had to turn up to receive the mild retribution due. 'Punny' usually consisted of changing into games kit, three minutes, a run round the Island, eight minutes, shower and change back, four minutes. This for a 'quarter', doubled for a half hour. It was all rather pointless unless you were in training for middle-distance running. I used to vary the routine with climbing wall bars in the gym and aerobics with chairs. Having power over others was not a good thing, and I abused it on occasions by working my captive Juniors over hard. How very near we all are to becoming sadistic. As we were afflicted, it is all too easy to afflict others.

My first act as a Prefect was to break a window in a snowball fight. Luckily the MOD of that moment happened to witness the event and Mr Hinton could see my genuine concern at my action. Beyond paying for the glass I heard no more of the matter. Once a week Murray Rust called all his Prefects to his study to discuss school affairs, lapses in discipline, disruptive pupils, how to deal with them and so on. One boy's name would come to the fore at the end of each session and 'Bunrab', as we called the Head, on account of the way he used to expose his false teeth and make a snatch at them, would cross his legs, smile wearily and say: "And now we come to the vexed question of Kumas Bezogma. Of course, his problem is his charm. He is such an endearing character BUT..." and he would stare at us and we would all laugh. Kumas was the spoilt son of a Persian oil magnate, an irrepressible clown with no intention of learning anything except English, and that osmotically. He was the charming bane of all staff and Prefects.

To an unfortunate member of staff, a certain maths teacher, Mr Mates, Kumas was a red rag to a bull. Mr Mates was a fair cop for anyone intent on baiting and disruptive behaviour, and Kumas' insolence was the last straw. Walking by the Lower Fourth form room in class time, one could hear the rumble of uproar and bellows of fury from Mr Mates. The door of the class room would suddenly open and Kumas would be catapulted out across the corridor to reel against the wall in well-feigned knock out, a beatific smile on his face. Meanwhile bedlam would rein on the other side of the door as Mr Mates, baited to breaking point, snapped his pipe stem off his pipe and beat his head on his desk in hysterical break down. A tense, tight, little man with a ginger moustache and short fuse, Mr Mates was clearly in the wrong profession, poor man, and he left after two terms, probably with a nervous breakdown.

At Sunday breakfast, the last meal before the allocation of the new butter ration, the Sixth Form boys would gather all left-over butter available, mostly by the girls who hardly ever seemed to eat their meagre 4oz a week. This, together with left-over sudsy marmalade, we would take up to the Prefect's room next to the Swamp, where we had a gas fire and could indulge in our own tea party (another perk), of hot buttered toast, marmalade and tea. Our butter consumption at these sessions was enormous, and health freaks would have had a field day with today's knowledge of polysaturated fats. To us it was simply a scrumptious indulgence.

The Sixth Form study room was separate from the school, a comparatively recent building alongside the subterranean boys 'bog' or 'loos'. We had a small garden in which we used to grow a few radish and lettuce. It was shaded by an old apple tree that never bore fruit but inhibited growth in the garden. The powers that be refused permission to fell it, so, with a judicious use of a brace and bit at the base of the trunk, and an application of sulphuric acid, plugged with a cork, and a liberal smearing of dirt, we sat back and observed the results. The tree seemed to lose its vitality and was leafless the next season!

Darts was a popular game in the study room, with the dart board right by the entrance door, a lethal position we never gave thought to until John Dunnicliff, coming into the room one day, was hit by a dart in his neck, narrowly missing his jugular artery. Dunnicliff went ashen with the dart hanging from his neck while someone tore off to find the MOD and get help. I forget the outcome except that Dunnicliff was OK, if justifiably upset by the accident, and we had to move the dart board to a less dangerous position.

As Seniors we attended the main Quaker meeting in the school hall. The chairs being all joined together in groups of four meant that if anyone moved there was a creaking noise that to me, at any rate, disturbed the repose of the meeting. We were always on the alert for someone to get up and relieve the tedium of the meeting by speaking. Some of the elders were always predictable in their mannerisms and good for a laugh. One old gentleman, a Dr Franks, who always wore a great coat with split tails, used to regularly get up, and with wire-rimmed, spectacled eyes almost on the page, thumb myopically through the Bible to his favourite prophet Ezekiel. "And Ezekiel said...", was always his opening salvo. He had a rasping voice like a clipped, dry, staccato, old crow, and having delivered his address he would part his coat tails carefully before sitting down again to doze the rest of the meeting away.

A tiny old lady used to attend the meeting with her large bucolic 'John Barleycorn' of a husband; a silent florid man who settled down in dormant stupor for the duration. She, on the other hand, would sometime during the meeting begin to get twittery and restless, finally bobbing up to deliver herself of some passionate message. As she spoke, the tears would well up in her eyes with the fervour, and trickle down her face. Her husband would surface a little at such time and herumph slightly with embarrassment at his weeping wife. A grand old lady called Mabel Foothill, with a lisp and deaf as a post, would often get up to speak, tuning her hearing aid at the same time, so that it wowed and whistled till she got the volume right. "Wath ith thucthess?" she would ask shrilly, twiddling her knobs. "Looking up to the hills ith thuckthess..." With the volume sorted out her shrillness would disappear and with a few more inconsequential observations she would sit down. On one occasion, we had a real loopy man in the meeting - an old, wild, white-haired fellow. About half an hour before he spoke, our observant eyes had spotted his agitation. With much wringing of his hands, he suddenly erupted from his chair and, apropos of nothing, declaimed with great emotion: "And my friend lay in the gutter with an eagle at his throat, but I thank the Almighty I am clear of his blood." And with that, looking about him in pain and despair, he blundered out of the meeting. A Quaker meeting certainly attracts some strange people!

We had some good lantern-slide lectures. By far the best was one delivered by Eric

Hosking, the wonderful bird photographer, on the Montagu's Harrier and the Barn Owl. It was whilst photographing Barn Owls that one had flown straight at him and pecked an eye out. We all noticed he had a glass eye! On another occasion, a well-known member of the ill-fated 1920's assault on Everest, when Mallory and Irvine disappeared, came and gave a talk and showed us slides of New Zealand.

Murray Rust instigated a reading competition. I went in for it first in the Upper Fifth. I had only ever reached the first round, usually a difficult, unseen passage, read to the Headmaster in his study. On my third attempt, I made the final, along with Hank. Murray Rust was a great admirer of Bunyan's *Pilgrim's Progress,* and the set piece unseen until the last moment, was the final paragraph where Christian cries out: "Death where is thy sting?" And, as he went down deeper: "Grave, where is thy victory? And all the bells rang for him on the other side." I got through my passage quite well and, listening to the others, was amazed at the different interpretation that could be put on the same passage. For the other half of the competition, we could choose a passage from any book that we liked. I chose the final two pages from *Tarka, the Otter,* the classic story of a wild otter, by Henry Williamson. Hank chose a passage from *Dandelion Days,* also by Williamson, depicting an amusing classroom scene from Willy Maddison's schooldays. I felt I had done my two readings justice, and on this occasion my confidence was justified as, third time lucky, I won it! At least I was good at something!

The Prefects used to read the 'lessons' or passages from various literary sources, in between hymns, prior to the speaker of that Sunday giving his evening address. I always took a pride in giving of my best on these occasions. Our old Latin master, Mr Peters, came back to the school to give the address one Sunday. I remember I had to read a long passage from Plato's *The Republic*. If I am honest I did not comprehend much of Plato's argument, but I read the passage dead slow and managed to convey a comprehension of what I was reading about that was mostly theatre! It went down well, and I was congratulated on my intelligent reading from two most unlikely members of staff, none other than John Russell, and Miss Philips, who normally had little time for me. ✤

Chapter 54
Eileen and the Sixth Form

Soon after my relationship with Topsy ended I formed a relationship of sorts with a girl in the form below me called Eileen Murray.

She had jumped up a form, being bright academically and was a consummate flirt, playing off one poor fellow against another so they did not know if they were in favour or out. As with Topsy, I took her too seriously and created an idealistic image she just did not fulfil. It was difficult to get beyond the superficial. Eileen always expressed a commitment to her adopted sect, and was a staunch proselytiser for the Christian ideal of service. In my cynicism, I came to view it as a sort of smoke screen, behind which she played fast and loose.

Her boyfriends came and went but I hung on, much to her puzzlement, often exasperated by her behaviour, but trying to convince myself that there was more to her. We met up after leaving school and I tried to further the relationship, but she was, by this time, adept at playing cat and mouse. Other young men kept coming on the scene, for instance, when I had planned a weekend on our own. She welcomed them all. I remember boating with her at Keynsham and en route we gathered two other young men and she invited them on board and flirted outrageously with all of us.

After we had left school I did manage to get one weekend camping with her at Wincanton where she had a living-in job with a family. I cycled down with a tent and all the gear and was her willing slave, putting up our camp on a farm while she watched. She was good at pretending she was a poor helpless female, and getting her willing men to do all the work. We passed an uncomfortable night, she casually, but zealously, guarding her virginity and myself frustrated to despair by her 'stop, go' ambivalence. Eventually, Eileen emigrated to America and became Mrs Blackburn and had a daughter. I saw her off in desolation one evening at the docks in Southampton and haven't seen her since.

Although I enjoyed my last year at Sidcot, I used the weekend walks to get away on my own into the delightful hills and commune with the larks and the silence. When we reached eighteen years of age and National Service loomed, we boys went to Axbridge and registered our intent at the Public Offices. At that time, when you reached eighteen, it was compulsory to serve two years in one or other of the armed forces. As an alternative to this, if one's conscience so dictated, one could register as a conscientious objector and do alternative service such as working on the land, or relief work abroad. Conscientious objectors in the First World War, many of them Quakers, had been vilified by the authorities, but their sincerity and persistence in the face of horrendous treatment had finally earned them a certain respect and dispensation. My generation was reaping the rewards gained by these brave men.

Learning how to kill someone seemed crazy to me, so I opted to register as a CO. Michael Pittard also decided on the same course and served his two years in the Friends Relief Service abroad. It was a Quaker organisation that did sterling work in reconstruction after the war. In retrospect, I wish I too had joined the FRS and expanded my horizons, but my homing instinct was too strong at the time. The rest of my form opted for the Forces. I don't remember anyone questioning my beliefs or I theirs, it was a completely personal matter.

I had to attend a tribunal in Bristol in the Easter holidays of my last year, and write out a declaration of my reasons for objecting to military service. Sid and Lyn Smith kindly drove me. There were several of us COs wishing to testify and we sat on a bench awaiting our turn. The lad before me was a Jehovah's Witness and he was given a very rough ride, partly because of his fundamentalist beliefs, but mainly because he was asking for an unconditional discharge and was not willing to undertake alternative service. His case was dismissed and he was ordered to join up on pain of imprisonment. He was a quiet fellow and I felt rather sorry for his position.

When it came to my turn to face the tribunal, I was required to stand in a witness box while grave, elderly men read my testament. My reasons were based on the Quaker principles that it was wrong to kill your fellow man or offer him violence and that it was contrary to Christ's teachings as interpreted by George Fox, the founder of the Quaker movement. I stated I was quite willing to serve society in some other constructive manner. My statement was read and my application for exemption from military training was conditionally accepted, without comment, providing I participated in a recognised alternative.

Starting with *Tarka, the Otter*, I had become captivated by Henry Williamson's writings, and Mother, always generous about literary enthusiasms, forwarded extra pocket money which I spent in Winscombe's very good little book shop. I followed Willy Maddison's life as depicted in Williamson's novels, and empathised with his pantheistic angst as he emerged from the trauma of the 1914-18 war to an ill-starred love affair, culminating in his drowning, just as he finds a romantic soulmate and literary recognition. Williamson's nature essays are gems of poetic observation of the natural world. In the sunny seclusion of the Quaker graveyard to one side of the school hall, I would read my newly discovered author by the hour, neglecting my revision for 'A' levels.

Irresponsible activities of this period included perfecting a simple sling from a piece of leather and a length of cord, which gave an incredible range to a pebble, even if no great accuracy. Across from the graveyard, towards the combe, was a large oak tree, the abode of a rook colony. I used to wing my projectiles the 300 yards or so into the branches of the tree to watch the rooks rise in protest at my long-range bombardment. By good luck, I never hit anything and the bombardment did little more than disturb the colony's repose from time to time. Hank, always of an inventive turn of mind, explored the mechanical advantages of the Aboriginal Woomera, or spear-throwing stick, that gave you added leverage by doubling your arm length. It, like the sling, gave a tremendous increase in projectile throwing range, and I managed to crack a tile on the Bursar's cottage on the far side of Newcombe Drive. I also relieved the tedium of cricket practice in the nets by bowling with my sling; it sent the cricket balls down towards the batsman at great speed but uncertain height, which was not appreciated!

Other boys made slings, and our groundsman Billy Hairs began to complain of stones in the outfield blunting his gang mower blades. I was not responsible on this occasion, I would like to record. To add a bit of variety to our diet at weekends, I snared rabbits on Sidcot hill. The rabbit population at that pre-myxomatosis time was huge. Before morning assembly and late evening, I would work my snare line, resetting any noose disturbed, or disposing of the odd lucky catch now and again. We made several tasty stews from the rabbits I caught, in the exclusive sanctuary of the Pree's room.

Like all momentous times in one's life, my final summer at Sidcot seemed to be full of sunshine as one contemplated emancipation from eight long years of school life. The choir sang Bach's *Coffee Cantata* in which I performed solos, taking the part of the despairing father whose daughter has become addicted to coffee. Eileen, who was really very musical and had a sweet soprano voice (another attraction), took the part of the wayward daughter which added a frisson to the event.

I had taken a fancy to learning the guitar, which was at that time an instrument still to be accepted as worthy of consideration in the conservative world of orchestral music.

Mother bought me a guitar of sorts, and a guitar teacher called Michael Watson, who lived in Bristol, took me on. Mr Watson earned his main income from dance band gigs and was something of a virtuoso in the Bert Weedon mould, being a master of many different styles, from acoustic Spanish finger playing to its electric cousin. Our first lesson was taken up with my tutor pointing out the irredeemable defects of my guitar, warped neck etc., and the cost of a good one. The superior tone of his private collection of instruments was obvious as he demonstrated his virtuosity. Mr Watson estimated that I would need a minimum of one lesson a week to begin with. So, fired with enthusiasm I rode back to school on the bus and asked the Head for dispensation to learn the instrument of my choice. I was met with a very lukewarm response and told that I could not have leave to go to Bristol more than three times a term. The Head would not budge from this for some reason known only to himself. Regretfully, my musical ambitions hit the dust. Reading later of Julian Bream's run-in with his principal at the Royal College of Music when discovered playing Bach that he had transposed for the guitar, I am not surprised at the lack of enthusiasm for my modest request for a weekly lesson. Segovia was to be the great ambassador for the guitar's rightful place in the realms of serious music. Interestingly, it is now taught at Sidcot as a standard instrument on a par with the violin. At least it saved my mother a great deal of money she could ill afford at the time.

In the Fifth Form, I had acquired the nick name of 'Chunky', for no apparent reason except that it went well with Charman. I had also acquired a second nickname, 'Charley Roe', used mostly by Hank, after a monosyllabic, myopic little man, who used to work at the slide in the kitchens, cutting up bread with a hand-operated slicer. His left hand usually had some unfortunate finger wrapped in bloody bandages, nicked in the slicer while pushing the last heel end of a loaf through its guillotine maws. Charley Roe was a domestic worker; I was a 'Char'- man and the connection was too good to miss. So Charley, or Roe, I became to my peers for the majority of my school days, and after.

A few more snippets from past years are now surfacing in my memory. One cannot forget Murray Rust's classic 'foot in mouth' announcement at the end of assembly: "Now, will everyone stay in their places please, until everyone has left the hall!" The Head also had the unfortunate habit, of which I am sure he was unaware, of running his fingers down his flies to check the buttons were done up as he entered the hall for assembly.

As well as experimenting with the Woomera, Hank had, on one of his visits to Cheddar, noticed that in the vicinity of the caves there was a Wishing Well into which people threw small change for luck. This inspired him to invent a patent, long reach grab, with which to fish out the change from the bottom of the well. I was not with him on the occasion of him trying the grab, but he told me he managed to retrieve about five shillings before being accosted by the local warden, who had a speech impediment, and who warned him off with the remark: "Don't you know this park's private. It's Private. Yer can't put yer bicycle here… It's all right if you want to go up change yer blaader, *(Jacob's Ladder, a local tourist route to get a panoramic view of Cheddar Gorge)* but thi'ith a private park." Hank beat a conciliatory retreat, five shillings better off and with enough material from the officious warden to use much later in a four-part madrigal, called inevitably *It's Private*. He took all the parts himself, tape recording them separately and overlaying them on the final tape which he had recorded on a vinyl record and gave to his friends. I have the scratchy recording still.

On the last half term, a group of us cycled to Weston-super-Mare and beyond, up the sludgy coast of the Bristol Channel to an area of sand dunes called Sandy Bay, with a few small bungalows and beach huts. Here we cooked ourselves an uncomfortable shade of red, lying out in the sun. Afterwards we headed for Bridgwater where, greatly daring, we visited the local cinema to see Cornel Wilde and Dorothy Lamour in *The Adventures of Nell Gwyn*. Going to the cinema was against the rules, as one group of pupils found out to their dismay when finding themselves in the company of some of the staff who happened to have gone to see the same film.

Our 'A' level exams were about three weeks from the end of the summer term of 1951. To fill in the remaining time left to us, members of staff generously gave of their time with lectures and informal classes. John Newick, I remember gave us some most interesting lectures on art history. What a difference between these latter informal teaching periods to what had gone before. Suddenly we were all adults together and felt like learning for its own sake.

Our form made up a cricket team and took on the village in evening matches at which I was prevailed upon to play. I remember being in last to bat, with about twenty runs to make to win the match. Play defensively, advised Stuart Linney, our captain, who was batting with me. "Just block the straight balls, and I will see what I can do at the end of the over." Which is just what we did. I curbed my instinct to swipe at the ball when facing the bowling and managed to stay in until Stuart got the bowling, and gradually he made up the runs with his sophisticated strokes until we achieved victory! I think I scored one run, but received a certain accolade for using what little talents I had cricket-wise on that occasion!

Our games field must have covered about thirty acres; it was superb and we were very lucky to have it. While I was at the school there was a vague rumour circulating that Somerset had wanted it for their County Cricket ground. The groundsman, Billy Hairs, made hay round the margins of the field which was used to feed the school horse, Bess. I used to enjoy helping him turn the swathes, wielding a wooden rake, something I already knew how to do from experience of haymaking at home.

Mary Hooper had introduced a lovely tradition of taking the Sixth Form leavers of each year on an evening's walk just before the end of term, to some tea rooms at Priddy in the heart of the Mendips. It was a joyous, carefree affair with 'Poppy' at her relaxed best. Our tea and cakes, which she so generously paid for, went down a treat! I remember a group of us sitting at a tea table pretending we were foreigners, talking in strangled mock German that caused some raised eyebrows among the other guests!

On our happy way back to the school in the evening light, we went into a field full of young heifers, and sitting on the ground in a circle we gave them a rendering in four-part harmony of Macbeth Bain's version of *The Lord's My Shepherd*. Gradually, from all corners of the field, the young cattle came galloping to gather round us row on row, to stare in inquisitive wide-eyed attention, a most appreciative audience! Whatever Mary Hooper thought of our lively, random, youthful behaviour that evening she let it ride. It was a most happy event that I shall always remember, and a fitting swan song to my boarding school days.

We put on *Thark*, a romp of a farce by Ben Travers, for our 'leaving' play. We produced it in two weeks, rehearsing all hours and enjoying every moment. I can't remember much about its content now, apart from firing off a duck gun at a portrait of one of my ancestors in a drunken frenzy, mistaking him for an intruder. Philip Hickson, a wizard at chemistry, used his expertise to make an explosive charge for the gun which, when I came to fire it in the actual performance, detonated with such force it nearly blew my head off and made my ears sing for days. In the euphoria of the moment, though, nothing mattered.

It was the tradition of leavers to stay up all night on the final day of the last term. I went to bed about midnight, as I planned to walk and hitchhike home on this final occasion, having sent my bike on in advance. For the last two years, on departure, I had welched on the obligatory handshake with the Head, on the one hand wanting to get cycling at the crack of dawn and also because I found the handshake perfunctory and without much meaning. To my surprise, Murray Rust had noticed my absence and taken the trouble to write to me, and I had responded and given my reasons for avoiding the formal goodbyes. It was noticeable from then on that the handshakes were much more personal.

Trooping out with the rest of the school that day, Murray Rust and Mary Hooper were extra fervent in their good wishes for our futures. I cannot say I felt nostalgic, I just felt a tremendous sense of relief and excitement as I took to the road. I was on my way back home to my roots. My journey home, I determined, would be governed by lifts offered spontaneously by drivers. I was not going to thumb lifts. I walked beyond Axbridge before the first driver slowed up and offered me a lift all the way to Frome, well on my way. I walked from there to Warminster, where a lorry driver took me in the late evening to the village of Nomansland in the Forest.

In the evening sunshine I walked to Fritham and bought my first beer at the Royal Oak, nostalgically wending my way to Eyeworth and the beech wood where Topsy and I had first kissed and embraced. I had jammed a charred stick in the fork of an old holly tree, close by the spot where we had made our fire when we left, and it was still there. I pulled it out and incorporated it in a new fire, and lying on my back looked through the canopy up at the stars in the night sky and dreamed impossible dreams. In the dawn of a new day, August 1951, I took another charred stick from the now cold embers of my fire, and replaced it in the cleft of the old holly for remembrance, and with a light heart walked home across the Forest to greet my mother. At that moment, I was immortal and life seemed infinite in its possibilities! ⚘

Returning to Godshill Pottery for the Easter holidays and in his last year at Sidcot, Chris went before a tribunal in Bristol in order to testify as a Conscientious Objector.

Chapter 55
The Festival of Britain

I left Sidcot in 1951, the year of The Festival of Britain. The Labour government had just got into power with a landslide victory and were trying to boost the moral of the country by celebrating everything that was British.

The winds of change soon to come had not yet made their presence felt and we were still (just), a power in the world. I went to London to visit the Festival, its graceful, sculptural, cigar-shaped, Skylon tower, and the Dome of Discovery, in which were exhibited the scientific and technological advances of the nation, designed to re-establish the country's belief in itself. I stayed with Topsy at her mother's home in Highgate. Topsy's mother, Pat, had just re-married; her new husband was a large genial man called Gilly Gilroy, who was able to overcome Pat's desperate deafness and hold an intellectual conversation or argument with her. Pat, now in her fifties, was determined that she was going to be able to have a child by Gilly, rather wishful thinking I had thought sadly. Topsy was living in a flat in Notting Hill and working in a bra factory. It was a job she did not keep long, she told me, as on an absent minded day, she made up several dozen pairs of bra using a left breast pattern for both left and right!

Topsy's younger sister, Beany, now fifteen, was in evidence as well, I remember. We all went for a midnight swim in Highgate Pond and visited the Festival the following day. I remember going on the big dipper with Topsy, who was dressed like a film star, and bumping into my ex-Headmaster who looked rather bemused at my company, taken aback at the two splendid young ladies I had in tow! We took a ride on the Far Tottering and Oyster Creek Branch Railway, built to the design of the cartoonist Rowland Emett. We were suitably impressed with the standards and innovations of British design exhibited in the Dome of Discovery, a pale forerunner of the Millennium Dome. Soon after, Topsy disappeared to go sailing around the world, or some such crazy Topsy adventure, only going as far as the Channel Islands, she told me years later. I spent a delightful week wandering round Highgate during the day and picking up Beany after she had finished work, who showed me other interesting parts of London.

Beany was a lovely young girl then, with no hint of the tragedy that was to overtake her later in her short life. She was to marry a successful travel writer called Ernle Dusgate Selby Bradford and they lived for a while in Godshill and had a son called Hugh. Ernle was a hard drinker and Beany became one too. Ernle and Beany moved to Malta to escape English taxes and enjoy the sun and the cheap wine. Little Hugh was something of an irritating appendage who knew sparse parental love and was put into nursery boarding schools from a very early age, becoming an introspective loner. Ernle developed a thrombosis in one of his legs and had to have it amputated. Despite this, he kept up the drinking, and the smoking, and died in his late forties of a massive heart attack. Hugh became a Buddhist and maintained a sort of relationship with Pat, his grandmother, before killing himself in a bout of depression. Beany almost died of alcohol poisoning and was temporarily rescued by Topsy, who looked after her sister until her death from cirrhosis of the liver. There was almost a sad inevitability about that family's demise. Even now, I cannot believe that such youth and talent could be so fatally damaged as to destroy itself so tragically. ❧

Chapter 56
The Arrival of Mr Harris

Alyndhurst farmer, Mr Harris, approached us in the autumn of 1951, wondering if he could rent the rough from us to corral two hundred or so cattle at night, with a view to ranching them on the open Forest during the day.

The three-quarters of a mile of fencing around the rough was on its last legs, time and fires having taken their toll on the galvanised netting and posts. Mr Harris said he would re-fence it as part of the deal, and after some discussion we agreed to his proposition. Seeing an opportunity for employment for the first leg of my alternative National Service, I asked Mr Harris if he would take me on to help with the fencing, and to mind the cattle when they arrived. He readily agreed and a few weeks later I was on his pay roll, clearing gorse and sharpening fencing stakes, helping his workmen to rebuild the long boundary fence of our rough. The piles were made out of all sorts, mostly hedgerow in origin, hazel, thorn, and ash, with no chance of defying rot for any length of time. However, any fence was better than the original. In a few weeks, it was completed and the cattle started arriving. I ended up with some hundred and fifty beasts, scrubby store cattle of all sizes and breeds that Mr Harris, who was a dealer rather than a farmer, had picked up cheaply in the local markets.

My job was to mind the cattle on the open Forest during the day from horseback, round them up each evening and put them in the rough, feeding them with a small amount of hay to supplement what nutritional herbage they had picked up off the Forest. This wasn't much, particularly in winter. The more robust animals survived this subsistence regime, but by March there were quite a few of the more scrubby animals that were in a weakened condition. Mr Harris was too greedy and unrealistic to see what was happening and wouldn't increase the hay ration. To cap it all, there was an outbreak of Foot and Mouth Disease locally, and eventually all cattle were ordered off the Forest. Fortunately the disease was contained around the edge of the Forest and never penetrated its interior.

In spite of the fact that the cattle were now confined to the rough, Mr Harris still did not organise more hay, and I began to lose cattle from starvation. I left one poor heifer out on the Forest, hoping she may find more nourishment. This was spotted by an official from the Ministry of Agriculture who treated me to a verbal assault that left me almost in tears, and I had to get the poor animal into the compound where she did indeed die. The organisation of hay supplies was appalling and spasmodic, the odd load coming all the way by tractor from Chitterne, one of Mr Harris's farms on Salisbury Plain, enough for three feeds for starving and bawling cattle.

The weeks want by and restrictions on movement of cattle went on and on. Finally, Mr Harris took the law into his own hands, and he and his two sons, John and Pat, and right-hand man Jack Dyer arrived at the crack of dawn one late spring day and drove the whole herd across the Forest to Lyndhurst and Angel Farm, Mr Harris's home, where there was plenty of grass. There were, amazingly, no repercussions from this quite illegal movement of cattle. Pulling all the Commoners animals off the Forest meant, of course, that fields normally laid up for hay had to be used for pasture. To compensate them for this loss of winter fodder, quite a few 'Lawns' in the south of the Forest were temporarily fenced off, fertiliser applied and hay made off them. The resulting fodder was then rationed out to each Commoner, according to his needs. The Forest continued to remain clear of infection, but dairy herds were decimated and despondency reined until, to everyone's relief, the disease burnt itself out.

After the cattle went, I continued to work for Mr Harris through the summer of 1952, bale carting on a large farm he owned at Stockbridge. The hay fields were several hundred acres and the bales dotted around to the horizon. The machine used by Mr Harris was an early round baler, made by Allis Chalmers, and the bales usually weighed about three-quarters of a hundredweight, only just within the limit of one's strength to lift and load on a lorry. Mr Harris liked the round bales as they shed the rain quite well and did not deteriorate too much from being left so long, unlike the rectangular ones which quickly became sodden unless stacked at an angle. It was heavy, hot work out on the unprotected rolling downs, under a broiling sun, and incredibly boring. Our puny efforts to clear the vast fields of their bales began to look like the task of Sisyphus. I worked with John, Mr Harris's oldest son, a pleasant enough fellow, a bit older than me, and Reg, a raw-boned strong fellow with a short fuse, and finally Ron, a quiet methodical worker, who always wore a black beret regardless of how hot the sun. Ron was to tragically die from Wiels Disease, contracted from a rat bite, a few years later.

1952 was the year of the coronation of Queen Elizabeth, and Godshill celebrated in a quiet way with junketings on the village green, and a procession. Danae skilfully made herself, and her pony Joey, the costume of a knight at a tournament, in red and black. They cut an authentic dash, going at full gallop in their heraldic apparel. There was a race amongst the older men, I remember, in which Uncle Aubrey came first, simply because of his forward dip finish. Jimmy Witt, his rival, a tall, thin man, was actually the faster of the two, but he ran leaning backwards, thus allowing my uncle to breast the tape first. It was a comic sight watching the two styles. A foot race from the Telegraph, approximately

Danae as a Tournament Knight on Joey for the Coronation celebrations in Godshill in 1952.

three miles, was inaugurated, which Sid Finch won, running in bare feet. I believe Martin Westlake took part and was crippled for days after. There was the usual bowling for the pig, donated by George Sturgess or Charley White, throwing the horse shoes, and other such innocent fête nonsense.

I didn't get to much of the celebrations having to do endless overtime, bale carting for Mr Harris. We finished the carting at the end of August, the last bales almost hidden by the new grass growing up round them. ❧

Chapter 57
Work on my Cousin Martin's Holding

With the end of bale carting, I left Mr Harris's employment and joined my cousin Martin, who by now had a small farm of his own, keeping chickens, pigs and a small dairy herd of six to eight pretty little Jersey cows.

The Westlake family were still living in Woodcot, originally built by Philip Oyler, a farmer, for his mother-in-law, then handed on to Forest School and finally, at the start of the war, to my cousins, to be their home for many years. The farm was only just solvent, so I agreed to work for a pound a week, my national insurance stamp, and my dinner. It was a happy time and I enjoyed working for my cousin Martin, who had completed his National Service stint doing farm work. He had served a tough apprenticeship under a local farmer called Jimmy Witt, during the hard bleak winter of 1947. Mr Witt had no tractors then, and all haulage and cultivations were done with three horses, Prince, Duke, and Molly. I believe Martin had a hard time of it, folding sheep in on root crops, the ground being so frozen that it was almost impossible to drive the stakes in for the hurdles.

I helped milk the cows in the little dairy each day, a useful manual facility acquired from our goat-keeping days. Martin had a milk round and there was a butterfat requirement which was checked by the Milk Marketing Board every so often to make sure it had not fallen below the required level. Jerseys produce some of the highest butterfat content of any of the milk breeds, so the inspections were usually a formality, although they did test for traces of antibiotic residues in the milk from mastitis treatment, because it interfered with cheese production. Martin's management was usually good enough to ensure the cows kept pretty clear of mastitis anyway. Spare milk, left over after the milk round, was put in a churn to be picked up each day by the milk lorry.

Martin grew a certain amount of dredge corn, oats and vetches which he harvested on tripods after cutting, making lots of small pook-like ricks, raised off the ground for the air to circulate and dry. If it rained, the steep pitch of the little ricks drained off most of the water. It was a very labour-intensive system, but produced a good quality end result, particularly in a wet harvest time. Likewise, hay could be cured in this manner; we had no pick-up balers then, of course.

Martin was farming on a shoe string, with never enough land to cope with the demands of his livestock. Hay was made on any land available, even if it was a graveyard and had to be cut with a scythe. Ken Harrod, Martin's uncle, who delivered flowers to Covent Garden for Hale Nurseries, was employed part-time to lend his expertise to anything from tinkering with tractors and reluctant engines, to sawing out wood and constructing yards, repairing Dutch barns, and doing general maintenance on the estate. He was a clever man with his own individual style of doing things and a godsend in diagnosing and repairing mechanical faults.

Sandy Balls' facilities were very basic in the early 'fifties. The war years had brought in a population of permanent caravan dwellers, but the holiday facilities were limited to delightful simple chalets placed strategically across the hillsides overlooking the Avon, tranquil and private amongst the pines and rhododendrons. The chalets had a table, chairs, Primus and bunk beds, a few cooking pots, and not much else. Water was carried from one of the stand pipes dotted around the various sites. A simple enamel bowl was supplied in which to do the washing up, and you poured your dirty water into a soakage pit filled with bracken and changed once every few days by the maintenance gang.

Sanitation was provided in the form of earth closets placed in blocks round the estate, the cubicles partitioned off from each other with hessian sacking tacked to wooden frames. I can tell you, from fifty years experience of an earth closet at home, bucket sanitation, or what ever you wish to call it, can be clean and reasonably sweet smelling, but it does need extremely thorough and careful maintenance. You need two buckets, one enamelled for urine, which you empty and scour regularly so no smelly lime scale builds up on its sides. The other bucket, for excrement, needs to be a galvanised, traditional oval latrine type. This too needs a good clean each time it is emptied. An adequate supply of saw dust, soil or ashes is vital to cover up each motion and keep the smell at bay. If the rules of thorough maintenance are carried out, all but those of the most squeamish sensibilities will find an earth closet quite acceptable.

The sanitation at Sandy Balls may have been all right according to my Uncle's theoretical ideas of the 'great cycle' and turn around of organic matter, but my year's stint with the estate's 'Honey Waggon' convinced me that you are never going to educate an urban population of holiday makers into the mysteries of a primitive system of sanitation. Our 'Maintenance' was cursory to say the least, the buckets being emptied into the 'Honey Waggon' at high speed with no cleaning at all. The urine buckets were caked with yellow smelly lime scale and the crap buckets were equally foul. Even on a domestic scale, the system needs watching, but it becomes totally impossible in the face of ignorance and abuse in a public context. We needed a relay of clean buckets and better facilities and care for a start. I cannot fault Uncle Aubrey on his composting of all the contents of the 'Honey Waggon' however; he was a meticulous compost maker producing prodigious quantities of sweet smelling manure that produced some really good crops of wheat.

Martin had two tractors, an early grey Ferguson and an antiquated two-cylinder John Deere that you started on petrol, later switching over to TVO (tractor vaporising oil), when the engine had warmed up. To achieve this quickly there was an adjustable blind that went over the radiator grill and blocked cool air being sucked through it by the fan. It was started manually by means of an external flywheel. Each cylinder had a decompression tap to make it possible to turn over the flywheel manually but, even so, it was a wrist-wrenching exercise if the engine flooded and refused to fire. I remember it had incredible traction for its size and we used to haul massive loads of timber up from the bottom of Sandy Balls with the front wheels off the ground, doing all the steering with individual wheel brakes. It had a hand-operated clutch, worked by a lever, which was very nearly the cause of my demise. One day, having picked up a load of long pine trees from the bottom of the wood, I was backing the trailer round to the wrack bench at the estate's saw mill, when the trailer began to jack-knife and one of the overlapping butt ends on the front end of the trailer swung across the clutch lever, preventing me from disengaging the engine. I just managed to bale out of the driving seat before another butt end could sandwich me between it and the steering wheel. Fortunately the engine stalled on the full jack-knife and everything came to a grinding halt. I have to say Martin seemed more concerned for his mangled steering wheel than for the fact that I had only just avoided being crushed to pieces. It was only later that I felt shaky at the thought of what might have happened. Ken found an old car steering wheel to replace the squashed one, and all was well again.

My favourite time was bracken cutting and carting in the Forest. Martin yarded up his animals in the winter and bedded them down on bracken. Martin, Ken and I used to go up the valley to Ashley Walk with our scythes and a picnic dinner, and choosing a patch of bracken, cut round and round it, one behind the other, until it was all cut and laid out in swathes. Dinner was a welcome ritual and a break from our labours in the autumn sunshine. I used to make a small fire and brew up a kettle of tea with Cuthbert's old kettle and eat date sandwiches with an apple and some cheese, and then we would doze until two o'clock. Then back to work, swinging the scythe rhythmically through the afternoon, watching the fem fall, with the occasional respite for one's back while you stroked an edge on the blade with your sharpening stone. Martin was an expert mower and could produce a good edge; with bracken, the edge did not have to be so keen as with grasses, the stiff stems stood up to the blade. My rhythm was good, but I never really mastered the art of getting the razor edge necessary for cutting grass properly.

After a week of cutting fern in the valley we took our prongs and pushed the swathes up into peeks, ready to load onto the tractor trailer. The colour soon went out of the bracken once it was cut. It was quite an art loading a trailer with loose fern or hay; one had to keep the load going up square and always remember to tie in the outer edges by keeping the middle full, yet always keeping it slightly hollow at the same time. It was an art one learnt intuitively by sensing disapproval from a competent expert. You were never instructed in so many words on how to load a waggon…

With a full load roped on, we carted it down to the farm yard to stack loose in a small Dutch barn, ready to be cut out, with a hay knife, in trusses for bedding the cattle down. Bracken makes good bedding for cattle as it has no weed seeds and is friable, making for easily spread dung. When green it is full of poisonous alkaloids and cancer-causing carcinogens, but withered it seems to be of no interest to cattle as well as being almost harmless. The old Commoners used to use fern for bedding their animals. Of course, mechanical cutting came eventually, on carefully reconnoitred patches to make sure there were no snags or stumps to break the cutter, and, wonder of wonders, the pick-up baler to compact and tie all the fern up in useful bales. But remembering our days of mowing bracken by hand, nothing quite compared with that steady work.

Martin gave me time off to go to Salisbury Technical College to learn a bit about farming techniques, milk production, maintenance rations, and supplements per gallon of milk yield. In the warm atmosphere of the College I used to find myself nodding off, only to be woken by a question from our long-suffering tutor. My college days were not a success. I learnt that mangolds and fodder beet, crops that Martin grew, were looked upon as an expensive way to cart water by agricultural experts. That they might contain valuable trace elements essential to animal health was never considered. I think Martin hoped I might gain some knowledge of dairy work to help him bump up the milk yields in his little herd. He offered me a penny for every extra half gallon I managed to coax from his cows. "Big deal," I remember thinking to myself. What his poor cows needed was lots of extra protein in cattle cake, too pricey for Martin to afford. So it was a no-win situation in which any financial reward seemed very far away.

Tragedy struck the Westlake family in the late summer of 1953. While we were getting in the corn harvest from a stony field at the extreme south end of Sandy Balls, news came of Keith's suicide. Keith, the eldest son of my uncle, a brilliant doctor and head registrar in one of the large London hospitals, had taken his life in an extreme bout of clinical depression. He left behind a young Scottish wife and two young daughters. My Uncle Aubrey, in his grief, unfortunately found a scapegoat in Norah, Keith's widow, and refused to have anything more to do with her. It was a hard time for Norah, to be suddenly widowed and blamed for a condition in her husband over which she had no control. My uncle had refused to recognise that Keith's recurring depressive states took him onto a knife edge from which he might slip off one day, if not diagnosed and helped. Norah was left to pick up the pieces of her life unsupported. In the end, Richard Westlake befriended Norah and gave her tremendous support, becoming an appreciated uncle to his two nieces, Carol Ann and Diana. A lukewarm reconciliation was effected with Norah and her in-laws, but it came a bit late for Norah. Forty years later, telling me about it, she still wept at the pain and injustice of her father-in-law's rejection.

Martin and I used to go to Sidcot to play rugby for the Old Scholars team against the school each year. Before we set off, I remember Martin drinking pints of salt water as a remedy to stave off cramp in the game to come. The family had an ancient, pre-war French Hotchkiss jeep which Martin would use to drive us to the school. None of the windows fitted and it was so draughty that it gave us stiff necks. In those days, we used to beat the school quite easily as we played club rugby at weekends and were fit as a result. I played for Southampton Trojans B team for a while, but gave up as the atmosphere was too public school and men, well into their forties, behaved like irresponsible adolescents. On a trip to play Streatham, in our tedious pub crawl back, we took a short cut and ended up with the coach stuck in a ploughed field. The whole team got out and with tipsy enthusiasm, pushed and heaved the vehicle back onto a metalled road. We got lost on small country roads, while the wags of the team sang the usual boring, smutty Eskimo Nell songs that seem to go hand in hand with rugby socialising. This 'Old Boys All Together' bonding was just too much for me and I left the club. Richard, Martin and I went on to join Wimborne Rugby Club later which was much more plebeian and to our taste.

By the autumn of 1953 it became necessary for me to begin earning a proper wage as £1 a week was simply not enough to keep me in clothes and pay my mother for food. My Aunt Marjorie couldn't understand my dissatisfaction with my working status, asking in puzzlement why I wasn't happy working with the family. I suggested moving on to a recognised wage, but was told the estate could not support it.

Reclaiming overgrown land at Godshill Ridge.

Chapter 58
Mr Bennett's Farm 1954

By a stroke of good fortune, a Mr Alec Bennett, former TT champion of the 1930s and car salesman in Portswood, Southampton, had bought a Godshill farm belonging to an old village family called Cutler.

The dry hill land had been in constant cultivation, but the land in the valley under Godshill Wood was boggy, derelict and covered in scrubby blackthorn. Mr Bennett had appointed a foreman called Stan Bacon, a native of Godshill, to oversee the reclamation of the farm, and needed another labourer to help him with the task.

After a slightly uneasy leave-taking from my cousin's employment, I started work early one frosty morning alongside Stan, cutting back overgrown hedges, and draining and re-fencing fields that had become almost derelict. Mr Bennett was cashing-in on all the Ministry of Agriculture subsidies of the time offered for land reclamation, and had hired Bert Mist, the only villager with a tractor, and his driver, Ron Langford, to plough up each field as it became cleared. A man from the Ministry came and analysed the soil, recommending a good chalking for a start to sweeten it, followed by a vast application of fertiliser. The fertiliser arrived in its component sacks - phosphates, potash and nitrogen. These had to be tipped out on the barn floor and mixed in varying proportions, according to which field was being treated. Why compound fertilisers were not bought ready mixed I have no idea, maybe they didn't exist then.

Ron Langford was ploughing all through the winter with his Fordson Standard, and trailed a two-furrow plough, putting two-thirds of the total acreage down to corn of one sort or another. The area allocated for pasture we seeded with a contrivance known locally as a Shandy Barrow, consisting of a nine-foot seed box with a revolving shaft going the length of its interior. The shaft had brushes every foot or so, coinciding with adjustable slots in the seed box. The grass seed was poured into the box and the revolving brushes forced it out of the slots in a controlled trickle. The whole contraption was pushed across the field just like a wheel barrow with a large front wheel, the hub of which had a toothed drive which engaged with a bevel-geared shaft, that in turn rotated the brushed shaft inside the seed box.

To make sure you covered all the field in grass seed, you had a nine foot stick with which to measure off the ground. As you traversed the field, you placed marker sticks in the ground with a bit of white rag attached so you could see them from the far end of the field. By pushing the Shandy Barrow in a straight line, with your eyes firmly fixed on the markers, it was amazing how accurate one could be. Sowing a field involved quite a few miles of walking, but there was also an element of novelty in using such an antiquated folk tool which, in spite of its age, was very efficient.

When the field had been seeded, Ron would come with his old tractor and, with an eternal fag stuck to his lower lip, he would course up and down with the light seed harrows to roughly cover the grass seed, and then finish by rolling it in. The quantities of fertiliser put on for the corn crops was astronomical. All the locals said it would grow too long and get laid by the weather, and it did, making much of the crop very difficult to harvest. However, the weather was reasonably kind. Ron and Bert cut the corn with an old reaper binder, sending it out of the machine in neat sheaves tied with twine. Stan and I followed behind, stooking the sheaves, or in local parlance 'hilling'. We gathered two sheaves under our arms, and banging down the butt ends on the ground, we leaned the heads of corn against each other so the sheaves stood upright to dry. Six sheaves made a 'Hile'. We harvested and built eighty mighty corn ricks that August. Old Mr Brewer came with his single-barrelled shot gun during the corn cutting, banging away with deadly effect at any rabbit that tried to make a run for it through the gradually diminishing stand of corn. When I asked him why he did not have a double-barrelled gun his reply was: "Why do you need two when one does the job?" to which there was really no answer as I never saw the old man miss his quarry.

I learnt a lot about corn rick building; how to arrange the sheaves and tie in the outer course, how to gently cantilever the walls outwards from the faggot base to drain the rain off, how to place the 'long end' and the 'short end' of the butt of the sheaf when making the pitched roof to the rick. Stan had a tremendous pride in a well-built rick and he would tap the butts of the sheaves into a perfect symmetry with a piece of board on the lane side, where passers by could see his handiwork. Ron Hayward, the local thatcher, was called in to add a temporary thatch on the finished corn ricks, made from wheat straw Stan and I had pulled from last year's straw rick. We worked our way round the loosely-built rick, pulling and laying out the resultant straight straw in a long line. When we had enough, we gathered it up in bundles, as much as we could encompass, then tied it with a twist of straw.

Stan and I worked, for the first four months, cutting back hedges and digging out old ditches, long clogged from lack of maintenance. The ditches were large, 3ft 6ins. deep, 3ft wide at the top, tapering to shovel width at the bottom. This was all done by hand. We must have shovelled hundreds of tons of earth making all those ditches. Mr Bennett bought a small grey Ferguson tractor, with all its tailor-made 'System' machinery - plough, grass mower, disc harrow, saw bench, front loader and hydraulic tipping trailer. Throughout the second winter, Stan and I dug gravel by hand and made a half mile of new road connecting the two parts of the farm, so doing away with the necessity of going on the public road. The tipping trailer was a boon for spreading the gravel as one just moved forward gently while the load slid off in an even layer.

Our gravel pit had been used by the tenant small holders of Godshill in the past to extract gravel for their annual communal patching up of Purlieu Lane. It provided gravel with just the right mixture of yellow sand bordering on clay, to bind the flint content for a good road surface. The ochres and reds in the various strata in the twelve foot gravel face were fascinating. Stan and I undercut the face with our picks until tell-tale signs from above suggested it was time to beat a hasty retreat, and with a sudden rumble, down would come a ton or so of fresh gravel, now loose enough to be shovelled onto the trailer. The clay element in the gravel used to build up on the shovel blade, I remember, and we each had a chisel-shaped piece of wood to scrape our shovels clean, providing a welcome half minute's rest from the rhythmic slog of loading.

Stan Bacon came from an old Godshill family, and in his youth worked as a gardener at Newgrounds for a genteel lady, Miss Sargent. Stan was in the RAF during the war years. He married and had two sons, Colin and Raymond, renting my mother's old weaving shed in the village for two shillings a week and turning it into a tiny home for his family. After the war he went back to earning his living as a jobbing gardener.

Next to the weaving shed, my mother had allowed an old lady, Miss Viney, to put up a tiny wooden bungalow where she lived out the rest of her life. She bequeathed the little house to Mother on her death. I remember, on a visit to the old lady with my mother as a child, being fascinated by a little 'weather house' that she had in her porch. It took the form of a model cottage with two doors out of which would come a lady if the weather was going to be good, and a man if it was going to be wet. The figures, as far as I can remember, swivelled on a central pin, the movement of which was governed by a piece of twisted gut which tightened up in warm weather making the lady appear, and relaxed in damp humid conditions, allowing the man outside the door to proclaim rain. It was more of a novelty than an accurate forecaster of the weather, but very intriguing.

A couple called Langley rented Miss Viney's old bungalow after the war. Mrs Langley was of Gypsy stock, her maiden name being Sheen. Mr Langley was a Londoner who drifted down to the Forest area soon after the war and never went back, a man of great energy, he too did gardening and odd jobs for a living. The Langleys had a son called Frank and a daughter who was tragically run over and killed on the dangerous corner at the village school. They went on to have another daughter, Cherry, many years later.

The Bacons and the Langleys were always at loggerheads, mainly because of the former family's prejudice against Gypsies. As Frank's mother was a Gypsy it followed, in terms of local prejudice, that Frank, half belonging to that infamous tribe, was automatically tarred with the brush of a 'no-good'. Class status on a village level. I think the youngsters got on well enough together, getting up to all sorts of pranks, but it was always at Frank the finger was pointed if they got caught. The roof of the Bacon's house was still thatched with heather in those days, and one night a group of boys, messing about with matches, set fire to the thatch. Luckily, Stan saw it in time to be able to put out the fire before it caught hold, so not much damage was done. Of course, Frank got the blame as the Bacons insisted that their two good boys could not possibly have been responsible for such an irresponsible act. Mrs Bacon, a woman of nervous disposition, complained that she could not possibly go on living in the house so long as it had a thatched roof. She persuaded Mother to re-roof the place with corrugated asbestos and the two families continued living next door to each other in an uneasy truce with the occasional flare-ups. When Stan Bacon was offered the foreman's job by Mr Bennett, it must have presented a great opportunity for him, as with it came the tenancy of the large old farm house of the Cutlers.

The crop of grass from the new leys and excess fertiliser was very heavy that first summer. Pick-up balers had not come on the scene at that time and all the hay went into ricks. Stan had a wooden hay sweep on the front of the Ferguson with which he swept up the raked-in swathes of hay into the base of the elevator worked by a little Lister engine. I pitched the hay by hand onto the elevator which carried it up onto the rick, where Bernard Target, another villager employed by Mr Bennett, built the rick. Stan was not too imaginative regarding how much hay he pushed up to the base of the elevator, or at what angle it came in at, often producing a hopeless tangle for me to sort out in my efforts to feed Bernard with a steady supply of hay on the rick. It was a sore bone of contention and irritation. Bernard Target was a likeable fellow, red-haired and good-natured, with a wife and two teenage children, a boy and a girl. Normally, he was chauffeur and general handy man for Mrs Bennett, cleaning shoes, chopping wood for the house, and so on. At haymaking, harvesting or thrashing, he was always pulled in to help, having a natural countryman's aptitude for farm work.

The corn was kept in ricks until it was needed on the farm, as in the case of oats, which we used to have crushed at Breamore Mill for fattening beef cattle mixed in with pulped swedes, or, in the case of barley or wheat until the price on the open market was right. Armfields, the local agricultural supplier and foundry at Stuckton, hired out labour and thrashing tackle. Up until the end of the war, it was towed from farm to farm with an ancient steam traction engine, which also powered the thrashing box by way of a long drive belt. The arrival of the traction engine heralded a dramatic and enthralling event, with its smell of smoke, hot steam and living, breathing energy. One of the foundry's traction engines, however, had run away when going down Fordingbridge hill and tipped over, scalding its driver to death with escaping steam from ruptured steam pipes. The old steam engines were very old and worn and, by the early 'fifties, steam power had given way to tractor power. Armfields now had a large TVO-driven David Brown tractor to power the old thrashing tackle. It was infinitely more manoeuvrable, and far less work to keep going, but a great loss to the romance of the job.

The thrashing team brought along a small mesh, wire-netting fence which they put all round the corn rick to prevent the rodent life, that had accumulated in the months after its building, from escaping. The thatch was stripped off the rick, and in the frosty gloom of an early winter's morning, the tractor started, and the giant drive belt brought the thrasher to life in a hum, whirr and clack of noise and movement. Thrashing was labour-intensive; it required two men on the rick to feed the man on the drum with sheaves, the butts in the right direction to facilitate a fluent reach, hook and cutting of the twine, to distribute the corn evenly into the maws of the drum. As each sheave hit the drum, the note of its hum lowered fractionally as the grain was flailed off its stalks, to rise again as the load lightened before the next sheaf. It required one man on the sacks to hook them to the grain chutes, weigh and tie them when full. Oats worked out the lightest per volume at 1¼ cwt to the sack with wheat at 2cwt, and barley the most at 2¼cwt. The sacks were always hired from the West of England Sack Company.

Two more men built the straw rick or fed the stationary baler which made 1cwt rectangular bales. Sid Gobels, the long-time tractor driver for Armfields, used to mind the baler, manually fishing the twine through with a pair of needles mounted in tandem, timing his dive for the twine to coincide with the late rammer being at its furthest travel away from the bail chamber. Having pulled the twine through, he would cut and hand-tie the ends for each bale, leaving enough slack for each one to expand as it left the confines of the bale chamber.

Last, but not least, was the poor fellow 'volunteered' to look after the cavings, or grain husks, and dust and general rubbish disgorged by the thrasher, rake it away and generally keep the machine clear of detritus. That made a total of eight men in all, quite a gang. I used to try and get on the corn rick with Bernard Target to pitch the sheaves to the thrasher feeder. It was good work, especially if one achieved a rhythm. If the rick had been a few months standing, a lot of rats and mice would appear as one neared the base. Some of the men had terriers who came into their own, making short work of the rodents as they tried to flee the shrinking rick, only to come up against the netting fence previously erected. I remember Queenie, Mr Bennett's Springer Spaniel gun dog tackling a large rat which clamped itself to her floppy upper lip tearing it quite badly. Sid Gobels had some penicillin ointment he put on the wound, I remember, in case of Wiel's Disease.

Finally, with the sun setting in the winter sky, we would get down to the last sheaf, and the drum would moan and slow for the last time as the final heads of grain were beaten and winnowed and sent on their way to the sacks, open ready to receive them. Then, with a final exploratory lift of the faggot rick bed, to expose any remaining vermin to the ever eager terriers, we shut down and covered the outfit up for the night, before wending homewards. ✢

Chapter 59
Pauline and Jimmy Nelson Enter Our Lives

Jimmy and Pauline Nelson were to make our home life in the early 'fifties interesting. A couple in their thirties, they were an odd pair, a down-to-earth builder from Ayrshire and a former cellist in the Hallé orchestra.

They had a little boy called Roddy. Jimmy was looking for premises to set up a pottery, and my mother in her usual open, generous way offered our facilities. Jimmy had been a conscientious objector and had served his time in the Quaker Friends Relief Service abroad. While there he developed severe food poisoning, resulting in a troublesome stomach ulcer he used to treat with a patent medicine, Aludrox. I remember the drug as Jimmy later used to colour one of his glazes with the medicament, producing a yellowish glaze with red flecks. The couple were very hard up, so they rented the Leek's old caravan from Olive who had bought it a few years before, and Jimmy began making pots from our native Forest clay.

To have someone around who was interested in making pots was heaven to me, and I spent all my free weekends in Jimmy's company, learning from his methods. I learnt how to do Japanese spiral wedging and the rudiments of glazing. Looking back, I now know that Jimmy's knowledge of pottery processes was fairly limited, but he certainly knew more than me, and it was so good to have a companion, rather like an elder brother, with whom to work on my pottery.

Verwood Village Pottery had fallen on hard times in 1951 and was about to close. Instead of keeping to the old traditional lines of pottery, they had brought in an electric kiln and employed a woman from Poole who was making very brightly glazed, industrial pots, quite divorced from the wonderful traditional wares. A timber merchant, Mr Thorn, was the last owner of the old pottery and he had been able to supply the wood to fire the huge up-draught kiln. With money short and enamel and aluminium kitchen ware, as well as plastic, coming into fashion, the old clay pitchers, washing bowls and cider costerels, were no longer in demand.

Jimmy made enough pots to fire our coal-fired kiln and we biscuited them. To save costs, he only fired them to 680°C and over half the larger pieces developed surface cracks on cooling. Jimmy blamed the clay, but I have since learnt that the too low firing was the cause. The rest he glazed with lead bisilicate and we repacked the kiln and fired it with a mixture of coal and offcuts of wood from a local saw mill. Coming up to temperature, the arch of the muffle cracked and fell in on the setting of pots, introducing smoke and a reducing atmosphere, causing all the lead glaze to bubble up. We did the best we could, carefully stoking to get the fire back to an oxidising atmosphere, and hoped for the best. The result when we came to unpack was pretty disheartening, with the majority of pots being bubbled and cratered. Not good news for a potter on the bread line.

We experimented with a brazier-like kiln, a simple box of bricks with air vents and an open top, and the muffle inside, raised on fire bricks with a six-inch gap all round. We tried building a coke fire round the muffle, gradually building it up and eventually over the top. This worked quite well but was a bit vulnerable to the vagaries of wind direction. Then we built a coke-fired kiln from the bricks of the old kiln and cast a muffle from ceramic cement which we incorporated into it, but the design was hopeless and we only just achieved red heat. With money running out, my mother offered to buy the electric kiln from Verwood Pottery. We were twelve years away from getting electricity on The Ridge, but Jimmy managed to find a villager, Bill Sevier, who was willing to let us put up a shed at the bottom of his garden to house the kiln near a transformer. Using the corrugated sheeting off the old Dutch barn from our fields, Jimmy constructed a shed, and we manoeuvred the ton of kiln into it. The electricity board wired it in and Jimmy had at last a reliable form of firing.

During the war years, a sand pit was opened up on the hill opposite us, under Godshill Wood. Over twenty years, it became an extensive working. In 1952 Jimmy, being dissatisfied with the local yellow forest clay that fired red, was looking round for an alternative. We were amazed to find a thin seam of white clay sandwiched between strata of yellow sand. For the price of a drink, the workmen in the quarry agreed to bring over a lorry load of this clay, and Jimmy started to make all his pots from it. Although slightly sandy, it was still a fat plastic clay, with hardly a trace of iron and, firing white, it was ideal for Jimmy to decorate with his coloured slips. Everything Jimmy made was turned at the base and he perfected a tapping technique for quickly re-centering his leather-hard pots on the wheel. His sense of form was good, but his decoration was lousy, and very rarely helped or enhanced the forms to which they were applied. When he was not using our old stand-up wheel, I made a few pots, and secretly thought I made a better job of decorating them than he did.

The new kiln took all the stress out of firing, but selling the finished ware at that time presented problems. People were still relatively poor in the country and car ownership a quarter of what it is today, which limited their mobility to get out and about, see craft

Chris digging clay at Godshill.

work and buy it. So, like my father with his carvings years before, Jimmy was confined to a few shops taking oddments of pots on a sale or return basis, with the occasional commission. Pottery did not seem a viable way to earn a living at that time if one was realistic.

Jimmy and Pauline got on reasonably well at this stage in their marriage. My mother offered them a piece of land on which to build a house and Jimmy knocked up a sectional bungalow, of necessity made out of the cheapest wood available which was elm planking on 3ins by 2ins frames, bolted together with a simple, single pitch roof. One could never accuse Jimmy of not being a hard worker, juggling pot making with house building. To me, it was all rather exciting, but then I was single with no care in the world. Jimmy with a family ought to have known that the days of house building without planning permission were long gone, but he was unrealistic enough to go ahead and build regardless. The elm boarding, green when cut, soon warped in the sun and weather, giving the thrown-up dwelling a real tatty, hillbilly feel. But the summer sun shone and various orchestral friends of Pauline's stayed for happy weekends enjoying the Nelsons' hospitality.

We tried dowsing for a water supply and the hazel twig seemed to twist and have a mind of its own for me at a certain point below the house. So we dug down into the subsoil for about ten foot, in yellow sand, until we came on a trickle of water. Jim bricked up the rather dangerous hole with bricks and the limited supply of water was pronounced as being sweet and pure enough to drink and make tea. The expense of the house brought the Nelson's finances to rock bottom and Jimmy took a job with the Forestry Commission, who were busy straightening the Forest stream in Black Gutter Bottom, from Newgrounds upwards. It was a drainage project without any merit, as the stream was only a winterbourne.

Jimmy had a little Bowen motor cycle with a 98cc Villiers engine and two gears that you changed using a lever on the handlebars. It was very similar to the James of the same period and made in Wales by disabled ex-servicemen. I expressed an interest and Jimmy, needing the money, sold it to me for £45 which was a fair price for the time. I was earning £4 10/- a week for a 44-hour week which included Saturday mornings. The motor cycle was rather badly maintained, but I polished it up and rode many thousands of miles on it over the next twelve years, having the engine rebored three times. When the MOT came in, in the mid-sixties, the front linkage to the forks was too worn and the braking system too inadequate for the machine to pass its test, and I sadly gave it up. On the level, with no head wind, it could do a good 35mph flat out, and 40 down hill There was just about enough power to get up most hills if one got a run at them. It ran on a petrol oil mix and did at least 65 miles to the gallon.

Pauline had a front-wheel drive BSA sports car that she used to drive in hair-raising absent-mindedness everywhere. I remember going to Bladon Gallery near Basingstoke to see the opening of an exhibition of Gypsy paintings by Forest artists Sven and Juanita Berlin. The Nelsons had become friendly with Augustus John who was President of the Gypsy Lore Society and who came along to open the exhibition. A tiny art shop, next to King's, the grocer in Fordingbridge, was in operation at that time, kept by a tall, thin man, Arthur Ballard who wore pebble glasses and had art dealer's long grey hair. He sold prints and the odd pot for Jimmy and lived with an artist called Maxwell Armfield, an ex-Sidcotian who had bequeathed a terrible painting of Goliath to the school which pupils had to view, it seemed, in perpetuity. The pair lived in Armfield's cottage on the edge of Woodgreen Common. Armfield was a specialist in working with tempera and had decorated the whole of his living room ceiling with exotic depictions of the solar system in conjunction with the signs of the zodiac. It was like a pagan temple to Merlin.

It was quite a party to Bladon Gallery, I remember. I went on the little motorcycle, while Augustus sporting a large brimmed hat and florid complexion, no doubt acquired from over-indulgence at the whisky, sat with Pauline in the front of the vehicle, while Jimmy, Armfield and Arthur Ballard sat as a threesome in the back. It was a merry load and weighed the car down so much I was able to keep up with it most of the time. Augustus John was magnificent with his generous introductions to Sven and Juanita's exhibition and the whole evening got off to a great start when some of the gypsy subjects of the paintings turned up to see themselves in paint. Sven painted in the naïve manner and with a very colourful palette; just right for his subjects.

Pauline and Jimmy's relationship began to deteriorate. The first spring of their optimism had resulted in Pauline becoming pregnant again, and Pauline, a sensitive lady, found Jimmy and his demands too hard to live with. She confided in Arthur Ballard. Jimmy got wind of their platonic liaison but was too jealous to be able to see it as such. In tears of high moral indignation at this apparent betrayal, he decamped to Ayrshire and his parents, taking Roddy with him. Poor little chap, at five he didn't really know what was going on, except that his father was upset. I was naïve and unworldly and could only see I was losing my new pottery colleague and friend; I too wept as I walked with Jim and little Roddy to The Fighting Cocks to see them catch the bus on the first leg of their long trip.

Jimmy wrote to inveigle me into acting as middle man between himself and Arthur Ballard. It was an invidious position, but being green I fell into it. Arthur, when I asked him about the situation was scathing of Jimmy's insensitivity to Pauline in the latter stages of her pregnancy and naturally not a little annoyed that I should concern myself with what he considered to be his private business. It was a sad, stressful time for both of my good friends. I could see both points of view, which made being a go-between untenable.

Pauline, deeply distressed at Jimmy's decision to take little Roddy away, dug deep into her spiritual resources and, presenting an amazingly serene front, stayed on at the bungalow by herself, knitting clothes for the coming child and getting bigger and bigger. As her time to give birth drew near, she was rescued by Arthur. It was a difficult birth but the baby, a daughter called Clare, with her father's strong determined jaw, wide mouth as well as an attractive personality, became a highly thought of osteopath. Pauline adopted Arthur's surname and he seems to have supported her and her children financially in the early years. They moved to Devon, where Pauline reconnected with the musical world centred around Dartington Hall, and I lost contact with her for some years. Jimmy emigrated to New Zealand a year after the break up and Roddy was able to return to his mother. Pauline told me he had such a broad Scottish twang he was almost unintelligible.

Jimmy went on potting, turning to industrial ceramics, insulators and so on, from which, by all accounts, he made a good living. Both Roddy and Clare as young adults went to stay with him and sadly found the experience painful, and living with their father impossible. Their unsettled childhood has left its mark, neither Roddy or Clare settling down with anyone. Roddy is one of those natural musicians, in the folk idiom, who can play almost anything at the drop of a hat, and socially is great fun. He has had many jobs, from making high class recorders to working for environmental projects. As Mother would have said, no doubt it was all meant to be!

After Pauline left, Jimmy's shack was demolished, by order of the planning authorities. Charles Leek said he would carry out the work in exchange for the wood. ❧

Chapter 60
Sid Finch

Sid Finch, who originally arrived on The Ridge with the Santis and who migrated to Olive Schaffer's, finally left her and went to stay in a loft room above a garage belonging to a cottage at Burgate Cross.

Here, he set up an austere bachelor pad and dabbled in pottery at Salisbury Art School, producing some original 'pinched' work with lively Galena glazes. To earn a living, he French-polished bar tops in pubs. Every now and again he held a party for his numerous colourful friends, myself among them, to partake of his organic vegetarian fare. It was with great pride that he used to show me his organic 'no digging' style garden at the back of his pad. Sid had a theory that if you dug the ground, you destroyed the soil structure. His method of getting a garden going was to cover the ground in hardwood sawdust as a light precluding mulch and plant out his cabbage plants or whatever straight into the uncultivated ground. I guess the theory was reasonably sound but Sid never seemed to take into account that his patch of land was full of the rhizomes of couch grass that no amount of sawdust was going to inhibit.

So amid seas of emerging grass, one or two cabbage plants could be seen struggling for survival, their meagre leaves eaten to lace by cabbage white caterpillars. Sid seemed unperturbed by the unequal struggle that his plants seemed to be having and laughed with unconcealed optimistic delight that I should express reservations about the prognosis for the cabbage ever reaching maturity. He was going through a vegan phase and used to expound at length, in an obtuse catarrh-choked voice, the advantages of a dairy-product-free diet. His bunged-up sinuses were not exactly a good advertisement for his nut cutlet and raw cabbage fare.

I remember a knock on the door late one New Year's Eve, and on answering it finding Sid on the doorstep in nothing but a pair of shorts. The night stars were sharp in the sky and it was freezing hard. I invited him in for a warm-up but, hugging himself, he refused, discoursing at great length and with teeth chattering on the efficacy of the ascetic life style. I got cold listening to him and was thankful when he cheerily 'Ho ho, well yes, ho, well cheerio'-ed his departure and, at a brisk jog trot, disappeared into the freezing night on his way back to Burgate. At that time of 'sack cloth and ashes', it was a ritual with Sid to see the New Year in on his own at the top of Pitts Wood, running from Burgate across the icy water-meadows and back in his bare feet. On that viciously cold night, he told me it took him two hours to thaw his feet out to gain any feeling and he was frightened he had got frost bite and would lose some toes. It was touch and go, apparently!

We all heaved a sigh of relief for him when he formed an attachment to a widow in Sandy Balls, Mrs Mary Fredericks, who took him under her wing and had a daughter by him. In his early days in Sandy Balls, this kindly man rescued an abandoned baby from a feckless vegan mother who hadn't enough breast milk to feed it herself and so was casually feeding the poor mite on nuts. The babe was a year old, weighed eight pounds and had a head like a coconut, with the large staring eyes of a famine victim. Sid saved its life with some good sensible feeding and put it in the hands of the local authorities, while the mother disappeared.

When Sid was making pottery in Salisbury Art School, he often used to give away pieces to his friends as Christmas presents. He gave me a porous 'Old Sarum Kettle' for dispensing water at table, which I treasured. A man of great enthusiasms, at one time Sid took up painting, organising his own exhibitions in the Godshill village hall from time to time. His paintings were shown in conjunction with his pottery. Having ceased making pots by this time and having given most of them away, he 'borrowed' them all back, my kettle amongst them, in order to have enough for his exhibition.

Sid's artwork was different to say the least, and it was presented to the public with a wonderful enthusiasm and totally childlike absence of any critical faculty. His talent for painting, using media ranging from coloured inks to lacquers, was notable for its distinctive naïve style, if nothing else. There were many tortured pictures of Mrs Fredericks in the nude in various poses, and Sid, as he took you round, would expound on the significance of these with cheerful enthusiasm. The shows were an unconscious ego trip for him that no one had the heart to disabuse. None of us ever had our pots back and we never had the heart to ask.

Living to be a spritely 95-year old (he died in 2013), Sid remained at Sandy Balls, taking pottery classes (Clay Play) in the summer with the holidaying children to whom he was a sort of good-natured 'Pied Piper'. ✦

Sid Finch at Sandy Balls with the artist Eryl (Jenny) Vize. (Photo: Courtesy Belinda Vize.)

Chapter 61
Work on Mr Bennett's Farm 1954 Onwards

Going back to life on the farm, it was in the days before myxomatosis, and the land was crawling with rabbits.

They did a good deal of damage, eating off the grass up to twenty yards into the hayfields, souring it with their urine and droppings. One field on the farm had an earthworks, referred to by the locals as Frankenbury; it dated from pre-Roman times and was called Godmans Cap Camp, according to the Ordnance Survey map. The earthworks, which surrounded the field, was covered in hazel coppice and honeycombed with rabbit warrens. Stan used to put up 100-yard long nets supported on poles round the outside of the bank, and then send down ferrets to bolt the rabbits into them. Mr Bennett and his friends used to blaze away at those that escaped the net and tried to make a break for it across the field, with their twelve-bore shotguns occasionally dispatching one. He was a poor shot, but enjoyed the adrenalin-charged sport.

When the corn was being cut with the reaping machine, old Mr Brewer used to come along with his single barrel hammer shotgun and wait for the rabbits to bolt out of the diminishing stand of corn. I never knew him miss his quarry and he was so fast at reloading his gun, I have seen him kill two rabbits, the last being at the extremity of his range, but a palpable hit none the less! As a last resort we had men from the Ministry of Agriculture to gas many of the warrens in the banks of the hedgerows. I never cared much for this method as it involved blocking off all the exits to the warren with sods and posting in cyanide powder with a tablespoon tied to a long stick. As soon as the powder was exposed to the damp and air, it gave off its lethal gas throughout the networks of galleries in the warren, and the rabbits died in a very painful way.

Haymaking was a chancy business with English weather. Before the days of satellite surveillance, forecasting was much more guess work than it is now. I remember one year when Stan timed everything very badly and we watched the hay weathering in the never-ending summer rains until it went black. In the end, we were forced to put it in a rick, just to get it off the ground to facilitate new growth of grass. Stan insisted the hay had some nutritional value and we had to bale it up from the rick with Armfield's Stationary baler in a constant cloud of black mould that left us, after a day's work, as black as chimney sweeps.

Those two days of baling without the protection of masks, inhaling that mould, did something to my immune system, and I developed a summer asthmatic condition that came on each time it rained. It laid me out, gasping for breath, fit for nothing and very frightened. For thirty years, I always dreaded a rainy day in summer because it heralded the onset of an attack. November to June was fine; indeed when I went cycling abroad I was as fit as a flea. My allergic reactions seemed to be linked with the Forest vegetation. I had the usual skin tests and reacted mildly to hay dust. I had courses of injections to desensitise my system, all to no avail. Summers were not looked forward to and all the medications I took had side effects that were almost as bad as the asthma. Since then, mild steroid inhalers have come on the market and made such a difference, I can now enjoy summers again.

Apart from corn, we grew kale, fodder beet, and swede; the latter was sold to the Cunard Line in Southampton. The roots, when harvested, we made into clamps, long rectangular heaps that tapered from a wide base to a pointed apex to allow for the run off of rainwater. We covered the clamp, first in straw and then earth, digging a shallow ditch around it, thus protecting the roots from the frosts. The majority of the root crop went to fattening Mr Bennett's herd of prize Hereford beef cattle, pulped and mixed with rolled oats also grown on the farm, and rolled and crushed at Breamore Mill. After the root crops were sown, it was our labouring job to single the plants out with a hoe, spacing each with room to grow to full size. I did not enjoy this 'singling' as it was called. It was boring, back-breaking work, each row being several hundred yards long. Stan Bacon seemed totally inured to the task, while I used to flake out at the end of each row and straighten out flat on the ground for a minute or so to ease the chronic back ache the hoeing induced!

A new eye disease, peculiar to the Forest, started hitting cattle in the early 'fifties. A small pin point of opacity appeared on the pupil of an animal's eye, usually only one eye, accompanied by copious weeping discharge. If left, the whole eye went opaque, like a poached egg, and an ulcer formed in the centre, which finally burst leaving the animal blind. It was very painful for the animal as well as being unpleasant to look at. Our Hereford herd got it very badly and we had to put them all through a cattle crush each day hnhand dose their eyeballs with antibiotic ointment. If caught early it could be arrested, and when healed it only left a tiny opaque dot in the centre of the pupil. It has become known as 'Forest Eye', and is largely spread by flies, though its incidence nowadays seems to be far less common.

George Combes joined our work force a year after myself, a small and wiry good-natured local from Blissford, much the same age. His mother was from the Sheen family of Gypsies and they lived in a converted railway carriage by the brook. George was short of stature and he could whittle out the root crops with no apparent back discomfort. He used to laugh at my ineptitude: "Ah, Chris, you see it sometimes pays to suffer from Duck's disease (*i.e. short stature*), then thee's don't have to bend so far, look see?"

After Mr Bennett bought his Fergusson tractor and all its associated tackle, Stan was to be seen working from a tractor seat more often than he worked alongside George and myself at the hard manual jobs. I suppose it was his privilege as foreman, but it did rankle on occasions, especially when he found fault with our work. Mr Bennett had an old army jeep which we used to drive from one part of the farm to another. George and I had a lot of fun belting up and down the gravel roads. It was a real gas guzzler doing eight miles to the gallon, but then we weren't paying for the petrol. The only time we had charge of the tractor, first thing in the morning when feeding the cattle, I would get George to drive flat out across the field while I off-loaded the hay and kale. The object was to see if one could keep on one's feet in the bed of the trailer at speed. Inevitably I lost my balance one day and pitched out onto the hard ground with a hell of a smack. George, concentrating on his driving, didn't look back until he was the other side of the field, when he did a double-take on seeing that the trailer was empty. His face was a study. Fortunately, I was only bruised, but the discomfort was enough to get us to desist from such foolhardy manoeuvres ever again.

Many of the fields on the farm in the valley under Godshill Wood were covered in scrub blackthorn, hawthorn, broom and gorse. To clear this, Mr Bennett employed a contractor, Mr Dennett, who came with a bulldozer and pushed all the invading growth into mounds; George and I were given the task of burning them. As there was as much earth as burnable debris in the heaps, it was gut-wrenching work, freeing up branches and roots submerged in a sea of soil and dragging them away for burning. We often thought how much easier the job would have been had we cut the scrub at ground level by hand, clearing the area for later bush ploughing out of the roots. However, we did it the hard way, and with the ground finally cleared, we then had to drain it. To this end, we laid land drains arranged in herring bone formation, with outfalls into the brook. The land drains were plain earthenware pipes, one foot long with a pinch bore, abutted against each other, about two foot down in a hand-cut trench and covered with a thick layer of straw to keep the loose soil out when one filled the trench in. These pipes carried the water from the natural springs occurring in the fields and away to the outfalls, so drying the field out for cultivation.

George always came to work on his pride and joy, a 350cc Enfield Bullet, which he would blitz about on with his cronies. One evening each week with his girlfriend, Deirdre, who took her life in her hands when sitting behind him on the pillion, they went to Pool Speedway to watch Pool Pirates. There was a gang of local 'cornstalks' in those days: Colin Bastable who rode a Douglas Twin, and who would yell at his girl to "lean over, gal!" when they took a corner at high speed, or weave dangerously in and out of traffic. There was George Vincent, mad as a hatter on a thumping Norton Single 500, and a "ton up" merchant called Ray Kenchington, cowman at Folds Farm, a young Brylcreem-ed Flash Harry who rode a Triumph Twin. And finally, John Friar, a powerful woodsman with a BSA Gold Star, and the steadiest of the bunch.

It was the last era of the British motor cycle before the Japanese, with their brilliant attention to accurate casting and fresh revolutionary technical design, started to corner the market and drive all British manufacturers to the wall, apart from Triumph, that still struggles on supplying a nostalgia market in America. I, fortunately, never had enough money or interest in motor cycles to get a powerful machine, although in those days, I must say, the roads were a lot less busy with traffic, which was just as well in view of some of the mad antics of my peers.

Chapter 62
My Social Life

My social life at this time was taken up with amateur dramatics. There was, an enterprising elderly lady called Miss Pat (actually Daphne St. George Sefton Pattinson, a former Gaiety Girl), who lived in a rambling house in Fordingbridge Church square.

Miss Pat ran a theatre group called Miss Pat's Players. She was producing an ambitious 'twenties musical, the classic *No No Nanette* and needed a male lead. As I could sing, I joined the group and took on the part of Tom, Nanette's boyfriend. Nanette's part was taken by a pretty girl called Betty Overill, the Catholic daughter of the local registrar. She had a beautiful and natural soprano voice, and great musical ability that could have taken her into the realms of professional singer.

Miss Pat always included a lot of youngsters in her productions, and this was no exception. The action was sardined with tap dance routines and a local man, Reg Tanner, who ran a good dance band which played at all the local hops. He and the band were co-opted to play for the musical, lending the production real class. The show was a great success; Betty in her sequinned 'twenties dress, and I reluctantly in tails, wowed the audience with our *Tea for Two* song and dance routine. I got to know Betty quite well and went to her house where she lived with her mother and we had some good evenings singing duets together. I always had the impression that her mother was giving me the once over, assessing me as a possible husband for her daughter. When she discovered that I was a Quaker, she cooled in her friendliness. It was all irrelevant anyway, as Betty was far too conventional and orthodox in her Catholicism for me to find much in common, apart from music where she left me standing in ability. In a moment of honesty, she told me her age, which was twenty-nine, six years older than me. I don't know if it was meant to be a turn off, but I did not pursue the relationship. I have often wondered what happened to her.

I was in quite a few productions of Miss Pat's, mostly her pantomimes which were chaotic affairs in which the dress rehearsal was usually the first performance owing to the theatrical infighting among the cast, until the reality of actual performance galvanised us all into a unity of purpose of sorts! Our Dame was always taken by a man called 'Fridgy' Brewer, a wiry man in his late sixties, rather like old man Steptoe, with a classic, bony, vaudeville face that he made up with bright rouge to accentuate his high cheek bones. He wore a horrible moth-eaten red wig and a voluminous dress with many ragged petticoats, which he would lift provocatively to reveal matchstick legs housed in red and white striped laddered stockings. 'Fridgy' was loud, predictable and coarse, and his audience loved him; indeed a pantomime without 'Fridgy' would have been unthinkable.

Miss Pat's Productions were mostly on the grand scale and centred around song and dance. She never produced a straight play. An elderly former teacher called Miss Robinson appeared on the scene and under the reluctant umbrella of Miss Pat (because she always liked to be at the centre of things), produced a 'twenties comedy called *Yellow Sands* by Eden Phillpotts. It was in Devon dialect and I remember learning my part before we even started rehearsals so I could enjoy the production. I played the part of a young country rip called Tom with rabid socialist principals, and very jealous of anyone who looked at his girlfriend. My 'girlfriend' was Brenda Bailey, married to a cornet player, who lived at Gorley. She was a sparky lady and obviously enjoyed our love scenes on stage, and we enjoyed a good flirt in the wings and at parties after the shows. Her husband was a bit jealous, I think, as when he came to pick her up she switched off instantly and became the attentive wife.

Chris 'Pandy' as the leading man in **No No Nanette,** *staged by the inimitable Miss Pat's Players of Fordingbridge.*

There was a stage fight, I remember. Phil Strange, my supposed rival, cunningly concealed a lipstick on his person and during my scrap with him, in which we exchanged furious simulated punches, he would surreptitiously give himself a good nose bleed, so realistic ladies in the audience were heard to whisper to each other: "Cor, he's given him a bloody nose, serve him right!"

Phil was quite a character. He earned his living as a window cleaner, but he always had a dream to be a big-time entertainer. There was a radio show on each week called *The Carroll Levis Discovery Show,* in which young hopefuls with various talents had their big chance. They came on, performed their act, and were judged by the volume of the applause registered on the 'Clapometer'. The act which achieved the most decibels was declaimed the winner and went on to greater things. Quite a few became famous via the 'leg-up' of that show, including Julie Andrews, Ronny Ronalde, the whistler, the duo of Albert and Les Ward, who played the washboard and electric saw, Bill Kerr, the comedian and many more. Phil Strange had been on the show but the 'Clapometer' sadly never gave him the lift to the big time, although he was a very talented working men's club entertainer. He had a brassy, tenor voice with which he could raise the roof, singing the various ballads of the day such as *Come Back To Sorrento.* He played the ukulele and banjo and did convincing impersonations of George Formby, as well as a routine in which he danced suggestively with a mop, crooning a passionate ballad to it as he insinuated his legs round the handle. It was as amusing as it was outrageous. Phil played gigs in pubs and clubs to earn a bit of extra money, and had a fund of risqué Max Miller-style jokes full of double innuendo. His small, bespectacled daughter was an accomplished tap dancer with Miss Pat, making up a trio of precocious young girls including Pat Combes and Jane Kenchington, who danced and sang in colourless, automated harmony like The Andrews Sisters.

Ron Thorn was another actor from *Yellow Sands* days, a confirmed bachelor at that time. When I knew him, he was an insurance agent collecting little premiums from house to house, riding on his moped, a hybrid cycle that you started by peddling. He had a lovely Hampshire burr to his voice and could 'tickle the ivories' on the piano to great effect. This made him indispensable in *Yellow Sands* as he had to sing a song which went thus: *"I'm rotten as a hen-pecked pear, Though only sixty-one I swear, Though rather short of teeth and hair, Sing tour-rool-looral lay, sing tour-rool loral lay."* His problem was that he couldn't act unless he had a few pints inside him, after which he was brilliant. He came to the dressing rooms on the night of performance with a carrier bag full of bottles of Double Diamond beer, consuming quantities of this while dressing and making up. Half the show went very well, but Ron did not stop when he had reached his optimum of alcohol consumption, he just carried on drinking when off the stage, so that by the time we got to the last act he was getting distinctly uncoordinated and it was touch and go as to whether we finished the play. Acting opposite him, I would see his eyes beginning to lose their focus and he would start repeating himself, stop, whistle a few notes of annoyance, and try again. Fortunately, the character he was portraying, Uncle Silas, was an old soak anyway, and the audience thought his muddle-headedness was all part of the act. It was a good job the play ended when it did.

Our faithful prompt over the dramatic years was a good-looking woman called Faith. She had suffered polio as a child, which had left her wheel-chair bound. She was cashier in the International grocers shop in the west High Street of Fordingbridge for years. *Yellow Sands* was a great break for her, as the cast required a lady in a wheel chair. Faith rose to the occasion and gave a great performance. She went on to have a happy married life, although further degenerating conditions in later life overtook her despite her indomitable spirit. With the production of *Yellow Sands* Miss Pat's Players went into decline, and a splinter group was formed to perform plays, as opposed to shows, under the steady hand of Miss Robinson. 🌱

Chapter 63
Working on the Land

As some of the tenant smallholders next to our orchard in the Purlieus, sold their land, my mother and father had bought them and we now owned the outside strip of fields bordering the Forest, amounting to seven acres.

The old orchard, from Grandfather Westlake's planting, after years of producing nothing owing to it being in a frost pocket, suddenly yielded a bumper crop in the autumn of 1952 which I bagged up and took to the Bat and Ball pub at Woodfalls where the landlord had a motorised cider press. The apples were tipped into a wooden trough and agitated for a bit to clean them, and then they were shovelled onto a bucket conveyor belt to the mill which, with a hum and a whine, reduced them to pulp. The landlord built up a 'cheese' of pulped apples, containing it with sacking cloths, engaged the press mechanism, and we watched as the juice was squeezed into a giant vat from whence it was automatically pumped to huge hogshead barrels in a warehouse next door. The whole unit was powered by a large, temperamental Lister Stationary engine, the plugs of which constantly sooted up.

Mother had acquired some old sherry casks to put our juice in, and it was with great pride that we came back from Woodfalls with 100 gallons of potential cider which we put in the old feed room of the stable to ferment, adding raisins and sugar to help the alcohol content. The resultant cider was good stuff, but with Hilda around it didn't last long. We discovered that the barrels we were keeping to mature, had only a third of their contents left when we came to broach them. Unknown to us, Hilda had been fortifying herself while at work in the St Ives café, taking half a gallon each day for several months. She never apologised or showed the slightest remorse and, as she had never given any help in our cider-making effort, I felt pretty aggrieved!

Another miracle crop to come only twice in my life, owing to the frosts, was from the old cherry plum hedgerow my grandfather had planted at the same time as the orchard on the boundaries.

I had been thinking of grubbing up the old orchard and reclaiming the strip of fields which were full of wild broom and blackthorn.

To this end, I began to work part-time for Mr Bennett, just enough to earn my keep and petrol for the motorcycle. First of all, I put up a new fence round the fields, cut hedgerow oaks with a crosscut saw and split fencing piles out of them with wedges, pointing them with an axe. I put up a three-strand barbed wire fence all round the lower boundary, the first new fence in forty years. This completed, I started clearing with bow saw, bill hook and axe, the scrub blackthorn, trimming out the larger wood for the home fire and making bonfires of the small trash. It was slow work on my own, but very satisfying to be reclaiming the neglected little fields.

As the Ministry of Agriculture was offering subsidies for land reclamation, Mother and I made use of the offer. Fencing, hedge-laying, putting in land drains, ploughing up old pasture, chalking and reseeding, all commanded small premiums which came in very handy for defraying some of the expenses. We had a contractor in to clear the orchard of its old apple trees, which was unfortunate as much of the wood that could have been used for the fire was burnt in the contractor's efforts to complete the job as quickly as possible. Trimming out the side branches was just too labour intensive to be economic.

Mr Dennett, the local agricultural contractor, was hired to chalk and plough up the orchard with his crawler tractor and prairie plough that turned over a two-foot furrow slice, one foot deep. He then disc-harrowed it, and I borrowed Mr Bennett's Shandy barrow and sowed the first field with a new permanent ley, with lots of timothy, rye and clover seed in it. It was a wet summer and a crop of Old Harry, a plant related to spinach, came up with the new grass, of which I cut a few swathes each day with a scythe to feed our ponies, Joey, Kelpie, Blonde and Pixie. Danae and I had converted the old lightweight caravan to a buckboard cart and, with Joey reluctantly in the shafts, it was very useful for carting small loads of fodder.

About this time Lt.-Colonel Prideaux-Brune, the owner of the Purlieus, died, and the valley was sold to pay off death duties, the existing tenants having first refusal to buy their fields at prices from £35 to £45 an acre.

It was a good time for farming, as we needed all the food we could produce in the aftermath of the war years. The fields next to ours were purchased by Bert Mist, another Godshill farmer, the first in the village to own a tractor, an old Standard Fordson. Bert was a short, tubby, florid man whose grown-up son, Fred, worked for the electricity board, blitzing in and out to work each day on his powerful motorcycle. Fred was not interested in the farm, much to his father's sadness. Bert's tractor driver, Ron Langford, worked the Purlieu fields, growing corn, mangolds, and short-term grass leys in rotation. Ron was a good, all-round worker and ploughman, pulling a trailed two-furrow Pearson plough and taking a great pride in his straight furrows and finish. By then I had acquired a good name for my ability to take on hard manual work and Bert often employed me to work with Ron, dung carting and spreading on the fields ready for the next crop. I enjoyed working and chatting with someone who had a vast knowledge of the old manual skills, such as laying a hedge, ditching and fencing.

When a field was put down to corn, Bert used to plant out a few rows of potatoes at one end, and Ron was also allowed to put some rows in. The method was to plough over two furrows, and then walk down the open furrow placing the seed potatoes one every foot along its length, just high enough for the tractor to miss them next pass. Ron then did another careful pass with the plough, lightly burying the seed potatoes, and repeated the process, the rows of spuds ending up two furrow slices apart.

Charley White of Jubilee Farm had bought a good percentage of the acreage, and taking advantage of the subsidies available, took out hedges, put in drainage, chalked and ploughed large areas and returned old derelict fields to cultivation. His farm prospered. Mr White's son, Robin, who had a milk round, was one of the few boys from the village school bright enough to gain a place at Bishop Wordsworth's Grammar School in Salisbury. However, his father never trusted Robin enough to hand over full responsibility of the farm to him, so Robin remained in a sort of limbo, eventually seduced by the unpredictable horse-racing world, to his detriment. It is doubtful whether the more academic education he had experienced was of much use to him, as it seemed to have made it harder for him to integrate afterwards, and adjust to the realities of village life. Married twice, with three sons, Steven, Flyn and Nathan, he was often to be found in The Fighting Cocks, adopting the persona of colourful local character and authority on Godshill history to any one who would listen.

Self sufficient - Chris digging potatoes.

Chapter 64
Danae's Progress

Danae on her two-stroke Excelsior 98cc motorcycle.

Danae left Sidcot a year after me, in 1952, expressing no wish to stay on into the Sixth form. Rather under Mother's influence she tried a spell at Salisbury Art College, but found she did not fit in with the art school milieu.

Her painting tutor was a Mr Barker, a local man who lived with his wife at Blissford with two children, Jonathan and Carol, who were in the same pony club as Danae. Besides painting, Danae also had her first taste of making pottery, which she enjoyed, but she never entered into the social side of art school life, it being rather foreign to her nature.

Rejecting the art school, Danae expressed a wish to work with animals and, with Mother's help, arranged a position with a Somerset farmer, Mr Snook. It was a live-in job on a dairy farm at Castle Cary, the other side of Wincanton. The venture was a great success and Danae came through her apprenticeship with flying colours, an ideal worker with her natural practical aptitude, strength and common sense. She bought herself a two-stroke Excelsior 98cc motorcycle with a hand change, two-speed, gearbox. On this she used to pay us periodic visits over the next year. The farm was in the transition stage, still using an old horse for the lighter jobs, that Danae said did everything at the gallop, and an old Standard Fordson for the heavier jobs.

Later on, she migrated back to The Ridge to work on a farm at Bramshaw for a Mr Price, of Prices Biscuits. Most of her work there was with pigs that were fed on whey, bought in as a by-product from cheese making. The pigs were housed in a long rectangular building with the trough which could be separated from them by a series of gates. The whey was run in and the meal sprinkled on top, the gate was then raised and all the pigs could scrabble noisily for their food. The noise was tremendous and the rancid smell in hot weather was overpowering. Often through lack of hygiene, or too much whey, the pigs got the 'squits' which added to the overpowering smell. It didn't seem to be too good a system for raising healthy porkers. The foreman, Mr Chalk, used to shoot invading deer on the farm with a .22 rifle and, occasionally, Danae used to bring home a bit of venison. Never one to shirk heavy work, Danae over did it carrying sacks of meal, put her back out badly and was incapacitated for some time.

Danae rejected art school and found her vocation working on farms.

Chapter 65
Pub Days and Village Characters

I used to spend my Saturday evenings in The Fighting Cocks, downing three or four pints of Strong's light ale at 1/5d a pint.

A pound in one's pocket was more than enough to get quite drunk in those days. I went to the pub primarily to talk to Jack Chalk, an octogenarian as spry as a flea. He and I seemed to hit it off. Jack was one of three brothers, the oldest, Henry, lived in School Lane with his son and daughter, John and Edie. Henry rented a field of four acres, which ran parallel with the lane from the school to his house, with its corrugated iron roof. He grew forests of rhubarb, along with the smallholder's stock crops of peas, potatoes, swedes, kale and cabbage.

All cultivations were done with a horse, and by hand. It was a real scratch-living, augmented by a pig for bacon and a cow for milk and butter. Son John also broke in ponies for riding, as had his father before him; John broke in all our ponies at around ten pounds per animal. He was thrown many times in the process and, in middle years, developed Parkinson's disease. The change in him was sad to see. His Dad, a tiny, cheery fellow, was good at treating ailments in horses. I remember him washing out a wound on one of our ponies that had become infested with fly maggots. "Don't thees worry, they gentils be good for a wound as they do eat up all thik bad stuff and do get it cleaned up, see? Wey up, my little beauty, there see?!" And the old man would clean out the fleshy wound with some warm water and there, sure enough, it was clean and pink and ready to heal. "Brimstone and lard be the best thing for thik cut, my maid," he used to say addressing Danae. He would get a bit of pig's lard and some powdered sulphur, and mixing the two together, apply it to the open wound. It was, indeed, a good disinfectant and kept the flies away.

The pace of life was slow for that branch of the Chalk family. They rented a few plots of water-meadow at Hollymarsh, just outside Fordingbridge, and thought nothing of spending a whole morning going from Godshill with a horse and cart to pick up a small load of grass, cut with a scythe from the water-meadows, with which to feed their stock. The old man would sit on top of the load, while John sat half asleep at the rear end of the shafts, rope reins slack in his hands, while the knowing old horse ambled its way back to the village. Daughter Edie was a diminutive spinster one would see on the bus every Monday and Friday, carrying a wireless accumulator needing to be charged at the back of Edwards and Smith radio shop. In those days at least ten people from the village would get on the bus to "go down Town". I remember a rather gentile elderly lady called Mrs Vize (the mother of artist Eryl (Jenny) Vize) who used to board the bus at Godshill Cross. She always wore a flamboyant, broad-brimmed floppy hat and had tear ducts that she could not control; as she theatrically greeted her friends with huge smiles, the tears would stream down her cheeks and she would dab at them unconcernedly with a tiny handkerchief.

Public transport was good, and it was needed. There were no official stops for the bus. You just stood by the side of the road and raised your hand to stop it, and when you wanted to get off you told the conductor, and he or she rang the bell at the nearest point to your house. The double-decker waited about a quarter of an hour before turn-around, just giving enough time for the villagers to do a quick shop. It was 2d for children and 4d for adults to go to Fordingbridge.

Old Jack, the middle brother of the three Chalks, was the most interesting of the family. He was still the same small wiry build he'd been in the Infantry in the 1914-18 war when he was posted to Gallipoli. He was part of the initial landing force that had been shot to pieces by the entrenched Turks as they tried to wade through the strong surf off the Dardanelles. As Jack graphically described it: "Gor, bugger, 'twas bloody murder, you! But then, what could you do 'cept keep going and hope no bullet had got your name on't. My mate, well, one moment he were there, and the next time I looked round he were gone, you. We was sitting ducks for they Turks."

After tremendous unnecessary loss of life, a landing was effected and the British army dug in. Later, in hand-to-hand fighting, Jack received a two-inch gash to his upper lip from a bayonet stab that still showed as a scar.

"I had him though, you; well 'twas either him or me, and I was bloody sure 'twasn't g'wain to be me!" And Jack would, yet again, try to light his foul old pipe and having got it going like a reluctant bonfire, he would gaze at me suddenly reflective. "But then s'now, if you stop an' think about it, he must have been some mother's son. What was it all about? Buggered if I knowed then, and buggered if I know now."

Jack would tilt his old cap back on his bald white pate, and chuckling to himself, take a good pull on his beer and smack his toothless gums, savouring it. "Arter Gliplie, I were batman for an officer in the Indian army up Dually. That weren't too bad, you. I travelled with him up to Mespot." (Mesopotamia, I think he must have meant.)

Jack was in his mid-thirties during his time of service and was referred to by his compatriots as "Old Man". But I gathered that the younger soldiers didn't dare to cross him too much, as he was an aggressive fighter. Because of his diminutive stature he could get in under the guard of a taller man who fancied his chances and lay him out in double quick time, with punches that had no regard to the Queensbury Rules. Jack was put on charge on more than one occasion. The love of his life, an amorous encounter that stayed with him, concerned a "pretty little Armenian maid, a real pretty little maid, she were too!" A second later he would lapse into his rakish mode: "Mind you, I've had 'em all" and he would chuckle wickedly. "Yes, I've left a few colts about the place," he would boast, as the various jungles of puzzling inter-related surnames testified round the village. He remained an unrepentant philanderer.

Jack had a small field he used to cultivate with a crossbred bay pony that pulled a light plough cultivator and harrows. He also shared a long narrow field known as Long Ground with his brother Abel which ran down from the rough below our house to Purlieu Lane. Here, he used to grow spuds, turnips, swede, peas, kale and a few marigolds. Jack was a dab hand with the mole trap, usually keeping a tally of the little creatures he caught by attaching their corpses to a sprig of willow branch he stuck in the ground at one end of his field, rather in the manner of a pheasant keeper's vermin pole. He caught deer too, with strategically placed nooses of wire: cruel, but effective. I helped him skin out a large fallow buck one winter, which we slung between two trees. He gave me a haunch for helping him which weighed fourteen pounds, quite a hunk of meat, which formed the basis for a great feast to which we invited all our friends. Jack used to cart dung all the way from Newgrounds where he lived, down to his fields in the Purlieus, which was quite a trip for the horse as the old cart weighed almost as much as the load. Jack looked after his land, keeping it clean, trimming his hedges and keeping his drainage ditches clear. He liked to keep everything up together.

While in the army, he developed pleurisy and was dosed with quinine which had the side effect of rotting all his teeth, so he claimed. He had never bothered to get false teeth. None of the old Foresters exposed their bodies to the sun and Jack was no exception. He would, maybe, take his jacket off as a concession to the heat and roll his shirtsleeves up to the elbows, but that was it. His face and neck were burnt and wrinkled with years of toil in the elements and the tips of his ears serrated where they had been frostbitten in the Gallipoli campaign winters. His forearms were covered with large black blotches, a legacy of the sun. Britches, boots with gaiters, jacket and a cap completed the outfit. Going to the pub, he always sported a red spotted neckerchief, to hide his lack of collar and lend a bit of dash to his persona.

Jack never had to pay for a drink on Saturday evenings in The Fighting Cocks as he was universally liked by the villagers. As the evening progressed and the drink began to take effect, his language and improper suggestions to nearby young women would become increasingly offensive. At closing time, Jack's last beers were fortified with a couple of whiskey chasers, and he would stagger off home merry and sozzled.

When he owned the Purlieus, Colonel Brune used to hold an annual supper in The George Inn in Fordingbridge, for all the tenant smallholders of Godshill. Jack always used to go with a wheelbarrow, because he knew he would be too drunk to walk back to the village, and he would rely on one of his less inebriated mates to wheel him back home. Another character, before my time, was Georgie Eldridge, who once lived in the house opposite the pub and would drink a good portion of his day's financial takings. Going into a drunken sleep on his cart, his old horse, who had travelled the route hundreds of times, used to bring him home without any supervision. (This happened to Jack too, on many occasions.) Georgie Eldridge wasn't past pouring a pint down his horse's throat, which used to make it lift its upper lip in stallion-like appreciation!

Abel, the youngest of the three Chalk brothers was another surviver of the 1914-18 war. He was in the trenches in France and was wounded in one leg, which left him slightly disabled. He lived with his sister, Polly Harris, on the far edge of the village green, overlooking Newgrounds. Although renting the same amount of land as Jack, he never had the energy of his brother to cultivate it to the same high standard. He was a kind, solid, little man but lacked the drive and adventurous spirit of his older brother. Flanders Field had been his one and only venture abroad in an otherwise very quiet life. Polly Harris, short of stature like her brothers, had two boys, John and Lionel. Lionel, who was at Miss Pask's school at twelve years old, slow and good-natured, was our postman for years, delivering the mail in fair weather or foul, always with a smile. He married and had three sons, sadly developing Parkinson's disease in middle years, dying at a comparatively young age. My last memory is of him driving his red Mini across the bumps and hollows of the village green in an alarmingly erratic manner, in pursuit of his independent-minded Jack Russell terrier. ⚘

Chapter 66
Real Farming and Bert Mist

With the fields cleared of blackthorn and finally fenced and ditched, I decided to try and buy a tractor and attempt a few cultivations of my own.

My attempts at reclamation had not gone unnoticed by the villagers and I had gained a certain respect. When I approached Bert Mist for advice on where to buy a secondhand tractor, he warmed to my interest in farming and offered to take me to a farm sale near Andover on the Hampshire downs.

All the farm machinery, or 'dead stock' as it is called, was laid out in rows, among which were some large blue Fordson Major tractors, the first powerful workhorses to be made after the war. They had a simple hitch and a pulley belt drive to power a saw bench, very basic compared to today's tractors. With Bert's paternal guidance and great daring, I bid for one of the tractors, and in a heart-pounding moment found myself the owner of one of the Majors. To me, the cost of £48 was an extravagant sum. It was well past its best years and what was left of the tyre treads did not offer much grip, but it was adequate for my needs.

There was no self-starter and you turned over the engine with a crank. The technique for getting the engine firing was to pull down the blind over the radiator, drain the carburettor of tractor vaporising oil (TVO) and then refill it with petrol from a small auxiliary tank. Then, at full choke and throttle, you turned the heavy engine over a few times with the crank handle until the engine fired. If you were fast enough in releasing the choke, the engine would then splutter into a roar and you could then throttle back. Like preheating a Primus stove, you ran the tractor engine until the temperature gauge on the radiator registered that it was hot enough to turn over from petrol to TVO. It was a thirsty monster, consuming 15 to 18 gallons of TVO a day when doing heavy cultivations. For run-around work, the tractor was a constant irritation, as unless it was pulling hard and very hot, one or another of the plugs tended to oil up and the engine would run unevenly at half power. My patience and handkerchiefs were worn ragged, cleaning oiled plugs and swinging the starting handle, trying to start the often obstinate engine.

I bought Bert's old trailer plough and a set of rusty old harrows and began ploughing up three acres of ground behind Miss Pask's cottage in the village. Ploughing up old grassland is very difficult especially if one has never done any ploughing before, and I had to learn by trial and error. To enter the ground, the plough has to have a good plough share attached at the base of the mouldboard. In front of the plough share is a disk called a coulter. As the share enters the earth, the coulter cuts the turf in front, allowing the continuous sod or furrow slice to be reversed and turned over by the mouldboard. Setting up the plough to the right depth, not too deep so that the furrow slices were thin enough to flop over and bury the grass side down, was quite a sharp learning curve, and I have no doubt that my first bumbling efforts afforded the villagers not a little amusement!

I borrowed Bert's disc harrows and succeeded in getting a reasonable enough tilth into which to plant a crop of wheat. I applied a compound fertiliser and contracted Jimmy Whitt to drill the seed corn for me. The corn came up reasonably well, but after a dry spell it began to look peaky and yellow and Jimmy hinted that I ought to roll the crop to help conserve moisture. The corn responded and I felt quite proud of my first efforts at real farming.

Although it was like getting blood out of a stone to get practical advice from the native villagers, I felt at least they had a grudging respect for my interest and bumbling persistence. No direct advice was ever given, it was only hinted at, and one had to read between the lines to glean information. They were fast enough to tell you if you were going wrong and I guess that was the way they had picked up expertise themselves, from their elders.

With Mother's help, I was able to purchase more fields next to ours, as the older villagers retired, sold up or "Put the fields in their pockets", as they used to quaintly phrase it. We bought a field from George Sevier of six acres, and I ploughed that up. This field had already been under cultivation and so ploughing it was easy compared to old grassland; I took great enjoyment from watching the friable earth folding in a wave behind me. I borrowed a trailed cultivator from my cousin Martin, and working up a good seed bed, put in a crop of oats, undersown with a ryegrass, timothy and clover ley.

The spring days spent in the fields made me feel good to be alive, the tractor pulled well with a deep throaty roar, and the heat from the engine infused with the faint odour of TVO blasted back at me. I stood to my driving a lot of the time and watched the gulls landing on the furrows, squabbling over the tasty leather jackets and wire worms. Life was good! The radiator of the Fordson took five gallons of water, and in the final few minutes before putting the machine away each night, I used to pull the radiator blind up to get the water nearly boiling, before draining it off into buckets to put in our bath for a hot, if somewhat rusty, warm wash. What a luxury that was! ❦

Chris was often to be found driving a tractor..'the spring days...made me feel good to be alive...'

Chapter 67
Riding Down to Sidcot on Horseback with Danae

After leaving Sidcot, I went back for a few Old Scholars Easter reunions, on one memorable occasion in the 'fifties with Danae, on horseback.

We rode to Somerset over two days, Danae on Joey, and myself on a newly-acquired, nine-year old crossbred of 13.2 hands, a bay gelding called Stormy. We rode to Wilton and through Grovely Wood to Hindon, staying the night in a farmer's barn, then on to Bruton and a dairy farm run by a young farmer called Dick Dyke and his new wife and jolly mother-in-law. Spring grass was in short supply that year, even on rich Somerset pasture, and Mr Dyke had only just spread his fertiliser a week before. But if we were willing to take a chance with possible nitrogen ingestion, he said, we were welcome to turn our horses into one of his fields for the night. As most of the fertiliser looked as though it had been washed into the ground, we took the chance and availed ourselves of his generous offer. After a winter of hay, the ponies thought themselves in heaven!

We were offered a cosy sleeping area in a barn attached to the house, and slept like logs in the straw. Next morning, with the sun shining we were invited into the farmhouse kitchen by mother-in-law and plied with fresh boiled eggs and crusty new bread, with home-made butter the colour of saffron. I can still remember the wonderful taste of it all. Dick Dyke and his wife came in from the dairy while we were enjoying our farmhouse breakfast and we talked farming. They were thrilled to bits that we worked on farms too and would not take a penny from us for the horses keep and generous breakfast. The ponies did not seem to suffer any ill effects from grazing a pasture with fresh nitrates on it, apart from an extra spiritedness from the infusion of fresh grass!

It was fun finding our way to Sidcot using Ordnance Survey maps and searching out the bridle tracks in order to avoid mettled roads as far as possible. Many of the tracks were shut off and we seemed to spend an inordinate amount of time unblocking gateways. We were 'observed', but no one actually said you cannot go through here. Maybe it was because we were so meticulous in shutting gates and leaving all barricades as we found them. We rode over the tops of the Mendips, coming to Sidcot from off the heights of Priddy. It was a very exhilarating way to travel and opened my eyes to the possibilities of a long pony trek.

At Sidcot, Danae stayed in the school, and I put up a tent in Hilly Fields, where a farmer let me graze the ponies and sold me some clover hay at an inflated price in exchange. It was a good weekend, and our arrival on horseback must rate as unique in the history of reunion! ⚘

Chapter 68
Horse Riding Days

Danae on Joey with Souki.

Danae and I did quite a lot of mad riding together after leaving school. Pixie, a 13 hands mare, and third generation from Mother's original Sappho, had given Danae endless fun before she went to Sidcot. She was a small bay pony, nothing much to look at, but she had a phenomenal fast trot, moving with a smooth gliding action. At seven, Danae was riding Pixie at all the local pony shows and winning numerous rosettes for gymkhana events. In those days, before the public became so safety conscious, there were many more adventurous events like trotting races, flat racing and musical poles. There was also a mad team game that originated in Afghanistan, where mounted tribesmen tried to carry the carcass of a calf on their saddle-tree over a certain line, while the opposing side did all it could, no holds barred, to stop him. Once caught, they would wrest the calf from him and gallop flat out for the opposite line. In our case, of course, it was not a calf, but a sack stuffed with straw. The game was fast and furious, attracting the more anarchical riders and undisciplined horses. There were lots of injuries and, after several cases of concussion, helmets became compulsory. Too dangerous manoeuvres resulted in disqualification. As a spectator sport it was great, but the conservative element in the riding establishment thought the game too dangerous to continue with as an event, so that was the end of that.

Danae won many trotting races on Pixie until a competitor came along who had taught his horse to run like a camel, front and back legs moving forward in unison on each side, the pacing gait that American trotting horses are taught for buggy racing. This gait should

Chapter 72
Danae and Australia

Danae and young John Harris 'drifted into an engagement'
before emigrating to Australia.

Danae's social life really was a bit limited at home, and she didn't seem to have any outside interests. Mr Harris had long been chewing over the idea of emigrating with his family to Australia as it offered a freedom and scope of opportunity for young people that was lacking in England in the 'fifties.

His eldest son, John, took a fancy to Danae and started to come over from Lyndhurst to take her out. Danae seemed to like him too, and as the Harris family got organised to emigrate to a cattle station in Broome, North Western Australia, she also expressed an interest in emigrating. It was all settled, and Danae and John drifted into an engagement. The Australian government were recruiting citizens and offering assisted passages to their country and Mr Harris, never a man to miss an opportunity when he saw one, made full use of the incentive. John Gray introduced himself to Mr Harris as having good experience of looking after cattle in the outback, and, taking the man at face value, Mr Harris offered to help finance John's passage back to Australia, give him a job as a stockman on arrival, on the condition that he would pay him back from his wages later.

So it came about that Danae set out on the great adventure of her life - to live on a cattle station in the tropical outback of the one-horse town of Broome. Broome had been noted for its Japanese pearls and pearl shell industry which was now in sharp decline owing to the Second World War. John Gray never fulfilled the bargain he made with Mr Harris. His stock work, unsurprisingly, was spasmodic and unreliable, and he sloped off eventually without ever having paid off his mentor a fraction of what he owed. At least, back here we had some respite from his presence as a guest who had somewhat outstayed his welcome, albeit not for long. ✤

Danae in Broome, in the North of Western Australia.

Feeding a kid goat, using a beer bottle.

Chapter 73
Armfields Agricultural Engineers at Stuckton

I cannot call these memories complete without mentioning Armfields' foundry at Stuckton, a family business that lasted over a hundred years.

Armfields forged and cast parts for all the water mills in the locality and were competent millwrights. They also cast, forged and machined their own designs of agricultural equipment, like chaff cutters, root pulpers, cider presses, harrows and so on. The casting had finished by the time I knew them, the tall smelting furnace chimney being the only reminder of a past activity. The machine shop, with its mass of solid Victorian machinery was driven by dangerous, unguarded belts off a main drive shaft running the length of the shop, hardly altered over the years. Three forge fires burned, and iron was heated, bent, flattened, pointed and shaped, to repair or make different artefacts. I even saw a set of wooden-framed harrows, perhaps destined for a museum, have new iron tines forged and fitted. The staff came as apprentices, young lads who started as general factotums taking the tea round, gradually rising in the ranks until they could handle almost any repair job within the agricultural spectrum. They stayed until they retired. It was a family firm that you could rely on to get everything from a gate hinge to a fertiliser distributor, and very useful to have on one's doorstep.

I was often caught on the hop at haymaking time, needing a running repair done, perhaps, to a power take-off universal joint bearing to drive the baler. I would go to Armfields and find Charley working at some routine job. I would explain what I wanted and Charley would stop what he was doing and gravely inspect my faulty item. "I suppose you want it done yesterday?" he would say, grinning, and he would drop whatever he was engaged in and do my repair while I waited.

But the times change, and from having eight to ten men on the payroll, Armfields' workforce dwindled to two or three. The stock changed, a tractor appeared in a new showroom, and Wellington boots, socks and cord trousers could be bought. A new proprietor bought the business and we had computerised stock taking. The fish-scale slates were sold off the machine shop roof and it was downhill from then on. Old Charley grinned enigmatically, playing the firm's economic situation very close to his chest, but in the 1980s an era ended, and Armfields was sadly sold off. One sunny day all the stock went up for auction and a hundred years of the sound of iron on iron, the clack of belts, the gentle roar of the forge fires, was gone for ever. All that knowledge, all that expertise, all that ancient stock of spare parts that enabled you to keep an antiquated machine in action, all gone under the auctioneer's hammer. The demise of Armfields was also a blow to convenience and a mark of the economic pressures of the times. Today's agricultural supplier, it seems, is not really interested in you unless you want new equipment. It is difficult trying to come to terms with the new values. ⚑

Chapter 74
Musical Fordingbridge

Social life at home, apart from the pub and Miss Pat's Players, included singing in the Fordingbridge male voice choir with my cousin, Martin.

Our choir master was the retired headmaster of Fordingbridge School, (now Avonway Community Centre) opposite the cinema. His name was Mr Brittain, a tall, white-haired and moustached old gentleman, who rehearsed us each week in the Methodist church in the square. Under his stern, but kindly, supervision we learned all the classical male voice choral pieces, ranging from *The Lost Chord* to negro spirituals, honing our expertise and balance towards an interpretation worthy of the male voice choir competition held each year in Bournemouth.

This was always a grand occasion and the whole choir went into town by coach. Mr Brittain grumbled and fussed about us like an old cockerel, making sure that our bow ties were straight and we were presentable. On one occasion, the head adjudicator was none other than the great choral expert and composer Herbert Howells. Lots were drawn for order of performance and we waited our turn to sing with nervous anticipation. Usually there was a set piece all the choirs had to sing, and then something of our own choosing. Listening to the other choirs, it was very easy to pick out the less sympathetic interpretations of pieces in which an egocentric tenor, maybe, would blast forth over the top of certain passages with total disregard for choral balance. When our turn came Mr Brittain would say: "Right lads, give it your best, you know what to do, don't let me down!" On the day, we achieved second out of twelve choirs, and both we and our kind mentor were over the moon with pride.

We always suffered from a surfeit of baritones and a constant lack of tenors, apart from a Mr Thurston who was the only true tenor we had. His high quality voice was a constant lifeline for our choir and he was a regular soloist. As one of the many baritones, I had a good enough voice to sing the odd solo part, but I was not the first choice. I enjoyed the spirituals more than anything; they escaped the sentimentality of some of the other pieces by being profound, simple sentiments of a downtrodden race, as well as full of life and humour. With the sad death of the inspiring Mr Brittain, the choir folded; he was the guiding light that had kept it going.

The other activity in which I indulged, was Old Time Dancing, held once a week in the Victoria Rooms, built by my great grandfather Thomas Westlake for the Fordingbridge community, as a benevolent gesture. A spritely old couple used to run the classes and provide the music, the wife playing the piano and the husband, the violin. They sounded a bit like Albert Sandler and the BBC broadcasts from the Palm Court Orchestra days. It was fun, and I learnt a large repertoire of old time dances. Mr and Mrs May, one of the families of butchers in Fordingbridge, used to chassé about the floor and, despite their size, performed the sometimes intricate steps with surprisingly precise dexterity, like well-trimmed galleons. A young lady called Janet West was usually my partner, a good-natured local lass. She worked in a library in Salisbury and was well read and interesting. Betty Overill came dancing too, as well as George Brewer and Ron Thorn. We had some merry evenings.

I became good friends with Janet who invited me, among others, to her twenty-first birthday party. She and her elderly parents lived in one of a row of semi-detached houses, and very welcoming they were. The party was a convivial affair, with a tremendous spread of food. Ron Thorn was there, and a man who Janet was later to marry, Vick Pinhorn, a cowman at Stallards Farm. Janet belonged to the Free church and was an interesting person. She was natural, a good sport and interested in abstract ideas. She, Ron and I hired a rowing skiff in Salisbury one summer afternoon, I remember, and idled our way up the Avon on one of its tributaries, trailing our hands in the weed-skeined water and idly putting the world to rights. We prevailed upon Betty Overill to join our threesome and used to play tennis doubles on a hard court we hired beside the Methodist chapel on the marsh at Breamore. Janet stayed the course, but Betty, I think, was bored by our company and soon gave up coming. ⚜

Chapter 75
Kate

So the years passed and one Easter, when I was twenty-four, I rode my little motor cycle down to an Old Scholars reunion at Sidcot, dimly aware of some unexpressed motive.

I attended the General meeting of the Old Scholars and suddenly realised that someone familiar was standing up and offering a vote of thanks to the President of that year for their address. It was delivered in a broad American twang ending with "We surely do thank you for your add-ress." I looked round the hall to see a soft, feminine and very attractive 19-year old Katie Duthie, and my heart gave a bound and I knew, just knew without a single doubt, this is the girl for me, this is the girl I want to spend the rest of my life with. I thought: "Go for it, man!!" The time was right, and the venue. I sought Kate out at the end of the meeting and it was as though both of us had been waiting for this moment. We arranged to go to the dance later, at Birds Assembly Rooms in the village, and never looked into anyone else's eyes all evening. She was so lovely, the chemistry was perfect and we had no need to say much that evening as we danced happily in each other's embrace. Meeting up the next morning I learnt that she was to go to art school in Winchester to take the National Diploma in design in fabric printing and weaving, that she had a horse called Starlight and loved riding, and that she lived in Bursledon within easy reach of the Forest. That was enough to go on with!

At the end of a memorable weekend, we made our way back home in tandem, Kate in her crazy little three-wheeled vehicle, a Bond Minicar, and I right behind on my Bowen motorcycle, both only capable of thirty miles an hour. We had a picnic on top of Pepper Box Hill, I remember, on the Downs, and lay dreaming in each other's arms in the afternoon sunshine, pledging to write to each other and arrange to meet again sometime soon. In the late afternoon we reluctantly parted and made our way to our respective homes, exultant in our newly-formed relationship.

Being in love is a form of heavenly madness where one's feet never quite touch the ground of reality. I felt I was the happiest man alive. I know Kate arrived at her home in a similar state of euphoria and when her mother asked her unnaturally preoccupied daughter how the weekend had gone, Kate had replied that she had met the most wonderful man in the world and that Kate's mother had thought: "O-Oh, here we go!" Kate told me later she did not wash her face for a few days after our parting so that my kisses would not be erased. Of what wonderful madness is new love made! I cannot remember what I told my mother, but she, with her usual generosity of spirit was probably enthusiastic for me.

It was a joyful day when Kate first came to our house in the Forest in her little car, all fresh and lovely and full of life. We caught the ponies Joey and Stormy, and I introduced her to the freedom of riding in the Forest. It was an eye-opening experience for her, as in the increasingly urbanised area of Bursledon horse riding was very compromised by busy roads, housing estates and blocked footpaths. The lack of restrictions as to where one rode and the infinite space of the Forest was a revelation to Kate.

We bade our reluctant farewells late that evening, and I watched Kate in her funny little two-stroke pop-popping car disappear into the night towards Southampton. It must have been quite an experience for Kate to visit our primitive little wooden house after the comparative splendour of her family's part share in a huge Georgian house with walled garden which I was soon to visit. It was rather splendidly called Ploverfield, a grand place with drive and lodge house. The Duthies had the largest half of Ploverfield, and a nice old couple, the Jacksons, the other. A modern side wing to the house was inhabited by two middle-aged brothers, Sid and Charley Ellis. Charley was disabled and in a wheel chair. Outside the Duthie's entrance to the house was a lovely magnolia tree and picnic table where the family would have their meals on sunny days. A former Royal Navy Commander lived with his new wife in the lodge house. A strange man, he was paranoid about 'Reds under the bed', and dry rot that he professed to smell a mile off. Ploverfield had three storeys, Kate and her sister Meg having, by choice, the attic rooms for their bedrooms. The rooms in the house were classical and spacious with high ceilings and large sash windows looking out on a lawn, flower beds and a monkey puzzle tree.

Kate's mother, Ruth, taught biology and zoology at Itchin Grammar School, and Kate's father Edward, a tall, thin, and totally bald man, was head pathologist at the Royal South Hants Hospital in Southampton. He was a man of considerable medical and scientific eminence, having worked with Flory in the research leading to the first production of aureomycin. This was the precursor to penicillin on a commercial scale, thus making it available to thousands of wounded servicemen and saving their lives. The persona he exhibited to his family was largely one of remote preoccupation with his work and he was not given to much small talk. His research work was his life, and the conditions under which he had to operate were always inadequate and underfunded. This produced an inordinate amount of stress in a man whose physique and nature were ill-equipped to cope with it. That said, he was a man with a strong sense of moral conscience for the underprivileged, and many varied interests in the fields of art and music. His knowledge of art and architectural heritage was considerable. When one was treated to his puckish sense of humour, it was like the opening of a window onto a whole new aspect of his character and for a moment the guard was down and he became accessible. I think, perhaps, he was essentially a shy man. Certainly not at ease with small children or stroppy teenage daughters.

Edward Duthie was the only son of a poor Kilkenny grocer. By dint of natural intelligence and hard work leading to scholarships, he achieved a good education, finally getting a place at Trinity College, Dublin, to study medicine. It was there that he met Ruth Patten, the oldest daughter of Canon Patten, the protestant rector of a church in the old medieval walled town of Fethard in County Tipperary, who also had scientific inclinations.

The couple were married in the mid-thirties, and Kate was born in August 1938. Ruth and Edward were living in Oxford at the outbreak of war. The threat of a German invasion appeared great at the time, and Harvard and Yale Universities in America offered to take on and find billets for the children of professors working in the Oxford faculty. Kate's mother, pregnant with her second baby, after consulting with Edward, decided to go to America with Kate, aged two, on one of the several boats crossing the Atlantic at that time. So it was that Kate was evacuated to America for the five years of the war. Kate's mother gave birth to another girl, a sister for Kate called Meg, and stayed to see her launched. It was not an easy time for Ruth as she had a severe bout of post natal depression after the birth. She remained a year in America to see her small daughters settled with their foster parent, and then sailed back to England to support her husband in his research. Kate and Meg were left in the capable hands of a New England psychologist, Peg Kennard who, although she had never married or had children of her own, was a more than fortunate choice of foster mother, "Udder Mudder" as the two Duthie girls called her. She was loving and kind, and the two girls became part of the large Kennard family, Peg's brothers fulfilling the role of indulgent uncles.

It must have been a huge decision for Kate's mother to make, to leave her two small daughters in America and go back to England, not knowing when she was going to see them again. It was not until forty years later that we knew just how tough it had been for her, when Kate in jest said to Ruth, apropos of some aspect of Kate's behaviour: "Well, I expect I am like that because you left me," at which point Ruth broke down weeping with the memory and guilt of that time. Such are the loadings we carry with us unexpressed through our lives. Kate, needless to say, was mortified at having hurt her mother. Maybe it was good for them both to face the past if only for a moment. In one sense, Kate and her mother were fortunate in that they actually reached America, as the next boat load of women and children to sail was sunk by a German U-boat and all lives were lost. The scheme of evacuating children to America was scrapped after that terrible tragedy, deemed as being too dangerous.

Peg kept the Duthie parents well informed of their daughters' fortunes and state of health throughout their sojourn in the States, and the fact that both girls developed into such competent and caring, balanced women is a tribute to their kind, perceptive American "Udder Mudder". They lived in New York, next to the Hudson River. Kate remembers roller skating in Central Park and in the holidays they took an overnight train to Connecticut, the town in New Hampshire of the Kennard's family home. Not having to take their clothes off when they went to bed on the overnight sleeper was the highlight, Kate remembers. Peg's brothers had their own children, so Meg and Kate started out their life with a large, happy, integrated family.

Kate and Meg returned from America in 1945, their parents meeting them off the boat at Liverpool. Kate was seven and Meg five, and they were dressed in fashionable navy blue coats with brass buttons with the American Eagle on, and little sailor hats. Kate was very unsure of her mother's identity for the first few days and very protective of her younger sister. She insisted on dressing Meg until, she said: "I'm sure you are my mother." Ruth sensibly let Kate dress her sister, ignoring the fact that most of the clothes went on back to front, or inside out. At the end of forty-eight hours, Kate had had enough of being Mum and abandoned her role, pragmatically accepting Ruth as her real Mum, if only because it meant less work! Edward Duthie had his problems too, with his scarcely known daughters. When Ruth was working late one night she asked him if he could put the girls to bed. When bed time came and he asked them to go upstairs and clean their teeth and have a wash, Kate broke down into sobs and howled. Poor Edward, who found small children difficult to deal with anyway, wondered what on earth he had done to cause so much misery. Kate, in between sobs, managed at last to tell him that: "Daddies don't put you to bed." Her experience of the Kennard uncles in America had fixed it in her head that the role of men was as entertainers, and only mother figures ordered you to wash and go to bed. At least the Duthie family were back together at last... ✤

Chapter 76
The Ploverfield Household, Bursledon and The Art School

Kate's father, Edward Duthie, 'a man of considerable medical and scientific eminence...'

Because Kate's parents worked full time during the week, they employed a part-time kitchen assistant to help prepare an evening meal for them.

This took the form of a lively old reprobate called Mrs Green, whose culinary expertise seemed to be limited to over-cooked boiled potatoes. Kate's Dad would groan on the nights that Mrs Green did the veg, as they were always overcooked or underdone, and Ruth more often than not had to organise the protein dish of the day, thus negating the very reason they had employed Mrs Green in the first place. She was a wiry, garrulous pensioner who used to insert old newspapers inside her dress or blouse to insulate herself against the cold, and always had a damp roll-up fag stuck to the bottom of her lower lip. These she manufactured from recycled butt ends, dried out surreptitiously in the lower oven of the kitchen's Aga stove. One eye was always permanently closed against the acrid smoke of her fags, and her fingers were permanently stained with nicotine. As she worked preparing food, an inch or more of ash would hang, ignored, from the end of the burning cigarette. Inevitably it ended up falling into whatever dish she was producing. Who knows what the tar content must have been of the fags Mrs Green recycled. I got on very well with Mrs Green - she was a dear old thing - and when I helped her with the washing up her admiration knew no bounds and I was her friend for life. in reality, she was more of a liability than an asset, but the Duthies kept her on because they knew she needed the extra cash. She was worth her small salary just for her cheerful company as far as I was concerned.

Kate took me riding round Bursledon on her horse, Starlight, a fine-boned 14.2 cuss of a bay gelding she loved dearly, and I quickly learnt to appreciate how unique the Forest was in comparison to the restrictions of the town and its environs. We walked a great deal down by the Hamble, viewing the boats bobbing on the tidal water or slumbering like stranded whales on the mud flats at low tide in the estuary of the river. The Hamble boating fraternity was pretty lively ashore in the evenings and a good pub to go to on the river was The Bugle that sold what it advertised as 'Home Made' wines. I think the term 'Home Made' was stretching it a bit, as the long list, from Birch to Parsnip, appeared to be made from grape concentrate with a specific artificial flavouring added, to try and differentiate the titles. It was a good selling point none the less.

Kate, having passed her 'A' level art exams at Sidcot, was exempt from the foundation year of a four-year course towards her National Diploma in fabric printing and weaving. In the summer of the first year I knew her, she did a lot of sketching in Winchester market, and also attended life classes. There were some gifted students in her year in the fabric printing and textile department. One, Peter Garland, was exceptional, and besides his artistic talents he was an accomplished self-taught pianist, with the nickname 'Seb' (after Bach, perhaps). A cycling 'anorak', an innocent abroad and gentle gay, he was universally liked by all. Mary, a large, exuberant and handsome blonde painter with lots of creative drive was, and remained, another of Kate's friends. Mary went to Jamaica and married a lively black Jamaican called Ossie Nelson, with whom she had three lovely children. After they married, they came to England, Ossie working in accounting for various establishments until his retirement. Saskia, their youngest daughter was born in England, her Jamaican appearance taking the midwife by surprise, much to Mary's amusement.

Another student of Kate's year, with whom we became good friends over the years, was Norman Runacres. Norman, a restless man, had led a chequered career doing many jobs including, at one stage, being involved in the design of Penguin biscuits. He was married to Betty who had to constantly put up with his loud, critical, public asides concerning her domestic inadequacies. The couple had two children, Karen and Simon. Because of an undetected Resus factor in the parents' blood groups, Simon, the second child, was born jaundiced and profoundly deaf. I will always remember the family coming to visit us on The Ridge for a meal and a walk in the Forest. Simon, because of his deafness was in a state of profound frustration, unable to communicate despite being highly intelligent. This frustration took the form of very wild behaviour, in the course of which he fell in a Forest stream and went right under, expensive hearing aid and all. Betty screamed, and Norman waded into the stream and fished out his drenched and frightened son and we all made for home as fast as possible to get him warm and into some dry clothes. The hearing aid was ruined. ❦

Chapter 77
Kate's Bond Minicar

Kate's little Bond Minicar was quite something and demands a chapter all to itself. You started it manually, rather like a lawn mower, by pulling a lever with a cable attached to it.

This was connected to a spring-loaded drum which engaged with the two-stroke Villiers engine and turned it over till it fired. It had tiny wheels and a box-like cab, and no reverse gear. Kate commuted from Bursledon to Winchester each day, some forty miles in all, and amazingly had no accidents. It could just take two people, and on rainy days we worked the windscreen wipers manually with two pieces of string. If stationary the wipers worked a treat, but perversely, the faster you drove, the slower and more inadequate the wipers were.

Coming back to Bursledon from an Art School party at two in the morning, the gears jammed in top. This meant that once on the move we had to maintain speed and keep going. The box cab had a sun roof, and every time we approached a crossroads or junction, I would stand up with my head and shoulders above the roof and try and spot any oncoming traffic before we buzzed the junction. Amazingly the gods seemed to be with us and the little roads at that hour were fortuitously free of other vehicles.

On another occasion, we drove to the Wrens at Oxshott for the inaugural Potters Day of the newly formed Craft Potters Association. Halfway there, the car seemed to develop a jerk in the transmission. Kate was registered with the AA, so we hailed some mechanics spotted in a lay by on their yellow motorcycle combination. In some puzzlement they looked it over, but they could find nothing wrong with it. Reassured, we continued on our way to Oxshott without, apparently, further mishap.

As always it was a happy time at the Wrens, dear Denise giving a warm welcome to Kate. We had a wonderful supper party, seated round a long refectory table in the main living room of Potters Croft, talking with potters from many different parts of the country. The Wrens were largely instrumental in the formation of the Craft Potters Association in 1958, which was to become a a great unifying force for potters in Britain, and also soon to provide a useful retail outlet in London for many of its members. A newsletter for full and associate members evolved into what has become Ceramic Review, an outstanding international magazine of ceramic art and craft. Over the sunny weekend, the tiny yard and premises of the Wrens hummed with interesting demonstrations and talks by various potters. Rosemary demonstrated her throwing skills, making large cider jars, and an old potter from Harnam made some pitchers. We had a lecture from Henry Hammond on Chinese brushwork and decoration, and there was much talk about the form that our new association should take. There was a great spirit of optimism, I remember, which over the following fifty years has proved to be well founded, as the CPA is thriving. The term ceramics has come to embrace a vast and varied world of fantastic artefacts made of clay that the more narrow world of the craft potter would never have come in contact with years ago. Even I, as a traditionalist, am excited by the vision and possibilities presented by some of the members.

Our stimulating weekend came to an end all too soon, and Kate and I jerked and clacked our way back to Ploverfield in the wounded Minicar. Something was very wrong with the transmission. It was a scary trip back in torrential rain, and we had some frightening moments being overtaken by articulated lorries that seemed oblivious of our presence on the road, driving us into the gutter. With our vehicle's small wheels it felt like being on a railway line from which it was difficult to extricate ourselves. All very stressful!

As we neared Bursledon, the transmission suddenly became even more jolting and harsh and we began to wonder if we were going to be able to finish our journey. On the final few hundred yards of the drive, there was a sudden grinding crunch and the car stopped dead. Only then did we discover that the vehicle was chain-driven and that the jerk had been caused by a tooth breaking on the rear drive sprocket. The situation had got worse as more and more teeth had broken until, in the drive, the entire sprocket had stripped. That we got home was something of a miracle.

Kate's Dad had the transmission repaired and all went well until the engine mounting brackets fractured, letting the engine fall down onto the front wheel when Kate was coming home through all the rush hour traffic of Winchester. The car, of course, stopped dead and Kate found herself surrounded by honking cars. She ran off to the nearest garage for help, leaving the Minicar in the middle of the High Street. On coming back with the breakdown lorry, to her dismay the car had gone, and she was left stuttering with embarrassment, trying to explain to the garage mechanic that her vehicle had been there a few minutes ago. Looking wildly around for clues she saw a nearby transport café and heard a few guffaws of laughter from within. Beside the café was a low wall, and a vase of plastic flowers protruding in surreal manner from behind it attracted her attention. Peering over the wall, she discovered her Minicar. While she had been away, some workmen in the café had bodily picked up the car, and putting it over the wall, had placed the vase of flowers on top of the bonnet as a requiem! Kate says she still remembers the acute schoolgirl embarrassment she felt at having to go into that now so theatrically silent transport café among all the hefty lorry drivers, and ask in her prim middle class voice for her car back. The silence was replaced by hearty laughter as six hefty lorry drivers got up and went to the door of the café. "You want your car back do you, darlin', right ho, no problem!" Out they marched, and deftly posted the poor Minicar back over the wall and into the street. The breakdown lorry was able to winch the front wheel off the ground and the last Kate saw of it was it being finally towed, ignominiously, away. The floral tribute was apt. We have dined out on this story for years to much amusement.

The Bond Minicar, having proved too much of a liability for his daughter, Edward bought a 1930's Ford from a friendly local garage. Safety-wise it was a much better bet, although its braking system was still only operated by rods. Kate called the car 'Norman' after the student in her year, and it gave some good service. It had the unusual advantage of having a windscreen that was hinged at the top so you could get plenty of ventilation on a hot day by opening it. When Kate and I got married we inherited 'Norman', the first car on The Ridge since my mother's Austin Seven. The engine was very simple and not easy to start when the weather was cold. I used to take a leaf out of my mother's book in dealing with the problem, by warming the plugs up on a Primus which usually had the desired affect of getting the engine firing. Sadly, with the advent of the MOT regulations, Norman, with its antiquated braking system became impossible to get through the compulsory test, and we sold it as scrap to a Gypsy family for five shillings. ✺

Chapter 78
Working Life at Folds Farm and for Self

After I had left Mr Bennett's employment I went to work for Mr Oliver Cutts, a Cockney businessman who had recently bought Folds Farm.

Its acreage bordered the north end of Sandy Balls and extended down into the Avon valley watermeadows. It was a dairy farm, boasting a herd of Friesian cows, looked after by a garrulous cowman by the name of Kenchington. He and his wife, son and daughter, lived in one of a group of tied cottages under Green Hill above the farm yards. The fences had gone to ruin under the previous owner, as had most of the rest of the farm. My job was to clear encroaching blackthorn from field boundaries and put up new stock-proof fences. Compared to Mr Bennett's farm Folds was a shambles. The ragtag of a constantly changing workforce had no commitment or pride in their work, and I found myself dogged by frustration at getting, keeping, and maintaining my hand tools for my work, as they were constantly disappearing.

The total acreage of the farm was in the region of 200 acres, the higher, dryer ground being used for kale, corn and hay crops, and the neglected meads for summer pasture. In the 17th century much of the Avon valley had been sculpted and engineered into watermeadows, utilising the River Avon and, by means of strategically placed hatches and sluices and engineered levels, it was possible to flood the pastures at will. Thus, in winter the grass was protected from frost, and at the same time the pasture was fertilised with a certain amount of river silt. By this means a very early bite of grass could be obtained. Water was drawn off in a controlled manner, passing down a comparatively raised spine of land called a drawn; it was then funnelled off into a herring-bone design of hand-cut shallow ditches onto the lower lying ground.

It was a very labour intensive system of grass management, requiring the full-time services of a 'Drowner', as he was known, as the small open carriers were often trodden in by the grazing cattle and needed to be re-dug frequently. All the hatches and sluices had to be maintained as well, of course. Meadows could be irrigated too in a dry season when grass was short. The disadvantage of a high water table was that it restricted carts from venturing too far onto the meads, for fear of breaking through the surface and getting stuck. Hay was made in the meads up until the Second World War. It was cut by gangs of mowers with scythes, all working one behind the other. When fit, it was carried out by hand on palliasses, to the horse-drawn carts waiting on hard standing. Again, very labour intensive, but then wages were only twelve shillings a week.

Our employer, Mr Cutts, was a former wrestler and a black marketeer during the war, and had made his pile buying up old bomb sites in London and building garages on them, putting managers in to look after them. Cutts paid £22,000 for Folds Farm which was considered a vast price at the time. Within a few weeks of buying, he brought a gang of builders down from London to modernise and refurbish the tied cottages. The gang had a novel time experiencing (many for the first time) life on a farm. They watched in awe, with open mouths, a difficult calving where we had to put ropes on the protruding calf's legs. The Friesian breed, although large animals, always seemed to have trouble owing to having a narrow pelvis in relation to the size of calf. "Cor, bloody 'ell, now I know what my missus musta gorn through!" said one of the men appreciatively.

To begin with the gang found the countryside fun and they enjoyed being 'all men together'. But after a couple of weeks they started to get randy and bored, the younger, single men going after the local 'talent' and the older, steadier men going 'AWOL' back to their 'missus' in London, and a pub with a bit more life than The Fighting Cocks. For a time it was quite an invasion in Godshill, a bit like it must have been when the Irish railway navvies were passing through. Oliver Cutts had a quick temper and would 'F and blind' at the slightest provocation. If he thought we were not working hard enough, he would charge across the field towards us yelling abuse. "Look out here comes old Ollie," we used to mutter to each other in anticipation of his latest entertaining piece of invective. We would stare at his boots when he lambasted us, which would make him even more annoyed and wild. Usually, after he had let rip and got rid of his fury, Cutts would change completely and become quite matey, taking a hip flask of whisky out of his jacket pocket and handing it round, while he subjected us to another of his vast fund of dirty stories.

Our first foreman employed by Cutts came from Woodgreen, another wiry, diminutive, little man called Jimmy Chalk. He lived in a thatched cottage in the village and earned part of his living growing an acre of raspberries which he harvested with great care each year. The mixed work force at Folds included some wild cornstalks straight from Burgate School. They did as little work as they could get away with and were alarmingly irresponsible at times, leading to potentially disastrous consequences. I remember one occasion when we were creosoting some fencing stakes. We had a 40-gallon barrel of creosote up on a ramp that had been used for putting the milk churns on to get them at the correct height for the milk delivery lorry. I had screwed a tap into the bung hole of the barrel and put it on its side to draw off the creosote into cans for application to the fencing stakes. The flow of creosote was a bit too slow for one of the lads and he, idiot that he was, unscrewed the tap from the bung to get a faster flow. It was a hot sunny day, and the lad was stripped off to his waist. The barrel was full, and of course when the bung was removed, a great gout of creosote hit the naked torso of the poor fellow, sousing him all over! Fortunately, it missed his eyes, but knowing how mere splashes of creosote can burn the skin we ordered an ambulance, and meantime got the youngster in the shade and wiped off as much of the creosote as we could with a rag soaked in paraffin. The lad survived but he must have had some weeks of extreme pain.

I was earning 3/6d an hour working part-time, just enough for my keep and modest wants and allowing me to keep on with my own land reclamation. Kate and I started to tentatively plan a riding holiday, originally to take place in Ireland, but common sense, expense and logistics prevailed, and we decided on a trip up through England and into Wales instead.

After leaving Folds Farm, I worked for a time on my own land reclamation, digging ditches, clearing scrub, thorn and broom and laying land drains. It was all heavy manual work but very satisfying seeing the fields cared for once again. With money getting low, Mr Harris fortuitously appeared on the scene again, asking if I would look after another batch of cattle over the winter months on the Forest. Because I thought I might have some time for my own work as well as looking after his animals, I agreed. To put out the daily ration of hay he supplied me with a Scotch cart on pneumatic tyres and a horse. It was a large chestnut cob with long feathering on its legs and I called it Horace. However, I had severe reservations about Horace's capabilities for minding the cattle on the Forest. He was fine when harnessed to the cart, but slow and very clumsy, and forever stumbling on the rough terrain. If I required a turn of speed to cut off some steer intent on getting away from the herd, getting Horace into a gallop was like asking for a response from a sack of corn. In the end, I just used Horace for carting hay, and either Joey or Stormy for minding the cattle. Joey used to bite the rumps of the cattle if they did not get a move on and he was fast and responsive when speed was needed.

By this time Kate was staying over at the weekends, arriving on Friday evening straight from art school. We looked after the cattle together, building a small fire to brew tea and have a picnic in some hollow, while keeping half an eye on the cattle. In the winter months, the cattle were reasonably settled, the promise of a bite of hay in the rough compound each evening being a good draw to hang around. I was able to get a certain amount of field work done at the same time, though on occasions, the whole herd would suddenly disappear. I would have to hastily bridle and saddle up Stormy and track them down, and with much yelling and whooping head them off and turn them back towards Godshill. When spring came, it was a full-time job stopping the herd from wandering off the Forest. There were no grids on the Forest boundaries at that time and when the grass started to grow on the verges outside, the underfed cattle could smell it and they were off! It became a battle of wills, requiring constant surveillance.

Prior to the grid system being introduced on the Forest boundaries to stop Commoners' animals straying onto adjoining farmers' land and crops, there was a lot of bad feeling between the two factions. Before the advent of the car, the boundaries had been gated to stop animals straying and the system had worked well, the gates being illuminated at night with a red paraffin lantern. With the increased traffic, the gate system became impractical and so they gradually went out of use and the Commoners' animals were free to roam. In the early 'fifties, I used to regularly see a herd of Forest ponies in the middle of Fordingbridge High Street at night with a policeman behind driving them out of the town. Dartmoor had a grid system before the Forest and I wrote to the area authority to find out if it worked. Back came a very favourable report and I, along with others, wrote to the Verderers and Commoners Defence Society, suggesting the Forest adopted the same scheme. The initial response was lukewarm, but as the bad feeling from outside the Forest increased, it was obvious that something had to be done and grids were finally brought in. It was wonderful not to have to continually search for our animals and retrieve them from angry farmers who fined us what they liked for our animals depredations. It heralded a new era indeed.

To return to Mr Harris and his cattle. He appeared to have learned nothing from his first bad experience of trying to ranch animals through a winter on the Forest. I was still supplied with insufficient hay, and calf heifers were dying from calving, getting into bogs and then not having the strength to get out. It was a depressing re-run of events, but at least we did not have the further complication of Foot and Mouth to contend with. It was with relief that my contract with him ended. ⚘

Chapter 79
Pony Trek in Wales

In late spring, Kate bravely rode her pony Starlight over from Bursledon one morning, via the floating bridge and through the outskirts of Southampton, to live permanently with our other ponies on The Ridge.

I went out on Stormy to meet her at Brook and escort her back. It was quite a day and a declaration of intent by Kate, and we were both very happy. We continued with our preparations for our intended pony trek to Wales.

I rescued an old, moth-eaten trooper's saddle from Charles Leek's stable (we were on good terms at that time), with 1914 Army Issue stamped on it, and had it refurbished by Mr West, one of Fordingbridge's saddlers. It was a wonderfully comfortable saddle, with high pommel and cantle, with lots of D-links from which to hang saddle bags. In the winter evenings I had converted some old army back packs into saddle bags, sewing D-links onto them and making up sets of straps to attach them to the rear of the flaps of the trooper's saddle. I also rigged up a harness that went under the horse's belly and was attached to the base of the saddle bags, to stop them flapping up and down when the horse trotted or cantered. This was a very effective feature of which I was very proud.

I visited, chatted to, and observed our local saddlers at work. There was a crusty, ancient saddler, Mr Thorn, living and working in a tatty, low-ceilinged property on the tight corner opposite the bank in Fordingbridge. Crippled with arthritic hips, and into his eighties, he still plied his trade, sitting at his bench doggedly sewing and repairing

Ponies outside Godshill Pottery, packed up and ready to go on the Welsh trek.

harness. Mr Thorn's first wife had died some years earlier, and it was a surprise to many when he married again, a comparatively young woman in her early fifties, and had a son by her who was about 12-years old at this time. Old Thorn used to chuckle over the event, telling me how his wife had gone to the doctor to ask why she appeared to be getting so fat round the middle. It was a great event in the lives of this elderly couple when their son was born, as old Thorn had no issue from his previous marriage.

I watched old Thorn roll his linen thread on his leather apron and wax it with a knob of beeswax and threading two needles, begin to sew. Holding the leather in a wooden vice between his knees, with a sharp bradawl, he'd make a small hole through which he passed the two needles, one from either side, so the thread ran in a continuous figure of eight, a looping stitch which when pulled up tight was very strong. Old Thorn's workmanship could not be said to be pretty, but it was robust. My mother had always had her odd bits of shattered harness repaired by him. He was slow, which could be maddening if you were depending on a piece of harness being ready at the time he invariably promised, hand on heart, it would be. When I knew him, he was an old man who could have retired from his work, but as he often said to me: "I'll keep on so long as my peepers will let me."

When I tried to buy leather from him for making our pony trekking harness, he would refuse to sell me any, for the spurious reason that the quality of modern leather, tanned with chemicals (as opposed to Oak bark) was too inferior. The same argument of quality appertained when I tried to buy needles from the old man. It was all part and parcel of his mind set, belonging to a different age.

Old Thorn's great delight was judging the cart horses at Fordingbridge Show each year, about the only time he left the confines of his dark and dingy workshop. You could see him in his latter years, determinedly hobbling about the showground with his two sticks, in his dark serge suit and highly polished boots, assessing the quality of the working horses of that particular year. Thorn was a man from a past age who viewed the advent of the tractor and artificial fertilisers onto the agricultural scene with dismay, and who honestly believed that one day soon the horse would come back into its own.

In the course of a conversation one day I mentioned Cobbetts *Rural Rides*, and Thorn expressed an interest. I had just bought a second edition, from Beaches secondhand bookshop in Salisbury, with a preface by Cobbett's great grandson. I impulsively lent the old man the first volume that included that part of the ride that took Cobbett through the New Forest. Thereafter, every time I asked Thorn how he was getting on with the book he would reply that it was very interesting but that his 'peepers' did not allow him to read more than a few pages at a time. This went on for a year and a half, until Thorn suddenly died and I realised that I had to resign myself to the fact that I was never going to get the precious book back. His old home and workshop became an estate agents, changing hands several times since.

Getting no joy from Thorn, I had turned to Mr West, the other saddler in Fordingbridge, a quiet, unassuming little man with white hair and a silver moustache. He kindly refurbished my trooper's saddle, putting new felt on the runners and replacing all the stitching that had rotted while the saddle had lain in a sea of cobwebs in Charles' old stable. Mr West was a wonderfully neat craftsman, but he did not seem to attract the custom of Mr Thorn, who in spite of his crusty nature, seemed to attract more work than he could cope with. Anyway, Mr West was only too willing to sell me leather, linen twine, and needles. When he realised my genuine interest for his trade he could not do enough, cutting strap leather for me from the hides he had at the back of the shop. It was a source of great pride to him that Charley, his son, had chosen to train in shoe repair and was working alongside his father. With the decline in demand for harness-making and repair, the diversification to shoes added a useful income. Mr West let me have a leather vice to hold my leather work. A useful adjunct, it had been given to Charley on completion of his shoe repair course, and was surplus to requirements. Charley, more or less retired now, was a great talker. When he joined his father, the shop became a focal point for Fordingbridge characters to congregate for good-natured gossip. Charley, about five years older than myself, was always a cheerful man. Kitty Trevelyan, who used to get her shoes repaired by him, called him Danny Kaye because he reminded her of that entertainer in the film *Hans Christian Anderson*. All the wrinkles of knowledge I gleaned from both saddlers stood me in good stead in making up our equipment.

Kate went on a search for a trooper's saddle for Starlight, and eventually tracked one down, arriving with it in triumph one weekend. She also wrote off to an obscure society called The Ancient Order of Pack Horse Riders, and from their archives they gave us an idea of a route we might take. From a small library of Ordnance Survey maps, one inch to the mile, a route was marked out westwards taking us across the Bristol channel on the Aust Ferry, and from there making our way up the Wye Valley and into Wales. As far as possible, we used bridle tracks and foot paths, avoiding mettled roads if we could.

In the meantime, as well as coping with all our trekking preparations, I had ploughed up and re-seeded Moss Field and the old orchard, and had only to make it into hay before we were free to make our epic trip. At this point in agricultural development, hay was still put into a rick and was very labour intensive. As I had no money for equipment, I had to beg, borrow and hire a tractor and mower from my generous cousin Martin, a tedder machine and side rake from Mr Bennett, and an elevator from Charley White. It was stressful and time-consuming gathering all this equipment together, as being hay-making time the owners were often using the equipment themselves. I finally got the grass cut and fit for carting, and with cousins Martin and Richard kindly lending me a helping hand, got it ricked. To keep out the rain, I bought a large black polythene rick cloth and, putting it over the top, anchored it with ropes. It was a catchy year for hay making, I remember and it was with a great sense of relief we got the job out of the way and were able to concentrate, with excitement, on our projected equine journey.

We asked Rodney Downer, our local blacksmith, to put some good stout shoes on the ponies, Joey, Stormy and Starlight, and set about testing our kit for size and utility. With our own Troopers saddles, Danae lending hers to to go on Joey, we had the necessary D-links to attach our saddlebags - expensive at £6 10s and £4 10s respectively - and blanket rolls. In case we had to stake out the ponies at night to graze on open ground, we had stakes with a swivel made for us by Furber, the blacksmith opposite Fordingbridge's Victoria Rooms. Our old cotton tent was a stalwart hand-me-down from Cuthbert Rutter, who had honeymooned in it thirty-five years before, but which was still waterproof. The groundsheets were dual-purpose, army surplus, doubling up as capes in wet weather. This was in the days before proofed nylon, Pertex, Gore-Tex and the like, or sewn-in groundsheets, so the weight of our kit was considerable.

We took a small petrol stove to use in the advent of really bad weather. One had to warm it with one's hands to produce adequate pressure in the fuel tank to extract enough petrol to preheat the burner, and for the petrol to vaporise into a weak blue flame. The stove had no pump to induce pressure, as on a Primus stove, but depended on the heat from the burner. Thus, while one was trying to cook on a feeble flame, by the time you had finished cooking the fuel container had grown quite hot and the burner, when you least needed it, was roaring away at full bore. It was a very frustrating piece of equipment.

In practice, we cooked for the main part on small camp fires made from dead twigs scrounged from the hedgerows, which forced us to pack our blackened billy cans in a protective bag. The fire was a lot more fun to cook on though, and well worth the inconvenience of blackened pots and pans.

The day came for our departure, and there was great excitement. The ponies were sleek and shining in their summer coats and looked great with all their tackle on; six

Joey, Danae's 'best ever' Welsh pony, complete with Trooper saddle, blanket rolls and saddle bags.

saddle bags with our food, spare clothes and cooking pots, Joey, with blanket roll and tent slung and strapped across the saddle tree. Kate's parents came to see us off on a fine July summer's afternoon on our first leg to Breamore House and over the downs to Coombe Bissett. I remember the landlord of the pub, The Fox And Goose at Coombe Bissett, was called Lock. He kindly let us have a pitch to camp on, and grazing for the horses in a little paddock to the rear of the pub. We drank a toast to our trip in the bar that night, and settled down in our little tent that was to be our home for the next five weeks. To give you an idea of the social mores of the time, Kate's mother suggested we take two tents, in the faint hope that we would sleep separately! We pointedly took a tiny Order of Woodcraft Chivalry tent my Aunt Marjorie had given me years before just to show willing, and used it to store our smelly saddles in.

I have written a diary of our journey through the countryside that far off summer, leisurely ambling 25 miles or so a day, and in the evening throwing ourselves on the ready hospitality of generous farmers. I took a guitar strapped to my back and would sing in the bar of whatever pub we visited in the evening, often getting a free pint as a reward. It was a wet summer, I remember, particularly in the hills of Wales, which in one sense was good as the farmers had plenty of spare grass for nomadic horse riders. I had one or two bad days with asthma, particularly on rain-swept days in bracken-covered country. I was trying homeopathic remedies at the time which did nothing for my condition, medication not yet available.

Our venture was a once in a lifetime trip, confronting us with all manner of situations and weathers. It was also a good test of our compatibility, we felt, as over five weeks one is bound to show some negative aspects of one's nature to one's companion, especially when conditions get rough, which they did at times. We achieved minor notoriety being discovered twice on our trip by roving reporters, one from the *Hereford Gazette* and the other from the *Welsh Argus*, for whom we provided some good copy. We seemed to appeal to the romantic nature in people we met, and they warmed to our enterprise constantly, as we clopped our way down the byways on our trio of ponies.

Travel with animals needs much more organisation and forethought than say, bicycles. Our first priority on finding a site was to check the fences and gates. This done, and we were sure there were no gaps through which the ponies could escape, we could unsaddle and leave the animals free to graze with confidence. We almost lost our mounts on one occasion, and never made the same mistake of not checking again. Care in looking after our horses was priority and we kept a good eye open for lameness, girth or saddle sores. Kate and I became accomplished campers, priding ourselves on setting up the tent and having a billycan of water over a fire within ten minutes of finding a field. We lived on £2.10/- a week and spent 2/- on the horses keep over the five weeks. Not bad eh?! It took a good few weeks to get back to normal life again after five weeks on the road and I found it almost impossible to sleep in a bed for a while, it was just too soft! 🌿

Chris and Kate on their 'once in a lifetime' trek across the Welsh hills, with Starlight, Stormy and Joey.

August 16, 1958

Kate cleans up the saddlery while Chris plays a ballad.

500-mile horseback tour will have cost them £35

A WISP of blue wood-smoke curled lazily upwards from the corner of a field on the outskirts of Abergavenny on Sunday morning. Then soft singing to the gentle strumming of a guitar floated over the hedge bounding the old Ross road. The ballad singer was 25-year-old Christopher Charman, of Godshill, Fordingbridge, Hampshire.

He and his twenty-year-old companion, Kate Duthie, an art student at Winchester College of Arts and Crafts of South Ploverfield, Bursledon, near Southampton, are on a 500-mile horseback journey which has taken them to remote parts and began a month ago.

Kate looked up from her task of oiling the saddlery and told a *South Wales Argus* reporter that they and two friends had planned for some time to tour Ireland on horseback. "But the arrangement fell through," she said, "so Chris and I decided to come to Wales by ourselves.

"The secretary of the Ancient Order of Pack-riders worked out a route for us, but we have varied it considerably, using our commonsense, and have had a wonderful time."

Chris briefly outlined the route they had travelled—from Hampshire across the Wiltshire Downs, by-passing Bath and Bristol, through the lower parts of Gloucestershire to Aust. They crossed the ferry to Beachley then on through Tintern. Ross-on-Wye. Ludlow to Montgomery returning through the Radnor Forest to Abergavenny.

Avoided towns

"We've skirted all the large towns," said Kate, "and tomorrow we move on again to Usk, Beachley then across the ferry again and in about a week we'll be home."

Chris, who runs a smallholding, makes pottery and collects ballads in his spare time. "I know about eighty ballads, and accompany myself on the guitar," he said.

"We almost lost the guitar at Kinnersley, Herefordshire," said Kate. "We left it behind after having a meal near the local church. We searched for it afterwards but could not find it then, that evening, thirty miles away it was returned to us by a cyclist. He had been working in the churchyard and found it and had cycled thirty miles to return it."

This adventurous young couple, weatherbeaten by their travels, have found no difficulty in finding camping sites and very little difficulty in finding tack for their three ponies, Starlight, Joey and Stormy. Only twice have they been asked to pay for feed for their mounts—2s. 6d. in one case and 5s. in the other.

Housekeeping

"By the time we return," said Chris, "the whole trip will have cost us about £30 to £35, but Kate looks after the housekeeping money."

"I've allowed £4 a week for food," explained Kate, "but we have managed on less. This week have spent only £3 3s. and last week our food cost only £2 10s. I do the cooking over an open fire when there is plenty of wood about. If there isn't enough wood we use a little petrol stove."

A great problem on the trip has been finding blacksmiths to shoe the ponies but in Abergavenny they were lucky when they called on the Price brothers in Lower Monk Street.

"Whenever Chris produces his guitar," said Kate, "we get a good welcome. Once we were given honey for a song and several times we have been offered beer for a ballad. Throughout the trip we have been met with universal hospitality."

The local press enjoyed the bohemian story of Chris and Kate's pony trek across Wales, singing ballads and playing the guitar to entertain their generous hosts.

Chapter 80
The Return of John Gray

After a year or so, John Gray was back from Australia, but a bit more fond of the booze than last time.

Sometimes, if my mother did not get in fast enough on Friday pay night, he did not have enough money over to give her his housekeeping. Jobs were harder to get as John ran through them and was fired. He did find one position at Woodgreen, minding the boilers that heated the large greenhouse complex of Hale Nurseries. On winter nights a lot was at stake in terms of flowers grown out of season for the Covent Garden market. John always called in at The Fighting Cocks on his way to Woodgreen to 'prime' himself for the night's work with an indeterminate number of pints of farmhouse cider. On the occasion in question, he is reputed to have 'gone on a blinder' and consumed twelve to fifteen pints, before weaving his erratic way to work on Mother's old bike. On reaching the boiler shed, he promptly fell asleep in a drunken stupor, to be found by the night watchman in the early hours with the boilers nearly out and thousands of pounds worth of flowers in danger of being frosted. John was fired forthwith.

Alcoholism was beginning to undo him, and lack of money was the only brake on it. He started to make his own cheap hooch, buying honey in bulk and converting it to mead, which he consumed before it was half way through its fermentation. He spent more and more time in bed, fully clothed, only coming out to shovel down his supper, without ceremony or thanks.

In a drunken state, John would read a newspaper article that was pro, say, bull fighting, and would work himself up into a high sentimental dudgeon, writing a letter to the editor saying he was willing to face the bull with nothing but his bare hands, and challenging the matador to do the same. The letter was then put out for the postman to collect in the morning. We were always amused when, early the next day, John would surreptitiously get out of bed and retrieve the inflammatory letter before the postman arrived, the relative sobriety of morning lending discretion to his confused mind.

Another pastime, when drunk and maudlin, was for John to read from the Australian poet Banjo Patterson, extracts from *The Man From Snowy River*, a long, narrative poem of sentimental pathos, that with the added influence of the booze, took John back to his youth in the 'twenties and 'thirties and his identification with the outback. As he read the ballad of the heroic ride, tears would stream down his face.

During this period of John's stay, I had become launched on my relationship with Kate. Out of respect for me, I like to think, I was not aware that John ever made any advances towards her although he had already established an unhealthy and booze-fuelled relationship with Hilda. Kate felt his vibes though, which were more pathetic, in her eyes, than a threat. To her, he was just unwholesome. When Kate's sister, Meg, paid a visit, he tried his charms on her, much to her disgust.

Having blown the Hale Nursery job, John finally got work as a baker's roundsman, delivering bread around the area. His visitor's driving licence had expired, but he managed to bluff his way out of that small consideration and held the job down for about a month. His rounds, which should have taken him less than a morning to complete, gradually took him longer and longer as he frequently stopped off at pubs on his circuit for a swift pint which, over time, turned into a slow five, or six, pints. Finally, the inevitable happened and John had a minor accident in which the police were involved. He was breathalysed and found to be well over the limit, and then, of course, it was discovered his licence was well out of date. So that was the end of that job, and a hefty fine had to be paid into the bargain. As it turned out, it was to be the last job that John was to find locally.

John's last escapade was to borrow Kate's horse, Starlight, very much against her better judgement, to go to the pub. Giving the spirited horse its head, he let it gallop down the main road with a loose rein, in his usual style. This time, the Gods were not with John, and Starlight slipped and fell on the tarmac, skinning his knees, but amazingly, nothing more. John, of course, fell with the horse and came back complaining of a pain in his leg. It wasn't until two days later he thought it ought to be looked at, and it was found to be broken. So we had the unedifying spectacle of six weeks of John in plaster on the sofa, in his pyjamas, eyes closed, jaw clicking, coming to occasionally to make some of his, by now predictable, remarks. We were all heartily glad when he recovered his mobility and, at last, applied for a job in Wales in construction work. We kept our fingers crossed that he would get the job, which would take him out of our lives once and for all, hopefully.

Kate and I were married by this time, and a babe was on the way. Kate mucked out John's bedroom as soon as he was out of the house and installed a lovely antique Georgian split-cane cradle, in anticipation of the birth. When John came back a week later from an unsuccessful interview, she quite fiercely and firmly told him he was not welcome any more as she needed his bedroom for her coming child, and that he must find some other place to stay. John capitulated fairly easily, seeing Kate's resolve was unshakeable.

Realising our need for a house, and that Kate and I had no prospect of ever having enough capital to buy one, my mother, with great generosity of spirit volunteered to move into a caravan at the end of the garden, using Mrs Gardener's old chalet as a bedroom. "I don't need much space nowadays, and it will be a blessing to get away from so much housework!" she said. The old weaving shed in the village which my mother had rented out over the years at 2/6d a week to various needy families, had finally become vacant. A large Gypsy family by the name of Sheen had been living in the place. The family had five children by then, all crammed into two small rooms. They had defaulted on their tiny rent and, as the family had increased, what had been a nice little bungalow became neglected. Fortunately, the Sheens were rehoused in Fordingbridge and Mother had vacant possession so she could refurbish the property fit for habitation again.

With Kate and I taking over The Ridge property, Hilda and Jenny needed rehousing, and Mother employed me to carry out the improvements required by the council planners for re-habitation, which I did in lieu of my keep. With Kate helping me at weekends we made the hut into a pleasant and cheerful little abode, painting and wall-papering the interior, installing a gas cooker and earth closet too, and refurbishing the electrical wiring. Hilda expressed her satisfaction at moving down to the village and immediately set about making a truly lovely flower garden that she kept up for many years afterwards. She also installed a small caravan in the garden as a spare bedroom.

John Gray moved in with Hilda, but after a month or so even Hilda had had enough. Amazingly, John unexpectedly fell on his feet. An elderly widow he had befriended in Northampton and helped over a crisis some years before had never forgotten his kindness. Having no relatives, she left her house and a small legacy to John. On her death, John departed to Northampton and we heard, a few years later, had ended his days there squandering his legacy on booze. He died from cirrhosis of the liver in his mid-fifties. The sad end to the saga of another strange character to cross our paths. ❦

Chapter 81
I Learn to Weave

On returning home from our epic pony trek, I was amazed to see lush grass, two foot high, at the top of our rough, the legacy of feeding hay to Mr Harris' cattle on it over the previous winter and a particularly wet following summer.

The ground soon reverted to its acid nature, originally being peat on a white gravel subsoil, and the gorse and bits of heather re-established themselves.

That winter, Kate taught me to wind a warp and weave. Together we retrieved and set up my mother's old floor loom in the upstairs bedroom on which, all those years ago, she had woven a cloth length for a suit for my father. After weaving some samples on a tiny Wendy loom and getting a good design worked out, we wound four yards of Harris warp on the roller, using a four-shaft lift. My mother's old string heddles had become old and moth-eaten, so I set up a jig with six-inch nails in a board, and with some strong string, knotted up a complete new set. I am proud to say it was quite a tribute to my dogged determination and persistence, as with six threads to the inch I had to make over two hundred of the fiddly items. It required much patience setting up the loom, hooking each thread of the warp through its correct heddle eye and reed and onto the roller, but with Kate's company and new found expertise, it was accomplished with no mistakes and a great deal of fun.

Throughout the winter I wove a few inches of cloth each evening, winding the bobbins for my shuttle on a mandril of paper wrapped round a knitting needle in a drill chuck. It was very remedial, throwing the shuttle across the bed of the warp threads on its shiny rollers, the weft thread unwinding behind it. This was beaten manually, hard up against its neighbour, by the reed beater which was mounted in a heavy, hinged wooden frame. The outer loops of the four banks of heddles were attached to parallel battens top and bottom, running in four banks, one behind the other. Each bank of threads in the heddles, called a shaft, could be raised or lowered by way of a pulley system attached to a set of foot-operated levers; this produced a gap, or shed, through which to pass the shuttle with its warp thread. The levers, operated in a certain designated sequence, determined how the weft threaded in and out of the warp, thus producing a repeating pattern already worked out on the Wendy loom. The loom is really the first primitive means of manually introducing a mechanical method of interlaying threads in a given sequence to produce pattern, texture and a utility fabric.

Eventually I amassed a twelve foot length of beautiful Harris tweed. Kate and I had considered it crazy to try and spin our own wool, and through contacts obtained from the art school had managed to buy spools of the most wonderfully mixed Harris yarn, in greens and blues. It certainly made up into a lovely cloth and, as the challenge of making that amount of cloth by hand was enough in itself, we were glad we made the decision we did. With high hopes we took the cloth length into John Colliers, the 'Fifty Shilling Tailors', to have it made up into a suit, but they would not touch it, saying it was too oily. I admit we had treated the threads with vegetable oil to make them run through the heddles and and reed better, but the cloth was not that oily. Nothing daunted, we put the cloth in the bath at home in some warm soapy water, trod out most of the oil and took it back to Colliers. Again they rejected it. We washed it again and finally, if reluctantly, they agreed to make up a jacket and trousers, saying that handwoven cloth was often difficult to cut. Came the day, we proudly went to collect the finished suit. They made a very good job of the tailoring, but all my initial design work went for nothing as the cutter had cut and made my suit with the cloth inside out, where I had done all my finishing off. That mistake too, after I'd pinned labels on the correct side to remind them. My complex four shaft design was confined to the inside face never to be seen. I suppose we ought to have complained, but considering it a bit late in the day for that, we resignedly took the suit back home. When I tried it on, to be honest, it didn't look too bad. By a stroke of luck, the lay of the weft, although having more vulnerable floats than on the correct side, was just as interesting to the eye. I got married in that suit and used it thirty years later, when it was back in fashion, to attend my niece Tessa's wedding. My mother lined the hairy legs of the trousers with old pyjama bottoms they were so itchy. The last time I got the suit out was for my daughter Ellen's wedding, but when I came to put it on, I found the moth had got into the plastic bag in which it had been stored and the only area the moths had got at was the fly of the trousers! Of such happenings are the warp and woof of life made.

Towards winter, we had several travelling Gypsies and their families passing by, asking if they could *poove* (or use our field) for a month or two at the end of the rough. After our trekking holiday I felt liberally disposed towards them and I thought I could trust them not to abuse my hospitality. They bought a few bales of hay from me for their horses, but obviously not enough to feed them adequately, and I should have had my suspicions aroused. One day, down in my fields, I thought I detected what looked like a hollow under the rick sheet at the top of my hay rick. On investigating, I discovered a whole lot of hay had been taken from the middle. Snow was on the ground and finding footprints leading from the rick to the Gypsy encampment, it was pretty obvious the Gypsies were the culprits. I angrily let them know of my discovery, to be met with: "Tidden me, mister, you know us buys hay from you…" said with injured innocence. I said if it happened again, winter or or no, they would have to leave their winter quarters. It was noticeable that from then on they began to buy a realistic amount of hay from me. To remove temptation, I hired Armfields Stationary baler and got the rick into bales.

Apart from this trouble, Kate and I got on quite well with these travelling Gypsies in their hooped, canvas-roofed vans, and they *pooved* quite frequently on several occasions. The Gypsy children or *chavvies* as their parents called them, used to roam the valleys quite freely, playing their games, but one dry March, out of sheer devilment, they set fire to the thick, gorse-clad hilltop overlooking Pitts Wood, which went up like a torch, threatening the enclosure. Within minutes the Gypsy families and their waggons were on the road to escape the inevitable confrontation and blame from the police, and we never saw them again.

I had tried to get them to keep their camp tidy, and they did appear to respect my request, until months later I discovered all manner of rubbish dumped in the middle of a gorse thicket. Out of sight obviously equalled tidiness, according to them. ❧

Chapter 82
CND, the Aldermaston March and Austin Underwood

The threat of the atom bomb hung over our idealistic youth like a thunder cloud. I was taking the paper *Peace News* at the time and got to hear of the Aldermaston March.

There had already been one march from London to Aldermaston Atomic Weapons Establishment, and the second one was being organised by CND, the Campaign for Nuclear Disarmament. This time the march was planned from Aldermaston to Trafalgar Square. Kate and I decided to take part and add our small might to the growing voice advocating unilateral disarmament by Britain, as prerequisite to getting the ball rolling towards international disarmament. It was all heady, idealistic stuff to young people.

We set off for Aldermaston on the appointed day, Easter 1959, and almost didn't get there, being involved in a minor accident. Fortunately, no one was hurt, but the cars were a bit dented. Still mobile, after exchanging addresses, we continued on our way. Finding a lay-by for the car at Aldermaston, we joined the swelling crowd around the entrance to the sinister-looking, heavily fortified site.

Politicians, church dignitaries, writers, actors and many other people were gathering behind a huge black banner with the CND symbol emblazoned across it. Rousing speeches were made, stirring propagandist songs sung: *"Can't you hear the H Bombs thunder, echo like the crack of doom...Men and women stand together, do not heed the men of war, make your minds up now or never, ban the bomb for ever more!"* The tall figure of Canon John Collins in his clerical robe, beside him the diminutive left wing socialist Michael Foot in his leather bomber jacket, J B Priestley, pipe in mouth with his flamboyant wife, Jacquetta Hawkes, sporting a broad-brimmed hat, and Brendan Bracken, a socialist and conscientious objector from the First World War, all stepped out in front of the banner. We followed behind in our thousands, stretching for more than a mile down the road. It was quite something to be part of that moment.

The organisation and groundwork that was put into organising that march was second to none; it had to be, with all the numbers involved. We billeted down on the floors of halls and schools to sleep each night in amicable order and unity of spirit. Mobile kitchens provided us with food and the general friendliness to our cause from the locals of the areas we marched through, was remarkable. Trad. jazz was all the rage, and the march had its own band that played lustily throughout the long weekend, raising our flagging spirits with rousing numbers like *When the Saints go marching in*.

It was a great spectacle to arrive, finally, marshalled by respectful police at Trafalgar Square, and soak up the atmosphere of what the entire national press said at the time was the largest peaceful demonstration ever witnessed in the country. There were many inspiring speeches made that afternoon, by well-known people from all walks of life, who for a few hours at any rate unified us into a beatitude of mind. If only we could sustain it, we thought, it might possibly bring peaceful change to the world. Impossible pie in the sky, of course, but none the less valid at the time.

One of our marshals, driving on ahead of us in his Morris Traveller, was a remarkable man called Austin Underwood, who we were to get to know well.

He had a public address system mounted on top of his vehicle, with two large speakers, which he used to issue instructions and blast forth the Aldermaston songs. One clever, pithy number was called *Old Man Atom*. It was spoken to a running banjo pick and started thus: *'I'm gonna preach a sermon 'bout old man atom, I don't mean Adam-in-the-bible Adam, I mean the atom Science liberated.'* It was written by a concerned

American journalist and had been taken up by Pete Seeger, the radical folk singer and protester. The final lines were: *'We hold these truths to be self evident, all men could be cremated equal!'*

Austin Underwood lived in Amesbury, in a council house with his wife and two daughters. He earned his living teaching woodwork at Bishop Wordsworth's Grammar School for Boys in Salisbury. An ardent socialist and town councillor, he supported many minority causes, where he considered the common man had had a raw deal.

Austin had fought in the Second World War in the liberating Allied Forces in Europe, and was one of the first to see the results of the horrors perpetrated by the Nazis on the Jews in Auschwitz and other concentration camps. Appalled by what he saw, the CND platform gave him a purpose, and a cause for which he worked tirelessly. He was to lead many crusades, including a memorable march to free the village of Imber in the middle of Salisbury Plain, which had been requisitioned by the War Office in the Second World War as a military training ground. The villagers had had no say in the matter, were evicted from their homes and farms and resettled, with the promise that the village would remain unharmed and they would be allowed back after the war ended. That promise was never kept, so Austin organised a mass trespass on MOD property to bring attention to the villagers plight.

It was a good demonstration, getting a lot of publicity in the national press, but the MOD, now they had possession of Imber, were not going to let it go, and have not, to this day, honoured their obligation. I don't suppose there are many of the original Imber villagers alive who remember their village. I cycled there one Boxing Day, a day when it is open to the public, and looked at the scarred remains of village cottages lining either side of the road, winding up through the middle of the hamlet. Far from being looked after, they are used for mock battle manoeuvres as the shattered, bullet-pitted, ruined walls testify.

The church is the only building surviving to any degree, and that only thanks to its absolution from gunfire and explosives. The building nestles in a fold of the downlands, the tombstones lying in a wild grassy, unkempt graveyard, dumb witnesses to hundreds of years of human life and activity under Wiltshire skies, now silent apart from the larks singing their inimitable paeans of continuity and hope. A service is held once a year in the church as a token gesture to the surviving villagers and their descendants. Maybe, one day voices will again be heard, and crops grown on these fertile ancient plains, when we have learnt to settle our differences by methods other than war.

After Kate and I got married, in 1961, and started a family it became impossible to take part in any further radical demonstrations, and we lost touch with Austin Underwood for a number of years. He called in to see us in the late sixties at the Pottery, looking rather bizarre having grown his hair to the fashionable Beatles' length, and sporting a moustache which fooled me as to his identity for a few seconds. He told me of the various minority causes he had tried to champion over the years and I showed him our embryonic pottery. One day, ten years or so later, I was coming out of the pedestrian shopping precinct in Salisbury when I saw a woman helping a very uncoordinated elderly man into their car. With a shock, it suddenly dawned on me that the elderly gentleman was Austin, with all the advanced symptoms of Parkinson's disease. To my everlasting shame, I was filled with self-centred embarrassment and confusion lest he should look my way and recognise me, and I retreated to the rear of the car while Austin's wife left to do some shopping. In a blind panic of indecision I risked a final look back to the car, to be confronted by Austin's face in the driving mirror staring straight back at me in recognition. It was only a moment, and I, Judas that I was, feigned the look of a disinterested passer-by and melted into the crowd, all because I could not handle the situation and say a friendly hello to this decent man in his affliction. I am still haunted to this day by my egocentric callousness when confronted with that chance meeting. I read of Austin's death in 1993 in the Salisbury Journal, and re-lived my nightmare.

As a more positive postscript to this incident, a confident young lady, with two lovely children, called into the Pottery with her husband one day. She said: "I don't suppose you remember me, I am one of Austin Underwood's daughters and I can remember visiting here when a child. We are on holiday and as we were passing we thought we would call in and see the pottery."

It was a heaven-sent chance for me to redeem myself, and as I expressed my genuine admiration for her father, and we reminisced about his involvement in CND and other minority causes, I could tell by the way she expanded that she was very proud of him. I said I would like to give her a piece of pottery in memory of her Dad, and the very profound affect he had had on my outlook at that period in my life. This gesture, from the positive way it was received, was obviously appropriate and it was a very happy family left the Pottery.

Chapter 83
Kate, and her Father Edward Duthie

In the first summer that I knew Kate she went on holiday to Venice with her father, a friend of his, and Sue, a local girl she was friends with at the time.

The party travelled by car and camped. Kate has a diary of this holiday which seems to be full of the rows and disagreements between herself and her father. At this stage, they were not good chemistry for each other and relations were strained.

However, other aspects of the tour were a great success, like the visit to Ravenna to see the glorious mosaics in the simple churches of that town. Venice, too, was an experience, the two young women getting separated from the two older men in the scrum of humanity that congregated for the Feast of Redentore in St Mark's Square. Being on their own, they immediately became targets for the pestiferous advances of Mediterranean males, getting their bottoms pinched and generally being harassed. What had been exciting at first, now became maddening, and it was with relief Kate sighted her father again, when their tormentors quickly melted into the anonymity of the crowd.

Kate and her father actually had a lot of common cultural interests. When she was twenty and established at the art school, they discovered this budding rapport and called in at The Ridge one day on their way to Dorset for a coastal walk over a long weekend Kate and her father were united and harmonious for once, and exuded a contentment and happiness that I had not seen before. Edward was smiling and uncharacteristically expansive, full of his puckish humour in anticipation of the walk to come. They went on their walk, and achieved a heart-warming breakthrough towards a loving father/daughter relationship.

The next Friday evening I motorcycled out to Winchester and joined up with Kate and we went to see Laurence Olivier in the film of *Henry the Fifth*, a rousing adaptation of Shakespeare's play. I then went home to the Forest and Kate to Bursledon, thinking to meet up for the weekend on the morrow. When I phoned the next morning, it was to be greeted by a tearful, distraught Kate telling me that her father had died suddenly after supper the previous evening, from a massive heart attack. Ironically, over supper, Edward and Ruth had been planning a holiday, contentedly discussing destinations in the sun, when he suddenly said he felt nauseous. This turned out to be a precursor to his fatal seizure. He was only fifty-two years old, and his eldest daughter not yet twenty-one, a man of so much expertise and medical knowledge cruelly cut down in his prime. Poor Ruth, her husband's sudden death came right out of the blue, and she was devastated. She had known her husband was not a well man and was aware of the stresses he was under at work, but Edward must have hidden from her the more critical aspects of his physiological condition. As the head pathologist at Southampton's Royal South Hants Hospital, he was only too aware of the dangers of high blood pressure, and Kate has told me that he used to treat himself for this condition.

I went to Ploverfield to give what comfort I could to Kate and her mother, and uttered the useless, empty platitudes that one does at such times. Nothing, but nothing, not even time, can ameliorate the finality of a death of a loved one, and we all knew it. Edward's friends and colleagues rallied round Ruth, shocked as she was at his premature death at a time he had so much more to offer the medical world.

At that time in my life I still nurtured the notion of the soul surviving death, and must have seemed to Kate, in her raw grief, an unrealistic and arrogant, cranky sort of comforter, not very compassionate in my certainty. Looking back one is sorry for so many shortcomings that youth doesn't recognise at the time. I didn't go to Edward's funeral and interment, which occasion, Kate said, piled on the collective agony of grief to almost impossible proportions with its ritual. I did however go to a very moving memorial service, where Edward's friends spoke of him in loving remembrance of the small ways in which he had helped them at various times in their lives, and how they had cherished his friendship. One Irish doctor, a friend for many years of the Duthies called Dr Leask, broke down in unashamed tears in his tribute to his friend and colleague, which somehow seemed fitting and lent an honest humanity to the proceedings.

Ruth appeared to weather the storm and took on all the responsibilities of looking after Ploverfield. Meg was in America at the time of her father's death. Having finished her school days at Sidcot, she was staying with her American foster mother, Peg Kennard, revisiting the haunts of the first five years of her life during the war, New York State and New England. It must have been a very strange experience to cope with the fact of her father's death from so far away, and to arrive home with him no longer there.

Chapter 84
Civil Disobedience

Kate and I had become members of CND and took part in another protest organised against the RAF base at Brize Norton in Oxfordshire, where bombers carrying nuclear bombs were based.

The protest took the form of a mass trespass on Ministry of Defence property bordering the airbase. Austin Underwood, closely involved with the organisation of the demonstration, drove Kate and myself to the airbase in his Morris Traveller. It was a lift to be remembered, as Austin drove at dangerous speed, often taking blind bends on the wrong side of the road. "Sorry about that! Learnt my driving in the army, gets you into bad habits," he apologised; it was amazing that we reached our destination without an accident.

With hundreds of other protesters gathering, we said goodbye to Austin and unloaded our expendable protest gear, consisting of a battered old army surplus tent. This we proceeded to put up, with speed and expertise born of experience, next to the main gates of the air base, while the other protesters floundered with theirs. We squatted determinedly in front, awaiting confrontation from the police, which wasn't long in coming. We were politely asked to move, a request with which Kate stoutly refused to comply. A reporter took a photograph of the two of us by our tent in the gathering dusk and, after refusing the request to move a second time, we were put under arrest for trespass with hundreds of other people like ourselves, bundled into police vans and taken to a specially convened court. Here we queued up and, one by one, faced a magistrate who confronted us with our misdemeanour. We managed to get in a few of our own lively reasons for our actions, but were remanded in prison for four days pending a more official hearing when the authorities would decide what to do with us.

I was separated from Kate, as were all the women from the men, she and her sister protesters going to Holloway Prison where they were put in solitary cells alongside other women who were incarcerated for thieving, violence, drugs and other crimes. From Kate's account of their time in jail, they had, by bad luck a much harder time of it than the men, who were all remanded in Bedford Prison. On arrival we had to empty our pockets of all items, which were noted and put into a bag for safe keeping. We were then paraded in front of a grim-faced, bored medic who gave us a cursory examination. A warder barked at us, like a sergeant-major, to lower our trousers and the medic walked along the rows of us giving our genitals a glance, and, pressing the lower abdominal muscles of our groin with his hand, demanded that we cough, presumably to test if we had a hernia. We were again shouted at, this time to pull our trousers up, and then marched to our quarters where we spent the next few days.

We ended up being lumped together in one communal room for the duration of our time on remand, sleeping side by side in rows on straw-filled palliasses on the concrete floor. Why is it that men with beards nearly always snore? I remember my nights in prison being ruined by various heavy snorers, and conducting my own survey I found that all the culprits were those protesters with facial hair! Being all together life was never boring as we could talk and debate amongst ourselves, but we were certainly not let off the strict regime governing prison life. One was expected to know the rules without being told what they were, which resulted in being shouted at by the prison warders if one inadvertently put a foot wrong or omitted the title of 'Sir' when addressing an officer. Our lavatory had no door, so you had to relieve yourself in full view of other inmates, but it was one up on buckets and the indignity of 'slopping out' we witnessed each morning, which other convicted inmates had to endure in their single cells. Food was basic: porridge with salt and a huge mug of tea for breakfast, mince and 'Smash' potato for dinner, and a hunk of bread and jam for supper. The kitchens were manned by the prison inmates and the tea was reputed to be laced with bromide to inhibit sexual libido. We were all barked into line twice a day, and marched into the oval prison yard where, under the surveillance of prison warders, we took informal exercise, strolling round and round its perimeter for half an hour, fraternising furtively with the long term 'criminals', curious as to why we were 'inside'. Interestingly, they all seemed sympathetic to our cause, probably because it was an action against the 'establishment', more than for the actual cause. One inmate, obviously a frustrated poet, smuggled us a poem written on two yards of toilet paper, that besides being entertaining, seemed to have quite a grasp politically of the entrenched powers and policies we were up against.

Bedford was a classic example of Victorian prison architecture, the main rectangular block housing prisoners in cells around a central hallway which is used as a collection point and recreational area. The cells extended, with their wired and railed landings in tiers, for several storeys, open treaded steel stairways leading from one landing to another. To prevent suicides, or for that matter inmates or prison warders getting thrown into the hallway below, steel safety nets were stretched across the whole danger area. Cell doors had a tiny peep hole through which the warden could observe the prisoner and the interior of each cell.

It was an interesting experience. In our eyes we had done nothing wrong and felt no qualms of conscience, so the few days in prison were more educational than a threat to our freedom. After four days on remand we were taken in police vans to a court hearing where we were informed we would be released in the knowledge we were bound over to keep the peace. Having made our point and brought it into national focus, most of us were pragmatic enough to go along with the Court's conditional dispensation. The police had generously made up coffee and ham sandwiches for us after we left the court. The more committed free-wheeling CND demonstrators, who in cases like Pat Arrowsmith, were to spend a lot of the next decade of their lives in prison demonstrating their beliefs against the national nuclear programme, immediately broke their cognisance, and received a term in jail. Whether their efforts in the years to follow, against the nuclear arsenal and its threat, ever made any impact on the policy of nations, is doubtful. Campaigning became a way of life for them, to the unbalanced exclusion of all else. In retrospect, time and Gorbachov have been the most revolutionary elements for change in the easing of world tension in relation to atomic weapons.

Now, writing in January 2003, five years on from when I first started this family history, we have other causes and concerns. America has been on the receiving end of terrorism when the Twin Towers were annihilated on 11 September, 2001, with the deaths of thousands of people. Muslim extremism and its alliance with acts of terror on civilian targets, has taken the place of the Cold War of the fifties and the last few decades of the 20th century. The response of the USA, with its overwhelming fire power against terrorism, has been predictably simplistic: to "Smoke out and destroy" those countries and people that they consider as part of an axis of evil, and thus defeat terrorism. In pursuing this policy of identifying tyrannical leaders of the world, they are treating the symptoms, and neglecting the causes of Muslim unrest. The results will be an escalation of terrorism, rather than a diminishing. With the gap between rich and poor throughout the world becoming greater each decade, it is imperative that those enlightened people of the radically better-off countries of the world, gave some thought towards implementing a more equitable division of the world's resources for everyone.

While Kate and I had been demonstrating, Kate's mother in Bursledon, still in the first fraught months of her bereavement, was alarmed and dismayed to find her daughter's photograph spread across the front page of the *Sunday Observer*, and hear of her arrest. She knew we had gone on the demonstration and, much to her credit, had not tried to stop us, but I don't think she realised at the time quite what it entailed or what the consequences for her daughter might be. So Kate's arrest and possible jail sentence must have been an additional stressful and alarming prospect for her. Her next door neighbour at the Lodge house, the former Commander, who she had considered to be a friend, was unkind with his remarks to her. He was of the opinion that our action was part of a Communist plot to upset the nuclear balance in the Cold War, and as such was despicable and amounted to treason, and that he would be unable to have anything more to do with her, or her family. We heard later that she had been ready to pay Kate's bail, or any fine that might have been imposed, to get her out of jail. As it happened it was unnecessary, but to our minds, well meant as it undoubtedly was, her intervention would have rather defeated the object of our protest.

Ruth never questioned our commitment to CND, but I know she had reservations as to what cranky cause I was going to lead her daughter into next. In retrospect, the simplistic tunnel vision of idealism can be, at base, rather selfish, and maybe we ought to have taken Kate's mother's feelings into account. We didn't, and our actions at that time must, therefore, bear a certain feeling of unease and regret. I remember Kate and I got home to The Ridge from our demonstration just in time to witness Olive Potter's old caravan go up in flames. It was quite a conflagration, with Calor gas bottles roaring like demented blow lamps and twenty foot high flames. We all thought 'Robin' would be distraught, but if anything, she seemed quite pleased and philosophical, because her ex-husband Stanley had offered to buy her a new modem caravan some months before; the fire was almost providential. So we came back to everyday life with a bump. ⚘

Chapter 85
Winchester - The Art School

Kate was now well-established at the Art School, and having a stimulating and creative time.

She was learning the craft and techniques of silk screen printing and weaving under the watchful eye of her tutor, Mrs Rendall, who was to teach many generations of students before her retirement. Equipment and facilities at the Art School were old and fairly primitive, but this factor only seemed to increase the determination of the students in her year to produce some remarkable work. Mrs (W)ren, as she was affectionately known (not to be confused with the potter), organised a visit to the cloth mills in the north of England, which was an eye opener for Kate and her fellow students, as the hard-headed commercial textile manufacturers of the real world had never heard of The National Diploma of Design. The mill management said they were only interested in taking on secondary school leavers with no preconceptions of design, whom they could train in their conservative standards; the height of their textile design was a repeat with a few roses. They were not the least bit interested in students already trained in creative fabric design that might rock their established market.

So much for the liaison of art schools with industry. It was a strange 'head in the sand' attitude and the writing was already on the wall, heralding the demise of the British textile industry. Continued use of antiquated Victorian machinery, coupled with poor, uninspired fabric design and quickly expanding overseas production, with its modern machinery and cheap labour, produced a complete turn around of trade, with most fabrics eventually coming from the Third World to which we once exported.

Another college visit of note for Kate was to Cookham to see the famous painter Stanley Spencer. He was in his latter years then, and Kate remembers him as a quiet, unassuming little man, in an old cardigan, surrounded by a muddle of paint brushes and paintings in various stages of completion. I remember her saying that she and the other students brought him a gift of a box of vegetables which he graciously accepted.

August 1959 marked Kate's 21st birthday and we celebrated at Ploverfield with a party. Kate's mother tactfully stayed with some of her friends, and left us the freedom of the house. It was lovely sunny weather and we celebrated out on the extensive lawn adjoining the house with a group of Kate's friends. Barbara Schneider, David Hoar and George Tonkin from Sidcot days were there and Hartmut, a friendly young German, the son of a young woman and fellow student Edward and Ruth had known in pre-war days at Trinity College, Dublin. Danae and John Harris came too, Kate was at her bubbly and animated best and we all had a most enjoyable evening.

The next day some of us went for a picnic, dinghy-sailing on the Hamble, returning in time for tea to find the larder bare and a visibly stressed Ruth wondering how to feed us. The company could sense Ruth's embarrassment and, after a cup of tea, the gathering broke up and we all went home. Her daughter's 21st, the bereavement, coupled with the fallout from our CND activities was just too much for her. ✦

Chapter 86
Dick Songer Arrives

In the late fifties, President Nasser of Egypt blocked the Suez Canal and Anthony Eden, the then Tory Prime Minister, sent a British force to Egypt to sort the Egyptians out.

This debacle was called the Suez Crisis, an overkill by the British resulting in Eden's resignation. A Fleet Air Arm pilot, Dick Songer, bought himself out of the service at this time in disagreement with British policy, and having an artistic ability, decided to apply to art school which happened to be Winchester. He met Kate and they became friends, and she brought him, one day, to The Ridge. We got on well as a threesome. Dick had been a Naval cadet at Dartmouth from an early age and trained as a pilot under the auspices of the Navy. He was intelligent, good at art and in his now liberated idealism, very interested to hear of our CND exploits. All three of us participated in another Aldermaston March to London. The numbers were even greater this time and the dense crowds that gathered in Trafalgar Square and all streets leading to it, were quite a sight.

Awareness of our dire situation in the Cold War seemed to be at last filtering through to the consciousness of the nation and we felt naïvely confident of change. Kate, in consideration of her mother, soft-pedalled on the protest front for a bit, while Dick and I went up to London for yet another demonstration to be headed by the ageing, but influential, philosopher and mathematician Bertrand Russell, now in his mid-eighties.

Dick had a flat in Winchester, and I had arranged to reach him by ten o'clock on the day of the demonstration, when he would take me on the back of his BSA 500cc single motorcycle, up to London. My old Bowen two-stroke was out of action, so I rode Danae's little Excelsior. The machine had developed an ignition fault which resulted in the engine cutting out unless one was going flat out. For some mysterious reason it would only re-start on a cold plug, so I carried a pocket of spares, which I had to change every time I came to a crossroads. I began to despair of ever reaching Winchester on time. I made it, however, and Dick and I blitzed up to London on his powerful motor cycle.

We joined the crowds demonstrating, and watched in awe the diminutive figure of Bertrand Russell leading the march to present a petition to Downing Street and, with other protesters, stage a sit-down in the street. At this point he was arrested and led away by police to a possible prison sentence. It turned out to be only a token arrest, of course, as someone of his great age and standing could not possibly be put in the clink without great public outcry. Bertrand Russell proved an excellent figurehead for the demonstration, bringing in lots of publicity for CND.

We slept the night on sofas in Topsy's large London house in Highgate, where she lived with her husband Larry Solon, the Jewish sub-editor of *Time Life* magazine, a large, horn-rim bespectacled, gentle bear of a man, and her four children, Simone, Marsha, Joel and Max. I can see now, in my mind's eye, Topsy opening the door to us and standing wide-eyed, petite, pale and child-like, with her two tiny boys clinging to her skirts, and Dick's comment that she looked far too young to be a mother of four. ❦

The Journal ends at this point, but life at The Ridge, Godshill, continued in its inimitable and traditional way. The epilogue that follows is a summary of 'what the Charmans did next...'

Epilogue

I knew from the age of ten I wanted to be a potter. Traditional village pottery has a life and a vitality other pots don't have. People who have made pots - something of them has rubbed off. The plastic nature of clay is fascinating - stuff you dig up and pummel it to an even consistency, moulds to your fingers and then you get this arrested plasticity fixed forever by the fire. It's amazing... I loved village style pottery, medieval slip ware, native African pots. Items that belong to everyone. I've always enjoyed the routine of making and the satisfaction of loading a whole tray of pots. It imposes its own discipline.

With the coming of electricity in 1964, our pottery became more durable. After the Verwood kiln was installed we added another and later an oil-fired kiln for stoneware. I used natural Forest colours for decoration, the greens, blues and browns from the metal oxides.

'...there to be used', a favourite motto of mine which I can also apply to the pieces we designed.

Godshill Pottery, resurrected from the remains of my mother's enterprise, eventually produced 45 lines - jugs, vases, cider pitchers, bread crocks, ashtrays, casserole dishes, plates among them. We built two showrooms and prepared to open to the public. They have been visiting ever since...It has been a satisfying journey.

When Danae's marriage ended and she returned from Australia she moved into the house we had built on The Ridge and, as she is a very practical lady, soon picked up how to throw. Among the pieces Danae made were characterful and very popular ceramic ponies.

Danae, and her new partner Peter Stammers, helped build and maintain further studios and workshops and worked with us in the all-important market garden which ensured our continuing self-sufficiency. From then on we never looked back.

Chris, Danae and Kate working in Godshill Pottery. Bottom right shows the chimney of the oil-fired kiln for making stoneware pots. (Photos: Salisbury Journal, 1971)

Margaret, pictured in 1974.

Left: Chris, Kate, Ellen and Tom.
Below: Chris passing on the love of outside living to Ellen and Tom.

he creative spirit continued. Kate and Chris with one of two ceramic knights made in the 1980s.
hey were based on the knights of the AA Milne poems. *Photo: Salisbury Journal*

The process of potting imposes its own discipline. Using clay from the New Forest, Godshill Pottery has produced over 45 lines including jugs, vases, cider pitchers, breadcrocks, casserole dishes and mugs - made to be used.

Our children Tom and Ellen came along in the early 1960s. Kate would work through the winter throwing pots and then, when the children were old enough, joined me full time, opening the showrooms to the public and decorating the pots herself.

Pursuing her painting career, she is a founding member of the Take 10 group of artists, winning acclaim and awards for her evocative New Forest landscapes.

Kate also became a key figure in the dramatic life of Godshill and has only recently retired as producer of the plays of Godshill Players as well as 'keeper' of the Village Hall. Cycling, another passion, has taken us all over Europe and beyond with Danae and Peter, long before the current surge of interest in the sport. Naturally I have kept a record of these travels!

Today, we, and the pottery, have reached retirement, yet the rural spirit of The Ridge, Godshill remains strong and is being carried on in our son Tom and his partner Tina, and our daughter Ellen.

My mother Margaret would have had something profound to say about that...

From me: Go Well, dear friends and family..."

July 2019

Photos left and opposite: Sonia Aarons-Green

Chris and Kate continuing the traditions of Godshill Pottery and celebrating their passion for craft and art.